£26.00

Schnitzler, Hofmannsthal, and the Austrian Theatre

Schnitzler, Hofmannsthal, and the Austrian Theatre

W. E. Yates

YALE UNIVERSITY PRESS

NEW HAVEN AND LONDON · 1992

Set in Bembo by Best-set Typesetter Ltd., Hong Kong
Printed and bound in Great Britain by St Edmundsbury Press

Library of Congress Cataloging-in-Publication Data
Yates, W. E.
    Schnitzler, Hofmannsthal, and the Austrian theatre / W.E. Yates.
      p. cm.
    Includes bibliographical references and index.
    ISBN 0–300–05742–3
    1. Austrian drama—Austria—Vienna—History and criticism.
  2. Austrian drama—20th century—History and criticism.
  3. Hofmannsthal, Hugo von, 1874–1929—Criticism and interpretation.
  4. Schnitzler, Arthur, 1862–1931—Criticism and interpretation.
  5. Theater—Austria—Vienna—History—20th century. I. Title.
PT3828.V5Y38   1992
832′.91209′9436—dc20   92–13125
                                                    CIP

A catalogue record for this book is available from the British Library.

Contents

List of Illustrations

These illustrations are all taken from Schnitzler's collection of cuttings in Exeter University Library. The underlinings in figures 5 and 6 are those of the 'Observer' agency in Vienna which supplied Schnitzler with cuttings.

Preface

Arthur Schnitzler and Hugo von Hofmannsthal were the principal
dramatists during the most exciting and turbulent period in the
intellectual and cultural history of Vienna. They reacted in very
different ways to the momentous changes taking place in the world
around them.

My subject is the interrelation between the two dramatists and
their historical and intellectual background; hence the book has a
dual focus. Schnitzler and Hofmannsthal are approached as complementary figures, whose contrasting dramatic work illuminates
some of the consequences of the intellectual upheaval at the turn
of the century and the political upheaval of 1914–18. Both their
writing for the theatre and the critical reception of their plays
reflect the shifting climate of cultural and intellectual life in Austria
(particularly Vienna) from the *fin de siècle* to the brink of Austro-
Fascism.

I do not pretend to be offering a comprehensive study of
Schnitzler and Hofmannsthal. The book is limited to their work
and reception as dramatists. In discussing individual plays in detail I
have moreover concentrated on key works rather than attempting
exhaustive coverage. I have not, for example, discussed the short
plays Hofmannsthal wrote in the 1890s – a reluctant decision,
but my aim is to concentrate on Schnitzler and Hofmannsthal as
theatrical dramatists, and these early playlets are not theatrical
works. The plays I have elected to dwell on all connect with some
of the principal issues of the time: anti-Semitism, double standards
in relations between the sexes, and the First World War and its
aftermath. Concentrating on these topics allows me to discuss some
of the two dramatists' best-known works. Those by Schnitzler are
Anatol, *Liebelei*, *Reigen*, *Das weite Land*, and *Professor Bernhardi*;
those by Hofmannsthal are *Elektra*, *Der Rosenkavalier*, *Der Schwierige*,
Das Salzburger große Welttheater, and *Der Unbestechliche*. I am en-

couraged to proceed selectively in this way by the conviction that the work of both dramatists is uneven in quality. Hofmannsthal's weakest writing in dramatic forms can be turgid and obscure, Schnitzler's lifelessly trivial. Schnitzler's work as a dramatist declined from the First World War onwards – possibly a consequence of his being worn down by controversy and prejudice, to which he was subject throughout his career. By contrast, Hofmannsthal's later development, including his involvement in the Salzburg Festival, exemplifies the role of the theatre in ideological myth-making.

The lives of the dramatists are treated mainly in chapter 2, which provides summaries of their careers concentrating on their dramatic and theatrical work and based largely on their letters and diaries. The intention of this is to give a factual biographical account in coherent form, so that the material need not be repeated in other chapters. Elsewhere the dual focus of the book means that I have had to give some space to significant features of the historical background. There have, however, been so many general accounts of 'Vienna 1900' that another would be otiose, so I have concentrated strictly on outlining those elements in the intellectual climate and social conventions of the time that bear directly on my argument. As well as elements of the intellectual climate at the turn of the century, discussed in chapter 1, these include the development of the various theatres in Vienna (outlined in the first section of chapter 3) and also reactions to the outbreak of the First World War and some of its political consequences (chapter 5). Throughout, I have tried not to lose sight of the wider cultural life of Vienna; in particular the satirical writings of Karl Kraus provide a salutary point of reference against which to measure the positions of Schnitzler and Hofmannsthal.

The final chapter reviews the uneasy friendship that the two dramatists enjoyed from the early 1890s onwards and surveys the fate of their reputation and works in the 1930s. I have kept this 'epilogue' short, but it is not a mere afterthought, for it concludes the story of the wider development traced in the course of the book: from the proclamation of a literary and artistic 'renaissance' (founded partly in a collapse of inherited values in an almost totally apolitical culture) to the disintegration of the Habsburg monarchy and the consequences of that disintegration, which included not only the cultural conservatism of Hofmannsthal but the subversion of cultural and political standards with the onset of Fascism.

The story inevitably requires detailed documentation, and the lack of complete editions of the works and letters of either dramatist makes this impossible to do as unobtrusively as I would have liked. I have, however, tried to avoid cluttering the text with disagreements with previous interpretations. So far as possible these are unloaded into the notes. Other secondary literature is referred to only when it supports or expands a point made in the main text.

In the belief that the material should be of wide interest, I have translated all quotations. When the passage quoted is in verse, the original German is given together with a literal prose translation. When the original is in prose, the German is quoted if the phrasing is of stylistic interest, if the meaning may be ambiguous, or if a passage is of especial significance.

Acknowledgements

It is a pleasure to acknowledge my debt to the libraries where most of the material has been gathered, in particular the Wiener Stadt- und Landesbibliothek and the Österreichische Nationalbibliothek in Vienna, the Institute of Germanic Studies, London, and Exeter University Library. In treating the reception of Schnitzler, I have been able to draw on his own collection of press cuttings, which is now held by Exeter University Library, and I have profited greatly from the work of Ingrid Leis, who organized and microfilmed the material in this collection.

Work in the Viennese collections would have been impossible without generous grants made by the British Academy and the University of Exeter; I also have to thank the University of Exeter for a period of study leave in 1990 during which the first draft was written.

The inception of the book goes back a number of years, and I remember with gratitude stimulating conversations about Hofmannsthal with Professor Martin Stern, Professor Brian Coghlan, and the late Paul Stefanek, all of which have borne fruit in the final planning. I owe thanks, too, to the editors of the various journals (especially *Colloquia Germanica*, *Modern Language Review*, and the *Publications of the English Goethe Society*) that have published articles and reviews in which I was first able to explore some of the themes of the book. I am also grateful to all the colleagues and friends who have kindly helped me by providing information and advice on various specific questions; I must in particular thank Mrs Sally McMullen, Peter Michael Braunwarth, Professor Martin Stern, Professor Peter Branscombe, Dr Klaus Heydemann, and not least Trevor Learmouth of Exeter University Library, who has given me resourceful and unfailingly patient support over the years and who helped me to trace several elusive details.

During the writing of the book I have been fortunate to receive encouragement and invaluable advice from Dr Robert Baldock of Yale University Press and from Professor Edward Timms. Finally, I owe an especial debt of gratitude to my wife, to my colleague John McKenzie, and to Dr Ritchie Robertson, all of whom read complete drafts of the typescript at various stages and were very generous in offering constructive and detailed criticism.

November 1991   *W. E. Yates*

List of Abbreviations

Note: The List of Abbreviations which follows is also a Bibliography of primary texts. (See Bibliographical Note, p. 247.)

Arthur Schnitzler

Works:

References are generally given to: Arthur Schnitzler, *Gesammelte Werke*, 6 vols (Frankfurt a.M., 1962–77), using the following abbreviations for the volumes referred to:

AB	*Aphorismen und Betrachtungen*, ed. Robert O. Weiss (1967)
DW	*Die dramatischen Werke*, 2 vols (1962)
ES	*Die erzählenden Schriften*, 2 vols (1961)
Jug.	Arthur Schnitzler, *Jugend in Wien. Eine Autobiographie*, ed. Therese Nickl and Heinrich Schnitzler (Vienna, 1968)
Tgb.	Arthur Schnitzler, *Tagebuch*, 10 vols (edition of the Österreichische Akademie der Wissenschaften) (Vienna, 1981–). Reference is given to the date of the entry in the following volumes: *Tagebuch 1879–1892* (1987), *Tagebuch 1893–1902* (1989), *Tagebuch 1903–1908* (1991), *Tagebuch 1909–1912* (1981), *Tagebuch 1913–1916* (1983), *Tagebuch 1917–1919* (1985)
Chrstk.	Arthur Schnitzler, *Hugo von Hofmannsthal. 'Charakteristik aus den Tagebüchern'*, ed. Bernd Urban and Werner Volke (Hofmannsthal-Forschungen, 3) (Freiburg i.Br., 1975)

Correspondence:

AS/Bfe. I

Arthur Schnitzler, *Briefe 1875–1912*, ed. Therese Nickl and Heinrich Schnitzler (Frankfurt a.M., 1981)

AS/Bfe. II

Arthur Schnitzler, *Briefe 1913–1931*, ed. Peter Michael Braunwarth *et al.* (Frankfurt a.M., 1984)

H/AS

Hugo von Hofmannsthal – Arthur Schnitzler, *Briefwechsel*, ed. Therese Nickl and Heinrich Schnitzler (Frankfurt a.M., 1983)

AS/Brahm

Der Briefwechsel Arthur Schnitzler – Otto Brahm, ed. Oskar Seidlin (Schriften der Gesellschaft für Theatergeschichte, 57) (Berlin, 1953)

AS/Kempny

Hedy Kempny – Arthur Schnitzler, '*Das Mädchen mit den dreizehn Seelen*'. *Eine Korrespondenz ergänzt durch Blätter aus Hedy Kempnys Tagebuch sowie durch eine Auswahl ihrer Erzählungen*, ed. Heinz P. Adamek (Reinbek bei Hamburg, 1984)

AS/Sandrock

Adele Sandrock – Arthur Schnitzler, *Dilly. Geschichte einer Liebe in Briefen, Bildern und Dokumenten*, ed. Renate Wagner (Vienna, 1975)

AS/Waissnix

Arthur Schnitzler – Olga Waissnix, *Liebe, die starb vor der Zeit. Ein Briefwechsel*, ed. Therese Nickl and Heinrich Schnitzler (Vienna, 1970)

Hugo von Hofmannsthal

Works:

HKA

Hugo von Hofmannsthal, *Sämtliche Werke*, ed. Rudolf Hirsch *et al.*, *c.* 37 vols (Frankfurt a.M., 1975–)

This edition is still incomplete; by the summer of 1991 nineteen volumes had appeared. References are given to HKA for quotations from the poems and lyrical dramas, from the moralities, from the operas (including *Der Rosenkavalier*), and from *Der Unbestechliche*. References for the other dramas and for the essays, aphorisms, and autobiographical notes are to the appropriate volumes in Hofmannsthal, *Gesammelte Werke in*

Einzelausgaben, ed. Herbert Steiner, 15 vols (Frankfurt a.M., 1953–70), using the conventional abbreviations, as follows:

A	*Aufzeichnungen* (1959)
D I	*Dramen* I (1953)
D II	*Dramen* II (1954)
L I	*Lustspiele* I (1959)
L II	*Lustspiele* II (1954)
P I	*Prosa* I (1956)
P II	*Prosa* II (1959)
P III	*Prosa* III (1952)
P IV	*Prosa* IV (1955)

Additionally, as an extension of the volume *Aufzeichnungen* above, reference is made to the edition of the notes by Ingeborg Beyer-Ahlert in: Hofmannsthal, *Gesammelte Werke in zehn Einzelbänden*, ed. Bernd Schoeller in consultation with Rudolf Hirsch (Frankfurt a.M., 1979–80):

RA III   *Reden und Aufsätze* III (*1925–1929*), *Buch der Freunde, Aufzeichnungen 1889–1929*, cd. Bernd Schoeller and Ingeborg Beyer-Ahlert in consultation with Rudolf Hirsch (1980)

Correspondence:

H/Bfe. I   Hugo von Hofmannsthal, *Briefe 1890–1901*, ed. Heinrich Zimmer (Berlin, 1935)

H/Bfe. II   Hugo von Hofmannsthal, *Briefe 1900–1909* (Vienna, 1937)

H/Andrian   Hugo von Hofmannsthal – Leopold von Andrian, *Briefwechsel*, ed. Walter H. Perl (Frankfurt a.M., 1968)

H/Beer-Hofmann   Hugo von Hofmannsthal – Richard Beer-Hofmann, *Briefwechsel*, ed. Eugene Weber (Frankfurt a.M., 1972)

H/Bodenhausen   Hugo von Hofmannsthal – Eberhard von Bodenhausen, *Briefe der Freundschaft*, ed. Dora von Bodenhausen (Berlin, 1953)

H/Borchardt   Hugo von Hofmannsthal – Rudolf Borchardt, *Briefwechsel*, ed. Marie Luise Borchardt and Herbert Steiner (Frankfurt a.M., 1954)

H/Burckhardt	Hugo von Hofmannsthal – Carl J. Burckhardt, *Briefwechsel*, ed. Carl J. Burckhardt (Frankfurt a.M., 1956)
H/Degenfeld	Hugo von Hofmannsthal – Ottonie Gräfin Degenfeld, *Briefwechsel*, ed. Marie Therese Miller-Degenfeld and Eugene Weber (Frankfurt a.M., 1974)
H/George	*Briefwechsel zwischen George und Hofmannsthal*, ed. Robert Boehringer (Berlin, 1938)
H/Haas	Hugo von Hofmannsthal – Willy Haas, *Ein Briefwechsel*, ed. Rolf Italiaander (Berlin, 1968)
H/Karg	Hugo von Hofmannsthal – Edgar Karg von Bebenburg, *Briefwechsel*, ed. Mary E. Gilbert (Frankfurt a.M., 1966)
H/Kessler	Hugo von Hofmannsthal – Harry Graf Kessler, *Briefwechsel 1898–1929*, ed. Hilde Burger (Frankfurt a.M., 1968)
H/Mell	Hugo von Hofmannsthal – Max Mell, *Briefwechsel*, ed. Margret Dietrich and Heinz Kindermann (Heidelberg, 1982)
H/Nostitz	Hugo von Hofmannsthal – Helene von Nostitz, *Briefwechsel*, ed. Oswalt von Nostitz (Frankfurt a.M., 1965)
H/Redlich	Hugo von Hofmannsthal – Josef Redlich, *Briefwechsel*, ed. Helga Fußgänger (Frankfurt a.M., 1971)
H/Rilke	Hugo von Hofmannsthal – Rainer Maria Rilke, *Briefwechsel 1899–1925*, ed. Rudolf Hirsch and Ingeborg Schnack (Frankfurt a.M., 1978)
H/AS	Hugo von Hofmannsthal – Arthur Schnitzler, *Briefwechsel*, ed. Therese Nickl and Heinrich Schnitzler (Frankfurt a.M., 1983)
H/Strauss	Richard Strauss – Hugo von Hofmannsthal, *Briefwechsel*, ed. Franz and Alice Strauss, revised by Willi Schuh (Zürich, 1955)
H/Wildgans	Hugo von Hofmannsthal – Anton Wildgans, *Briefwechsel*, ed. Norbert Altenhofer (Heidelberg, 1971)

H/Zifferer

Hugo von Hofmannsthal – Paul Zifferer, *Briefwechsel*, ed. Hilde Burger (Vienna, n.d. [1983])

Anthologies:

JW

Das Junge Wien. Österreichische Literatur- und Kunstkritik 1887–1902, ed. Gotthart Wunberg, 2 vols (Tübingen, 1976)

Marb.

Jugend in Wien. Literatur um 1900, ed. Ludwig Greve and Werner Volke (Sonderausstellungen des Schiller-Nationalmuseums [Marbach], 24) (Munich, 1974)

WM

Die Wiener Moderne. Literatur, Kunst and Musik zwischen 1890 und 1910, ed. Gotthart Wunberg and Johannes J. Braakenburg (Stuttgart, 1981)

HUK

Hofmannsthal im Urteil seiner Kritiker. Dokumente zur Wirkungsgeschichte Hugo von Hofmannsthals in Deutschland, ed. Gotthart Wunberg (Frankfurt a.M., 1972)

Fiechtner 1949

Hugo von Hofmannsthal. Die Gestalt des Dichters im Spiegel der Freunde, ed. Helmut A. Fiechtner (Vienna, 1949)

Fiechtner 1963

Hugo von Hofmannsthal. Der Dichter im Spiegel der Freunde, ed. Helmut A. Fiechtner (Berne, 1963)

Resonanz

Resonanz. 50 Jahre Kritik der Salzburger Festspiele, ed. Max Kaindl-Hönig (Salzburg, 1971)

TR

Günther Rühle, *Theater für die Republik 1917– 1933 im Spiegel der Kritik* (Frankfurt a.M., 1967)

Periodicals and Newspapers:

F

Die Fackel (Vienna, 1899–1936)

MSF

Mitteilungen der Salzburger Festspielhaus-Gemeinde (1918–1922)

NDR

Neue deutsche Rundschau

NR

Neue Rundschau

NZZ

Neue Zürcher Zeitung

NFP

Neue Freie Presse (Vienna)

WAZ

Wiener Allgemeine Zeitung

CHAPTER 1

Fin-de-siècle *Vienna:*
Irrationalism and Renaissance

'Jung Wien' and the Café Griensteidl

In the early hours of 21 January 1897 the Café Griensteidl closed for the last time. It stood on a prime site on the Michaelerplatz, at the corner of the Herrengasse and the Schauflergasse, only a few yards away from the imperial Palace (Hofburg). It was to be demolished to make way for a larger, modern commercial building. (Recently, nearly a century later, a new restaurant was opened on the ground floor, exploiting the old name.) Strategically placed near where the Burgtheater (the court theatre and national theatre) had stood until its new building on the Ringstrasse was inaugurated in 1888, the original coffee-house was the regular meeting-place of the writers of 'Jung Wien'. Artistic figures of several generations gathered for the final evening, 'celebrities of yesterday,' so the *Neues Wiener Journal* reported the next day, '[. . .] wanting to bask in the light of the celebrities of today and perhaps even of tomorrow'. The closure and demolition are now remembered because of Karl Kraus's satire of the 'Jung Wien' circle, *Die demolirte Litteratur*. But when the news of the impending closure was first known, it was a matter not just of national interest but of international concern. The Café Griensteidl, readers of the *Berliner Tageblatt* were reminded on 9 November 1896, was 'both the birthplace and the battleground of the whole literary and artistic development of modern Vienna'.

The capital of a vast empire that would disintegrate after the First World War, the Vienna where Schnitzler and Hofmannsthal both grew up in what has justly been called 'one of the most cultivated and subtly civilized middle classes to be found anywhere in the world'[1] is widely recognized as a crucible of the modern mind. The upsurge of creativeness that developed in the 1890s and lasted up to and beyond the First World War produced one of the most remarkable periods of imaginative activity in the history of Europe. In a city celebrated for its theatrical culture, it was natural that modernism ('die Moderne') was launched in the theatre, in the

1

so-called 'Ibsen week' in April 1891, when the great Norwegian dramatist himself came to Vienna at the invitation of Max Burckhard, the director of the Burgtheater, to attend the première of *The Pretenders*. (Both Hofmannsthal and Schnitzler attended banquets in his honour.)[2] Within the next few years the spirit of innovation spread through the other arts, including the visual arts and music. The Viennese Secession was founded by Klimt and others in 1897; it was also in 1897 that Mahler's ten years as director of the Opera House began. And in the early years of the twentieth century it was again in Vienna that some of the most influential revolutionary developments were made, in music and architecture especially.

The beginnings of the group that made the Café Griensteidl the centre of literary modernism in Vienna are recorded in Schnitzler's diary in the spring of 1890 (Tgb., 2 April 1890). By the following March the name 'Jung Wien' was well established; and at the end of 1891, reviewing the progress he had made that year, he noted that the other principal figures of this 'stimulating circle' were Hofmannsthal, Felix Salten, and the dramatist Richard Beer-Hofmann, and, as later additions, Hermann Bahr and a journalist and painter, Ferry Bératon (Tgb., 31 December 1891). Karl Kraus too was a regular coffee-house companion from November 1893 to December 1894, and it was not until a year later that Schnitzler noted that they no longer met him (Tgb., 6 November 1895). Kraus would become the implacable satirical opponent of the 'Jung Wien' circle, in particular of what he saw as the intellectual corruption of Bahr and the pretentiousness of Hofmannsthal; Schnitzler appeared as one of the witnesses in a court case brought against him in February 1901 by Bahr and Emerich von Bukovics, the director of the Deutsches Volkstheater (Tgb., 22 February 1901). Other regulars in the Griensteidl circle included the dramatist and decadent lyric poet Felix Dörmann; from 1893–94 onwards Hofmannsthal's friend Leopold von Andrian, also a poet and in 1895 the author of a highly-acclaimed story *Der Garten der Erkenntnis*; and Rudolph Lothar, a journalist and dramatist friend of Schnitzler's. Though Schnitzler's characterization of Lothar in his autobiography stresses his 'superficiality' (*Jug.*, 284–5), he too would become a figure of influence around the turn of the century as the editor of the literary weekly *Die Wage*, launched in 1898, as the author of a history of the Burgtheater (1899), and as a prolific playwright. Other figures who belonged to the 'Jung Wien' generation, though not all of them were devotees of the Café Griensteidl, included Peter Altenberg, writer of prose vignettes, Otto Stoessl (journalist and poet), Raoul Auernheimer (dramatist and theatre reviewer), and the poet Paul Wertheimer.

The central figure at the Griensteidl gatherings was Hermann Bahr, and though Schnitzler and Hofmannsthal did not meet him until April 1891, it was he who was the self-appointed leader of the 'Jung Wien' group. 'Bahr', wrote Hofmannsthal in April 1891 in a review of Bahr's drama *Die Mutter*, 'is the most lively of us all' (P I, 15). Hofmannsthal's judgment of the actual play is negative; and though he also built a reputation as a dramatist and novelist, Bahr's importance lies mainly in his activity as an ebullient journalistic essayist and generous critic who adopted a critical strategy of eclectic receptiveness – what in his autobiography he called being 'quite uncritical'[3] – and was swift to scent each new shift in the wind of literary and artistic fashion. His virtuoso ability to anticipate the developments and changes of successive post-Naturalist movements made him a vital standard-bearer in Vienna of *avant-garde* ideas and an important 'literary catalyst'.[4] He was also co-founder of the weekly *Die Zeit*, which provided the modernists with an organ they had lacked – a lack that Schnitzler had explicitly bemoaned to Hofmannsthal two years earlier (H/AS, 18: letter of 27 March 1892).

Despite all his outstanding talent as a publicist, Bahr features as erratic and indiscriminate in *Die demolirte Litteratur*, and though both Schnitzler and Hofmannsthal remained fond of him, their respect for him was at best qualified. Schnitzler perceived an element of charlatanry in him at their first meeting (Tgb., 27 April 1891); and though by June 1894 they had become friends, by mid-March 1895 he was again summing him up as no better than 'a common swindler' ('ein ordinärer Schwindler': Tgb., 14 March 1895). Hofmannsthal, who spent a lot of time with Bahr in the early summer of 1891 discussing art and literature,[5] was slower to see through him. Twenty years later he would warn Richard Strauss clearly enough against being taken in by Bahr's nature as a 'turbulent [. . .] renegade' (H/Strauss, 125: letter of 26 July 1911); but looking back in 1918 in a letter to Andrian, he admitted ruefully that it had taken him fifteen years to grasp that Bahr was 'extremely rancorous and extremely jealous, albeit not in a vulgar way', and remarked on the weakness of Bahr's creative imagination ('gestaltende Phantasie') by comparison with Max Reinhardt (H/Andrian, 283–4: letter of 9 September 1918).

It was in fact Schnitzler and Hofmannsthal who were generally recognized as the leading creative figures of the 'Jung Wien' group, a standing summarized, for example, by Alfred von Berger in a long article on Hofmannsthal that appeared in the *Neue Freie Presse* on 16 July 1905: 'Hofmannsthal, and next to him Schnitzler, are obviously the models for our younger and youngest writers'

(HUK, 138). Stefan Zweig in his memoirs stresses the fascination that Hofmannsthal in particular had for a whole generation, a 'unique phenomenon' seeming to incorporate, despite his youth, the attainment of 'absolute poetic perfection'.[6]

Despite Kraus's satire, the leading figures of 'Jung Wien' were not mere coffee-house dilettanti. Highly productive and seriously committed, they frequently met for private readings and discussions of one another's work. Writing to Hofmannsthal on 1 October 1919, Schnitzler remembered their first readings as powerfully heightened hours ('Stunden der kräftigsten, belebtesten Atmosphäre': H/AS, 285). When Schnitzler read his story 'Geschichte von einem greisen Dichter' on 26 December 1894 to a circle including Hofmannsthal, Salten, and Beer-Hofmann, his diary records that it lasted over three hours. Their correspondence and diaries show that throughout their careers they kept up these readings, which were often long and taxing. This emerges from numerous examples, like the afternoon of 18 November 1903, when Hofmannsthal read his drama *Das gerettete Venedig* to Bahr and Brahm, or the occasion in August 1905 when Schnitzler read to Hofmannsthal and others not only a draft of *Zwischenspiel* but also *Der Ruf des Lebens*.[7]

With the exception of Bahr, the 'Jung Wien' writers were largely unpolitical in their interest. In this they were typical of their time and class, but it is all the more remarkable in view of the threatening changes taking place in the Austria in which they came to maturity. The headlong political decline of Austria following its defeat by Prussia in the Seven Weeks War in 1866 was accompanied by equally dramatic social changes within Vienna which included rapid industrialization, with a corresponding mushrooming in the size of the city. (The population of Vienna quadrupled in size in about fifty years, from 420,000 in mid-century to over one and a half million in 1900.) Together with this went an inevitable growth of urban poverty, exacerbated by overcrowded housing and exploitative working conditions; a striking increase in the Jewish population; and the tensions produced by the Stock Exchange crash of 1873, in which, as Schnitzler recalls in his fragmentary autobiography, his father was one of many who lost all their savings (*Jug.*, 48). The squalid living and working conditions of the poorer classes are recorded in various memoirs, including the autobiography of the philosopher Sir Karl Popper, who was born in Vienna in 1902; in his early childhood, he recalls, one of the main problems that agitated him was still 'the sight of abject poverty [. . .]: men, women, and children suffering from hunger, cold and hopelessness'.[8] When a big workers' demonstration took place on May

Day in 1900, the sixteen-year-old Hofmannsthal wrote a short ironic poem dismissing the turbulence of the common 'rabble' as ephemeral by contrast with the lasting life of beauty ('schöne Wahrheit': HKA II, 22); and a letter written in 1895 to a friend, Edgar Karg von Bebenburg, records his continued lack of understanding at that stage of the reality of the whole 'social question', and his ignorance of the poorer classes, the 'Volk' (H/Karg, 80: letter of 18 June 1895). By 1907, when he had become much more interested in political questions, he looked back at the former lack of a whole 'class' of independent-minded people with that degree of concern (H/Redlich, 7: letter of 22 February 1907). In Schnitzler's novel *Der Weg ins Freie*, which is set around the turn of the century, the Social Democrat activist Therese Golowski is inspired to research into the hostels and soup kitchens of the poorest quarters (ES I, 840–1); but that is a work that was not published until 1908. It was because the writers of 'Jung Wien' in the 1890s steered clear of social problems and their political implications that Karl Kraus could ridicule Bahr's volume *Die Überwindung des Naturalismus*, pointing out that Austria had never had any Naturalism needing to be 'superseded'.[9] Indeed the detachment from political commitment is faithfully reflected elsewhere in *Der Weg ins Freie*, in a context of direct relevance to the theatre: Schnitzler's fictional dramatist Heinrich Bermann considers planning a comedy on political life precisely because after attending a protest meeting with Therese Golowski it seems utterly unreal to him, a world of fantasy (ES I, 806).

At the time, even among those alive to the speed of social change, there was no sense of the impending collapse of the entire political structure. One of Hofmannsthal's notes made in 1894 records a fantasy of Vienna destroyed, the current artistic generation succeeded by a new barbarism (RA III, 383); but it is a cultural, not a political, decline that this note imagines. Stefan Zweig would remember the years of his youth – admittedly with nostalgic idealization – as a golden age of security. As late as 1913 Henry Wickham Steed, the Vienna correspondent of *The Times* from 1902 to 1913 (and subsequently its Foreign Editor and then Editor), published an account of the Habsburg monarchy which Hofmannsthal described two years later as intellectually the most significant recent book about Austria (P III, 227), and the preface of which ends with a confident disclaimer of impending collapse:

I have been unable to perceive during ten years of constant observation and experience – years, moreover, filled with struggle and crisis – any sufficient reason why, with moderate foresight on the part of the Dynasty, the Hapsburg Monarchy should not retain its rightful place in the European community.[10]

And Josef Redlich – historian, politician, and later a friend of Hofmannsthal's – also stressed that no one at the time saw that the writing was on the wall for the monarchy.

Redlich would date the inevitable downfall of the monarchy from the disturbances of November 1897, when nationalist feeling, coming on top of unrest about the blocking for eighteen months of Karl Lueger's election as Mayor of Vienna, led to the fall of the Badeni government.[11] Beer-Hofmann was even arrested during the disturbances; but when Schnitzler noted in his diary entry for 30 November, after a meeting with Beer-Hofmann, Hofmannsthal, and others, that *even they* were talking politics ('Sogar wir politisirten') it is clear how exceptional an occurrence this was. Indeed, Stefan Zweig's memoirs confirm how not just the young men of letters but the average middle-class Viennese of the time turned to the newspapers not for news of political events or reports of the latest debates in parliament but for details of what was on in the theatre.[12]

Schnitzler made his name with plays centring on the amours of leisured young men about town; Hofmannsthal made his with poems and short playlets, 'lyrical dramas', imbued with what he himself came to look back on as a 'magically' easy command of language. And indeed throughout their careers their work would have at best limited political effect; themes of love and language would remain of central significance. Nevertheless, their writing even in these early years was not entirely hermetic, but on the contrary closely tied to the whole climate of their times. This is something of which they were well aware; the realization is expressed, for example, in the opening lines of one of Hofmannsthal's poems from the year 1896:

> Merkt auf, merkt auf! Die Zeit ist sonderbar,
> Und sonderbare Kinder hat sie: Uns.
>
> (HKA I, 68)
>
> Take heed, take heed! The times are strange,
> And strange their offspring too – ourselves!

Irrationalism

What was distinctive about the times was a sense of insecurity that was at once disturbing and exciting. Even writers blind to the imminence of political change were keenly aware of living in an age of intellectual transition. The optimism on which the liberalism of the 1870s had depended had rapidly evaporated; Bahr describes his own eventual shaking-off of the 'superstitious' faith in progress in which he had grown up.[13]

The intellectual climate has been the subject of such close analysis, notably in Carl E. Schorske's seminal study *Fin-de-siècle Vienna* (first published New York, 1979), that there is no call to rehearse the material at length here; rather I shall concentrate on indicating those elements that are of especial significance for the work of Schnitzler and Hofmannsthal. In brief, until the late nineteenth century, the predominant optimism sustained an idealistic faith in the power of human reason, as evidenced especially in the power of education and of art and in the confident advance of science. The cultured bourgeoisie, as Arthur J. May writes, 'heartily believed in the religion of progress, in the optimistic faith that there was an iron law of inevitable human improvement'.[14] Over a century after the French Revolution, the assumptions of the Age of Enlightenment were still largely in place until the fall of the European empires in 1918. The widespread survival of this unquestioning optimism at the end of the nineteenth century is summarized by Stefan Zweig in his memoirs: 'Radicalism and violence seemed to have become impossible in an age of reason.'[15]

According to Hermann Broch, writing in the 1940s, the crisis that followed arose from the 'value vacuum' (WM, 86) of the period 1870–90, the essential artistic temper of which, Broch argues, may be seen in the characteristic 'non-style' of its architecture. Broch presents the period as an age not of art but of *Kitsch*, with Vienna the very capital of cultural vacuity; but in fact it was one of substantial achievement: the realist drama of Anzengruber; the witty late prose of Kürnberger and the novellas of Ferdinand von Saar; the operetta of Johann Strauss, the symphonies of Bruckner; the artistry of the Burgtheater company in one of the most celebrated periods of its history; the international reputation of the medical school, where both Freud and Schnitzler trained and which provided a powerful base for Freud's theories.[16] What was much more disruptive was the rapid change in the fabric and social structure of the expanding city – a process of change that continued past the turn of the century in the modernizing reforms introduced under Lueger's mayoralty.

The social changes and the pressures they produced underlay further political developments, notably the rise of anti-Semitism as a powerful political force in Austria, which confirmed the demise of the rule of reason; the political history of the period can indeed be seen as a downward spiral into irrationalism. It was in the early years of the twentieth century – first on a visit in 1906, then as an aspiring painter from 1908 to 1913 – that Hitler was in Vienna, learning his populist anti-Semitism from the politics of the city; the most hysterically irrational of political movements was being born.

The central role played by the large Jewish population of Vienna in every branch of its cultural life, both as patrons and as practising artists, was a subject of raucous resentment in the anti-Semitic press. It is characteristic that the two leading dramatists were of Jewish or partly Jewish extraction. Schnitzler was born into an assimilated Jewish professional family. Though Hofmannsthal was baptized in the Karlskirche and brought up and educated as a Roman Catholic, his paternal great-grandfather, on whom the title 'Edler von Hofmannsthal' had been conferred in 1835, was a silk merchant from Bohemia, Isaak Löw Hofmann, who had become a prominent member of the Viennese Jewish community.

In intellectual life too the inherited rational norms were under threat. Two disruptive forces that Bahr picked out in 1903 were the 'destruction of the ego' by Ernst Mach and the 'destruction of language' by Fritz Mauthner.[17] Mauthner, a journalist and philosopher who worked in Berlin but came from Prague, was the author of a three-volume work, *Beiträge zu einer Kritik der Sprache* (1901–2), in which 'criticism of language' is defined as fundamental to all theory of knowledge. It is known that Hofmannsthal had read the first volume by the time he wrote the 'Chandos Letter', the most celebrated document of the 'language crisis' of the early twentieth century, in 1902: he himself told Mauthner that he bought it as soon as it appeared, and an excerpt also appeared in the weekly *Die Wage* in January 1901.[18] In the case of Mach, whose lectures Hofmannsthal attended in 1897, what Bahr had in mind was his conception of knowledge as being essentially restricted to our subjective experience of 'sense impressions' ('Empfindungen'), in effect a reduction of the whole individual mind and personality to the sum of its sensations and impressions. In 1891 Bahr defined the latest phase of the modernist search for truth as consisting in 'sensations, nothing but sensations, momentary impressions of the rush of events on the nerves'.[19] Bahr himself subsequently re-hearsed Mach's theory in an essay first published in the *Neues Wiener Tagblatt* on 10 April 1903 and reprinted the next year in his volume *Dialog vom Tragischen*, proclaiming the 'irrecoverable ego' ('Das unrettbare Ich').[20] The most seismic influence of all, how-ever, was that of Freud, whose most resonant work, *The Inter-pretation of Dreams (Die Traumdeutung)*, appeared late in 1899 and was drawn to the attention of the literary world by a long two-part review by Max Burckhard in *Die Zeit* in January 1900 (JW II, 1047–59) – a review that Freud himself found 'uncommonly lacking in understanding'.[21]

Freud's immense contributions to the treatment of mental and psychic disorders – his definition of neurosis as authentic disease distinct from physiology, and his invention of psychoanalysis as an instrument of therapy – were based on theoretical writings that were highly controversial. This is true especially of the central emphasis in his work on sexuality, resulting from his theory that most neuroses derive from the repression of unconscious drives, especially sexual drives, and their conflict with the ideas of the conscious mind. He not only diagnosed the prevalent social ethics as being repressive and so inducing neurosis, at a time when Victorian taboos and conventions of sexual behaviour were only beginning to be brought out into the open and broken down; most fundamentally, by unlocking the mysteries of the unconscious mind, he also helped to revalue the irrational element in Man, seeing it no longer as essentially negative, an 'animalistic' side to be overcome, but as the very deepest layer of our mind, and even – when 'sublimated' – as contributing to our highest artistic achievements.

Schnitzler read *The Interpretation of Dreams* soon after it had appeared,[22] and in his own treatments of the human psyche, especially in his prose fiction,[23] frequently travelled along similar paths to those of Freud's theoretical writings. His interest in psychological literature was not limited to Freudian theory;[24] nevertheless, Freud so admired his psychological insight that in 1922, writing on the occasion of Schnitzler's sixtieth birthday, he admitted to regarding him as a kind of *Doppelgänger* (WM, 652). Hofmannsthal too was a lifelong reader of psychological literature. He too owned a copy of the first edition of *The Interpretation of Dreams*, though he seems not to have read it until 1903, the year in which he wrote his *Elektra*;[25] five years after that, in a letter to Oscar A. H. Schmitz, he wrote of Freud as someone all of whose writings he knew.[26] His works include a series of explorations of problems of personality, developing and undeveloped. In Mach's Vienna it is characteristic that Hofmannsthal should have shown particular interest in the idea of the split personality and in dislocations of personality. In the mid-1890s, for example, after discussing the actress Adele Sandrock with Schnitzler, he noted their conclusion that her conscious self ('ihr bewußtes Ich') and her 'dreamlike' histrionic self seemed unconnected (A, 115), and formulated the idea that this splitting of the self seemed to be inherent in the 'reproductive genius' that acting required ('Diese Spaltung des Ich scheint die Daseinsform des reproduzierenden Genies zu sein').

His further interest in psychological ideas, and psychoanalysis in particular, in relation to literature and drama seems to have been stimulated not least by Alfred von Berger, who reviewed the *Studies in Hysteria* by Breuer and Freud in the *Morgenpresse* of 2 February 1896 and also published a long critical article on the dramatization of psychological phenomena ('Ueber dramatische Darstellung psychischer Phänomene') in *Die Wage* in August 1900 (JW II, 1116–23).[27] Hofmannsthal's interest in psychological problems continued into the new century. By 1904, in connection with his planned adaptation of Calderón's *La vida es sueño* (*Das Leben ein Traum*), he wrote to Bahr of the problem of 'plumbing the deepest depths of the dubious subterranean kingdom of the ego' ('in die tiefsten Tiefen des zweifelhaften Höhlenkönigreiches "Ich" hinabzusteigen': H/Bfe. II, 155). In 1907 the 'biographical study in abnormal psychology' *The Dissociation of a Personality* by the American psychopathologist Morton Prince (New York, 1906), a case history of multiple personality, provided one of the chief inspirations for his early work on his novel *Andreas*.[28] And as for Freud in particular, though in his letter of January 1908 to Oscar A. H. Schmitz he refers disparagingly to Freud's non-specialist (that is, non-medical) work, by September 1922, when he wrote the second of his 'Vienna Letters' for the American monthly *The Dial*, he was very warm in celebrating the perceptiveness of Freud's work and the influence he had exercised (A, 289–93); and in 1924 he again acknowledged his seminal importance (H/Burckhardt, 161: letter of 12 September 1924).

The innovatory impetus of the modernist movements born in the 1890s – the poets and dramatists of 'Jung Wien', the painters and architects of the Secession – derived from a sense of liberation from the past. The Moderns were, as Bahr put it in his review of the production of Hofmannsthal's *Elektra* in the Theater an der Wien in 1905, a 'new generation with a great longing for freedom ('dieses neue Geschlecht der großen Sehnsucht ins Freie').[29] This liberation was to be achieved by a revolutionary search for truth. 'Let us become true,' proclaimed Bahr in 1890, in an essay on 'Die Moderne': 'Let us shake off the rotten past, long withered, which is suffocating our very spirit in its rotten foliage. Let us be of the present!' ('[. . .] Gegenwart wollen wir sein': JW I, 31). This is a spirit reflected in the work of Klimt, whose *œuvre* as a whole exemplifies his coming to terms with the intellectual and cultural upheaval of his times. A drawing of the figure of *Nuda Veritas* 'holding up the mirror of art to modern man' (Schorske) appeared in the third number of *Ver sacrum*, the journal of the Secession, in 1898, with flowers growing at her feet – 'vernal symbols [. . .] to express the hope of regeneration'.[30] The fifth Secession exhibition the next year included an oil depicting the same figure, but now with a snake at her feet – a painting that Bahr himself would purchase.[31] The phrase 'Nuda veritas' comes from Horace (*Carmina* I.24.7); the pose, a female figure with her right arm reaching upwards holding a mirror, derives from Botticelli's 'Calumny of Apelles', which hangs in the Uffizi. This is a figure to which attention is specifically drawn towards the end of the Botticelli chapter in Walter Pater's *The Renaissance: Studies in Art and Poetry*, a book on which Hofmannsthal wrote in *Die Zeit* in 1894 (P I, 202–3). *Nuda veritas* was a familiar artistic topos of the late nineteenth century: a painting by Jules-Joseph Lefebvre was shown in the 1870 Paris salon (it is now in the Musée d'Orsay), and the figure reappears on the river façade of the Palais de Justice. What Klimt distinctively adds in his 1899 oil – a suggestive token of the importance of sexuality in the whole climate of turn-of-the-century Vienna – is the sinister figure of the serpent entwined around her feet. In the third and most radically subversive of the three Faculty paintings commissioned from Klimt by the University of Vienna, 'Jurisprudence', the disintegrating intellectual order is again symbolized in a female figure, in this case functioning as the sensual embodiment of irrationality, the new threatening power substituted for the rationality of law. (It is pertinent to recall that it was in another great Habsburg city, Prague, that Kafka was at this very time growing up.)

The disintegration of stable value systems broke down the coherence of traditional perceptions of life. This breakdown is reflected in the fictional hero of Hofmannsthal's 'Chandos Letter'. Chandos has previously felt part of an integrated spiritual order, perceiving 'the whole of existence as one great unity' (P II, 10) – the idea of a 'lost unity' goes back to Bahr's essay 'Die Moderne' of 1890 (JW I, 31) – but this has now dissolved: 'Everything broke down into separate parts, then the separate parts into further parts, and single concepts no longer served to describe anything' ('Es zerfiel mir alles in Teile, die Teile wieder in Teile, und nichts mehr ließ sich mit einem Begriff umspannen': P II, 13). If the phrasing of the first part of that sentence reads like an echo of Mach's reduction of the individual to sense-impressions, the second spells out the consequences, the inadequacy of inherited modes of expression.

Two months after the appearance of 'Ein Brief', Hofmannsthal returned to the subject in a dialogue 'Über Charaktere im Roman und im Drama', which he published in the *Neue Freie Presse* at Christmas 1902. It takes the form of an imaginary discussion between Balzac and the Viennese orientalist Joseph von Hammer-Purgstall, in which Balzac is made to argue that because every generation is 'more aware' than the one before it, a 'peculiar chemistry, which operates with every drawing of breath, will increasingly fragment life', so that every experience, 'even the loss of illusions', will 'fall into the deep well of the soul not in one piece but [. . .] in atoms', to such an extent that 'around 1890 or 1900 what was meant by the word "experience" [Erlebnis] will no longer be understood at all' (P II, 44–5).

The sense of discontinuity was so acute that identity itself often seemed under threat. There are many testimonies to the new sense of fluidity: Hofmannsthal writing in 1891 that his own self of yesterday was of no more concern to him than that of Napoleon or Goethe ('Mein Ich von *gestern* geht mich so wenig an wie das Ich Napoleons oder Goethes': A, 93); Andrea in the opening scene of his first lyrical drama, *Gestern*, proclaiming that 'yesterday is false, today alone is true' ('Das Gestern lügt, und nur das Heut ist wahr!': HKA III, 13); a similar line in a sonnet by Otto Stoessl (who moved on the fringes of the Griensteidl group and subsequently associated with Karl Kraus), 'Wir sind nicht heute, was wir gestern waren' ('What yesterday we were, today we are no longer').[32] In this context, the chameleon-like character of Bahr as a critic seems not unnatural but symptomatic. Strategies to counter the threat to the very integrity of the personality range from Karl Kraus's construction of a fixed but essentially fictional satirical persona[33] to Schnitzler's cataloguing of the daily events of his life in his diaries: 'I have', he noted in his entry for 4 August 1890, 'a strange need to record [or "capture"] myself psychologically' ('Ich habe ein sonderbares Bedürfnis, mich psychologisch festzuhalten').

The disintegration of stable systems of values is reflected in the disorientation in modes of artistic expression characteristic of the period, the symptomatic search for new 'languages' in all the arts. The most conspicuous example, which provides Schorske with the starting-point for his analysis of the decline of Liberalism, is architecture, the abandoning of the Victorian historicism of the Ringstrasse and the fashioning of new styles, which developed gradually towards functionalism (pioneered in Vienna by Adolf Loos). But there are equally potent parallels in the other arts: the successive modes adopted by Klimt in painting, followed by the contrasting Expressionist styles of Schiele and of Kokoschka; Schönberg's adoption of atonality in music; the 'language crisis' in literature, with its parallel in philosophical language criticism

('Sprachkritik'), a concern that continued to occupy Hofmannsthal in his forties in *Der Schwierige*.

The ideological disorientation had specific implications for drama. Schnitzler perceived that with the collapse of inherited ideological certainties the very prerequisite of traditional drama had disappeared – a late Viennese counterpart to the European phenomenon of the 'death of tragedy'. Writing to Otto Brahm, he once defined the 'fundamental dramatic defect' of one of his own plays, *Der Ruf des Lebens*, as lying in the 'undramatic world-view' ('die undramatische Weltanschauung') underlying it (AS/Brahm, 203: letter of 16 March 1908). His collection of aphorisms, *Buch der Sprüche und Bedenken*, published in 1927, still contains a definition of 'the existence of a definite world-view and the acceptance of certain established ethical values' as 'a necessary precondition of drama' (AB, 101). In particular any endangering of the idea of the inte-grated personality had implications for dramatists, undermining as it did the traditional notion of character development. Hence a vogue for one-act plays, explorations of psychological moods rather than elaborations of complex actions. The popularity of the genre led to critical discussion of its aesthetics; Rudolph Lothar, for example, reviewing three Schnitzler plays in *Die Wage* in March 1899, argued that since the one-act form allowed no time for exposition, for events building up the motivation of the action, its essence lay in creating atmosphere ('Stimmung'), evoking a milieu and so illuminating the characters from without (JW II, 971–5). But that is to describe the effect rather than the cause. Not only had the whole conception of character become insecure, the episodic form also lent itself to conveying the fragmented quality of per-ception in a life unsettled by the new discontinuity.

In 1913 Steed recorded rather plaintively that Vienna had in recent years 'adopted with snobbish alacrity the unintelligible canons of "modern Art"'.[34] But to the practitioners themselves the conversion must have seemed undetectable. The resistance to modernism, by critics and the public alike, was deep-rooted. Even Bruckner's Eighth Symphony was attacked in 1892 by Eduard Hanslick as a nightmarish caterwauling; Hanslick added that if this was the music of the future he did not envy the future.[35] And the bolder experimentation became, the shriller the abuse. 'Philosophy', the first of Klimt's three Faculty paintings (all eventually destroyed by fire in 1945), was denounced in a petition signed by over eighty professors when it was first shown in 1900. In the musical sphere, Hofmannsthal's warning in his letter of 7 October 1908 to Strauss that the Viennese public were 'still as resistant to anything new' as in Mozart's time (H/Strauss, 41) was borne out the next year when a reviewer in the *Fremdenblatt*, Richard Batka, savaged what he deemed the 'pointless ugliness' of Schönberg's three *Klavierstücke* Op. 11, and summed up his opinion in the dictum that if that was art, then art was art no longer, while in 1913 a performance of Berg's Altenberg songs, conducted by Schönberg, ended in a near riot.[36] In December 1910, in the most famous *cause célèbre* of all, the house on the Michaelerplatz designed by Loos, just across the road from where the Café Griensteidl had stood, was attacked in the *Neue Freie Presse* for a tasteless bareness, blatantly at odds with the older buildings around it,[37] and its bare front earned it derisive notoriety as the 'house without eyebrows'. Even among the erstwhile moderns there were those whose conservatism was antagonized by the development toward functionalism in architecture: Andrian, for example, wrote to Hofmannsthal on 18 September 1913 referring to Otto Wagner as a 'barbarian' insensitive to the destruction of Old Vienna (H/Andrian, 203).

These examples illustrate the characteristic ambience of the period, its tension between innovation and conservatism. Even within the modernism of the 'Jung Wien' circle, the forward-looking, would-be revolutionary momentum coexisted with a nostalgia for the Vienna of the past – most often Biedermeier Vienna, as for example in Hofmannsthal's essay of 1893 on Bauernfeld (P I, 159–64), or further back the age of Maria Theresia.[38] The nostalgia is characteristically for a lost innocence – the loss of innocence paradigmatically suggested in Hofmannsthal's well-known sonnet 'Die Beiden' (HKA I, 50). Written in 1895 or 1896, this poem was reprinted with very minor modifications in 1899 in *Ver sacrum* with an illustration by Friedrich König that suggests a medieval setting. In the gesture with which the two figures exchange the goblet, passing it from one to another, the poem evokes a moment of communication – in the event, of failed communication. The tension that has had this disturbing effect, disrupting the youthful confidence suggested in the quatrains, is clearly the product of the experience of love. The poem finally becomes one about the loss of innocence; with the erotic encounter the magic of innocence, and also its command, are past.

As the old order was passing, the intrusion of modernity made the past seem a Paradise before the Fall, from which man had in the modern world been excluded – a paradise lost recurrently conjured up in images of a garden, most notably in Hofmannsthal's trochaic 'Prolog zu dem Buch Anatol' (HKA I, 24–5), the playful yet evocative celebration of the grounds of the eighteenth-century Belvedere palaces that he wrote as a preface to the published edition of Schnitzler's *Anatol*. Carl E. Schorske, commenting on this poem, justly observes that 'the image of the garden [. . .] served as the artificial preserve wherein the functionless and cultivated could live sundered from a world they neither made nor cared to know'.[39] In the early dramatic fragment *Der Tod des Tizian* the great painter Titian is described as having built a garden surrounded by high walls, so that the outside world cannot even be seen (HKA III, 46). Other poets of Hofmannsthal's generation who evoke gardens as places not just of solitude but of solitary nostalgia include Paul Wertheimer and Joseph August Lux.[40]

Paradoxically, however, it is also characteristic of the temper of the period that escapist nostalgia is counterbalanced by a constant sense of forward-looking excitement – the sense, encapsulated in the title of *Ver sacrum*, that the modernist period is one of rebirth, a modern Renaissance.

Renaissance

In September 1898, noting the importance of the Renaissance in connection with d'Annunzio and his 'attitude to world civilization', Hofmannsthal used the phrase 'the renaissance of the Renaissance' ('die Renaissance der Renaissance'), adding cryptically 'in connection with everything' ('auf alles bezüglich': HKA II, 426). The Renaissance idea was indeed pervasive.

In the visual arts, Renaissance settings had been fashionable since the 1870s, associated in Vienna with Hans Makart in particular. But by the 1890s fashion had changed. Early in 1897 Berta Zuckerkandl, writing in *Die Zeit*, ridiculed the tastelessness of pseudo-Renaissance interiors in the Makart manner (JW II, 669); the next year Adolf Loos, in his attack on the 'Potemkin city' in *Ver sacrum*, rejected as sham the imitation Renaissance buildings of the Ringstrasse era such as the university, the museums, and the Opera House (JW II, 870–2).

Although artistic historicism was under fire, the Moderns were captivated by the notion of their own age as a second Renaissance – a period both of rebirth and of decadence. The parallel between the late nineteenth century and the historical Renaissance was explicitly drawn in 1892 by Marie Herzfeld, an influential Viennese critic, in a long review of Hofmannsthal's *Gestern* that appeared in the *Allgemeine Theater-Revue für Bühne und Welt*. The setting was 'the overripe time of Renaissance and dissolution, whose basic spirit has features in common with our own' ('die überreife Renaissance- und Auflösungszeit, deren geistiger Grundtypus mit dem unserigen manchen Zug gemeinsam hat': JW I, 322; HUK, 42).

The appeal and the supposed affinity of the period lay partly in the fascination of the artistic life, and partly in the perception of the Renaissance as a climactic expression of individualism in which achievement was coupled with unrestrained abandonment. Marie Herzfeld, for example, used the term 'Renaissance strength' ('Renaissance-Kraft') as a critical description in a review in *Die Zeit* in 1896 (JW I, 630). Hence Rudolph Lothar's description of Nietzsche in 1898 as a 'Renaissance man reborn';[41] so too Alfred von Berger, writing in *Die Wage* after Nietzsche's death in 1900, wrote that he toyed 'with the vision of a splendid heroic person-ality, of utmost genius, invincible power and strength of will, modelled on the brilliant but infamous great figures of the Italian Renaissance, a personality that feels beyond good and evil' (JW II, 1130).

By comparison with other parts of German-speaking Europe, however, Nietzsche had a relatively weak following in Vienna.[42] Certainly the late nineteenth-century view of the Renaissance derived mainly from Jacob Burckhardt's classic study *The Civil-ization of the Renaissance in Italy* (*Die Cultur der Renaissance in Italien*), which had first been published in 1860 and went through seven new impressions in the period 1885–1908. Schnitzler, for example, completed writing his drama *Der Schleier der Beatrice*, which is set in early sixteenth-century Bologna, shortly after reading Burckhardt (Tgb., 15 May 1899). The main source of the fascination the Renaissance had for Hofmannsthal was Walter Pater's book *The Renaissance* (1877), which appeared in German translation in 1902; in his 1894 essay 'Walter Pater' he argues that Pater gives an account of the very nature of the artist unmatched in understanding even by Goethe (P I, 202–3).

The stock picture of the period distilled from these sources was a simplistic one. It is attractively captured in a lively verse comedy set in mid-sixteenth-century Italy and entitled simply *Renaissance*, which was written by a Viennese dramatist and producer, Franz von Schönthan, in collaboration with Franz Koppel-Ellfeld. First produced in 1896 in the Hoftheater in Dresden, where Koppel-Ellfeld was employed as dramaturg, this play seems to have been read by Schönthan, in Schnitzler's presence, in a Viennese coffee-house, probably the Café Griensteidl, in the same year (Tgb., 28 October 1896). At the end of the following year it was staged in Vienna at the Deutsches Volkstheater, and on 31 October 1900 in the Burgtheater, where it survived in the repertory until 1920. The central character is a painter, an apostle of sensual pleasure, who teaches whole-hearted commitment to life as the very substance of art, and conceives of art as serving the beauty of the world. The power of his exuberance is shown by the impact he has on two other characters: a widowed Marchesa, whose heart he wins, and her son Vittorino, an aspiring young artist, whose education he takes over and who under his tutelage learns to see art as the very purpose of life.

In most of German-speaking Europe, the Renaissance was much used from the mid-1870s onwards as a dramatic setting. A series of dramas appeared on the Borgias, Marino Falieri, Raphael, Savonarola, and the like.[43] It was because of this vogue for using the Renaissance as mere décor that in April 1906 Hofmannsthal would tartly dismiss a suggestion made the previous month by Richard Strauss that he should write a libretto with a Renaissance setting, centring on Cesare Borgia or Savonarola. Hofmannsthal rejected the setting as hackneyed, adding that he could think of no other epoch so far removed from the present in the quality of its life (H/Strauss, 18–19).

In fact, despite all the interest in the Renaissance idea, it was not a subject much exploited by the Viennese 'Moderns' in the theatre. The critic Hans Sittenberger, writing in 1898 about contemporary Austrian drama, attempted to argue otherwise, crediting them with a fondness for Renaissance dramatic settings (WM, 254); but this is not borne out even by his own evidence. The only example he discusses, apart from one act of Rudolph Lothar's pseudo-Faustian drama *Der Werth des Lebens*, is Hofmannsthal's *Gestern*.[44] And indeed almost the only important plays in Renaissance settings written up to that point by members of the 'Jung Wien' generation were those by Hofmannsthal, and they are very different from the quasi-Nietzschean heroics of fashionable Renaissance tragedies. Moreover, while *Gestern* met with a very favourable critical reception (even Karl Kraus, later hostile to Hofmannsthal, wrote a review in *Die Gesellschaft* in June 1892 praising the psychological perception, the classical perfection of the verse, and the authenticity of the rich atmosphere),[45] it was not performed in Vienna until 1928. The fragment *Der Tod des Tizian*, printed in 1892, was not staged until 1901. The short tragedy *Die Frau im Fenster*, first printed in 1898, was performed in Berlin that year but was not seen in Vienna until June 1900, when it was performed in the Deutsches Volkstheater by Brahm's visiting company from Berlin. Rudolph Lothar's one-act tragedy *Cesar Borgia's Ende*, performed in Frankfurt am Main in 1892 and published the following year, was not staged at all in any of the principal Viennese theatres. Among later works with Renaissance settings, Schnitzler's *Paracelsus* was produced in the Burgtheater in March 1899 but was given only twelve performances in just under two years; *Der Schleier der Beatrice*, first staged in Breslau in 1900, was not produced in the Burgtheater until 1925.

Sittenberger's analysis carries more conviction in his scepticism about the supposed kinship between the *fin de siècle* and the Renaissance. The Moderns lacked the psychic energy of the Renaissance, he argued; they aspired to the ideal of the immoralist superman but could achieve only decadent self-indulgence (WM, 254–6). Marie Herzfeld had said much the same thing in 1892 in her review of *Gestern* (JW I, 322–3; HUK, 42–3). Indeed, the whole idea of the *fin de siècle* as a time of renaissance stands in contradiction to how the period is more usually regarded, as one of apocalyptic decline – the 'joyful apocalypse' diagnosed by Broch in *Hofmannsthal und seine Zeit*. Broch's study is strongly influenced by Kraus, but in Kraus the image of impending apocalypse is used in a profound polemical sense: the true apocalypse, as outlined in the 1908 essay 'Apokalypse', is the demise of imagination, producing an uncivilized humanity (F 261, 7). Broch's concern, by contrast, is with a particular culture in decline – a decline that eventually coincided with the downfall of the Habsburg dynasty.

Just when that downfall became inevitable is debatable. Perhaps from the Austro-Prussian War in 1866 and the creation of the Dual Monarchy the next year; perhaps from the suicide of Crown Prince Rudolph at Mayerling, in an atmosphere of suppressed scandal, in 1889; perhaps from the fall of the Badeni government in 1897. But at the time, as we have seen, there was no sense of imminent collapse. This may explain why dramatic presentations of the Renaissance are seldom tinged with a sense of impending destruction; only rarely, as in *Der Schleier der Beatrice*, where the infidelities are played out in a city under attack by Cesare Borgia, does approaching doom colour the atmosphere, making the present moment doubly sweet (DW I, 678–9).

It was in a cultural sense that there was a feeling of living at the end of an epoch. The Viennese of the late nineteenth century were, in a word used by Hermann Menkes in an essay in *Die Zeit* in 1895, 'Verfallzeitler', 'men of an age of decay' (JW I, 541). This is the feeling underlying the argument of Paul Wertheimer, writing in October 1897, that the true historical analogue to the new Austrian renaissance lay in the *end* of the Renaissance (JW II, 780–90); similarly Hofmannsthal noted a preference for Rome in its time of decay ('Rom der Verfallzeit') – a city of epigones ('Spätgeborene': P I, 205). The sense of being 'epigones' is a recurrent one, from Hofmannsthal (P I, 147) to Kraus, who uses the term in the poem 'Bekenntnis', written during the War (F 443–444, 28).

The work in which the Renaissance is given its most searching treatment as an intellectual phenomenon bearing on artistic creativity is not a drama at all but the 'Chandos Letter' ('Ein Brief', 1902). Though it has often been printed among Hofmannsthal's essays, it is not an essay but fictional. This is borne out by his subsequent inclusion of it in 1905 in his collection of stories *Das Märchen der 672. Nacht und andere Erzählungen*.

In it, as he wrote to Andrian on 16 January 1903, he adopts 'eine historische Maske' (H/Andrian, 160) – a mask, that is, chosen in order to give artistic expression to a specific view of intellectual history. The choice of an English Renaissance setting – he was beginning work in the summer of 1902 on *Das gerettete Venedig*, his adaptation of Otway's *Venice Preserv'd* – is explained in part by the association of the period with creative facility, as in his lyric dramas. But in *Gestern*, as Rolf Tarot has shown,[46] the Renaissance also serves as a symbol for a specific stage in individual development, the awakening of the conscious personality. So too in the letter Chandos is confronted with a development of self-awareness; one of the projects he has abandoned was to be a collection of apophthegms, bearing the programmatic title *Nosce te ipsum*. His crisis has been induced by a confrontation with self-knowledge, which has threatened his very sense of individual identity; one of the very first points he makes in his letter is that he scarcely knows whether he is the same person as the one to whom Bacon has written (P II, 7).

Hofmannsthal's choice of Francis Bacon as the Renaissance addressee to whom Chandos looks for understanding has the function of articulating the rational principle which suddenly governs Chandos's mind, breaking down the world of his perceptions analytically.[47] That is to say, Hofmannsthal has Chandos confront an analytical rationality associated with the historical original of his addressee; he is addressing the rational principle that has destroyed the unity of his world-view. His abandoning of specific projects illustrates his rejection of the rationalist and scientific activities of the Renaissance period, symbolized in the (Baconian) works he is giving up (P II, 8–9): his history of the early years of Henry VIII's reign, his treatment of myths and fables, and the *Apophthegmata* on subjects conducive to self-knowledge, whose model is clearly Bacon's *Apophthegmes New and Old* (1625).

The quest for a new 'language', appropriate to authentic experience, on which Hofmannsthal's Chandos embarks (P II, 20) is the direct consequence, then, of his rejection of the spirit of Bacon. His inability to write Latin prose, to write a historical work he has planned, and to use classical myths – these are all symptomatic: the first, of a breakdown in the cultural order; the second, of a loss of continuity and tradition, for continuity is enshrined in language (this would be one of the themes of Hofmannsthal's essay 'Der Dichter und diese Zeit' of 1907); and the third, of the undermining of spiritual certainties, for one of the functions of myths in imaginative literature is to express fundamental and timeless truths. Together, these three failures demonstrate a conviction that the institutions of the past, exemplified and expressed in language, are hollow.

What Hofmannsthal has set out in a Renaissance setting in 'Ein Brief' is unmistakably a set of symptoms of his own age: a disruption of values associated with an undermining of intellectual certainties. But he goes further. By building up the parallels between the fictional Chandos and the historical Bacon, he not only suggests the kinship of the Renaissance and the modern period, he also suggests a causal historical link between the two periods.

Underlying his fascination with the Renaissance was a historical sense, an emerging view of cultural history.[48] The undermining of intellectual and spiritual certainties had been the product of advancements in learning, going back not just to the Age of Reason but to the Renaissance itself. This is essentially the point rehearsed by Bahr at the end of his essay 'Das unrettbare Ich' (1904): 'Reason overthrew the ancient gods and dethroned our world. Now it threatens to destroy us too' (WM, 148). Hofmannsthal saw the Renaissance, the Reformation, and the French Revolution as signifying a disintegration in the traditional order: with the emancipation of the individual, a hitherto cohesive cultural unity had been sacrificed. This view would later form the basis of the belief he developed (under Andrian's influence) about the role that should be played by Catholic Austria in the process of cultural restoration – the 'conservative revolution' – which he championed after the First World War and to which I shall be returning in chapters 5 and 6. The roots of the process of decline, as he perceived it, lay in the Renaissance. The changes it launched – political nationalism, the rise of the bourgeoisie, an increased historical awareness – were all developments that he could regard as having reached their climax in the nineteenth century.

By the end of Hofmannsthal's life, this grand overview of the decline of European culture had become an orthodoxy. It is summarized by Egon Friedell in his *Kulturgeschichte der Neuzeit*,[49] the first volume of which appeared in 1927, and in which the Renaissance is described as 'the second – and true – Fall of Man'. What Friedell regards as the true apocalypse is, in Krausian spirit, the First World War; but in tracing the progressive triumph of the human intellect he explicitly draws a line leading from 1500 to 1900. In the Renaissance, with the expansion of intellectual inquiry, lie both the beginnings of the rise of science and, in the German-speaking centres, the roots of the Reformation, which together were to destroy the intellectual authority and the political unity of the medieval church. In the choice between beauty and goodness, as Friedell puts it, the Renaissance chose beauty, and he draws a parallel with Wilde's *The Picture of Dorian Gray* – a book which in the mid-1890s Hofmannsthal had found 'surprisingly' reminiscent of the outlook of his own circle.[50]

The Chandos Letter represents a turning-point in Hofmannsthal's creative work in anticipating, at least embryonically, his later cultural politics, which informed his work for the Salzburg Festival and are expounded in the address 'Das Schrifttum als geistiger Raum der Nation', which he delivered at the University of Munich in January 1927. The final paragraph of that address (P IV, 412–13) presents the 'conservative revolution' as a counter to the 'intellectual revolution' in European thought that had begun in the Renaissance (see pp. 183–4, below).

The Renaissance was widely admired around the turn of the century, catching the imagination of artists who saw it as a climactic period of individualism and artistic creativity. As such it provided a parallel to the belief in a rebirth of art that informed the Moderns' search for new styles. They sensed an affinity not so much with Renaissance achievement as with the example the period presented of a *revival* of culture and creativeness – a model for the programme of regeneration proclaimed in the title of *Ver sacrum*. It is in this sense that Bahr wrote in 1893 of the Austrian 'Moderns' ('das junge Österreich') as being influenced by the 'hope of a renaissance' (JW I, 364) and that Wertheimer, discussing Bahr's volume entitled *Renaissance* in October 1897, argued that it was legitimate to speak of a kind of 'Renaissance' led by Bahr ('von einer Art Bahr'scher "Renaissance"': JW II, 783). But the crucial link was that in the historical Renaissance, love of art went together with the beginnings of the breakdown of certainty, a disruption of values whose final stages the Moderns sensed in their own age.

'Naturalist' and 'Neo-Romantic'

In responding to the intellectual and social crises of their time, Schnitzler and Hofmannsthal adopted contrasting strategies in their dramatic writing. That their methods made them complementary opposites was indeed seen as early as 1906, when the Berlin theatre critic Alfred Kerr wrote that Schnitzler's way of writing attempted to be forward-looking, Hofmannsthal's backward-looking.[51] He meant that by contrast with Schnitzler's realistic depiction of the *mœurs* of the present day ('Schnitzler seeks to continue the technique of Ibsen') Hofmannsthal was clearly out of sympathy with

Naturalism, the movement which was most in line with the
progressive political thinking of the times and which had long been
thought of as the main 'modern' movement – 'the modern movement, which came from the north a decade ago', as Karl Kraus put
it in *Die demolirte Litteratur*.[52]

In 1893 Ferdinand von Saar published his *Wiener Elegien*. Saar
was one of the central figures in Josephine von Wertheimstein's
salon in Döbling on the north-western outskirts of Vienna, where
Hofmannsthal was a welcome guest. The fourteenth of the elegies
includes a satirical portrait of fashionable 'modernity', evoking
among other things a young budding dramatist of the future:

> Dichtest du etwa schon jetzt an einem veristischen Drama,
>   Das in der Klinik beginnt und am Seziertisch verläuft?[53]

> Have you been working away on some veristic drama,
>   Set in a clinic and played round the operating-table?

Two years after the 'Ibsen week', this is clearly a dig at the 'clinical'
style of Naturalism. 'Hospital poetry' ('Spitalpoesie') was the term
Paul Heyse had applied to *Ghosts*.[54] There was considerable justice
in Kraus's sceptical riposte (already quoted) to Bahr's volume
Die Überwindung des Naturalismus, to the effect that there was no
Austrian Naturalism; but if there was a Viennese dramatist whom
Saar might have had in mind, it was probably Schnitzler, whose
Anatol, including the scene *Die Frage an das Schicksal* with its use of
hypnotism, had been published late in 1892. Schnitzler was from
the first associated with the realist camp. When one of the *Anatol*
playlets, *Abschiedssouper*, was first performed in Bad Ischl in 1893,
the report in the *Wiener Allgemeine Zeitung* on 18 July referred to
him as 'a young Viennese writer of the Naturalist school', and by
the time his first major success in serious drama, *Liebelei*, was
produced in the Burgtheater in 1895, reviewers took it as established fact that he was 'the boldest of the Viennese "Moderns"' and
that *Liebelei*, itself 'terrifyingly modern', was 'drawn directly from
the life of Vienna'; the Burgtheater was even seen as taking a daring
risk in experimenting with such full-blooded realism.[55] The play
treats love across the class barrier. Ludwig Speidel, reviewing the
première in the *Neue Freie Presse*, emphasized Schnitzler's 'truthfulness'; another critic wrote that he had depicted the milieu of
the young Viennese men about town with 'almost photographic
accuracy'.[56] When Julius Bab, surveying stylistic trends in contemporary German drama just before the First World War, named
Schnitzler among lesser followers of Gerhart Hauptmann, Schnitzler
marked the passage in his offprint in red crayon, indicating his

dislike of the categorization.[57] But even after his death, a number of obituaries still summed up his work as having its roots in Naturalism – whether he was seen as having outgrown or extended it or as having been subject to its limitations.[58]

By 1931 there were dissenting voices, including now Bab, whose tribute, published in Berlin, associated Schnitzler rather with Hofmannsthal as a neo-Romantic.[59] But in fact their difference in approach was always fundamental. Throughout his career Schnitzler's writing is characterized by ironic objectivity in his observation of the world around him. Hofmannsthal, by contrast, had Balzac observe in his imaginary dialogue with Hammer-Purgstall:

> There are no experiences except the experience of one's own self [das Erlebnis des eigenen Wesens]. That is the key that opens for every one of us his lonely prison cell, the impenetrably thick walls of which are, it is true, hung with the phantasmagoria of the universe as with many-coloured tapestries. No one can escape his own world. (P II, 38)

Whereas Schnitzler's drama registers the realities of the external social world, Hofmannsthal's affirmation of subjective imaginative experience proclaims his affinity with the neo-Romantics. Hence the antipathy with which a committed left-wing critic such as Franz Mehring would judge him in 1899, seeing his talent as 'foppish' (HUK, 58).

The contrast between the two dramatists is reflected in the language of their early writing. Whereas Hofmannsthal adopted a distinctively atmospheric poetic idiom, Schnitzler's idiom, as Josef Körner perceived, was not an individual one but on the contrary borrowed from real life, the conversational language of Viennese society.[60] The difference would also determine the allegiances they developed in the theatre. Schnitzler would develop close ties with Otto Brahm, the leading director associated with German Naturalism, who was a byword for scrupulous fidelity to the dramatic text, while Hofmannsthal gave his loyalty to Max Reinhardt, who notoriously subordinated the text to the totality of theatrical effect.

This contrast suggests the superficiality of Kerr's analysis of Schnitzler as the more forward-looking of the two dramatists. By 1906 Reinhardt had already succeeded Brahm in charge of the Deutsches Theater in Berlin and it was becoming clear that the innovative potential of Brahm's style of production had been largely exhausted.[61] Hofmannsthal's distinctively anti-Naturalist view of the poet's task can be seen in a very early essay on Eleonora

Duse, first published in 1892. He describes her art as lying in 'playing not just realistic reality, but the philosophy of her role [die Philosophie ihrer Rolle] as well'; and from this he goes on to define the fundamental distinction between 'the creative poet and the Naturalist, in that the latter treats the human soul scientifically' ('[. . .] der Wissenschaft von der menschlichen Seele treibt'), as if it were something that could be physically observed (P I, 74).

Both the charm and the limitation of Schnitzler's work, whatever its subject (infidelity, prejudice, honour), are that it is tied to the physical world and the attitudes of turn-of-the-century Vienna; Hofmannsthal, even in his comedies, would work for timeless effects, bringing out what he would designate the 'mythical' quality of his material. The significance of myth was discussed in *Die Wage* in 1901 by Otto Stoessl in an article ('Die Erneuerung des Mythos') stimulated by the appearance of Spitteler's *Olympischer Frühling* (JW II, 1160–6). Stoessl defines the creation of myth as the very origin of poetry and indeed of all art, and argues that the urge to mythicize is still universal, a 'religious, mythical impulse' that is identical with the artistic impulse. He not only gives examples from world literature, including Dante's *Inferno*, some of the plays of Shakespeare, and *Don Quixote*, but also cites Bismarck as an example of a political figure who has acquired the status of a 'mythical hero'. To Hofmannsthal this 'mythical impulse', or more precisely a mythopoeic impulse – not just using myths (he had in fact already begun to treat material drawn from ancient myth in *Alkestis*) but actually *making* myths – lay at the very heart of poetic creativity: 'The poet creates new myths', he noted in 1894, the year of *Alkestis* ('Der Dichter schafft neue Mythen': RA III, 382). It was an aim of which he would remain entirely conscious throughout his career in his approach both to creative writing and to the (ever-endangered) self: 'Individual and times perceived as myth', he noted in 1921 ('Der Einzelne und die Epoche als Mythos gesehen': A, 233). Hence his eagerness in 1913 to revise the first version of *Ariadne auf Naxos*, jettisoning the adaptation of Molière's *Le Bourgeois gentilhomme* with which it was originally linked and so breaking, as he put it to Richard Strauss, the 'unnatural coupling of the dead with the living' (H/Strauss, 199: letter of 3 June 1913) – the dead being the prose comedy, the 'living' his reworking of the mythical material of the opera.[62]

The character of his distinctive approach to reality, by contrast with Schnitzler's ironic realism, is expressed in an aphoristic observation included in his *Buch der Freunde*, to the effect that anyone who takes the phenomena of society and social interaction other than symbolically is wide of the mark ('Wer das Gesellschaftliche anders als symbolisch nimmt, geht fehl': A, 21). In one of the section of his notes *Ad me ipsum* that were written after the First World War, he compared the creation of myths to the chemical process of crystallization, adding that 'at the crucial moment everything becomes mythical [. . .]' ('Mythenbildung ist wie Kristallisation in der gesättigten Salzlösung: es wird dann im entscheidenden Augenblick alles mythisch [. . .]': A, 233).

CHAPTER 2

Biography in Letters and Diaries

Documentation

Schnitzler and Hofmannsthal were on first name terms from spring 1892, and saw each other frequently. They twice took holidays together, cycling in Switzerland in August 1898 and spending ten days together in South Tyrol (then still part of Austria) in July 1907. They never, however, advanced to using the intimate form of address, and the more time passed the more uneasy their friendship became. Hofmannsthal's moods were variable; Schnitzler, jealous of his own reputation, easily grew suspicious and even envious. Some of the reasons for this will emerge in the course of this book, and will be discussed in the final chapter.

Despite their personal differences, however, and despite the fundamental contrasts in their approaches to dramatic writing, they had much in common. They both enjoyed practical work in the theatre, observing rehearsals and collaborating with directors. They were both very widely read (Hofmannsthal exceptionally so, in many languages, even while still at school); and they both travelled a lot throughout Europe, while maintaining homes on the outskirts of Vienna.

They were both, moreover, given to hoarding papers and records. In Schnitzler's case particularly, this characteristic is revealing of his whole view of himself and his work (see pp. 58–62, below). But both were also given to repeated revision of their works, many of which had long gestation periods. Two of their best-known plays may serve as examples. The first ·conception of Schnitzler's *Professor Bernhardi* probably dates back to 1899;[1] the main spell of work then started in October 1909 and was completed in the spring of 1912. The earliest plans for Hofmannsthal's *Der Schwierige* go back to 1909, and the final version was not ready for publication until 1921.[2]

The result in Hofmannsthal's case is that though the standard edition of his works launched in 1975 was originally intended to provide comprehensive documentation of the genesis of every one of his works, that proved totally unmanageable and had to be abandoned.[3] (Just how unmanageable it was may be gauged from one of the first volumes to be published, Volume XIV, which is devoted to a fragmentary comedy entitled *Timon der Redner*. The volume contains twenty-eight pages of consecutive text, a further fifty-nine pages of draft scenes, and 413 pages of notes and variants.) In Schnitzler's case too the danger was that works would never be completed. The most substantial example is a 'tragicomedy' entitled *Das Wort* centring on a coffee-house *littérateur* based loosely on Peter Altenberg. The first notes go back to 1901, and he read a draft to Brahm in May 1907, but when he reread his manuscript two years later, he decided that though there were good details, the work as a whole was still 'unusable' (Tgb., 7 September 1909). Plans for changes are noted in his diary on 25 April 1920; he reworked the text in 1927 and reread it in May 1931, only a few months before his death, but was never satisfied with it.[4]

The dramatists' hoarding of papers provides not only their editors but also their biographers with rich sources of material. It is not surprising that the lives of such prominent figures in the artistic life of Vienna are well documented; what is unusual is the extent to which they provided the documentation themselves. The main sources are Schnitzler's diaries and Hofmannsthal's letters.

Schnitzler kept a diary for over fifty years. The earliest extant diaries go back to 1879, when he was not yet seventeen, and the very first entry (19 March 1879) refers to a still earlier one. He was also a prolific letter-writer, though often from duty rather than for pleasure – as he admitted, for example, when he wrote to his young friend Hedy Kempny lamenting the tedium of having had to write nearly twenty letters the previous day (AS/Kempny, 95: letter of 21 August 1922). For Hofmannsthal, writing long and personal letters was a fundamental part of his life, which he pursued indefatigably; the number of his recorded letters exceeds 11,000.[5] A feature of his letter-writing is the varied voices he adopts, gearing his style to his addressee. A letter of 19 May 1896 to Felix von Oppenheimer begins with a revealing apology: he has not written for so long, he says, because he did not know in what surroundings to imagine his addressee (H/Bfe. I, 195). He liked to write, as he expressed it to Beer-Hofmann on 23 May 1919, 'at the dictate of spontaneity' (H/Beer-Hofmann, 166). This not only makes his letters fascinatingly personal documents; the skill they show at adopting ever-changing styles and registers is also a key to one of the features – perhaps one of the weaknesses – of his work as a dramatist, the variety of forms and styles he adopts. There is in his less successful work (including the ambitious tragedy *Der Turm*) an unmistakable element of pastiche.

In the outlines of the two dramatists' careers that follow, I have tried to make full use of the diaries and letters, so that their very different personalities may as far as possible be allowed to speak through their own records and in their own words. The final section of the chapter will then consider the essentially autobiographical impulse underlying not only Schnitzler's lifelong devotion to keeping a diary and preserving his old diaries but also Hofmannsthal's various attempts at critical analysis of his own career, an impulse deriving in both cases directly from their views of their lives and work.

Arthur Schnitzler

Schnitzler was born on 15 May 1862; ten days later, Nestroy died. The supreme satirist of the life and follies of Vienna in mid-century was succeeded, as it were, by the ironic chronicler of the life and follies of the expanding Vienna at the end of Franz Joseph's long reign. The comparison between the two dramatists – Schnitzler recreating and illuminating the Vienna of the turn of the century as Nestroy had done for the Vienna of the Biedermeier period – was drawn in the year of Schnitzler's death in the final volume of Friedell's *Kulturgeschichte der Neuzeit*.[6]

The elder son of a prominent laryngologist, Schnitzler followed in his father's footsteps in studying medicine in Vienna, graduating in 1885. After three years as a junior hospital doctor in the Allgemeines Krankenhaus he was appointed in 1888 to an assistantship in the Allgemeine Poliklinik, of which his father was the director. From 1887 onwards he was also an editor of the *Internationale klinische Rundschau*, which his father had founded. Though he took over this responsibility with 'no pleasure' in the prospect of 'journalism' (Tgb., 24 November 1886) he became a regular contributor over the next eight years, writing several reviews each year. His attention, however, was increasingly divided between medicine and writing. From the mid-1880s onwards he published small contributions to literary magazines, including a number of poems published under the pseudonym 'Anatol'. In 1888 he began work on a cycle of playlets about a philandering but introspective man-about-town, to whom he gave the same name, Anatol.

Increasingly he moved in literary circles, and he grew ever more conscious of what in his diary he defined as the 'medicine –

literature' conflict ('Medizin – Poesie': Tgb., 18 September 1889).
His insistent awareness of what he called the 'pronounced conflict'
between his profession and himself (Tgb., 20 September 1888) led
to a strain in his relations with his father that almost certainly
contributed to the self-doubts about his actual literary achievements
which dogged him throughout his life. After his father's death in
1893, his medical work was restricted to his private practice.

It was in 1890–91 that he got to know Hofmannsthal, Salten,
Bahr and the elegant Beer-Hofmann. Though it was Hofmannsthal's
creative work he rated highest, it was Beer-Hofmann's character he
most admired. He was also on particularly relaxed terms with
Salten, whom he found the 'most agreeable' in everyday contacts
(Tgb., 21 December 1895). Schnitzler was the oldest of the circle:
when the *Anatol* cycle was published in book form late in 1892 he
was thirty. By the end of the century he was already critical of the
tone of these playlets. On 4 January 1899, for example, he wrote to
his fellow-dramatist Ludwig Fulda that one of them, *Agonie*, was
unperformable and that the dialogue in another, *Denksteine*, read as
though it had been translated from French (AS/Bfe. I, 365). Internationally, however, it was first and foremost as the writer of *Anatol*
that he was known: after his death, a headline over the obituary
notice in *The Scotsman* on 22 October 1931 still summed him up
simply as the 'Austrian Doctor Who Created "Anatol"'. In Berlin
the following morning Julius Bab's appreciation in the *Berliner
Volkszeitung* was similarly headed 'Der Dichter des "Anatol"'.

The amorous pursuits of his young heroes had their basis in his
own frenetic pursuit of women. His diaries enumerate his conquests, and record his infidelities and his jealousies. A succession of
mistresses provided him with experiences that he would exploit in
his imaginative works. Some were affectionate girls of humble
origins and without ties or prospects, such as one Jeanette Heeger,
whom Schnitzler first met in September 1887, the type of sweet
young thing ('süßes Mädl') celebrated by Anatol. Others were
connected with the stage, like Marie (Mizi) Glümer, a minor actress
who displaced Jeanette Heeger as his mistress in 1889–90; another
early play, *Das Märchen*, was consciously planned as a reflection of
their relationship:

> Began to write *Das Märchen*. 'The Tale of the Fallen Woman'.
> Liberating myself. – Psychological material from my relations
> with Mz. [Mizi] – many external circumstances also. (Tgb., 30
> November 1890)

The actress Adele Sandrock, who played the main part in the first
production of *Das Märchen* in the Deutsches Volkstheater, identified

the play at once as the story of Schnitzler's affair with Mizi Glümer (Tgb., 25 November 1893). The discovery of Mizi's infidelity contributed to his cynicism about promises of female fidelity[7] – an example of the double standards of the time (see pp. 116–19, below), but a factor that only added to his congenital insecurity. Hence the ironic self-stylization in an imaginary epitaph: 'He was fortunate with women, but was loved only by one, and by her only after she had deceived him' (Tgb., 5 May 1896).

Though *Das Märchen* was not a success – Schnitzler himself recognized that it was a 'fiasco' (Tgb., 17 December 1893) – it played an important part in his life in bringing him into contact with Adele Sandrock. Emancipated and temperamentally demanding, she came to be regarded by Schnitzler as typifying feminine sensuality; 'Dilly, the bayadère', was what he dubbed her in a diary note of 30 December 1894 after discussing her with Hofmannsthal in the coffee-house. This conversation is the same one that led Hofmannsthal to reflect on the split personality as characteristic of the 'reproductive' artist (A, 114–15). The relationship between Schnitzler and Adele Sandrock is satirically reflected in the scene between the poet and the actress in *Reigen*.

Another 'Mizi', Marie Reinhard, succeeded Adele Sandrock as his mistress in March 1895. A singing teacher from a respectable Jewish home (her father was a prosperous businessman), she first came to him as a patient in 1894. Shortly after she had become his mistress, he devoted a long diary entry to reviewing his affairs with a number of women:

> I do not think Mz. Rh. and I love each other. Love is really always a symbol of something else. For me, Mz. Rh. [represents] 'salvation' (from Dilly), for her I represent the idea of a man. Jeanette was sensuality, Olga[8] a *grande passion*, Fifi relaxation, Jenny and Minni frivolity, Fännchen 'young love' (so certainly not love), Dilly the sensation of having a famous woman (though God knows I was not proud of that!), Mz., it is true, my virtue, youth – so love itself, 'true love'. (Tgb., 4 May 1895)

Less than six weeks after seducing Marie Reinhardt he resumed his relations with Mizi Glümer, who had been patiently badgering him into renewing their affair, and within a year, though still finding Marie Reinhard 'nice and sweet and pretty', he was longing for yet another new lover (Tgb., 19 January 1896). By early 1898 he had convinced himself that he simply loved both Mizis (Tgb., 28 February 1898).

Nevertheless, Marie Reinhard and her parents pressed him to marry her – an outcome that he could contemplate only at moments of loneliness.[9] After she became pregnant he spent six weeks with her in Paris in April–May 1897 – weeks which were still to some extent marred by his distaste for marriage (Tgb., 7 May 1897) but which, he realized, would probably turn out to be among the happiest of his life (Tgb., 14 May 1897). In September 1897 she bore him a stillborn son, but marriage seemed at least possible; her sudden death in 1899 (of complications after a burst appendix) filled him, as he confessed to Hofmannsthal, with 'a loneliness beyond compare' (H/AS, 120: letter of 22 March 1899). A fortnight later Hofmannsthal summed up Schnitzler's grief in a letter to Edgar Karg von Bebenburg: 'During the first performance of my plays [*Der Abenteurer und die Sängerin* and *Die Hochzeit der Sobeide*] the mistress of my friend Schnitzler died: just as dreadful a loss, of course, as if she had been his wife, for that has for years been exactly what his relation to her has been like' (H/Karg, 138). For thirty years Schnitzler would continue to record the anniversary of her death in his diary.

Schnitzler recognized that his promiscuity was a weakness (Tgb., 5 January 1895), and would accuse himself of 'heartlessness' (Tgb., 30 July 1897) or even of being by conventional moral standards a corrupting force (Tgb., 15 March 1896) – so that, Anatol-like, he would worry himself out of wholehearted pleasure: 'I do not even have healthy frivolity enough simply to enjoy the lovely creatures' (Tgb., 26 February 1895). It was only realistic for him to regard himself as unsuited for marriage: 'If I am honest with myself, what I should like best is a harem, and then not to be further disturbed. It is doubtful that I was made for marriage' (Tgb., 6 May 1897).

Four months after Mizi Reinhard's death, however, he met another young actress and singer, Olga Gussmann. Not the least of her attractions was that she was his social equal and that she had had no previous lovers (Tgb., 30 April 1901). His first report to Hofmannsthal, contained in a letter of 17 July 1900, was not entirely promising: 'Every day I chat for a few hours with a young actress, a beginner, not pretty but incredibly sharp for eighteen' (H/AS, 141). Nevertheless the affair developed, though their relationship showed early signs of the stresses that would eventually undermine it, arising from her worries about his past affairs and about her own career: 'the two spectres that stand over our bed – my past and her future' (Tgb., 5 May 1901). From Schnitzler's diary it is clear that she did not at first press for marriage (Tgb., 12 January 1902), but she bore him a son in August 1902; they then married the next year and had a further child, a daughter, in 1909. In 1910 they moved to a house in the Sternewartestrasse in the eighteenth district of Vienna, where Schnitzler lived for the rest of his life. But the marriage deteriorated, as they gave vent to quarrelsome mutual recriminations. She would accuse him of a 'monomania' that had hindered her singing career, he would blame her for his unproductiveness. 'You know that it isn't the political situation but our relationship that makes me incapable of working', his diary records him having told her on 2 October 1919. The marriage finally ended in judicial separation in June 1921.

By the time he married, his literary career was well established. In 1895 the story *Sterben* (first serialized the previous year in three issues of the monthly *Neue deutsche Rundschau*) was published in book form by the firm of S. Fischer, who would remain Schnitzler's principal publisher for the rest of his life. In the same year he also made his real breakthrough in the Viennese theatre when *Liebelei* was given its première in the Burgtheater. It was a play which, after a number of false starts, Schnitzler had written at great speed in September and October 1894. After reading it to Hofmannsthal and Salten on 14 October, he submitted it on 29 October to Max Burckhard, who had been director of the Burgtheater since 1890 and was trying to foster the new *avant garde*. By 18 January 1895 it had been accepted, and the first performance took place on 9 October. The part of the betrayed heroine Christine was played by Adele Sandrock, newly engaged at the Burgtheater, that of her father by Adolf Sonnenthal, a member of the company since 1856 and one of the most celebrated actors associated with the style of the pre-Ringstrasse company of the 1880s. The first Berlin production was in the Deutsches Theater just over a fortnight later (4 February 1896) and was if anything even more successful than the Viennese première; Schnitzler's fame was secure.

When Burckhard was succeeded in the Burgtheater by Paul Schlenther, things at first went less smoothly. A set of three one-act plays (*Paracelsus*, *Die Gefährtin*, and *Der grüne Kakadu*) was produced in March 1899, but although Sonnenthal's playing in *Der grüne Kakadu* met with critical acclaim, that play was withdrawn in December, apparently under pressure from Court circles. It was a work that Schnitzler had begun to write within three months of the unrest that had brought down the Badeni government in November 1897.[10] Set in July 1789 against the backdrop of the French Revolution (the action takes place on the very day of the storming of the Bastille), it is rich in implications for the society of 1899, especially in the depiction of self-centred aristocrats and a hedonistic stage audience for the play within the play on which the action turns. It had already been banned by the Berlin censor the previous year.[11] The following September *Der Schleier der Beatrice*, which is written largely in verse, was rejected;[12] and by the end of 1901, during discussions about the casting of his plays in the Deutsches Volkstheater, he noticed that it seemed to be common knowledge that the Burgtheater was now closed to him (Tgb., 28 November 1901). His attitude to Schlenther would remain reserved: his diary note for 1 May 1916, written when Schlenther had just died, shows that he regarded him as having harmed his career considerably. In principle, however, Schlenther was sympathetic to modern realist drama; an old friend of Otto Brahm, he had been Brahm's successor as theatre critic on the *Vossische Zeitung* in Berlin and had been co-founder with Brahm of the Freie Bühne in Berlin. From 1905 onwards other new Schnitzler plays were again performed in the Burgtheater, by casts including leading members of the company.

Typically Schnitzler's work continued to centre on love and infidelity. Examples staged in the Burgtheater included the comedy *Zwischenspiel*, which was performed in 1905 with Josef Kainz, the pre-eminent actor of the Modernist generation, as Amadeus, and for which Schnitzler received the Grillparzer Prize in 1908; the tragicomedy *Das weite Land* (1911), one of his most accomplished works (known to present-day English-speaking audiences in the version by Tom Stoppard, *Undiscovered Country*); and *Komödie der Verführung* (1924), in which Raoul Aslan – according to Stoessl 'the sole living reminder of Sonnenthal and his forerunners'[13] – played the part of Falkenir. The evening of the première on 11 October 1924 was a remarkable one: while *Komödie der Verführung* was being played at the Burgtheater itself, the other theatre belonging to the company, the Akademietheater, was also devoted to Schnitzler, presenting two early plays, *Liebelei* followed by *Literatur*, a one-act comedy which treats the exploitation of experience in autobiographical literature (see figure 1). *Literatur* forms part of a cycle entitled *Lebendige Stunden*, which Schnitzler regarded as the best thing he had written so far (Tgb., 4 September 1901).

In box-office terms, however, the most successful of Schnitzler's plays launched in the Burgtheater was a historical drama set in the Napoleonic period, *Der junge Medardus* (1910). Directed by Hugo Thimig, it was the principal hit during Alfred von Berger's fairly brief spell in charge of the theatre; Schnitzler recorded proudly in his diary that it had set a new record for the Burgtheater box-office (Tgb., 21 March 1911). He subsequently received the Raimund Prize for it in 1914. But it was overlong and expensive to stage, and when Karl Schönherr's *Der Weibsteufel*, an earthy dialect drama involving only three characters, was given its première in 1915, the twice-weekly satirical journal *Kikeriki* was quick to point to the contrast. A cartoon appeared on 18 April 1915 showing Thimig

1   Poster for the Burgtheater and Akademietheater, 11 October 1924.

(who had succeeded Berger in 1912 as director of the theatre) embracing Schönherr for having written a play really suitable for wartime, economical on characters, costumes, and décor, while the figure of Schnitzler and the cast list of *Der junge Medardus* provide a pointed contrast in the background (see figure 2). In 1926 Schnitzler learnt that the text was being cut in performance, and wrote to the then director of the theatre, Franz Herterich, demanding that the cuts be reinstated and the play restored to its full four-and-a-half-hours' length (AS/Bfe. II, 437: letter of 8 April 1926). But the play disappeared from the repertory at the end of the following year, and a revival in 1932 was given only four performances. Schnitzler's postwar excursions into verse drama, the comedy *Die Schwestern oder Casanova in Spa* (1920) and *Der Gang zum Weiher* (1931), were both much less successful, though he was particularly fond of *Die Schwestern* and regarded *Der Gang zum Weiher* as technically one of his most accomplished works.[14]

„Der Weibsteufel" von Karl Schönherr.

Burgtheaterdirektor Thimig: Komm Karl, laß' dich küssen, Du hast ein echtes Kriegs=Theaterstück geschrieben, hast gespart mit Personen, Kostümen und Dekorationen.

2   Cartoon from *Kikeriki*, 18 April 1915.

From about 1909 he came to be associated more closely with the Deutsches Volkstheater. In 1909 a 'Schnitzler year' was organized there, the programme including the première of a one-act satirical comedy, *Komtesse Mizzi*. The following year the *Anatol* cycle was first performed complete; in 1912 the cycle *Marionetten* was first performed; in 1917 a comedy about journalists, *Fink und Fliederbusch*, was quite warmly received by the audience but slated by most of the journalists reviewing it; and 1929 brought the last play that Schnitzler published during his lifetime, *Im Spiel der Sommerlüfte*. By 1917 he was registering the particular importance of the Deutsches Volkstheater for him. As events had turned out, it now mattered more than the Burgtheater (Tgb., 17 August 1917). It was in this theatre that *Professor Bernhardi* received its first Austrian production in 1918, and many new productions followed in the 1920s (including *Das weite Land* and *Der einsame Weg* in 1925, and in 1926 the cycle *Komödie der Worte*, which had first been produced in 1915 in the Burgtheater).

A number of his plays, however, were given their premières not in Vienna but in Berlin, mainly in the theatres (first the Deutsches Theater, then from autumn 1904 the Lessing-Theater) directed by Otto Brahm, with whom he had become friendly in 1895. In 1896 Brahm produced *Freiwild*, a play about the conventions governing duelling. It had previously been rejected by Emerich von Bukovics, the director of the Deutsches Volkstheater, who as a former army officer was sensitive to the offence it might give.[15] The first Viennese performance eventually took place in the Carltheater on 4 February 1898 and led, as Schnitzler noted, to 'violent attacks in the anti-Semitic and militarist press';[16] even when the play was eventually performed in the Deutsches Volkstheater in 1905 the police still stipulated that the uniforms worn must not resemble either those of the Austrian army or those of any of Austria's allies.[17] Other plays that Brahm produced included *Das Vermächtnis* (1898); the cycle *Lebendige Stunden* (1902); *Der Schleier der Beatrice* (1903); in the following year *Der einsame Weg*, a work that Hofmannsthal later saw as having ushered in a 'second phase' (that is, a more mature, complex stage) in Schnitzler's creative career (H/AS, 238: letter of 24 July 1908); and in 1906 *Der Ruf des Lebens*. Brahm and Schnitzler developed a firm friendship, writing regularly and even holidaying together in the Tyrol in 1908. When *Professor Bernhardi* received its première on 28 November 1912 in Viktor Barnowsky's Kleines Theater, it was the first major Schnitzler play to be first performed in Berlin other than under Brahm. On that very evening Brahm died, to Schnitzler's great sadness.

Schnitzler was in Berlin at the time to attend the first night, which, as he was able to note in his diary the next day, was mostly well received by the reviewers. But *Professor Bernhardi* is a work that was the subject of bitter controversy. Indeed, Schnitzler's career was dogged by controversy, three works in particular occasioning spectacular scandals. The first of these was the story *Leutnant Gustl*, a *monologue intérieur* which presents a satirical picture of a worthless young subaltern. It was first printed (under the title 'Lieutenant Gustl') on 25 December 1900 in the Christmas supplement of the *Neue Freie Presse*. Three days later articles defending the honour of Austrian officers and attacking Schnitzler as dishonourable appeared in two right-wing papers. One, which is mentioned in Schnitzler's diary, was in the *Reichswehr*, which was directed principally at a military readership; the other was in the Christian Social *Reichspost*. The affair became a *cause célèbre*, with much of the press comment virulently anti-Semitic.[18] It ended with Schnitzler, who had been a reserve officer since the 1880s, being cashiered *in absentia*.

Reviewing the scandal towards the end of 1901, one commentator justly observed that nowhere in the Viennese press had it received unbiased objective treatment;[19] on the other hand the very attention drawn by the military to the story provided publicity and guaranteed its success. Nor was this lost on satirical commentators: a cartoon in *Der Floh* on 7 July 1901, for example, depicted Schnitzler not appealing against the verdict but expressing his thanks for the advertisement (see figure 3). The same held equally true of controversies sparked off by censorship, and indeed the point became common currency. A reading of Heyse's *Maria von Magdala* two years later, for example, brought an ironic comment in the *Neues Wiener Tagblatt* for 7 May 1903 to the effect that the banning of that play in Berlin had presented it with extraordinary popularity. A further ten years later Robert Hirschfeld made exactly the same point, in a passage heavily marked in crayon on Schnitzler's copy, about the censoring of *Professor Bernhardi*.[20]

The second famous scandal centred on *Reigen*, a sexual morality play which eventually became known worldwide under the title of Max Ophüls's (very free) film adaptation, *La Ronde*. *Reigen* is another of the products of Schnitzler's thirties that he wrote quickly; his diary records that he began it on 23 November 1896, completed it the following February, and read it to Hofmannsthal, Beer-Hofmann, Salten and others on 17 March 1897. It was privately printed in 1900, but not published until three years later, when it appeared under the imprint of the Wiener Verlag, which specialized in modernist publications. In 1904 the publication was banned in Germany. A stage production in Hungarian was banned in 1912,

3 'Schnitzler, the sometime regimental surgeon': cartoon from *Der Floh*, 7 July 1901.

Ehrenrichter: Was wollen S' denn, Sie — Sie — Sie Civilist Sie? Das Ehrengericht hat Sie ausgestoßen — da gibt's kan Recurs .. Arthur Schnitzler: Pardon, ich will ja gar nicht recurriren; ich komme bloß mich für die schöne Reclame bedanken, die Sie meinem Buche gemacht haben. Jetzt geht's!

and the work was not performed until 1920, in Berlin (Kleines Schauspielhaus). When it was first produced in Vienna in February 1921, at the Kammerspiele (which belonged to the Deutsches Volkstheater), fighting broke out during one performance and it was banned again for a year in the name of 'public order'. A week after that, there were public protests in Berlin, which led to a prosecution of the theatre company, including its directors, Gertrud Eysoldt and Maximilian Sladek, for creating public disorder. (In November of the same year the plaintiffs were found not guilty.)[21]

In October 1912 a production of *Professor Bernhardi* which was planned in the Deutsches Volkstheater was forbidden because of the play's allegedly 'distorted' depiction of Austrian public life. The matter was raised in parliament at the end of the month in a formal question (*Interpellation*) to the Minister of Internal Affairs, and a protracted controversy developed in the Austrian press, which was kept going partly by argument along ideological lines (including a lot of anti-Semitic comment), and partly by attempts to circumvent the ban (see pp. 98–9, below). Plans were hatched to mount a production in Pressburg, just across the Hungarian border, but at the end of April 1913 this too was banned by the local authorities.

That it eventually took a world war and the collapse of an empire to make performance of the play in Austria possible was an irony that did not escape Schnitzler, who made the point in his diary as soon as the censorship was lifted (31 October 1918). So too did Auernheimer, the chief theatre critic of the *Neue Freie Presse*, in a long article published two months later (24 December 1918).

In Schnitzler's later years, many of his most successful publications were works of prose fiction. He had published fiction throughout his career; stories issued in book form by Fischer included both *Frau Berta Garlan* and *Leutnant Gustl* in 1901, and in 1908 he published his first long novel, *Der Weg ins Freie*, about the Viennese Jewish community. This appeared in book form after first being serialized in the *Neue Rundschau* (the continuation of the *Neue deutsche Rundschau*). So too did other works: *Frau Beate und ihr Sohn* (1913); *Casanovas Heimfahrt* (1918), the genesis of which is linked with that of *Die Schwestern*; and *Fräulein Else* (1924), a study of a young woman who commits suicide. The last, strongly influenced by Freudian symbolism, was published by Zsolnay in Vienna. After being popularized by a silent film with Elisabeth Bergner in the title part (1929) it became a bestseller as the 'book of the film', with a picture of Elisabeth Bergner on the dust-cover. Other stories that were serialized in various magazines and journals and then published by Fischer include *Doktor Gräsler, Badearzt* (1917), *Traumnovelle* (1926), and *Spiel im Morgengrauen* (1927).

Further publications included the *Buch der Sprüche und Bedenken* (1927), a collection of Schnitzler's occasional aphoristic work going back in part to the 1880s and widely published in newspapers. In 1915 he began writing an autobiography, based on his early diaries; but though he worked on it until 1920 it remained uncompleted and takes the story of his life only up to the turn of the century. It was not published until 1968, when it appeared under the title *Jugend in Wien*, edited by Schnitzler's son Heinrich in collaboration with Therese Nickl.

Schnitzler was a very sociable man. His pastimes, together with voracious reading, included playing cards (poker, often with heavy losses, in his youth and early manhood); music-making (he was a competent pianist, and played duets, including some of the newest music, with his son), theatre-going, walks (often in the company of friends), and long conversations discussing the artistic and political affairs of the time. He had a wide circle of acquaintances, and knew not only most of the leading figures from the artistic, literary, and theatrical world in Vienna but also – partly through his younger brother Julius, a surgeon – many prominent medical men as well.

That he had no close contact with Freud until 1922 was the exception to prove the rule, and was by Freud's choice. It was, Freud explained, his admiration for Schnitzler's psychological insight that had led him to avoid a meeting out of apprehension at encountering a kind of *Doppelgänger* ('aus einer Art von Doppelgängerscheu': WM, 652).

Among the men of letters whose friendship Schnitzler particularly valued, besides Beer-Hofmann, was the German novelist Heinrich Mann, whom he first met in 1910 (Tgb., 21 April 1910). He also enjoyed conversing with the Tyrolean realist dramatist Karl Schönherr, a fellow doctor. But literary reflections were often double-edged. Even in his earliest literary reviews, published in the fortnightly *Moderne Rundschau* in 1891,[22] he had shown himself to be an unsparing critic, and his diary reveals that he was a harsh critic of his own writings, full of sharp self-doubts. In 1896, after falling asleep while reading through *Freiwild*, he gloomily recalled that he had occasionally fallen asleep even while writing it (Tgb., 9 April 1896). He constantly accused himself of being second-rate in achievement and in mind, and this tendency increased after the turn of the century, as he began to find it harder to work quickly.

It was also in 1896 that Hofmannsthal reported a conversation with Berger about Schnitzler's similarity to Grillparzer. Schnitzler was pleased (Tgb., 27 February 1896). Certainly there is something of Grillparzer, whose *Gespräche* he read as they came out in August Sauer's edition from 1904 onwards, in the anxious self-analysis recorded in his diary on 2 January 1909, apparently deriving from a conversation with his wife: 'Hypochondria, in every sense, my severest defect: it spoils my happiness and my capacity to work.' It is after another such conversation with his wife two years later that he summed up his view of his artistic achievements:

> Ich weiß, daß ich nicht zu den großen Dichtern zähle; nie ein absolutes großes Kunstwerk schaffen werde; – fühle aber stark die Merkwürdigkeit meines Gesammtwesens, in dem auch dichterische Elemente ersten Ranges sind – die nur als ganzes keine Dichterkraft ersten Ranges bilden. (Tgb., 3 January 1911)

> I know that I am not one of the great writers, that I shall never create a great work of absolute art; but I have a strong sense of the remarkable quality of my capacities as a whole, in which there are also poetic elements of the first rank – only they do not add up to a poetic power of the first rank.

Schnitzler's hypochondriac self-scrutiny also extended to his physical well-being. Most of his ailments were minor, but he had genuine problems with his hearing from his early thirties onwards. He had his first consultation about his ears on 30 January 1894, and from late 1896 onwards his diaries contain ever more frequent plaints about the 'roaring' in his ears which sometimes seemed never to have left him 'for a single second' (Tgb., 4 December 1902). Depression about his hearing started in April 1897, and a series of notes in 1900–1901 record its continuing deterioration. At times he felt he was 'hearing worse with every passing day' (Tgb., 18 April 1900). On 4 October 1898 he lamented in a letter to Hofmannsthal, 'Such insidious, ever-present and unstoppable things are how old age and destruction most perfidiously announce their approach' (H/AS, 113). Two years later he was reading Beethoven's letters from the time of the onset of his deafness (Tgb., 20 September 1900).

Difficulties with his hearing cast an increasing shadow over his life from his early fifties onwards. At the same time the widespread jingoism of the early war years, added to ever-growing anti-Semitism in Austria, made the whole climate of opinion unsympathetic to his work. One consequence of this was that his earnings fell. He had had financial worries for some years; they had, for example, disturbed his work on revising *Der einsame Weg* (Tgb., 28 December 1902). But now things worsened sharply, and by the time the war had entered its third year he was so frightened about his declining earnings that it seemed as though he were heading for 'certain ruin' (Tgb., 17 November 1916). The cumulative effect of the hostile climate, coming on top of things like the ban on *Professor Bernhardi*, is reflected in his reaction to the critical reception of *Fink und Fliederbusch*, that never before had an author been so abused in the course of his career (Tgb., 19 November 1917).

The critics had long tended to typecast him as the author of works of erotic dalliance such as *Anatol* or *Liebelei*, an author whose creative strength, as numerous reviewers would repeat, lay in the erotic field. Plays on other topics, such as *Fink und Fliederbusch*, tended to be dismissed as being simply un-Schnitzlerian (see pp. 86–7, below). In the war years he felt he was regarded with 'immense incomprehension on all sides' (Tgb., 16 January 1916). After the war he was increasingly regarded as *passé*. As early as 1917 a reviewer of *Doktor Gräsler, Badearzt* wrote in what was meant to be an admiring passage: 'With admiration we appreciate how young this old master Arthur Schnitzler still is, how he has preserved all the qualities of his youth, his glowing love of subtle eroticism, his wit, his unerring delicacy of taste.'[23] The entry in his diary that evening shows how depressed he felt to be described as an 'old master' (Tgb., 6 October 1917).

The postwar years brought new friendships, including that with an enterprising young professional woman, Hedy Kempny, who poured out confidences to him in a long correspondence. The publication of another novel, *Therese*, in 1928 brought generous praise from Hofmannsthal (H/AS, 308: letter of 10 July 1928). He was also involved in a number of silent films based on his works. But his last years were a time of depression and isolation, the deepest personal tragedy being the suicide of his daughter Lili in July 1928, just a year after her marriage. He wrote to Hedy Kempny that he was seeking refuge in work but that it all now seemed pointless (AS/Kempny, 275–6: letter of 24 August 1928).

Schnitzler died suddenly on 21 October 1931, and on the following day a black flag flew over the Burgtheater – a gesture normally reserved for the death of a member of the company, and the first time, it was reported, it had been done to commemorate the death of a dramatist.[24] One further final stir in the press was created by the reading of his will:

> By a codicil to his will, dated April 29, 1912, Dr. Arthur Schnitzler, the dramatist and novelist (whose death was reported in *The Times* yesterday), ordered that his heart be pierced before burial, and that no wreaths be placed on his grave or printed notification of his death posted to friends or published in the Press. He also wished that his funeral should be of the pauper class, that the money saved should be distributed among hospitals, and that no funeral orations should be held. No accessory rites or ceremonies were to be performed after his death, and no mourning observed.[25]

He was buried in the Jewish cemetery in the Zentralfriedhof, on the eastern outskirts of Vienna.

Hugo von Hofmannsthal

Hugo von Hofmannsthal was born on 1 February 1874, the son (and only child) of a prominent Viennese banker. His poetic talent matured very early, and his poems began to be published under the pseudonym 'Loris' (or 'Loris Melikow') when he was only sixteen and still at school. It was in the autumn of 1890 that he was first introduced to the Griensteidl circle, where Schnitzler and Beer-Hofmann made the most lasting impression on him. This is the subject of an emotional letter he wrote on 12 June 1912 in honour of Schnitzler's fiftieth birthday:

> Many people have been close to me since then, and I am still no more blunted, no more insensitive to the approach of another

human being. But what I derived from the first contact with you and Richard is something that can never be repeated. For me above all it was a moment the like of which could never return. I was stepping out from the absolute solitude of my youth precociously mature but infinitely inexperienced [Frühreif und doch unendlich unerfahren], and you were for me not just a human being, a friend, but a new link with the world; you yourself were for me a whole world. (H/AS, 266)

The first of his lyrical dramas with a Renaissance setting, *Gestern*, was written in July 1891. A long letter of 13 July to Schnitzler records the difficulties he had with the final scene (H/AS, 8) – not the last time the ending of a play would give him problems – but *Gestern* appeared safely in the autumn of 1891 in the *Moderne Rundschau*, under the pseudonym 'Theophil Morren'. It is the first of a number of short pieces, essentially dramatic poems, evoking the self-indulgent life of the aesthete and at the same time suggesting its limitations. Five years later, in a letter of 20 June 1896 to the journalist Ria Schmujlow-Claassen, he would describe *Gestern* self-deprecatingly as 'rather precocious and not very pleasant' ('ziemlich altklug und nicht recht erfreulich': H/Bfc. I, 203). But at the time it made his name. In her long review, which appeared in mid-May 1892, Marie Herzfeld described it as 'a psychological study of rare concentration and striking individuality, in gracefully constructed and elegant verse' (JW I, 322; HUK, 41).

Towards the end of 1891, still not eighteen, Hofmannsthal was sought out by Stefan George, who was on a visit to Vienna. By 27 December Schnitzler's diary reports that Hofmannsthal had read poems by George to their usual circle (Salten, Bahr, Bératon, and himself) in connection with a discussion of symbolism. But Hofmannsthal never allowed himself to be sucked completely into the circle of George's disciples. Their first encounters are reflected in a sonnet 'Der Prophet', in which George, himself only twenty-three at the time, is evoked as a figure of stifling authority (HKA II, 61). Though George included a second verse play, the fragment *Der Tod des Tizian*, in the first issue of the *Blätter für die Kunst* in October 1892, relations between the two remained tense,[26] and in mid-1893 Hofmannsthal distanced himself from George's exclusive circle, to George's disillusion. Reviewing their relations in May 1902, after an almost complete break of three years (there had been one brief encounter in Munich in 1901), George expressed his conviction that together they might by their writings have exercised a 'salutary dictatorship', and reproached Hofmannsthal for associating with all manner of minor writers and for avoiding being linked with him (H/George, 150). George was a formidably severe correspondent. Hofmannsthal's long reply to this letter was met with a stony rebuttal in July: there was scarcely a point within it, George declared, where his feelings were not diametrically opposed to what Hofmannsthal had written (H/George, 158). They remained in touch only until 1906.

In 1892 Hofmannsthal began to attend the salon of Josephine von Wertheimstein, where he was fêted as a prodigy until the death of the elderly hostess in July 1894. It was also in 1892 that he enrolled at the University of Vienna, where he read law until 1894. After a year's break for military service with a dragoon regiment (following which he was promoted to the reserve of officers) he changed to Romance literature. Among the lectures he heard over the next four years, those given by Berger on aesthetics made a particularly strong impression. They included a course in 1895 on 'Psychology and Art', and Berger seems in particular to have stimulated his interest in psychoanalysis in relation to literature and drama. His lasting respect for Berger is attested in an obituary tribute written for the *Neue Freie Presse* in 1912 (P III, 143–4).

While studying he continued to write short verse dramas. The most famous, *Der Tor und der Tod*, appeared in Otto Julius Bierbaum's *Moderner Musen-Almanach* for the year 1894. It is, as he later noted, linked to *Gestern* in treating the 'danger' of a life of self-centred isolation ('Gefahr der Isoliertheit, des selbstischen Erstarrens': A, 241). In a variation on the opening scene in Part One of Goethe's *Faust*, the aesthete Claudio realizes the emptiness of his life and commits himself to ethical responsibility, summed up in the idea of 'constancy':

> Ich will die Treue lernen, die der Halt
> Von allem Leben ist [. . .]
>
> > (HKA III, 73)

> I want to learn constancy, the mainstay of all life.

In his self-analytical notes *Ad me ipsum*, which were written from 1916 onwards, Hofmannsthal would write that these lines in *Der Tor und der Tod* had expressed a 'decisive' crux (A, 228). Claudio's resolution summarizes Hofmannsthal's rejection of art for art's sake and of the doctrine that 'no artist has ethical sympathies', as Oscar Wilde had expressed it in the preface to *The Picture of Dorian Gray*. Hofmannsthal's view of the aesthetic movement was summed up in a letter of 1896 to Bahr which includes, in a possible essay title, the formulation 'the Cul-de-sac of Aestheticism' (H/Bfe. I, 206), and in *Der Tor und der Tod* especially, one of the central concerns of his later work, the moral development of the individual through ethical commitment, is already clearly in evidence.

Military exercises in eastern Galicia in 1896 and 1898 helped to widen his experience and outlook, while a fortnight in Varese, in north-west Italy, in the late summer of 1897 allowed him to plunge into work on further lyrical plays, *Die Frau im Fenster*, *Die Hochzeit der Sobeide*, and *Das kleine Welttheater*. He wrote with a fluency he would never recapture; he told his mother on 8 September that he had written nearly two thousand lines of verse in a fortnight (H/Bfe. I, 232). In later years he would look back on these charmed weeks of work as having been perhaps the happiest of his life (H/Burckhardt, 282: letter of 11 May 1928) and as the end of a whole phase in his work: 'Youthful phase: magic [Magie]. Varese. Later, artistic shaping [or "structuring"]' ('Gestaltung': A, 232). The next two years also saw the composition of *Der weiße Fächer* (like *Die Frau im Fenster*, partly in prose) and the trochaic *Der Kaiser und die Hexe* (1897); *Der Abenteurer und die Sängerin* (1898), based on the memoirs of Casanova; and *Das Bergwerk zu Falun* (1899), which remained unpublished.

It was *Die Frau im Fenster* that provided him with his first theatrical première, which took place as a matinée at Brahm's Deutsches Theater in Berlin on 15 May 1898. Four months earlier Brahm had rejected *Der Kaiser und die Hexe* – ruefully reported by Hofmannsthal in a letter to Schnitzler (H/AS, 98). Then in March 1899, *Die Hochzeit der Sobeide* and *Der Abenteurer und die Sängerin* were given their première in the Deutsches Theater and simultaneously in the Burgtheater in Vienna. The reception, however, was very disappointing, all the more so in that in Berlin Kainz was appearing in *Der Abenteurer und die Sängerin* – a point to which Hofmannsthal had proudly drawn George's attention in advance (H/George, 142: letter of 23 November 1898). Hofmannsthal had a forlorn report to make to Schnitzler when he wrote to him on 23 March 1899: his 'poor plays' had been 'slaughtered' in the press and had been taken off after three performances (H/AS, 120). That same year he published all three of these plays in a collective volume under the title *Theater in Versen*, a formulation indicative of his developing interest in theatrical performance.

The political and social problems of the time still do not impinge on these short plays of the late 1890s, but far from expressing a naive aestheticism, they continue the critique of the aesthetic life which also informs the best-known of his early short stories, *Das Märchen der 672. Nacht* (1895). This was seen clearly by perceptive readers in his own time, notably by Berger. In a substantial article on Hofmannsthal that he published in the *Neue Freie Presse* on 16 July 1905, Berger wrote:

In the works of his first period Hofmannsthal wallows in his subjectivity, enjoying it to the full – but always (and this is what raises him high over the pack that merely follow the *Zeitgeist*) in a clear awareness of the inadequacy and incompleteness both of this spiritual condition [der Unzulänglichkeit und Halbheit dieses Seelenzustandes] and of the art that reflects it. (HUK, 141)

Nevertheless, despite the increasing detail and incident in his work, his technique was not yet really theatrical. This point was put to him frankly by Count Harry Kessler (with whom he had made contact as a result of publishing poems in the *Jugendstil* journal *Pan*, to whose editorial board Kessler belonged). Writing on 11 July 1898, Kessler observed that *Die Frau im Fenster* had made less of an impression on him in the theatre than when he had read it (H/Kessler, 6).

Hofmannsthal was now facing crucial decisions about his future. In 1898 he successfully submitted his doctoral dissertation on the language of the Pléiade poets (his *viva* was held on 23 June), and in 1901 he submitted a *Habilitationsschrift* (a dissertation submitted to gain recognition as a tenured university teacher [*Dozent*]) on Victor Hugo. This, however, was not immediately accepted, and at the end of the year he withdrew his application, giving as his reason his constitutional inability to stand the pressures of combining professional work with his poetic and dramatic writing.[27] This decision, coming as it did at a time when the vein of his purely lyrical work was drying up and he was increasingly looking towards other forms, represents a major turning-point in his career.

Socially Hofmannsthal had the poise of his patrician background. He spoke 'in aristocratic Viennese German, with a rather nasal voice and a slight drawl'; the phrasing is Berger's, and is supported by numerous other accounts.[28] When Kessler first met him in Berlin on 11 May 1898, he summed him up in his diary as a 'short, jolly Viennese', adding a few days later that he was 'vain and socially ambitious'.[29]

A man of intense friendships, which are documented in his letters, Hofmannsthal was also, however, susceptible to severe depressive bouts. Throughout his career his letters repeatedly testify to his hypersensitive nervous disposition. At times he would work so intensely that he drove himself to the edge of collapse, as when he wrote to Schnitzler on 20 July 1899 that his nerves had never been worse (H/AS, 127); at others, he would lose all his appetite for creative work, as he did, for example, in the spring of 1897.[30] When Hofmannsthal fell victim to what he described to Stefan

George in 1902 as 'one of his bad deep depressions' (H/George, 162: letter of 24 July 1902), one effect always was that it interfered with serious writing. His correspondence with Schnitzler shows evening invitations to the Sternewartestrasse being declined because of the working time he would lose though the resulting 'nervousness' ('Nervosität': H/AS, 232; letter of 1 November 1907); in the summer of 1908 he could not even write letters in the Austrian Alps 'for fear of stress and insomnia' (H/AS, 237: letter of 24 July 1908), and a spell in south-eastern Switzerland produced 'a nervous depression or irritation of the nervous system' (H/AS, 240: letter of 14 September 1908).

When Hofmannsthal was trying to secure his release from military service in the early months of the war, there was nothing incredible about his request to Schnitzler to put him in touch with a psychiatrist who might secure him leave on account of his 'truly absurd nerves' (H/AS, 277: letter of 31 March 1915). A few months after that, when he had been complaining that he had not achieved any really satisfactory work for five years, Schnitzler noted that he was again 'depressed' (Tgb., 23 August 1916). Eight years later another depressive attack cost him the friendship – admittedly always volatile – of the German poet and essayist Rudolf Borchardt. On 4 February 1924 he wrote a long letter attacking the introductory 'epistle' Borchardt had contributed to a *Festschrift* in honour of his fiftieth birthday (H/Borchardt, 183–6) – a letter for which he then apologized three weeks later as 'completely absurd' and as having been written 'in a condition of crisis that was equivalent to an illness' (H/Borchardt, 186–7).

One period of particularly sustained depression afflicted him in the years 1899–1902, most acutely in the eight months from December 1901 to July 1902. The main underlying cause of his malaise in this period was his planned *Habilitation* and his sense of having reached a crucial turning-point.[31] Abandoning any thought of an academic career and dedicating himself instead to a full-time literary career was a major commitment, and his worry about his consequent inability to settle down to satisfying, serious writing kept surfacing in his letters and conversations. On 1 December 1901, for example, he wrote to Richard Dehmel that he often found himself unable to write even a single poem (H/Bfe. II, 61). On 14 February 1902 he wrote to another poet, Rudolf Alexander Schröder, of a 'terrifying [. . .] paralysis' of his productive powers (H/Bfe. II, 67), and on 15 March he told Eberhard von Bodenhausen (another friend whom he had originally met through *Pan*, of which Bodenhausen was co-editor) that he had had an 'enormously unproductive winter' (H/Bodenhausen, 20). His letter of 24 July to

George describes his condition as a state in which he was painfully bereft 'not only of every ray of inner vision but also even of clarity of thought' (H/George, 162–3). One day after writing that letter he spoke to Schnitzler on the same subject, complaining, so Schnitzler recorded, 'of his deep depression that – and because of which – he had not worked properly since 1899 [von seiner tiefen Verstimmung, dass er und durch die er seit 99 eigentlich nicht recht gearbeitet], though without personal and material worries' (Tgb., 25 July 1902). These plaints immediately preceded the writing in August of the Chandos Letter ('Ein Brief'), which was conceived as one of a series of 'imaginary conversations and letters' and first published in two issues of *Der Tag* in Berlin, on 18 and 19 October 1902. When he sent George a copy on 14 December 1902, Hofmannsthal again wrote of having suffered in recent months an inner 'paralysis' ('Erstarrung': H/George, 173).

Much of the experience of this whole period is recorded in his letters to Leopold von Andrian – one of several friends, all men of high culture, who came from the minor aristocracy. The two had first met, so Andrian later recalled, in 1893 when Hofmannsthal, already 'shrewdly concerned with nurturing his burgeoning fame', called on the literary historian Oskar Walzel, who was Andrian's tutor.[32] Their acquaintance got off to an inauspicious start, when Hofmannsthal committed the social solecism of replying to a formal letter from Andrian in an informal style, addressing him as 'du'. Andrian commented rather superciliously in his diary: 'He must have observed that that is more *du monde*, but on the other hand it shows once again that when even the cleverest people want to be fashionable, they commit acts of stupidity or tactlessness.'[33] Nevertheless, with Andrian Hofmannsthal came to enjoy one of the closest and most important of his friendships, a lifelong bond which also produced one of the most revealing volumes of his correspondence.

In two letters in particular, those of 9 November 1902 and 16 January 1903, Hofmannsthal spells out that the Chandos Letter is informed by personal experience (H/Andrian, 157–61). In particular, Chandos's loss of faith in the language of his past writings forms a rather imprecise parallel to Hofmannsthal's disillusion with the predominantly lyrical idiom of his work in the 1890s, the 'verbal magic' ('Wort-magie': A, 215) still in evidence in his lyric dramas. In his late teens words had seemed mysterious, 'sealed prisons of the divine breath, of truth' (A, 105). Their power, as he had written in an even earlier note dated 21 October 1891, is a life-giving one, so that the poet is 'a Midas in reverse' (A, 93). The same point is made again in the anti-realist essay 'Poesie und

Leben', which was published in *Die Zeit* in May 1896: words serve the poet to invest experience with a 'new existence' (P I, 263). This faith is reflected in numerous poems of the mid-1890s: the poet's words are 'magic spells' ('Zauberworte': HKA I, 43); in his command of them he is a 'magician', and they express his communion with a whole world of experience and beauty transcending individuality. What the 'magician' ('Magier') creates is a world apart, splendid and mysterious (HKA I, 52: 'Ein Traum von großer Magie'). The essay 'Poesie und Leben' too spells out explicitly that there is no direct interconnection between poetry and 'real' life, the life of everyday experience (P I, 263). By 1902, with his reading of Mauthner (see p. 8, above) a further influence, the 'magical' command Hofmannsthal had enjoyed over poetic language – what in *Ad me ipsum* he would in retrospect define as 'magical command over word, image, and symbol' ('die magische Herrschaft über das Wort das Bild das Zeichen': A, 215–16) – appeared suspect. If the power of words went beyond truth, language itself was suspect as a medium of expression. This topic was the basis of a conversation with Bahr in March 1902 – a very early signpost of the theme of the comedy *Der Schwierige*, on which he did not begin work until 1909 – 'about the powerlessness of words and people's inability to communicate with others through words'.[34]

By contrast with the fictional Chandos, however, Hofmannsthal had never stopped writing altogether. Even in the letter to Schröder he interpreted the difficulties he had been going through as no more than an effect of inner change, 'the difficult transition from the production of youth to that of manhood' (H/Bfe. II, 67). Indeed, it has been suggested that the true model for Chandos may have been Andrian, in whom, as has rightly been observed, Hofmannsthal saw 'his own most pressing concerns and problems reflected, often in an exaggerated form'.[35] Beginning in 1893, when he was eighteen, Andrian had enjoyed two years of productive poetic activity, but in 1895 it abruptly stopped. He wrote to Hofmannsthal on 22 September 1895 of the change that had taken place within him and the sudden sense of aging that he felt (H/Andrian, 56), and by March 1899 he was suffering a depression so deep that he reached the point of telegraphing Hofmannsthal that he thought he was losing his sanity – a crisis that Hofmannsthal at once reported to Schnitzler (H/AS, 121: letter of 26 March 1899).

Though Chandos claims hyperbolically that he has lost the 'ability to think or speak coherently about anything at all' (P II, 11), what he has actually lost is his faith in certain kinds of 'literary' activity (P II, 7). Hofmannsthal's publication of 'Ein Brief' as one of a series of pieces in daily newspapers (in which he had not published for five years) betokens his determination to work in a more accessible idiom and to achieve contact with a wider public. It is the beginning of what he would later call his 'cultivated journalism' (P III, 68); he was adopting a conscious public manner, or mask. In his long letter of 22 June 1902 to Stefan George, in a defensive account of his writing, he described himself tellingly as using 'the disguise of a certain journalism' as one of his attempts 'to get through to the spirit of our confused age by the most various routes and in the most various disguises' (H/George, 154–5).[36]

In the light of these new priorities, his lyric dramas now appeared insufficiently dramatic to present the conflicts of real life. Since the mid-1890s he had, he felt, been edging closer towards what in 1894, while working on a translation of Euripides' *Alkestis*, he called 'dramatic drama' (H/Andrian, 23: letter of 21 February 1894). While still working on his *Habilitationsschrift* he wrote to Brahm that he sometimes longed to write something for the theatre (H/Bfe. I, 324: letter of 21 December 1900), and by the time the Chandos Letter was written he had been planning larger-scale dramatic works for some time. In particular his plans to adapt Sophocles' *Electra* and Calderón's *La vida es sueño* went back to October 1901, part and parcel of what he would later define as his attempt to find his way into large-scale dramatic form ('Anschluß an große Form': A, 370).

In the meantime, in June 1901, he had married. Five years earlier, in the winter of 1896–97, he had imagined himself close to marrying Minnie Benedict, the daughter of a wealthy Viennese businessman. He described her background on 13 February 1897 in a letter to Andrian as being 'a similar circle to the Schlesingers, perhaps even more clearly that of *small* Jewish finance' (H/Andrian, 98).[37] She was also friendly with Schnitzler (indeed on 6 March 1897 Schnitzler noted in his diary that she was obviously bitter that *he* did not want to marry her himself). When Hofmannsthal was not yet nineteen he had confided to Schnitzler over supper that the writings of Schnitzler and other friends made him afraid of women (Tgb., 23 October 1892). His attitude to women always remained very different from Schnitzler's. In particular, so Schnitzler recorded, he had no experience at all of women with a past, like Fanny Theren in *Das Märchen* (Tgb., 14 January 1897). It is to this note that Schnitzler added the observation that Hofmannsthal was toying with the idea of marrying Minnie Benedict.

When he finally did marry, his bride was another young woman from the *Geldaristokratie*, Gerty Schlesinger, a member of the family that he had mentioned in the letter to Andrian (her father was the Secretary General of the Anglo-Austrian Bank). Indirectly

it was through Andrian that Hofmannsthal had first met her;
Andrian was a schoolfriend of her brother Hans and had introduced
Hofmannsthal to him in 1894.[38] A month after the wedding the
young couple moved into an eighteenth-century house in Rodaun,
then still a village on the south-western edge of Vienna. One rather
malicious satirical account suggested that the purpose of this move
was to escape from Gerty von Hofmannsthal's many aunts, who –
typical of their leisured class – had nothing to do and so wanted to
pay constant visits; Rodaun was distant enough to keep them at bay
and leave Hofmannsthal in peace to get on with his writing.[39]
Rented on a long lease, the house was to be Hofmannsthal's home
for the rest of his life, where his three children were brought up and
where, having finally given up the notion of academic work, he
devoted himself to literature – with the added benefit, from 1916,
of a modest *pied-à-terre* in the Stallburggasse, near the Hofburg.[40]
The Rodaun household was a stable home, founded on a happy
marriage. On 10 September 1926 Hofmannsthal wrote to one of the
closest and most sympathetic friends of his later years, Carl J.
Burckhardt, that he could not imagine life without marriage,
and he added that all his thoughts about it were expressed in his
comedies ('Es ist alles was ich davon denke in meinen Lustspielen
gesagt': H/Burckhardt, 226).

Though Hofmannsthal turned mainly to various kinds of drama in
his search for a suitable medium for larger-scale creative writing, he
also kept up his essayistic activity – the journalistic 'disguise' or
'costume' he had defended to George in June 1902 when admitting
that his poetic powers were mixed with 'other intellectual urges'
(H/George, 154–5). His resistance to George's authoritarian influence was itself symptomatic of his determination to work on a
broader canvas; significantly, the final break in 1906 came shortly
after his first meeting with Richard Strauss. It is also just after this
that he would later date a 'third stage' in his development as a
dramatist, in which, from about 1907 onwards, a clear aim emerges
to meet 'traditional requirements of theatricality' ('die Erfüllung
traditioneller theatralischer Forderung': A, 370).
. One of his key pieces of essayistic writing in the early years of
the twentieth century was the lecture 'Der Dichter und diese Zeit',
delivered in various German cities in December 1906 and published
the following year. In the central part of this address (P II, 230–44)
he rehearses the mystery, the 'magic', by which poetic language
works and tries to suggest the visionary exaltation from which art
springs. But he also takes stock of the relation of the poet or
imaginative writer to his own age, an age of overpopulated cities

that are 'vast wastelands', and stresses his responsibility towards the generality of people: precisely because the whole continuity of a culture essentially depends on those few who have creatively shaped its language, the poet has a responsibility to exercise 'leadership'.

His concern both for the cultural responsibility of the artist and for the relation of the individual to the wider community fostered his increasing interest in the theatre as the most 'social' of art forms. In it the human interaction of which drama essentially consists is acted out before an audience functioning as a microcosm of the whole community. At the same time his scepticism about the limitations of language took him towards various kinds of non-verbal theatre. He became interested in the symbolic force of mime and gesture (elaborated on in the 1911 essay 'Über die Pantomime'), and also in dance.[41] For Grete Wiesenthal, whom he met in October 1907, he composed two dance libretti in 1910–11. His best-known ballet, however, was *Josephslegende* (1912), which was written in collaboration with Kessler to music by Richard Strauss for Nijinsky ('the greatest genius [. . .] among all mimes': P III, 145) and Diaghilev's Russian Ballet company, and which received its première on 14 May 1914 in Paris.

Music, like dance, added a further expressive dimension to verbal language. Hofmannsthal's partnership with Richard Strauss was formed at a time when both were at something of a crossroads in their artistic careers, unsure of the direction in which their work would develop.[42] What brought them together was one of the most intense of Hofmannsthal's dramas, *Elektra*, which had been composed in the summer of 1903 and first performed in October that year in the Kleines Theater, Berlin, with Gertrud Eysoldt in the title role. The production was by Max Reinhardt, the first of many Hofmannsthal productions that he would undertake. It was through Bahr that Hofmannsthal had met Reinhardt in May that year in Vienna, so that Bahr was later able to take satisfaction in Hofmannsthal's first real public success.[43] Strauss, fresh from the *succès de scandale* he had enjoyed with *Salome* (1905), was attracted by *Elektra*; Hofmannsthal reworked the text as a libretto, and Strauss was delighted to discover in him 'a born librettist' (H/Strauss, 33: letter of 6 July 1908). The finished opera received its first performance in Dresden on 25 January 1909, and so began a long and fruitful collaboration, which is documented in their celebrated correspondence – so comprehensive a documentation of artistic partnership that in 1926, while they were both still working together, they published a selection (stopping short at 1918). Since then there have been successive fuller editions of the correspondence, in which we can follow the genesis of all their operas and their striving to achieve a perfect match of music and text, 'fitting like hand and glove', as Hofmannsthal himself put it (H/Strauss, 582: letter of 13 August 1928). The greatest success of all was *Der Rosenkavalier*, in the conception of which a seminal part was played early in 1909 by Kessler. It too was first performed in Dresden, on 26 January 1911, with sets and costumes by Alfred Roller; the Viennese première followed a few weeks later on 8 April.

Strauss and Hofmannsthal were temperamentally too different to become close friends. Strauss seemed, so Hofmannsthal wrote to Bodenhausen's sister-in-law Countess Ottonie Degenfeld, 'a remarkable but utterly alien being, as if from another planet' (H/Degenfeld, 69: letter of 20 January 1911). Their differences are often in evidence in their correspondence. Strauss's first reaction to Act One of *Der Rosenkavalier* was that it was 'perhaps a bit too subtle for the masses' (H/Strauss, 48: letter of 4 May 1909), to which Hofmannsthal replied eight days later that the action was simple and would be 'comprehensible to the most naïve public' (H/Strauss, 49). Strauss would urge Hofmannsthal that the public had to be made to laugh, not just to smile (H/Strauss, 62: letter of 20 July 1909); indeed eventually it came to seem to Hofmannsthal that Strauss just kept repeating that (H/Strauss, 606: letter of 7 May 1929). Hofmannsthal would urge him to tone down crude effects,[44] and long after *Der Rosenkavalier* was completed wrote (though did not send) a letter attacking the crudity of the score (H/Strauss, 291–3: letter of 11 June 1916), but he would also thank Strauss for producing effects that worked well theatrically (H/Strauss, 63: letter of 26 July 1909).

Similar differences came to the surface during their work on their next joint project, *Ariadne auf Naxos*. Strauss had difficulties grasping the symbolism, which Hofmannsthal then explained in a lengthy letter of mid-July 1911 (H/Strauss, 113–16); a subsequent letter formed the basis for an interpretative introductory essay, the so-called 'Ariadne-Brief', which Hofmannsthal published in a musical yearbook in 1913 (P III, 138–42). The first version of the opera was designed to be performed as the *divertissement* following a version of Molière's *Le Bourgeois gentilhomme*, and was performed, in Reinhardt's production, in Stuttgart on 25 October 1912. This combined production had mixed success and also posed practical problems: since it required separate casts of actors and singers, for example, it was always going to be expensive to mount. In December 1912 Strauss and Hofmannsthal decided to write an independent musical prologue ('Vorspiel') to replace the Molière, Hofmannsthal in particular being increasingly hostile to the original 'improvisational misalliance', as he called it, between the opera and

prose comedy (H/Strauss, 200: letter of 12 June 1903).[45] The
reworked version was finally given its première on 4 October 1916
in the Opera House (Hofoper) in Vienna.

Most of Hofmannsthal's major plays also received their first
performances outside Vienna. Up to the First World War, like
Schnitzler, he was dependent on theatres in Berlin. *Das gerettete
Venedig* was produced by Brahm in the Lessing-Theater in January
1905, with sets designed in part by Edward Gordon Craig.[46] The
prose comedy *Cristinas Heimreise*, which grew out of an idea for a
Strauss opera, was produced by Max Reinhardt in the Deutsches
Theater on 11 February 1910, with a cast headed by Reinhardt's star
actor, Alexander Moissi. In response to criticism of the final act in
this production Hofmannsthal then altered it,[47] and in this short-
ened version it was one of the plays that Reinhardt's company
performed in May of the same year in Vienna (Theater an der
Wien). The next major dramatic work was the morality play
Jedermann. The initial stimulus had apparently come as early as 1903
in a letter from a composer friend, Clemens zu Franckenstein,
reporting on a performance of the English *Everyman* he had seen in
London, mounted by the Elizabethan Stage Society (HKA IX,
233–5). Hofmannsthal adapted the material, drawing also on a
mid-sixteenth-century German play by Hans Sachs.[48] The finished
work reflects his sense of disintegrating values in a materialist world
– an attempt, as he put it in 1911 in the essay 'Das Spiel vor der
Menge', 'to contrast an intact world order with the infinitely fragmented conditions' of the time (P III, 64–5). The play was first
produced by Reinhardt on 1 December 1911, again with Moissi,
and again in Berlin (in the Zirkus Schumann).

In the next five years Hofmannsthal engaged in intense reading of
Molière. One product was a very free reworking of *Les Fâcheux* in
1916, *Die Lästigen*. Another was his translation of *Le Bourgeois
gentilhomme*, which he composed in 1917 and which was first performed on 9 April 1918. The central part was played by a brilliant
Viennese comic actor, Max Pallenberg, but the performance once
again took place in Berlin (at the Deutsches Theater). His failure to
establish a niche in the Viennese theatre, and more particularly the
failure of the Burgtheater, under successive directors, to build his
work centrally into its repertory, rankled with Hofmannsthal
throughout his career. This is most openly expressed in two letters
written to Andrian on 28 August and 2 October 1918. In the dying
months of the monarchy Andrian had been appointed director-
general (*Generalintendant*) of the court theatres, and that provided
the spur for Hofmannsthal to pour out his resentment of how he
felt he had been 'systematically mistreated' by the Burgtheater
(H/Andrian, 288: letter of 2 October 1918).

As an officer of the reserve, Hofmannsthal had been called up at the outbreak of the First World War, but he was soon transferred to a desk job in Vienna, and from May 1915 was released to engage in propagandist journalism ('eine besondere publizistische Aufgabe').[49] He produced a series of patriotic essays and addresses, arguing what he perceived as the cultural mission of Austria – what in the title of one essay of 1917 is called 'the idea of Austria' ('die österreichische Idee'), a formula derived from his correspondence with Andrian (see pp. 170–73, below). He also functioned as general editor of the *Österreichische Bibliothek*, a series of twenty-six slim volumes designed to represent the character of Austrian culture. In 1915 he was sent on 'political' – in effect, propaganda – missions on behalf of the Austrian Foreign Office to occupied Poland and Belgium; in the summer of 1916, he lectured in Warsaw at the invitation of Andrian, who had been posted there as Austrian envoy; and further lecture tours abroad followed, to Scandinavia at the end of 1916 and to Switzerland in 1917.

Towards the end of the war, consciously taking up threads from his earlier imaginative work, he turned again to comedy. *Der Schwierige*, by common consent his masterpiece and one of the greatest of German comedies, was largely written in 1917. The first version was completed in late 1919 and serialized in the *Neue Freie Presse* between April and September 1920. After further revision the first edition in book form was published by S. Fischer the following year. While it continues to reflect the cultural concerns informing his essays, its composition marks another major change of course in Hofmannsthal's work, a return to dramatic writing and the theatre after his polemical and journalistic work in the first three years of the war. Hofmannsthal wanted it to be performed in the Burgtheater, ideally by Reinhardt's company. On 25 January 1921 he told Andrian that it made no sense to launch a play like *Der Schwierige* in Berlin or Hamburg (H/Andrian, 319), and on 14 February he wrote to Anton Wildgans, who had taken over the direction of the theatre a fortnight before, that he had withheld the play from theatres in Germany and clung to his wish to see it first performed in Vienna (H/Wildgans, 30–1). But the Burgtheater rejected the play, to Hofmannsthal's dismay. Where was he supposed to bring out a Viennese comedy, he asked Marie Luise Borchardt over Easter – in Hanover perhaps, or in Bochum? (H/Borchardt, 159). The première eventually took place in the Residenztheater in Munich on 8 November 1921, with Gustav Waldau and Elisabeth Bergner in the main parts. When it was performed in Berlin three weeks later, the hostility of the press response[50] confirmed all Hofmannsthal's doubts about launching it in northern Germany. But when Reinhardt took over the Theater in der Josefstadt, one of the highlights of his first season was a new production (premièred on 16 April 1924), with Waldau again playing Hans Karl and with Helene Thimig as Helene Altenwyl, Hermann Thimig as Stani, and Egon Friedell as the academic celebrity Professor Brücke.

By then Hofmannsthal was deeply committed to the Salzburg Festival. He was involved in consultations as a member of the artistic advisory committee ('Kunstrat') from February 1919. At the first festival in August 1920 *Jedermann*, produced by Reinhardt, was performed in front of the cathedral, and it remained a focal point of the festival thereafter, being performed again in 1921 and at every subsequent festival from 1926 onwards, except for the years 1938–45. In 1922 and 1925 Hofmannsthal's second morality play, *Das Salzburger große Welttheater*, was performed instead. The première in 1922 took place on 12 August in the Kollegienkirche, again produced by Reinhardt, and again with a cast headed by Moissi. It was one of the projects on which Hofmannsthal worked with the greatest conviction – indeed, so intensely did it occupy him in the autumn of 1921 that he missed the première of *Der Schwierige* in Munich. His enthusiasm for the festival, and for the ecclesiastical settings of Reinhardt's productions, accorded with his own commitment to the idea of Catholicism, not so much as a personal religion (he was, indeed, not an observing Catholic as an adult)[51] but as a fundamental part of the continuity of cultural tradition that he saw enshrined in the 'idea of Austria'. His loyalty to this idea of Catholicism was strengthened by his correspondence with Andrian and also by his family background: his brother-in-law Hans Schlesinger became a Dominican monk and celebrated his first Mass in 1919.[52]

Like Schnitzler, Hofmannsthal was hard hit by the economic depression of the postwar years. He wrote with bitterness to his wealthy young Swiss friend Carl J. Burckhardt of the humiliation he felt at being 'reduced to an absolute beggar' (H/Burckhardt, 10: letter of 27 March 1919), and after the massive inflation of 1922 he told Andrian that the basis of his ordinary daily life in society had been 'suddenly shattered' (H/Andrian, 335–6: letter of 23 November 1922). Financial insecurity forced him to keep up his journalistic writing. He lamented this in a letter to Schnitzler: 'For the sake of earning my daily bread I am taking on work almost beyond my capacity – essayistic work, that is, not poetic work, for I almost have to suppress that' (H/AS, 295: letter of 28 January 1922).

In fact he continued to undertake a wide variety of writing in his later years. The prose works of the period include the fragmentary novel *Andreas*, the first version of which dates back to 1907. He resumed work on it in the summer of 1913, then again intensely in 1918 and 1919, and reworked it again in 1924–25. The *Buch der Freunde*, a collection of aphorisms and quotations, was first published in 1922. (It was reissued posthumously in 1929 in an enlarged edition, with an afterword by Schröder.) There were also more Strauss operas. *Die Frau ohne Schatten*, a dramatized fable about fertility, can be seen as presenting, in the meeting of the childless empress and the dyer Barak and his wife, an allegory of the development in Hofmannsthal's own work: his commitment to linking his creativity to the substantial concerns of society.[53] It was first performed on 10 October 1919 in the Opera House in Vienna (now Staatsoper), of which Strauss had been co-director since May 1919. There followed *Die ägyptische Helena* (first performed in Dresden in 1928) and finally *Arabella*, on which they were still at work when Hofmannsthal died; he sent Strauss a revision of Act One with the very last letter in their correspondence, dated 10 July 1929. (*Arabella* was eventually performed in Dresden in 1933, under the baton of Clemens Krauss.)

The last of Hofmannsthal's comedies, *Der Unbestechliche*, which is set in pre-war Austria, is built round a central role, that of a masterful servant, that was written for Pallenberg. The première took place on 16 March 1923 in Vienna, in the Raimundtheater – an unfashionable late nineteenth-century foundation, now under the enterprising direction of Rudolf Beer but still far removed both in locality and in tradition from the Burgtheater to which Hofmannsthal had always aspired. A production later the same year in Berlin (Lessing-Theater) was a failure.[54] He never completed a final revision of the play, so that it was not published in his lifetime, but the version used in rehearsals has survived in a duplicated typescript (*Bühnenmanuskript*), as has a version of the first act that was published in the *Neue Freie Presse* two days after the première.

Hofmannsthal's last years were filled with gloom at developments in a postwar Europe marred, as he saw it, by materialism and the disintegration of the political continuity that had been symbolized in the Habsburg monarchy. Writing to Redlich in 1928 he compared conditions to those leading up to the Austrian defeats of 1859 and 1866 (H/Redlich, 97: letter of 28 May 1928); in another rather self-pitying letter written the same year to Andrian, he lamented that his 'higher and better' aspirations left him 'isolated' in face of an 'appalling world' (H/Andrian, 406: letter of 2 April 1928). In the Munich address 'Das Schrifttum als geistiger Raum der Nation' he formulated his commitment to the idea of a 'conservative revolution' in the sense of a restoration of cultural values; the tragedy *Der Turm*, on the other hand, depicts a society dominated by material values and violence. Successive versions of *Der Turm* were worked on in the 1920s. The first version was completed in 1924 – an achievement recorded with relief in a letter to Strauss (H/Strauss, 455: letter of 8 November 1924) – but reworking started almost at once, prompted by Reinhardt, and the revised version was performed in Munich (Prinzregententheater) and Hamburg (Deutsches Schauspielhaus) on 4 February 1928, achieving at best a *succès d'estime*.[55]

On 13 July of the following year Hofmannsthal's elder son committed suicide at home in Rodaun, and two days later, leaving the house to go the funeral, he himself suffered a fatal stroke. In accordance with a wish he had expressed as a young man, he was buried in the Kalksburg cemetery, just west of Rodaun, in the habit of a Franciscan monastic order of which he was an honorary member.

The Autobiographical Impulse

Schnitzler's diary for 1917 contains a revealing entry in which he tries to explain the particular regard he felt for his friend Richard Beer-Hofmann:

> A truly noble human being. How many others are there like him? Some greater poets – indeed basically it may be that he is not what we call a 'poet' at all? What are categories, opinions, even talent? The only thing to be respected is that mysterious quality we call personality. (Tgb., 11 April 1917)

In no way are both Schnitzler and Hofmannsthal more clearly children of the Vienna of their times than in their concern with 'personality', with the integrity of individual identity. Hence the craving for self-knowledge which Schnitzler noted in himself in his late twenties (Tgb., 4 August 1890). Each of them was repeatedly concerned to define the very character of his own development; each of them – Schnitzler in his diaries, Hofmannsthal in *Ad me ipsum* and related notes – endeavoured to impose a coherent form on life and work, in defence of identity itself.

Schnitzler's proneness to searing self-criticism meant that he was inclined to view his whole character as flawed. (This is not a tendency Hofmannsthal shared.) By the time his career as a dramatist had been launched, he was naggingly aware of the discrepancy between his sensibility and high aspirations on the one hand and the shallowness of his life-style on the other (Tgb., 29 January 1894). When he was forty he would still define a major 'flaw' of his life as 'not being totally confident in anything' ('Fehler meines Lebens, in nichts totale Sicherheit zu haben': Tgb., 26 August 1902). It was, as he himself realized, to build up a 'necessary contrast' to his 'inner disorder' that he carefully preserved and arranged documentary records of his life, letters, press-cuttings, and so on (Tgb., 28 March 1896). That the maintenance of his diaries was a similar defence against insecurity is confirmed by his emotional investment in their preservation. When he set to work on his autobiography during the war, that took on the same importance for him – so much so that by contrast with his habitual exposure of his other works in private readings, he kept it secret at first from everyone.

The style of the earliest diaries is self-consciously literary; he himself, rereading them when working on his autobiography, found an element of 'posing' in those of the early 1880s (Tgb., 5 April 1916). For a long time the entries are occasional rather than daily; the pattern of regular daily entries was not established until 1890.[56] But as he gradually worked out his strategy, he was in effect learning to give shape to the very record of his life. The diaries became a 'work' of the utmost significance for him, and the thought that they might get lost filled him with 'strange fear' (Tgb., 30 March 1904). In 1918, as the end of the war approached and he reread his diaries of the 1890s, reliving his memories of his relations with various women (Marie Reinhard, Adele Sandrock, and Mizi Glümer are among those he names), he noted his 'burning wish that they should not be lost' and asked: 'Is that vanity? In part, certainly. But somehow a feeling of obligation also. And as though it could liberate me from my painful inner isolation if I could be sure of friends after my death' (Tgb., 22 August 1918). This takes up an earlier note, written on 18 April 1915, a few weeks before he began 'systematic' work on his autobiography (24 May 1915), which mentions his 'need for complete honesty'. It is a recurrent concern in the last thirty years of his life. As early as 1901 he wrote: 'I do not know whether the urge to be truthful to myself was in me from the first; but it is certain that it has intensified with the years and indeed that it is now the strongest and most constant of my inner urges' (*Jug.*, 324). Several aphorisms on truth and truthfulness are included in the *Buch der Sprüche und Bedenken* (AB, 51).

The 'need' for truthfulness was doubtless one of the impetuses behind the diary, and is reflected in many entries both in his frank criticism of others (including Hofmannsthal) and also, more painfully, in his severe self-criticism. The next sentence of the diary entry for 24 May 1915 reads: 'Autobiographical yearnings, not from vanity but rather from a feeling of isolation.' Isolation is a condition of insecurity, which derived in Schnitzler's case partly from recurrent self-doubts about the quality of his achievement and more fundamentally from doubts about his very identity as an artist.

'If only I were as much an artist as I have an artistic temperament' ('Wenn ich nur so sehr Künstler wäre, als ich Künstlernatur bin'), reads the entry for 2 January 1880; and the theme recurs again and again over the years. 'If I am really an artist', he wrote in 1895 when worrying about the unsatisfactory quality of his various plans, 'ideas commensurate with my personality must come to me' (Tgb., 17 December 1895). The 'if' is highly revealing, given that the entry was written two months after the première of *Liebelei*. Nearly thirty years later an entry records his attendance at a recital on 18 March 1915: 'As I move to go into the "artists' room", the portress asks: "Are you an artist, sir?" And I reply: "If only I knew!"' Implicit in this answer, albeit typically ironized, is still the same fundamental doubt about his identity: he does not enquire whether he is a *good* artist but in effect admits his uncertainty as to what kind of a person he is.

From an early point Schnitzler clearly had the eventual publication of his diaries in mind: his friends knew about them, and Hofmannsthal, for example, told him in 1903 that he almost envied those who would one day be able to spend weeks reading them, imaginatively reliving Schnitzler's experience (H/AS, 170: letter of 19 June 1903). In his will Schnitzler stipulated that they should only be published complete.[57] This reflects his conviction that they had an autonomous importance as a 'work' – that is, a creative work. On 22 May 1905, while he was rereading entries of twelve years earlier, he wrote that 'individual parts' of his diary seemed to be the only thing he had written that had 'power' ('Mir ist, als wären einzelne Partien dieses Tgb. das einzige von meinen Sachen, worin Kraft'). More than twenty years later he still judged that parts of it were more substantial than any of his imaginative or fictional writings ('wesentlicher als alles, was ich "gedichtet" habe').[58] According to Alma Mahler-Werfel, indeed, towards the end of his life he was confident that his diaries, 'if ever they should be published, would have an importance comparable to the works of the greatest' ('daß diese Tagebücher, wenn sie einmal herauskommen sollten, sich an Bedeutung mit den Werken der Größten messen können').[59]

It is clear from these various indications that he saw their 'power' as something creative: he recognized that in building up the record of a life shaped day by day by imaginative selection, the diary is a kind of running autobiography, and has the same fictionalizing quality as autobiography has. What he was creating in the quasi-documentary form of the diary was a life of imagined historicity, a cumulative substitute for the integrity he admired in Beer-Hofmann. For all its laconic and factual manner, the diary is not merely the distillation and record of a life – it actually *creates* a life, shaping it out of the passing moments experienced but not held fast by the (ever-changing) ego. Cumulatively it creates a personality more real, because more circumstantial, than the characters of the dramatic and narrative fictions, more secure than the identity of its author.

It was only natural that Schnitzler's artistic aspirations also made him constantly concerned for his reputation. His early insecurity in this respect was vividly expressed in a dream that he recorded on 7 September 1893, in which he had appeared in a Schillerian cloak kissing the hand of a Hanslick-like Goethe. Part of his 'burning wish' that his diaries should be preserved, recorded in the entry for 22 August 1918, was certainly connected to the natural interest of the creative artist in posterity. This interest, which he admitted on 25 December 1917 in his review of the outgoing year, was all the more sharp at a time of diminishing public success. But exactly the same concern underlies the collection throughout his career of press-cuttings concerned with his own work.

From about mid-1898 he engaged press-cutting agencies, chiefly the 'Observer' agency in Vienna, to supply him with cuttings.[60] The very earliest items in the collection go back still further, to 1891, and include several of the first reviews of *Anatol* mentioned in his diary between 10 November and 19 December 1892. He assiduously maintained the collection, which is now in the University of Exeter Library,[61] and it contains in all some 23,000 items. Many of these are only brief reports or announcements, even incidental mentions; many relate to the various controversies in which Schnitzler was involved. There are also a number of photographs, theatre bills and programmes, and copies of early critical essays. But it is in the reviews, many of them bearing the marks of Schnitzler's underlinings, that the importance of the collection chiefly lies. Schnitzler realized this; it is mentioned in his testamentary disposition of his *Nachlaß*, dated 16 August 1918, as being, 'especially in that part which rejects my work, not without interest as a document of literary or rather cultural history'.[62]

In so far as his diaries comment on the notices he received, they confirm that he longed to find in them the kind of praise that would provide reassuring black-and-white evidence of his artistic achievement. *Professor Bernhardi* will serve as an example. It is a play for which he had a special affection: 'There are works of mine I like better,' he wrote in his diary on 27 March 1918, 'but nowhere do I like myself better than in *Bernhardi*.' The one review of the first

Viennese production in 1918 that he singled out in his diary on 24 December of that year as 'excellent' was a long and extremely positive piece by Raoul Auernheimer that had appeared that day in the *Neue Freie Presse*.

His preservation of his collection of cuttings is in keeping, then, with his preservation of his diaries: both documented his life and achievements and so provided a defence against his lifelong uncertainty about his very identity as an artist. By contrast, Hofmannsthal adopted the very opposite approach to critical reception: he deliberately avoided reading press reviews, except those of chosen critics.[63] But he wholly shared Schnitzler's interest in the integrity of artistic identity. Significantly, he never lost his interest in Schnitzler's diary-writing. Seventeen years after his letter of 19 June 1903 imagining future readers, Schnitzler recorded a joint walk in which they discussed precisely his diaries and autobiographical writing (*Chrstk.*, 45).

Hofmannsthal's approach to the problems of artistic identity and critical reputation took the form of retrospective notes on his own work, in which he attempted to impose a unifying pattern on his entire literary production. In his view of human potential for achievement his work does indeed show great consistency. One of his central themes is formulated in his very first published essay, which was printed under the pseudonym 'Loris' in February 1891; this is the idea of 'self-education to human integrity' (P I, 10). In that context it still has a Nietzschean connotation, but the idea of spiritual wholeness is also put in Goethean terms, alluding to the eighteenth-century topos of the dualism of Man: 'Unity of the soul in contrast to the two-souls-in-one-breast disease – that is, self-education towards becoming a whole man, an "individual" in the Nietzschean sense' ('Einheit der Seele im Gegensatz zur Zweiseelenkrankheit, also Selbsterziehung zum ganzen Menschen, zum Individuum Nietzsches').

It is increasingly a Goethean conception of harmonious integrity of the personality that he advances as an ideal. He recurrently expresses this ideal by quotation of an aphorism that Lichtenberg had noted from the *Spectator*: 'The whole man must move together.' (In most cases Hofmannsthal slightly misquotes it in the form 'The whole man must move at once'.) It crops up in notes of 1906 (A, 151), and again the same year – ascribed to Addison – as the epigraph to a letter to Bodenhausen (H/Bodenhausen, 78: letter of 7 June 1906). In the '*Novelle* in letters'[64] *Die Briefe des Zurückgekehrten* (1907) it is quoted as 'one of my great truths' (P II, 281). It is found again in notes dating from about 1910,[65] and in 1912 it is quoted in the Introduction to a four-volume anthology *Deutsche Erzähler*,

again ascribed to Addison, and with a rider citing as 'more pertinent than ever' Lichtenberg's dictum that every German should
write it on his fingernails (P III, 111). The translation Hofmannsthal
gives is 'der ganze Mensch muß sich *auf eins* regen'; fifteen years
later, in the address 'Das Schrifttum als geistiger Raum der Nation',
when he quotes it again, and again refers to Lichtenberg, he offers a
different translation, 'Als ein Ganzes muß der Mann sich regen' (P
IV, 409), echoing the Goethean term 'Ganzheit' ('wholeness'). He
repeatedly resorts to eighteenth-century vocabulary in defining his
ideal of achieving and maintaining a full humanity, for example
when writing to Strauss about *Elektra* during their work on *Ariadne
auf Naxos* in July 1911: 'preserving one's self in every transformation, remaining a human being, not sinking into an animal existence shorn of memory' ('in der Verwandlung sich bewahren, ein
Mensch bleiben, nicht zum gedächtnislosen Tier herabsinken':
H/Strauss, 115).

From about 1916 Hofmannsthal was increasingly concerned to
establish the coherence of his work – what by the mid-1920s he
had convinced himself was the 'impressive unity' of his work
('Formidable Einheit des Werkes': A, 237), and he would collect
his thoughts on this theme ('Über den Zusammenhang meiner
Arbeiten': A, 235), at first under the title *Spectantia ad me*,[66] which
was then superseded by the title *Ad me ipsum*. One attempt to
organize these notes coherently was begun in the spring of 1916, as
the basis for an introduction to the opera *Die Frau ohne Schatten* that
he had decided the previous year to entrust to Max Mell.[67] Mell
wrote the essay in the summer of 1916 and sent it to Hofmannsthal
at the beginning of November; Hofmannsthal's reaction was to
respond to an earlier request and send him a version of his notes
Ad me ipsum (A, 220–3).[68] Another version of *Ad me ipsum*, also
drafted in 1916 (A, 213–19), was shown to the Viennese scholar
Walther Brecht in 1919.

In 1917 he drew up a brief summary of his life, divided into three
stages (A, 232), and on 18 April 1921, in a letter to Max Pirker, he
attempted a much fuller schematic survey not of his dramatic writing but of his own development as a dramatist from *Gestern* to *Der
Schwierige* (A, 369–70).[69] It is in this letter, which was designed to
provide Pirker with a basis for an essay on Hofmannsthal's career as
a dramatist, that he identifies the 'fulfilment of traditional theatrical
demands' as becoming a 'clear goal' from about 1907 onwards.

Two years later, in the summer of 1923, he planned to rework
Ad me ipsum, dividing it into numbered sections (A, 234). And
in 1927, in Aussee, he drafted an 'imaginary letter' to Carl J.
Burckhardt about his early works, again using the title *Ad me ipsum*

(A, 240). These separate drafts are complemented by a series of autobiographical and self-analysing notes, which he continued to write up to 1928.

The self-interpretation in *Ad me ipsum* and related notes and essays (including, for example, the 'Ariadne-Brief') has a significance out of all proportion to the actual length of these works, which amount to a very small proportion of his total work. This significance lies in the contribution that his self-interpretation made to his development, and particularly to his understanding of his aims as a dramatist. It is in that sense an integral part of his work. *Ad me ipsum* has also, however, exerted an overstrong influence on Hofmannsthal scholarship, which has too often adopted Hofmannsthal's own theoretical and rather abstract vocabulary and has also tended to accept his presentation of how his work evolved. His comments can, of course, be both interesting and fruitful; after all, they are authentic records of how he himself saw his work. But it is important not to forget that Hofmannsthal's own view of his works constantly involves a *re*interpretation, a back-projection of his later concerns. The point has been put well by Ritchie Robertson:

> In these retrospective comments, Hofmannsthal does not speak with unchallengeable authority, but has the same position as any other commentator on his works; his greater intimacy with them is balanced, and sometimes outweighed, by the bias resulting from his desire to see his literary career as a coherent whole.[70]

At times hindsight demonstrably distorts the truth, and we need to be watchful about such distortion, which characteristically takes the form of a simplification – a stylization – of his development.

What this stylization also shows is Hofmannsthal's concentrated commitment to that integrity of effort that Schnitzler, by contrast, feared he himself lacked. Schnitzler once wrote that his 'main sin' was 'not to be able to enjoy the present – always preferring to do something else' (Tgb., 30 July 1896). Seventeen years later another entry returns to the theme:

> Nm. [Nachmittag] spazieren gehend tiefes Bewußtsein meiner Immoralität. Denn gibt es eine schlimmre, ja eine andre, als stets in Sorgen zu sein, – nie den Augenblick – oh, nicht genießen – *haben*! (23 July 1913)

> Afternoon, walking: deep consciousness of my immorality. For is there any worse – indeed any other – immorality than constantly worrying, never – not just enjoying, but *possessing* the present moment!

Experience, the very stuff of personality, is elusive. In post-Machian Vienna, it is a familiar theme (see pp. 8–12, above). But it also bears on that confident integrity that Schnitzler admired in Beer-Hofmann. In his total, even obsessive, commitment to a conception of art founded partly on an eighteenth-century ideal of human potential, Hofmannsthal had a bulwark against disintegration, even amid the political disintegration of postwar Europe. This strength of purpose found expression in his letters too, in a way that was generously recognized by Alfred Polgar, reading his collected correspondence in 1939:

> You cannot imagine how moved I was by these letters, by the constant striving of the writer to draw into himself the very maximum of world and spirit and to force out of himself the very maximum achievement [von dem unablässigen Bemühen des Schreibers, ein Maximum an Welt und Geist in sich hineinzutun, ein Maximum an Leistung aus sich hinauszuzwingen]. He placed the highest demands on himself and did what he could to meet those demands. Anyone of whom one cannot say the same has lived his life wrongly.[71]

CHAPTER 3

The Theatre

The World as a Stage: Theatre in Vienna

There is an old Viennese popular song entitled 'Die Welt ist ein Komödienhaus', which explores the time-honoured metaphor of the world as a stage.[1] If, as has often been observed, it is in Vienna that life most frequently seems to be seen as theatre, that is a consequence of the central importance long accorded the theatre there.

In the first half of the nineteenth century, when the song was written, Vienna enjoyed a paramount position as the major theatrical centre in the German-speaking countries. Throughout that time there were five permanent theatres. Two were court theatres within the walled *Innere Stadt*: the Theater nächst dem Kärntnertore functioned as the opera house; the Hofburgtheater, the home of the classics and serious modern drama, was regarded as the premier theatre of German-speaking Europe. The Hofburgtheater (Burgtheater for short) maintained its distinguished reputation during the third quarter of the century, under the direction first of Heinrich Laube and then, after a brief gap, of Franz von Dingelstedt. The other three permanent theatres were all in districts just outside the walled centre. The largest was the Theater an der Wien, the smallest the Theater in der Josefstadt, and the oldest the Theater in der Leopoldstadt, which was rebuilt in 1847 and reopened, much enlarged, as the Carltheater. These were all commercial enterprises, the traditional homes of Viennese dialect comedy.

Despite the proverbial enthusiasm of the Viennese for the theatre, the number of theatres did not increase while the population of the city was doubling between 1800 and 1855. The incoming population from the far-flung provinces in the early stages of industrialization had no attachment to the local genres of dialect comedy, and when new theatres finally began to be built it was mainly to provide homes for operetta, light vaudeville comedy, even variety. There were two exceptions. One was the Theater am Franz-Josefs-

66

Kai, which opened in 1860 and had dialect comedy as well as operetta in the repertory (it was, indeed, where Nestroy made his final appearances in 1862), but which burnt down in 1863. The other was the Harmonie-Theater in the Wasagasse, north of the centre. Opened in 1866, it is remembered mainly as one of the earliest works of Otto Wagner, and it was quickly changed into a music-hall.

Two major new foundations of the 1870s were also short-lived, both falling victim to fire. The Komische Oper, opened on the new Schottenring in 1874 and renamed the Ring-Theater in 1878, burnt down in 1881 – one of the great disasters of theatre history, in which nearly four hundred people lost their lives. The Wiener Stadttheater, which opened in 1872 in the Seilerstätte, in the centre of the old city, was burnt out in 1884. The Stadttheater was an adventurous experiment, born of the optimistic cultural idealism and free enterprise of the Liberal era; its very opening was yet another disproof of Broch's conception of the Vienna of the 1870s as a cultural vacuum. It began, under the direction of Laube, with a repertory of serious drama, and was intended to provide com-petition for the Burgtheater. But its financial position was under-mined by the Stock Exchange crash of 1873, and when the shell of the building was reconstructed after the fire it was as a variety theatre, the Etablissement Ronacher, which became notorious for the frivolous triviality of its programme. It is to the Ronacher that Schnitzler's philistine Leutnant Gustl recalls having gone on his first evening after being posted to Vienna (ES I, 348); in another early Schnitzler story, 'Exzentrik', a young woman cultivates as her admirers a series of performers appearing in circus acts there: a dwarf, a giant, and a clown (ES I, 562–7).

By the time the careers of Schnitzler and Hofmannsthal got under way, the Viennese theatre was in the throes of expansion and change. Of the old dialect theatres, the Theater in der Josefstadt was increasingly run-down. When we learn in Schnitzler's *Liebelei* that Christine's violinist father works there (DW I, 221), the informa-tion signals their depressed social status and living conditions. Its standing and importance would pick up only after the First World War, when it was taken over by Max Reinhardt. The Carltheater had a varied programme under a rapidly changing succession of directors. It was here that the work of Offenbach had been intro-duced to Vienna by Nestroy, helping to pave the way for the development of Viennese operetta by Johann Strauss the younger and others. In the Carltheater itself operetta featured prominently in the repertory, especially in the 1870s and again in the 1890s, and from the end of the century it was essentially an operetta theatre, though overshadowed by the Theater an der Wien, where the repertory was dominated by operetta from the 1870s onwards. Hit followed hit in the Theater an der Wien from the 1870s and 1880s into the last years of the monarchy, from *Die Fledermaus* in 1874 to Lehár's *The Merry Widow* (the biggest commercial success of all) in 1905.

In the 1870s the success of operetta spelled box-office failure for Anzengruber, the one dramatist who made a serious attempt to adapt the conventions of dialect comedy to treat contemporary problems, and who in Berlin, indeed, would be recognized as a precursor of Naturalism. The more acute urban poverty became, the more the new theatre-going public took refuge in the escapism of operetta. *Die Fledermaus*, it is true, unmistakably reflects the social stresses of the time: financial insecurity, moral laxity, hedonism, the hypocrisy of the mask (the 'Hungarian countess'), and the ultimate hollowness of the frivolity underlying the scandals and deceptions. But its topicality was exceptional, and in general Broch is right in pointing to the lack of satirical substance in Viennese operetta (WM, 96). In 1885, the year of another of Johann Strauss's successes, *The Gipsy Baron*, a polemical booklet appeared under the challenging title *Wien war eine Theaterstadt* ('Vienna was once a City of Theatre', with the emphasis on the verb in the past tense). The author, Adam Müller-Guttenbrunn, was a rising critic of pan-German Nationalist views. The nub of his message in *Wien war eine Theaterstadt* was that the old vitality of Viennese theatrical life, founded on the close association of playwrights, directors, actors, and audience, was a thing of the past. Twelve years later, looking back from the very different position that obtained then, he repeated that by the middle of the 1880s theatrical life had descended to the very nadir of intellectual vacuity.[2]

Müller-Guttenbrunn's critical view of the 1880s was coloured by his ideological position: he regarded the taste of the 1880s as being corrupted by a repertory dominated by imported French farces and operettas. Other (and better) judges took a different view. Karl Kraus, for example, would look back on the 1880s in his poem 'Jugend' of 1917 (F 462–471, 180–4), recalling with affection a series of operettas by Offenbach and others. He also celebrated the company of the pre-1888 Burgtheater as an ideal against which he judged the performers of later generations and found them wanting. To some extent, no doubt, this idealization, which is most fully set out in the 1914 essay 'Das Denkmal eines Schauspielers' (F 391–392, 31–40), is a satirical device, symptomatic of a nostalgia characteristic of his generation;[3] but the Burgtheater was also a genuine source of early inspiration to that whole generation, including both Schnitzler and Hofmannsthal.

Both were particularly indebted to the polished comedy of manners (*Konversationsstück*) traditional in the Burgtheater. Because of the risqué subject matter of his early work, Schnitzler, however, was open to suspicion of being infected by French examples. The report in the *Wiener Allgemeine Zeitung* for 18 July 1893 on the première of *Abschiedssouper* in Bad Ischl described the playlet as reminiscent of Murger's *Scènes de la vie de Bohème*. The jibes continued even when *Liebelei* was produced in the Burgtheater in 1895. The play was widely credited with a realist intention (see p. 22, above), but a review in the Social Democrat *Arbeiter-Zeitung* on 11 October, signed 'e.w.' (Edmund Wengraf), found the characters insufficiently Viennese, and linked this charge with an innuendo about social class, saying that was how the ordinary people of Vienna were imagined to be in educated homes where the children were allowed to speak only French. Nine days later *Der junge Kikeriki* re-used the point about the characters, taking over the description of the female characters as 'grisettes', and dismissing the play as presenting 'the love-life of Paris, artificially translated into Viennese'. That some of these doubts may have struck a chord with Schnitzler himself is suggested by the letter to Fulda four years later in which he writes disparagingly of the dialogue of *Denksteine* as reading like a translation from French (AS/Bfe. I, 365).

Even in later years, the much-admired ease and lightness of his dialogue was still sometimes traced back to a debt to French salon comedy. On 23 February 1924, for example, a critic in the *Neues Wiener Tagblatt* ('H.T.'), reviewing a production of *Professor Bernhardi*, praised the 'authentic Schnitzler dialogue [. . .] which sounds so Viennese that we have long forgotten how much he learnt from the French comedy of manners'.

There were indeed French models in the Burgtheater; throughout its history high comedy had been represented in the works of Molière, and from the mid-nineteenth century a series of plays by Scribe and by Sardou were added to the repertory with considerable success. Hofmannsthal revered Molière in particular as the dramatist in whom all the elements of comedy were united ('Molière vereinigt die Elemente des Komischen': RA III, 512–13). There were also German models, notably Gustav Freytag's *Die Journalisten*, which was a firm favourite in the Burgtheater from the mid-1850s onwards. A new production in 1909, with Hugo Thimig in the part of the cynically adaptable Schmock, was still in the repertory when Schnitzler's *Fink und Fliederbusch* was performed in the Deutsches Volkstheater in 1917, and several reviewers, including Auernheimer (NFP, 15 November 1917) compared the two plays.

But the classic dramatist of the *Konversationsstück* was a Viennese, Eduard von Bauernfeld, to whom Hofmannsthal devoted an appreciative essay in 1893, after Saar had published a selection from Bauernfeld's *Nachlass* (P I, 159–64). Bauernfeld, a friend of Grillparzer's, provided the Burgtheater with a succession of these light comedies of manners from the 1830s onwards, and the most successful of them were still being performed when the old Burgtheater was closed in 1888. This kind of comedy, characteristically set in spas and salons and recapturing the conversation of elegant society, was a natural model for aspiring dramatists at the end of the century. Bahr was one who explicitly compared his own comedies to Bauernfeld's.[4] Hofmannsthal's debt to the genre is to be seen at its strongest in his masterpiece, *Der Schwierige* (see p. 186, below); and Schnitzler's plays too, from *Anatol* to the 'tragicomedy' *Das weite Land*, have their roots in the same genre. The language of the characters was justly summarized by Josef Körner, in the most substantial critical study published during Schnitzler's lifetime, as 'the conversational tone of Viennese society'.[5] Towards the end of his life, when Körner made a similar observation in the course of a comparison with J. J. David, Schnitzler reacted bitterly to the reduction of his style to a conventional 'salon language'.[6] But just a year after Körner's monograph was published, Hofmannsthal made the same point about Schnitzler in the first of his 'Vienna Letters' in *The Dial*, explicitly pointing to the connection with the *Konversationsstück*, 'the drama of conversation as it was nurtured in the Burgtheater [. . .] in the years between 1860 and 1890', when the genre 'was just at its height on this stage'.[7]

The other court theatre, the neo-Renaissance Opera House on the Ring, opened in 1869. By the turn of the century, with Mahler in charge, it was in the middle of ten of the most brilliant years in its history (1897–1907). The move of the Burgtheater from its relatively intimate home on the Michaelerplatz proved more difficult, partly because of the much larger size of the new building, partly because it exemplified the difference that Adolf Loos would later hammer home between functional effectiveness and decorative effect. (The young Klimt had been one of those who had worked on the ceiling paintings over the ornamental main staircases at the north and south ends of the building.) As late as 1910 Schnitzler's diary notes a conversation with Max Burckhard, a former director of the theatre, and Hugo Thimig, a future director, about its 'huge defects' (Tgb., 16 November 1910).

Nevertheless, under the direction first of Burckhard and then of Schlenther, modern subjects and concerns entered the repertory. The plays of Ibsen were staged in the 1890s with star-studded casts, and the strength of the impression they made on the 'Jung Wien' circle is reflected in Hofmannsthal's early essay 'Die Menschen in Ibsens Dramen' (1893). The production of *Liebelei* two years after that – the first play in Viennese dialect to be performed in the Burgtheater – marked a further incursion of conscious modernity and earned Schnitzler the description he is given in *Die demolirte Litteratur* as the dramatist who introduced the working girl to the Burgtheater ('der Dichter, der das Vorstadtmädel burgtheaterfähig machte': WM, 650).

It was Burckhard who in 1899 engaged Josef Kainz as a member of the company. Kainz was, in Rudolph Lothar's words, 'a veritable classic of modern acting' (WM, 631), 'a Romantic of the nerves'.[8] His joining the company was widely seen as a token of Burckhard's determination to complete a modernist revolution that had been begun five years earlier, centring on the acting of Friedrich Mitterwurzer; Kainz was indeed generally regarded, as Kraus recorded, as Mitterwurzer's successor (F 10, 19). For Hofmannsthal he was the actor who most spoke to the Modernist or Impressionist generation, as Emanuel Reicher had done to those associated with the realism of Brahm's company in Berlin. The point is made in a letter of 19 March 1892 in which he apologizes to Schnitzler for breaking an appointment in order to visit Kainz instead: 'Please remember that Kainz means to me what Reicher does to you' (H/AS, 18).

Karl Kraus, himself an actor *manqué*, contrasted the acting of Kainz and others with the quality of speaking he remembered in the smaller Burgtheater of the 1880s. In 1901, when the question whether Nestroy was really worthy of being performed in the Burgtheater ('burgtheaterfähig') was being discussed, he turned the question round and expressed a perceptive doubt as to whether the Burgtheater was up to performing Nestroy ('ob das Burgtheater Nestroyfähig sei': F 75, 22) – an antithesis that he would expound again nearly a quarter of a century later in his long polemical essay 'Nestroy und das Burgtheater' (F 676–678, 1–40). His concern with the primacy of language, with fidelity to the text not just in letter but in spirit, led him to launch what he called 'theatre without décor', 'dekorationsfreies Theater' (from the mid-1920s he would introduce the title 'Theater der Dichtung'): that is, one-man readings of an international repertoire of drama, including a succession of Nestroy texts, in challenging contrast to what he saw as the trivializing spirit of contemporary theatre, whether in Vienna or in the elaborately staged productions of Max Reinhardt.

Reinhardt did not have a permanent base in Vienna until he took over the Theater in der Josefstadt in 1923. At the end of the war Hofmannsthal was involved behind the scenes in attempts to bring him to the Burgtheater. Once those efforts had broken down, the Theater in der Josefstadt offered him an ideal alternative. He rated its acoustics very highly, and it was well situated, within walking distance of the Ringstrasse. With financial support from a wealthy banker, he had the premises reconstructed and refurbished, and re-opened the theatre in 1924 with a programme designed to demonstrate the ideal of a harmonious acting ensemble (*Ensemblespiel*). The company was billed as 'The Actors in the Theater in der Josefstadt under the Leadership of Max Reinhardt' ('Die Schauspieler im Theater in der Josefstadt unter der Führung von Max Reinhardt'), and this formulation was retained until 1938, though in practice Reinhardt ran the theatre himself only until the summer of 1926. *Der Schwierige* was the third production of his first season and, in addition to his other work in Salzburg and elsewhere, he himself produced some two dozen plays there between 1924 and 1937[9] – an exciting time in the Viennese theatre, since he had a dynamic rival in Rudolf Beer, who staged a number of serious modern works (Wedekind, Brecht, Werfel) in two other theatres.

Even critical opposition such as Kraus's both to the Burgtheater and to Reinhardt is symptomatic of how the idea of theatre remained at the heart of Viennese attention, an institutional focus for better or worse for the whole of Viennese culture. At its best theatre provided a stimulating variety of dramatic experience and a wide range of vocal critical opinion, at its worst it afforded an outlet, even in wartime, for frivolous escapism, such as Kraus would satirize in his documentary drama *Die letzten Tage der Menschheit*. But Stefan Zweig's account of how the middle-class Viennese of the late nineteenth century turned to the newspapers for news not of politics but of the theatre is not just indicative of a lack of involvement in politics, it also bears witness to the real importance accorded to the theatre.

Its centrality in the Viennese view of the world is reflected in the constant recurrence of the metaphor of the world as a stage, with many different overtones. In Hofmannsthal's morality play *Das Salzburger große Welttheater* the overtone would be a moralistic one, coloured by postwar disillusion. At the end of the nineteenth century, if life was seen as play-acting, the implications were anything but moral:

> Also spielen wir Theater,
> Spielen uns're eig'nen Stücke,
> Frühgereift und zart und traurig,
> Die Komödie uns'rer Seele [. . .]
> (HKA I, 25)

In the same way we too are actors, acting out our own dramas, precocious, tender, sad – the comedies of our souls.

The lines from Hofmannsthal's prologue to Schnitzler's *Anatol* sum up a conception of life exemplified in *Anatol* itself – life as a series of episodes, life viewed in ironic detachment from moral involvement or moral judgment. Similar images recur in the early work of both dramatists. In Hofmannsthal's fragment *Der Tod des Tizian* one of the disciples of the dying Titian recounts how the great artist has taught them 'to enjoy the ebb and flow of every day like a play' ('jedes Tages Fließen/Und Fluten als ein Schauspiel zu genießen': HKA III, 48). Claudio too is, or has been, an 'eternal play-actor' ('Ewigspielender': HKA III, 76), and Schnitzler's *Paracelsus* ends with a reduction of all experience to 'play'. What in earthly life is not mere 'play', Paracelsus asks in his last speech, however important and profound it may have seemed: 'We know nothing of others, nothing of ourselves; always we are play-acting, and wisdom lies in knowing that':

> Was ist nicht Spiel, das wir auf Erden treiben,
> Und schien es noch so groß und tief zu sein!
> [. . .]
> Wir wissen nichts von andern, nichts von uns;
> Wir spielen immer, wer es weiß, ist klug.
>   (DW I, 498)

It is also characteristic of the centrality of theatre to the cultural life of Vienna that the poems in which Hofmannsthal writes most directly about the very nature of art are those he wrote, twelve and a half years apart, in commemoration of the deaths of Mitterwurzer (HKA I, 82–3) and Kainz (HKA I, 108–10).[10] In both poems he conjures up the commandingly 'magical' effect of the great actor: Mitterwurzer 'Der Zauberer, der große, große Gaukler', Kainz 'ein niebezauberter Bezauberer'. In each poem he sketches the impression made by some of the best-known roles of the actor concerned, suggesting the transforming power essential to his art. This effect was observed in 1908 by Josef Hofmiller, who described the poem on Mitterwurzer as being, together with Hofmannsthal's poem on another actor, Hermann Müller (HKA I, 89–90), 'perhaps the most apposite poetic statement of the born actor's capacity to be transformed' (HUK, 170). In the poem on Kainz again Hofmannsthal celebrates this mystery of 'transformation', '[das] Geheimis/ Wollüstiger Verwandlung'. As an agent of transformation the great actor also represents artistic creativity.[11] Like the creative artist – like Titian, who has brought the woods to life, weaving divine figures where before there was nothing (HKA III, 47) –

he is a source of life ('Gewalt des Lebens, diese war in ihm': HKA I, 83). Like the dramatist himself, he breathes life into the figures he creates, the Promethean effect suggested in the poem on Mitterwurzer by the image of a salamander. In these two poems, the Burgtheater actors most characteristic of the new artistic expressiveness are celebrated as representative of the modern artist *tout court*.

Outside the privileged world of the court theatre, very different developments took place at the end of the nineteenth century. In the years 1889–98 three further ambitious new foundations, all placed outside the wealthy centre of the city, were associated with an ideological commitment to the maintenance of popular culture. All three are still standing, though only one of them survived very long as a theatre devoted to spoken drama. This was the Deutsches Volkstheater (the nearest to the Ringstrasse), which was planned in reaction to the loss of the Stadttheater. A group of writers, including Anzengruber, met with the aim of founding a 'popular' theatre which would avoid competition with the Burgtheater and would give priority to cultivating dialect drama.[12] The expectation was that the theatre would provide a base for Anzengruber himself, but he died within three months of its opening in 1889. The first director, Emerich von Bukovics, presented a programme that included both dialect plays (Raimund and Nestroy as well as Anzengruber) and realist drama – Anzengruber, Ibsen (who attended the Austrian première of *The Wild Duck* there in 1891, seeing Mitterwurzer in one of his most celebrated roles), and Schnitzler (*Das Märchen, Freiwild*). It was here that Schnitzler's last play, *Im Spiel der Sommerlüfte*, would be staged in 1929, under Rudolf Beer, who was in charge of the Deutsches Volkstheater from 1924 to 1932. From 1921 to 1932 he controlled the Raimundtheater as well.

The Raimundtheater opened in 1893, with Müller-Guttenbrunn as its first director. Schnitzler was among those present at the inaugural performance of Raimund's *Die gefesselte Phantasie* (Tgb., 28 November 1893). It too was intended as a home for dialect drama and local comedy, but it was much less well placed, in the farthest south-western corner of the Mariahilf district, not far from the Westbahnhof. Müller-Guttenbrunn's successor was a Berliner, Ernst Gettke. He ran an orthodox dramatic repertoire until 1907, but it then became another operetta theatre, a fate from which it was only temporarily rescued by Beer. Another substantial theatre that was opened in 1905, the Wiener Bürgertheater in the Vordere Zollamtsstrasse, east of the centre, went the same way, switching to a repertory of operetta within six years; the Johann-Strauss-

Theater, which opened to the south of the centre in 1908, was run as an operetta theatre from the first. By that time the focus for more experimental writing had moved to cabarets: Friedell, the journalist Alfred Polgar, and Kokoschka were all involved in the Cabaret Fledermaus which opened in 1907.[13]

The third foundation of the 1890s was much the most contentious. This was the Kaiserjubiläums-Stadttheater, which opened on the Währinger Strasse, north-west of the centre, in 1898. Its name commemorated the golden jubilee of the Emperor's accession. It was the largest theatre in Vienna after the Opera House. Initially under the direction of Müller-Guttenbrunn, it was founded with the support of Christian Social circles and was conceived as an 'Aryan' (that is, anti-Semitic) theatre – built, as Müller-Guttenbrunn would later declare, as 'a creation of the united anti-Semitic and national German parties'.[14] While the venture was, of course, viewed critically by the Liberal press from the outset, it was also subject to attack from the Right for being insufficiently anti-Semitic in its repertory. *Kikeriki*, for example, was very hostile in its criticism of the theatre by its second season.[15]

The theatre reports that appeared in *Kikeriki* around the turn of the century illustrate the elevation of anti-Semitism to an absolute criterion of judgment. On 8 May 1895, for example, its report on a première in the Carltheater appeared under the epigraph 'Fort mit den Juden!' ('Away with the Jews'); it contrasted the play performed with the 'Jewish botches' of Dörmann, Schnitzler, and Herzl and rejoiced that at last the work of a 'Christian German author' had had a turn. Five and a half years later, on 27 October 1901, it carried a piece in which the anonymous writer claimed to be still looking forward to the performance of plays that were '*really* Aryan, really Christian' plays and that 'pilloried the Jews'.

Müller-Guttenbrunn lasted five years in charge of the Kaiserjubiläums-Stadttheater, struggling with a budget in constant deficit. At the end of December 1902, when bankruptcy was approaching, he wrote a defensive memorandum to Lueger, the Mayor of Vienna, which he later leaked to Karl Kraus, who printed it in *Die Fackel* on 11 November 1903 (F 146, 10–21). It puts the blame for the financial crisis on lack of support for the ideological function of what he still defined as 'a Christian, Aryan theatre' free of immoral material translated from French, and on the opposition of the Jewish Liberal press. After his resignation in the summer of 1903, Kraus drew the moral: the whole idea of an 'anti-Semitic' theatre was an artistic nonsense; institutions born in party-political spirit were incapable of survival (F 145, 23).

Müller-Guttenbrunn's successor, Rainer Simons, accepted appointment subject to a less binding commitment to an anti-Semitic policy.[16] This produced a heated and outspoken debate at a general meeting of the theatre association held at the Rathaus on 30 October 1903. The honorary secretary of the association gave an assurance that Simons had promised to remain true to the 'tradition of the Christian theatre' and not to employ any Jews. Robert Pattai, a prominent anti-Semitic politician since the early 1880s, argued in favour of supporting the theatre under its new director, in resistance to the 'Judaization' of society and in particular the theatre. The German word *Verjudung* carries much stronger pejorative overtones than any possible English translation, suggesting a society and theatrical life overrun by Jews, a development for which, Pattai claimed, the 'extraordinary power of the Jewish press' was responsible. Challenged by a Viennese priest, J. Dittrich, to commit himself to continuing the theatre as a 'German, Christian, Aryan stage for German artists and German authors', Simons answered by referring to the terms of his contract, which bound him to upholding the 'Christian' traditions of the theatre.[17] But the anti-Semitic forces were unconvinced; the *Deutsches Volksblatt*, for example, reporting the confirmation of his appointment on 31 October, commented that it was an outcome with which Simons and his 'Jewish protectors' could be well satisfied.

Under Simons, the repertory quickly began to change in character, with operas added from September 1904. The designation 'Volksoper' was added to its name, and by 1908 it too had come to specialize entirely in light opera and operetta. By contrast with what was perceived as an ideological sell-out, Müller-Guttenbrunn's régime was viewed more favourably by his erstwhile critics in the anti-Semitic press, and when the time came to celebrate his seventieth birthday, *Kikeriki* was ready to laud him as the pride of Vienna.[18]

However briefly Müller-Guttenbrunn's régime lasted, the very foundation of the Kaiserjubiläums-Stadttheater on the basis of a racist ideology was a sinister example of cultural anti-Semitism. In the arguments surrounding Müller-Guttenbrunn's managership, lines of battle were drawn that would re-emerge repeatedly in controversies to come. The central importance of the theatre in anti-Semitic polemics was most clearly expressed, perhaps, in an article entitled 'Judentheater und Theaterjuden' which was signed 'W.R.v.P.' and published in the *Deutsche Zeitung* at the end of 1899. This article succeeded so well in summarizing anti-Semitic sentiment that the next day the *Deutsches Volksblatt* printed excerpts and praised its excellence.[19] It argues that the theatre was a victim of an international Jewish conspiracy which aimed to achieve Jewish domination and worked through the medium of the Jewish press.

The corrupting effect of this influence was already widespread in society, and the theatre as an institution was especially vulnerable to 'Jewish terrorism' because of its moral function. Instead of inspiring the indigenous population, theatres were being reduced to vehicles of propaganda for the alien Jewish cause, and were in the hands of paid Jewish hacks. The article concludes with a call to Christians and Aryans to treat the Jewish press with contempt.

In 1902 anti-Semitic invective in the right-wing press was inflamed by two theatrical flops. One was a drama by Carl Bleibtreu, *Weltgericht*, in the Raimundtheater, the other an evening of one-act plays by Antonie Baumberg in the Deutsches Volkstheater, a theatre that was especially subject to criticism for providing an insufficiently 'national' programme. Bukovics's withdrawal of Antonie Baumberg's plays from the repertoire was followed by her suicide. *Kikeriki* was quick to place the blame on Jewish influence. It published a piece lamenting the 'fate of these two outstanding Aryan writers', printed a cartoon showing the Jewish press holding a pistol to Antonie Baumberg's head, and summed her up as 'a victim of the Jewish press clique'.[20]

The world of the theatre had changed since the mid-nineteenth century, as the world reflected by the theatre had changed. While there were also good things to come (especially when both Reinhardt and Beer were based in Vienna in the 1920s), the rising current of anti-Semitism was a constant part of the critical climate in which Schnitzler and Hofmannsthal worked.

Anti-Semitism and the Press

The history of the growth of political anti-Semitism in Austria in the years following the Stock Exchange crash of 1873 is well known in outline: Schönerer's leadership of the German National movement from 1879, the addition in 1885 of the 'Aryans clause' ('Arierparagraph') to the nationalists' Linz Programme of 1882, and the election of Karl Lueger as Mayor of Vienna in the mid-1890s.[21] One of the consequences of the process was that the long-established assimilation of Jewish families was brought into question. Because so many of the most cultivated circles were dominated by people of Jewish or partly Jewish extraction, all assimilated, the distinction between Jew and non-Jew had not been particularly important; Schnitzler, for example, recalls in his autobiography how in successive generations of his own family interest in the Jewish religion had declined and evaporated (*Jug.*, 19). But organized prejudice restored a sense of separate identity in Jewish families who had largely lost it (*Jug.*, 328).

The most radical reaction was the Zionist movement. Herzl had been born into a prosperous and assimilated Budapest family; Schnitzler traced the route that led him towards Zionism and the publication of *Der Judenstaat* in 1896 back to the rise of anti-Semitism in the 1880s and his expulsion from the student *Burschenschaft* 'Albia' in 1883 (*Jug.*, 155–6). They talked over the 'Jewish question' together in 1895; Schnitzler's diary note that they had discussed Herzl's 'idea for a solution, in which he seriously believes' (Tgb., 4 November 1895) betrays his own scepticism. But the traditional uncomplicated pattern of assimilation had been irredeemably replaced by a climate of racialism, mistrust, and nagging insecurity. In the first winter of the war, when Schnitzler observed that the Germans had joined the Jews and the Austrians in being misunderstood, he told his sister-in-law Elisabeth Steinrück that he himself felt all three in equal measure (AS/Bfe. II, 68–9). By the end of his life, when he published a short piece entitled 'Das Gute am Antisemitismus' in the *Neues Wiener Journal* for 8 September 1931, he could even argue that the 'benefit' of anti-Semitism lay in its giving Jews more self-awareness (AS/Bfe. II, 1123–4).

It is one of the sharpest ironies of modern European history that while the great explosion of cultural innovation in turn-of-the-century Vienna was taking place the government of the city passed into the hands of the anti-Semitic Lueger. What no one can realize who is not familiar with the press of the period is just how rampant anti-Semitism was in Vienna, and in what ferociously extreme and abusive terms it was publicly expressed. Even a very few examples will be too many, but abhorrent though they are, they are necessary in order to give an impression of the climate of opinion.

It must be borne in mind that in the right-wing press the very term 'anti-Semitism' carried no pejorative overtones at the turn of the century. It was at this time that the Austrian Anti-Semitic League (*Österreichischer Antisemitenbund*) was founded.[22] On 30 June 1901 *Kikeriki* appeared with a cartoon on the front page entitled 'Der neueste Watschenmann' (figure 4): the latest much-abused fairground Aunt Sally is the anti-Semite, and the caption asks how long the anti-Semitic Viennese will have to put up with the indignity. Or again two years later the morning edition of the *Deutsches Volksblatt* for 28 October 1903 contained an article in praise of the substantial successes of the anti-Semitic movement in the Lower Austrian parliament (*Landtag*): there was now a solid anti-Semitic majority, and support had dropped away from those who betrayed the anti-Semitic cause by allying themselves with Jews and their supporters.

Examples such as these illustrate how proudly the slogan of anti-Semitism was adopted by those of either a clerical or a pan-German

4 *Kikeriki*, 30 June 1901: 'The latest Aunt Sally'.

nationalist persuasion. The growth of anti-Semitism had gone hand-in-hand with the waning of liberalism. The Liberal party had not in fact been dominated by Jews;[23] nevertheless in the eyes of anti-Semitic commentators the very notion of 'liberalism' had become inseparable from that of Jewish influence. So too was the Social Democrat movement on the Left, which attracted anti-Semitic opprobrium as liberalism declined. From the turn of the century onwards the champions of anti-Semitism consistently presented themselves as standing firm against these two threats, and the 'Jewish press' was pilloried for its resistance. *Kikeriki*, for example, appeared on 1 August 1901 with a front-page cartoon entitled 'The height of mendacity', showing the 'Jewish press' as a comic figure, with a caption to the effect that it was preventing proper recognition of the achievements of anti-Semitism in the provincial parliament. The most scurrilously outspoken of the daily newspapers was the Christian Social *Österreichische Volks-Presse*, which was edited by Hermann Bielohlawek, a member of the *Landtag* and a tireless campaigner for the anti-Semitic cause. Its readers were bombarded with statements to the effect that the Liberal *Neue Freie Presse* was the 'most despicable rag in the world', the chief organ of information of the Israelites ('das Haupt- und Intelligenzblatt Israels'), and that this 'organ of the stock-exchange crooks' far outdid all the other Jewish papers in villainy. The principal Social Democrat newspaper met with similar treatment. Regularly referred to as 'the Jewish *Arbeiter-Zeitung*', it 'wallowed in orgies of lies'; written by 'lying Jews', it systematically printed untruthful reports on Catholic institutions that were written by 'paid Jewish scoundrels of the vilest kind'.[24]

The vocabulary of the time may be illustrated by just two more examples from the summer of 1901. On 30 June the *Österreichische Volks-Presse* reprinted a report from the *Neue Tiroler Stimmen* about an incident in Bozen, in South Tyrol, between an officer and the local population. The article in the *Österreichische Volks-Presse*, signed 'P.', comments on the inflation of the incident by the 'Jewish press', not only in Tyrol but also by 'the Viennese Jewish papers, in particular once again the organ of the Rothschilds'. This last allusion is to the *Neue Freie Presse*, in which Schnitzler's story *Leutnant Gustl* had appeared at the end of the previous year. The article reminds readers that the scandal it had caused had culminated when a court martial cashiered 'the Jewish *littérateur* Schnitzler' ('den Literaturjuden Schnitzler'):

This was occasioned by the disgraceful piece *Lieutenant Gustl*, in which, as in all this Jew's other rubbishy productions [wie in allen anderen Schunderzeugnissen dieses Juden], the honour of officers is treated in a Jewish spirit.

No officer thinks, speaks, or acts in the way ascribed by the Jew Schnitzler to 'Lieutenant Gustl', unless the officer concerned is himself a Jew, as can unfortunately be the case.

The piece continues in the same vein and concludes by stressing that the greatest enemy of the officer class is the prostituted and unpatriotic Jewish press ('die vaterlandslose, prostituierte Judenpresse').

Just under a fortnight later, on 12 July 1901, the morning issue of the *Deutsche Zeitung* carried a report of a debate in the Lower Austrian parliament, in which both Lueger and Victor Adler, the Social Democrat editor of the *Arbeiter-Zeitung* and himself a Jew, took part. Adler was taunted by reminders of the support he drew from prostitutes in the Novaragasse in his constituency. At one point, attacking Lueger's Christian Social party, he was talking of political morality and when he was interrupted, Lueger himself interjected, 'Let the member for the Novaragasse have his say about morality!' Adler protested vehemently against Lueger's insinuation, whereupon another member called out, 'Impertinent Jew!' Adler continued his attack on the Christian Social party as endangering the political morality of the population, and was met with cries of 'That's a Jew's view!' and 'A Jewish verdict on the Christian people!' So it went on, and the paper itself inveighed against what it saw as Adler's malicious attack: 'From his Shylock-like visage it could be seen [. . .] how he relished at long last being able to indulge his long-standing resentment and openly to attack the anti-Semites he hates.' The allusion to Shylock was topical: *The Merchant of Venice* had been one of the plays produced at the Kaiserjubiläums-Stadttheater in its second season, and the production had been the subject of outspoken debate in the press.

In the next three decades, anti-Semitism in Vienna continued to flourish. By 1914, according to Pulzer's analysis, 'the organization of anti-Semitic movements and the penetration of anti-Semitism into social life had gone much further than in Germany'.[25] At the very beginning of the war it was given a further boost by reactions to a new influx of refugee Jews from Galicia, a phenomenon that Schnitzler discussed with the Saltens and the music critic Richard Specht (Tgb., 18 December 1914). After the war, prejudice was further stoked by the precarious economic position of the new republic. In the run-up to the elections in October 1920, which returned the Christian Socials as the strongest party, *Kikeriki* presented Austria as an 'Eldorado' for the Jews and the *Reichspost* carried full-page advertisements on behalf of an 'organization of many thousand like-minded German Austrians' ('Die Vereinigung vieler Tausende gleichgesinnter Deutschösterreicher') calling on the electorate to cast not a single vote for the 'Jew-ridden' Social Democrats ('Keine einzige Stimme der verjudeten Sozialdemokratie!'), demanding the removal of the 'Jewish socialists' from the government and the election of a 'Christian German government' rather than one led by men 'alien to the people' ('von Volksfremden'); anti-Semites were patriotic people working for the removal or reduction of the 'destructive and baleful Jewish influence' in the interests of intellectual and moral progress, and all German Austrians were called on to shake off the 'Jewish yoke'.[26] *Kikeriki*, though by this time less dominated by anti-Semitic material than it had been twenty years earlier, continued to snipe at Jewish influence in the press, in the financial world, and in intellectual life;[27] it also issued an annual almanac and carried regular advertisements for this 'widely-known and popular *vade mecum* of every Christian and anti-Semite'.

Hofmannsthal's family had been Catholic for two generations – since the conversion of his grandfather – and he did not regard himself as Jewish at all. Indeed he seems to have felt little affinity for the Jewish elements in Austrian cultural life. In 1894, imagining the destruction of Vienna and the replacement of the current generation of artists by a new barbarism, he defined that threat as 'a great barbarism, a sensual, Slav and Jewish world' (RA III, 383). His political development towards Catholic conservatism was not impeded by the anti-Semitism endemic in Austrian clerical politics; early in the war Schnitzler talked with Specht and the Saltens about his unwillingness to admit the 'evil effects of Catholicism' ('die üblen Wirkungen des Katholizismus': Tgb., 18 December 1914), by which they must primarily have meant the anti-Semitism of the Christian Social party. After the war, when Willy Haas had included an article on Hofmannsthal in a volume of essays on Jews in contemporary German literature, Hofmannsthal wrote to him frostily repudiating the treatment of his work in that context and reminding Haas of the rest of his ancestry: his grandfather had married into an old Italian family, and his father had married the daughter of a Viennese lawyer who was from an old Lower Austrian country family on her father's side, while her mother's family came originally from Swabia (H/Haas, 46–7: letter of 4 June 1922). The point was made not, of course, with hostility to the Jews (his friendship with Max Reinhardt, for example, was at its height) but rather in keeping with the internationalism he espoused after the war. It was in the same spirit that in 1925 he wrote to the

essayist Otto Forst de Battaglia protesting at being classified as a
'Jewish' writer and stressing his international ancestry.[28]

Since he did not satirize sacrosanct institutions such as the
Austrian army and since after the appearance of *Jedermann* he had in
any case been identified with traditional Christian teaching, he was
a less promising target for direct abuse than Schnitzler was, though
even he was subject to occasional smears. In 1902, for example,
after the failure of Bleibtreu's *Weltgericht* in the Raimundtheater, an
article in *Kikeriki* wrote that Bleibtreu was far superior to the
protégés of the Jews, 'to say nothing of the true Jews pure and
simple – Bahr, Schnitzler, Hirschfeld, Hofmannsthal [misspelt] –
and still lesser Jewish youngsters'.[29] In 1912, Bleibtreu himself
belittled Hofmannsthal's eclecticism as an attempt, born of a Jewish
opportunism ('sein jüdischer Anlehnungssinn': HUK, 238), to cash
in on different styles, and in particular picked out this 'Jewish'
opportunism that delighted in international literary trading as having dealt dishonestly with Otway's *Venice Preserv'd* (HUK, 240).
But it was only when the Salzburg Festival pushed his collaboration
with Reinhardt into the limelight that he came regularly under anti-
Semitic attack, especially in the years 1922–24 (see pp. 214–15,
below).

Schnitzler, by contrast, was always identified as a Jewish writer.
His diary shows that in the late 1890s he discussed the growth of
anti-Semitism as a hostile factor in Viennese literary life with his
friends: with Beer-Hofmann on 6 March 1897 and again with Salten
on 3 February 1898 after the final rehearsal for the Carltheater production of *Freiwild*. A week after the latter conversation, *Kikeriki*
published an abusive attack on the play as the product of a 'cowardly
Jewish spirit', expressing 'Jewish attitudes' unqualified to treat the
honour of Aryan women;[30] Schnitzler noted the attack in his diary
(Tgb., 10 February 1898) and the following day recorded his anger
at the 'infamous attacks' to which Jews were being subjected ('die
infamen Angriffe, denen man als Jude ausgesetzt'). He was also
particularly upset at the end of that year by the reviews of *Das
Vermächtnis* (Tgb., 1 December 1898). In a damning notice in the
Deutsche Zeitung that day, for example, Albert Leitich reported that
the play had been applauded merely by a well-organized claque from
among 'the literary Jews of Vienna' ('die Wiener Literaturjuden').
The whole drama was false to Viennese life:

The main point in Schnitzler's tedious comedy is the Viennese
girl from the poorer classes, the type that the Jewish literary
pillagers [die literarischen Marodeure des Wiener Judenthums] are
proud of having discovered but that in fact has long been there in

our literature, albeit in its genuine form and not the false form
that the Jews as aliens in the life of our people [die Juden als
Fremdlinge in unserem Volksleben] have forced upon it.

Other events that attracted anti-Semitic criticism in the right-wing
press included the award of the Grillparzer Prize in 1908. The
Reichspost for 16 January 1908, for example, reported the decision to
bestow the distinction on the 'decadent' author of the 'pornographic'
Reigen, rather than on Schönherr, as a disgrace explicable only by
the determined Jewish domination of Viennese literary life.

Despite these attacks, Schnitzler still had no sympathy with
Zionism. In 1902 a conversation with a Zionist, David Wolffsohn,
was cursorily summed up in a note to the effect that he had
convinced Schnitzler just as little as all the others had (Tgb., 1
November 1902). But the appearance of *Der Weg ins Freie* in 1908
brought him increasing public prominence as a major figure in the
Jewish community, both in Vienna and internationally, until in
September 1923 he was even voted one of the 'twelve foremost
Jews in the world' by readers of the New York *Jewish Tribune*.[31]
This prominence meant that he was more than ever exposed as a
target of anti-Semitic smears. For a newspaper like the *Reichspost*,
Reigen in particular provided a focal point that could constantly be
referred to. After the première of *Das weite Land*, the *Reichspost*
carried a cartoon of him on 22 October 1911 as a dancing figure (see
figure 5) with a verse caption about how 'all Israel' had applauded
his new play, because it loved the 'round dance' of filth. At the end
of that year Josef Karl Ratislav published an essay on him that
Schnitzler read as soon as he received it (Tgb., 4 January 1912). It is
indicative of his sensitivities that the sole passage marked in pencil
in his copy is one that describes his work, in contrast to that of J. J.
David, as being distinctively Jewish.[32] Nor would the anti-Semitic
attacks let up after the war, for the scandals triggered by the
performances of *Reigen* in Berlin and Vienna provided the *Reichspost*
with ample opportunity for further vilification.[33]

Schnitzler's almost obsessive concern with the reception of his
works, reflected in his systematic collection of reviews for forty
years (see p. 61, above), indicates how vulnerable he was to
what he felt was unsympathetic or unfair criticism. His papers
include a substantial body of aphoristic and essayistic notes on the
phenomenon of criticism, which he may or may not have been
planning to organize and publish. By 1908 at the latest his scepticism towards professional critics was deeply ingrained (AB,
404–5), and the notes and aphorisms reflect the same discontent.

„Das weite Land".

Hier der Dichter Schnitzlerleben,
Seines Volkes Stolz und Glück.
An der „Burg" hat man gegeben
Jüngst von ihm ein neues Stück.

Seinen Beifall zu bezeigen
Ist ganz Israel hingerennt.
Denn es liebt den alten „R e i g e n",
Den man vulgo „Sautanz" nennt.

5 Cartoon from the *Reichspost*, 22 October 1911.

The qualities he found reflected in newspaper criticism were 'self-importance, arrogance, and malice' (AB, 418) as well as ideological bias (AB, 447); he drafted descriptions of the various tricks by which critics distorted their material and warped their judgments. Among the leading reviewers in the later part of his career, he particularly mistrusted Alfred Polgar, who wrote for the *Wiener Allgemeine Zeitung* and whose reviews also appeared in leading newspapers in Berlin (*Vossische Zeitung*) and Prague (*Prager Tagblatt*). Schnitzler had never liked him: as early as 1898 he had described him contemptuously in his diary, together with Stefan Grossmann, as one of Peter Altenberg's 'repellent disciples' (Tgb., 2 June 1898). Twenty years later the review that Polgar wrote of *Professor Bernhardi* (WAZ, 23 December 1918) seemed to him simply malicious, 'full of uncontrollable envy' (Tgb., 24 December 1918). Writing to Körner on 8 April 1931, when Schnitzler was nearly seventy, he still referred sourly to the criticism that appeared in the daily press as 'corrupt in spirit and in character' ('die nach Geist und Charakter korrupte Tageskritik unserer Zeitungen': AS/Bfe. II, 778–9).

In 1912, reflecting on the reception of *Professor Bernhardi* in Berlin, he confided aphoristically to his diary his resignation to critics' inherent tendency to misunderstand at least living writers (Tgb., 5 December 1912). One misunderstanding that particularly dogged him was that the critics' expectations seemed to be immutably determined by the nature of his early successes.

He did not dispute the character of his early work. When he was analysing his 'literary development' in 1897 he himself saw a 'straight line' leading from *Das Märchen* through *Liebelei* and *Das Vermächtnis* to the novel *Der Weg ins Freie*, all treating relations between the sexes, and *Freiwild* by contrast as a 'sidetrack' (Tgb., 29 June 1897). But he wearied of being constantly expected to treat nothing but erotic themes and being constantly typecast (and denigrated) as the author of *Anatol* and *Reigen*. Not even *Der Weg ins Freie* escaped reduction to the cliché; Stefan Grossmann, for example, concluded his review in the *Arbeiter-Zeitung* on 16 July 1908 by saying that it might just as well be called *Liebelei* since it was only a more pretentious variation on Schnitzler's usual theme.

One of the critics' tricks, Schnitzler noted, was to use the title of a work against its author; *Liebelei* could just as well have been called *Christinens große Liebe* ('Christine's Great Love': AB, 463), but it was as the master of dalliance that he was irrevocably typecast. A year after *Professor Bernhardi* had made an impact as a controversial play of ideas, he found it necessary to insist to Robert Roseeu that though it was different from *Anatol*, it was just as authentically

'Schnitzlerisch' (AS/Bfe. II, 34: letter of 17 December 1913). But the next year even a review of the first English translation appeared under the heading 'Arthur Schnitzler writes a Play without a Woman in it'.[34] The same kind of reaction awaited *Fink und Fliederbusch* in 1917. Marco Brociner, the theatre critic of the *Neues Wiener Tagblatt*, wrote on 15 November that the play lacked that 'breath of eroticism' with which Schnitzler created his most authentic effects; four days later a review by Bernhard Neufeld in the *Sonn- und Montagszeitung* conjured up a picture of the difficulty he must have found in banishing Anatol and the 'süßes Mädel' from his work, and referred to him as the 'master of erotic frivolities' ('[der] Meister der erotischen Spielereien'). Schnitzler's anger at this 'shameless' description is recorded in his diary entry for that day.

When *Professor Bernhardi* was finally produced in Vienna, Brociner returned to the theme. Writing in the *Neues Wiener Tagblatt* for 22 December 1918, he made amusing play with the idea that Bernhardi was no more than Anatol in another guise, his love affairs behind him – a leading physician, but still the old Anatol when it comes to standing up for a matter of principle. (This passage is angrily marked in crayon on the cutting in Schnitzler's collection, and it is also quoted in his diary for that day.) Two years later a letter to Dora Michaelis, in which Schnitzler resentfully quotes the same review, shows him still complaining that critics behaved as though he had never written anything except *Reigen* and *Anatol* (AS/Bfe. II, 221–2). It is precisely the stereotyped expectation of 'eroticism' that he picked out in his satirical summary of the critics' view of *Professor Bernhardi* in the poem 'Meine Kritiker', in which he puts into the mouths of the critics the couplet:

> *Bernhardi*, pfui Teufel, ein Thesenstück
> Und ohne Weiber! er geht zurück.
> (AB, 296)

> *Bernhardi* – ugh, a problem play,
> No women, either! He's had his day.

Ends and Means: Professor Bernhardi

Professor Bernhardi is the play in which Schnitzler came closest to confronting the issue of anti-Semitism head-on. His dramatization of political issues is expressive of his view of politics as a whole, and revealing of the limitations of that view.

It is a work largely composed of argument, which turns on opposite views about responsibility. These are expounded principally in dialogues in the last two acts between the central figure,

Bernhardi, and two other characters, both from outside Bernhardi's hospital. One is a Catholic priest, whose interest is in the criteria of moral decisions. The other, Flint, a government minister, is concerned with achieving practical political results.

Bernhardi is the Jewish director of a Viennese hospital, the 'Elisabethinum', where an election to a vacant consultancy is about to take place. When a nurse, Ludmilla, summons a priest to administer the last rites to a patient who is unaware that she is dying after an abortion, Bernhardi refuses to admit him to the bedside as it would destroy her euphoria. Ludmilla, however, tells the patient that she has sent for a priest. This does indeed disturb her, and while Bernhardi and the priest are arguing, she dies, the last rites still not administered. For this the priest at once blames Bernhardi. In order to deflect criticism from the hospital Bernhardi is at first willing to issue a conciliatory statement, but then the Deputy Director, Professor Ebenwald, a pan-German nationalist, tries to exploit the position by arguing that he could prove he is innocent of any anti-Catholic sentiment by agreeing to the appointment to the vacant consultancy of a non-Jewish candidate, Hell, rather than Wenger, who is Jewish. Bernhardi, convinced of Wenger's greater scientific ability and expertise, refuses to agree to this. After Ebenwald has left, he tears up the statement he has drafted. The matter quickly becomes a *cause célèbre*, fought out in the press and in parliament, until eventually Bernhardi feels bound to resign. He is tried on a charge of insulting religion, found guilty, and sentenced to two months' imprisonment. He refuses to appeal, and serves his sentence. After his release the nurse, who has been a key prosecution witness, admits to having perjured herself in her account of his behaviour. Together with an anti-Semitic medical student, Hochroitzpointner, she has accused Bernhardi of having actually struck the priest, whereas he has in fact only touched him lightly on the shoulder. The play ends with his reinstatement as a practising physician – a moral victory – but he declines to appeal for compensation or indeed to pursue the matter publicly further in any way.

Set in Vienna 'around 1900', the play is full of authentic touches suggesting the close connection between the fictional action and the real world. The very name of the hospital is modelled on that of the Josephinum, which was founded in the late eighteenth century by Joseph II and was used in the second half of the nineteenth century as a training school for army doctors. (Schnitzler's variant is suggestive of the Empress Elisabeth, who was assassinated in 1898.) As director of another hospital, the Poliklinik, Schnitzler's father had held a position similar to Bernhardi's, and though Schnitzler played down the parallel – notably in an open letter in *Der Merker* in February 1913 in reply to an article by Georg Brandes in the previous number[35] and in a private letter to Brandes, written on 27 February 1913 (AS/Bfe. II, 12–13) – when he took the decision to complete the play in the autumn of 1909 one of his first steps was to read his father's papers in connection with the Poliklinik and the intrigues surrounding it (Tgb., 29 October 1909). Other details, too, had their basis in his experience. In his autobiography he recalls in particular that the figure of Hochroitzpointner is based on two young doctors he had known in the 1880s, one Tyrolean, one anti-Semitic (*Jug.*, 158).[36] Within the play itself, moreover, we are repeatedly reminded that the events in the Elisabethinum reflect the realities of political life. When Ebenwald reflects, early in Act Three, 'We are living in such a confused age – and in such a confused country' (DW II, 395), the signal is clear: the drama is not confined to a fictitious hospital but is really about the Austria of Schnitzler's own time.

The issue of anti-Semitism as it affects Bernhardi's case is openly discussed in a key argument in Act Two between two of the senior staff of the Elisabethinum (DW II, 366). Dr Löwenstein, a Zionist paediatrician, says that the affair has been blown up into a matter of public interest only because Bernhardi is a Jew; the gynaecologist Professor Filitz instantly exculpates himself with standard excuses: *he* is not anti-Semitic, he even has a Jewish assistant, and in any case there is no prejudice against 'decent' Jews. He accuses Löwenstein of having a persecution mania and of actually having a provocative effect by his constant suspicion of anti-Semitism on all sides ('Antisemitenriecherei').

What is revealing about this argument is that neither is wholly right or wrong. It is clear that there is a strong element of anti-Semitic prejudice working against Bernhardi. Within the hospital it first shows early in Act One when Ebenwald alludes to his Jewishness, commenting on a correct diagnosis with a sourly sarcastic 'Great rejoicing in Israel!', and then Hochroitzpointner, emboldened, alludes to Wenger's language and accent (DW II, 343–4), and it comes out more openly in the dialogue between Ebenwald and Dr Schreimann in Act Three (DW II, 395). Outside the hospital, we learn from Löwenstein's report of Flint's speech in parliament that there have been interventions about Jewish influence in the university, shouts of 'Verjudung der Universität!' and the like (DW II, 408) – a detail entirely consistent with parliamentary behaviour at the time (see p. 81, above). After the trial, so Bernhardi reports in Act Four, there have been anti-Semitic catcalls among the crowd (DW II, 423), and when, after his release from prison, he is met with demonstrations of support, Flint brushes these aside with the dismissive remark that the demonstrators must have been Zionists (DW II, 450). On the other hand, even Bernhardi's supporter Professor Cyprian regards Löwenstein as being obsessed with an *idée fixe* (DW II, 419). Prejudice and obsession are equally destructive of dispassionate judgment.

This is typical of the even-handedness with which Schnitzler tried to balance the forces in the opposing camps. Another example is the way the voting in the election between Wenger and Hell runs across racial or confessional lines. That confirms that the issue goes beyond anti-Semitism and has to be seen in wider terms of individual and corporate responsibility. It is also revealing of the whole strategy of Schnitzler's characterization. Just as Flint is a caricature of self-seeking, and Filitz and Hochroitzpointner are caricatures of anti-Semitism, so the obsessional Löwenstein is a caricature of committed opposition to anti-Semitism. Schnitzler himself referred to his character (in a long letter of 4 January 1913 to Richard Charmatz, a historian) as being presented almost as a caricature (AS/Bfe. II, 3). Indeed, the whole cast of the play consists of a series of satirical caricatures. In a way that is difficult to grasp after the Holocaust, what governs the play's presentation even of anti-Semitism is not moral outrage but satirical amusement. That is precisely the approach of the fictitious dramatist Heinrich Bermann in *Der Weg ins Freie*, who envisages treating anti-Semitic wranglings in a political comedy (ES I, 847). In his autobiography, Schnitzler recalls that in his early twenties he had become interested in the 'psychological side of the Jewish question' (*Jug.*, 96). He was the most humane observer of his fellows, and *Professor Bernhardi* reflects his unflagging psychological interest – an amused curiosity even about the workings and manifestations of anti-Semitic prejudice, which formed part of the wider satirical evocation of the slogans, prejudices, and machinations of the political scene as a whole.

This dispassionateness is also characteristic of Schnitzler's even-handed disposition of characters in the pro-Bernhardi and anti-Bernhardi camps. Of the whole gallery of comic figures, the only two who come out of the play well are on opposite sides of the argument: the practical Cyprian on the side of the unpractical Bernhardi, the idealistic (and half-Jewish) Dr Adler, a stickler for the proprieties, consistent and truthful, helping to unseat him.

That otherwise the characters are inadequate – weak, scheming, venal, obscurantist – does not, however, vitiate the arguments they advance. The play is made up of the wrangles of individuals; but since the question of Bernhardi's conduct towards the priest becomes inextricably intertwined with the election of Hell or

Wenger, the real issue is a political one. The point is made explicitly in Act Two when Ebenwald feigns regret that 'in Austria all matters to do with appointments finish up as political issues' (DW II, 379).

Bernhardi summarizes at the end of Act Four the principles on which he has exerted his authority and kept the priest from his patient: 'My job is to make people healthy – or at least to convince them that I can' (DW II, 441). The qualification in his rider moves his position away from his purely diagnostic and curative function, in respect of which his expert authority is unchallengeable, into the realm of psychology. That is what makes his moral position shaky. Schnitzler could have simplified the whole issue by making the priest's appearance the direct cause of his patient's death; but he does not do that.[37] Factually, Bernhardi's purely medical diagnosis is correct; her death is certain and inevitable. At issue are the rival claims of her emotional comfort, which Bernhardi sees it as his duty to protect, and her spiritual salvation, which the priest sees himself as responsible for securing. We do not know whether she is in fact a believer; though the nurse gives evidence that she has demanded 'the comforts of religion' (DW II, 400), her evidence is untrustworthy. But what Bernhardi sets against the priest's conviction of a spiritual requirement is basically only short-term humanitarian kindness.

His consistent claim is that he has merely done his duty. This is what he says to the priest when consoling him for having failed to reach the bedside in time: 'It isn't your fault. You only wanted to do your duty. So did I' (DW II, 358). The clash of standards represented in this conflict of 'duties' is emphasized when Hochroitzpointner consoles the nurse with exactly the same argument as Bernhardi has used with the priest: she too has only done her duty (DW II, 359). And since Bernhardi has indeed acted in accordance with what he conceives his duty as a physician to be, even the priest comes to admit in Act Four that he could not have acted otherwise:

> Ich sehe mich aber nun veranlaßt, Ihnen zuzugestehen, Herr Professor, daß Sie in dem speziellen Fall – verstehen Sie mich wohl, Herr Professor – in dem speziellen Fall, um den es sich hier handelt, in Ihrer Eigenschaft als Arzt vollkommen korrekt gehandelt haben, daß Sie innerhalb Ihres Pflichtenkreises, geradeso wie ich innerhalb des meinen, nicht anders handeln konnten. (DW II, 430)

But I find myself constrained, Professor, to concede that in this particular case – you understand what I am saying – that in the particular case at issue you acted with complete correctness in

your capacity as a physician, that within your area of responsibility you could not act otherwise, any more than I could in
mine.

The awkwardness of the wording suggests the embarrassment the
priest feels: he knows Bernhardi has been wronged. He does not
concede that Bernhardi was right to act as he did, only that he did
nothing improper. But in referring to his duty, putting it on a par
with his own, he effectively repeats the very point Bernhardi has
made to him in Act One. It is an improbable concession from a
priest in whose view the dying patient's eternal salvation was at
stake; by having him accept Bernhardi's 'correctness', Schnitzler
weights the scales of the argument heavily in Bernhardi's favour.

This scene, in which the priest and Bernhardi come face to face
and finally shake hands, was a late addition to the play, drafted in
September 1911 and completed only in the spring of 1912. After
he had dictated his first version of it, Schnitzler even wondered
whether it was dramatically necessary at all (Tgb., 23 September
1911). It is true that it does not advance the action, but in a play not
of action but of argument, this is where the threads of the argument
most clearly come together, and it works well in the theatre.
Desmond MacCarthy, reviewing a London production in 1936,
wrote of it as 'the deepest scene in the play':

> The priest [. . .] has come to tell Bernhardi that he thinks that he
> (Bernhardi) – as *a doctor and a sceptic* – acted rightly. The professor
> asks, with some irony, why then he did not say so in court a few
> hours ago. It was not lack of courage, Father Reder replies; God
> had told him that for the sake of the cause which is more precious
> to him than anything in the world he must withhold the ex-
> pression in public of his private judgement, which would be
> misinterpreted. He owes it, however, to Bernhardi to tell him
> personally what he thinks [. . .][38]

Bernhardi is quick to spot the flaw: what cause could be more
sacred than that of truth? The priest's response is that the particular
truth in this instance would actually work against the greater truth
he represents (DW II, 431). Similarly two speeches later he talks
of his obedience to the church as a 'supreme law' that overrides
individual morality.

Clearly set out here is the central issue, a conflict between distinct
levels of responsibility: on the one hand, the instinctive humanitarianism of Bernhardi, on the other, the morality of the institution,
which makes wider claims beyond the private morality of the
individual. This wider kind of responsibility is claimed not only by

the priest. It also underlies the arguments of Löwenstein, on behalf of Zionism; of Ebenwald, on behalf of the clinic; of the journalist Kulka, on behalf of the press; and of Flint, the champion of medical education.

In Act Five, in conversation with the civil servant Winkler, Flint concedes his sympathy for Bernhardi, on the level of the 'heart' (DW II, 448); and it is at that same level that Cyprian defends him at the meeting of the management committee in Act Three, where he says that Bernhardi's only mistake was 'daß er seiner ärztlich-menschlichen Eingebung gefolgt ist' (DW II, 405) – roughly translated, that he followed the dictates of his heart as a doctor and as a man. It is the only argument in Bernhardi's defence, and we learn in the next act that it is not seriously advanced at all at the trial. But it is open to two substantial objections: first, that this morality of the heart is more 'menschlich' than 'ärztlich', more humanitarian than medical, and secondly, that moral judgments cannot depend on vaguely benevolent intentions but also require consideration of the predictable consequences of one's actions. The real case against Bernhardi's stance is put not by the priest in Act Four but by Flint in their final confrontation in Act Five: his conduct has been self-indulgent, nothing but a 'tragicomedy of obstinacy' (DW II, 456).

In Act Two, when Bernhardi is still willing to compromise by issuing a conciliatory statement, he describes himself as not being of heroic stuff (DW II, 375). It is a typically ironic understatement. His last conversation with Winkler, when he recounts how his plan to write a polemical piece against Flint while in prison has been watered down into writing a philosophical treatise (DW II, 461), will confirm how little stamina he has for controversy. He does not say precisely why he tears up the draft statement after his interview with Ebenwald. It looks like an act of irritated distaste. The most favourable explanation that can be advanced is that to issue the statement would be to capitulate to the standards of schemers such as Ebenwald and so to compromise his own integrity,[39] and certainly from that moment on he keeps insisting that the affair is a personal one and nothing to do with politics. But the distinction is understood neither by Cyprian, his strongest supporter within the Elisabethinum, nor by his lawyer, both of whom think him just obstinate (DW II, 420–2); and indeed his refusal to fight the case out means that he ducks the moral issue, the real claims of public responsibilities as against personal scruples.

The most powerful argument ranged against him is that long-term ends may justify means, that individual judgments and sensibilities have to be seen in the context of a wider whole. When Kulka tells Bernhardi towards the end of Act Four that 'lots of personal affairs carry within them the germ of political ones' (DW II, 439) he is in effect spelling out the fact that public and private issues intertwine, and that it is impossible to cocoon oneself wholly from public responsibility for one's private actions. Cumulatively, the argument is put from all sides: by Ebenwald and by Cyprian, both arguing for the prosperity of the Elisabethinum; by the priest; and above all by Flint.

Flint makes the distinction in his conversation with Bernhardi in Act Two (DW II, 384), where he admits that Bernhardi is more of a 'decent human being' than he is but sets against that private decency the good of public achievement ('das Wohl eines großen Ganzen'). It is this, he says, that matters most; to sacrifice the opportunity of large-scale achievement ('das Wirken im Großen') for the sake of moral conduct in a particular instance is immoral in a higher sense ('im höheren Sinne unmoralisch').[40] He repeats exactly the same argument to Bernhardi to explain why he has gone back on his word in parliament, failing to support Bernhardi in order to preserve his own position (DW II, 455–6). But he has also used that argument to explain why when he and Bernhardi were both young doctors in training he once fought shy of having the courage of his diagnostic convictions rather than risk courting the disfavour of his professor, allowing the protection of his long-term career to justify his failure to save a patient's life (DW II, 383–4).

By putting the political case against Bernhardi in the mouth of this apostle of expediency Schnitzler has again weighted the argument unfairly in Bernhardi's favour. Flint is visibly a performer, something of an actor. We glean this from his scene in Act Two, when he tells Bernhardi how he holds his audience in his hand in parliament, as once he used to as a lecturer (DW II, 389). In Act Five again, talking to Winkler (DW II, 446–7), he speaks in terms of performance and effect. In this conversation he reveals his belief that 'conviction' is actually out of place in politics, which necessitate constant concessions and compromise. This no doubt reflects Schnitzler's disillusioned view of the level of political debate in early twentieth-century Austria. But as a general principle, while compromise may be the stuff of politics, it does not necessarily imply lack of conviction. In Flint, political morality is shown in its worst colours. What Bernhardi has suggested in conversation with Cyprian, that Flint has no convictions beyond the argument of the moment (DW II, 374), is steadily confirmed in the course of the play. To Bernhardi he argues that his own political survival is important for reform (DW II, 457), but his practical realism serves no grand design based on considered principle; the hollow jargon he mouths reveals him as self-seeking, and in the theatre, audiences laugh at him as an all too recognizable political type.

Flint's opportunism is paralleled among Bernhardi's opponents inside the Elisabethinum. An example is the sophistry of Ebenwald's argument that the committee must not show ingratitude to the trustees by supporting Bernhardi's financially dangerous policies (DW II, 406), without invoking the same criterion of gratitude in relation to Bernhardi himself. As Robert A. Kann observes, the 'poisonous' atmosphere of political life has penetrated the academic world and the academic profession;[41] the result is that the deceptions enacted within the hospital reflect the political and social life of the nation.

This is why the play was banned, as presenting the whole currency of Austrian political life as corrupt. In 1910 Karl Kraus coined the aphorism 'Satires that the censor can understand deserve to be banned' (F 309–310, 40), implying that anything that was really worth censoring would by definition be something no censor could ever understand, but in this case the authorities had entirely grasped the point. It is Hochroitzpointner who first reminds Bernhardi that they are living in a 'Christian country' (DW II, 359), a term suggesting all the pressures that affect the interests of the hospital, including both the authority of the church and also the anti-Semitic prejudice engrained in clerical politics. Bernhardi replies with a New Testament allusion, paying Hochroitzpointner back in his own coin: 'Der Herr verzeihe ihnen – sie wissen verdammt gut, was sie tun' ('May the Lord forgive them; they know damned well what they do'), a pointed invocation of moral standards against the calculation of institutional and political interests.

Commentators who defend Bernhardi's conduct, stressing his incorruptibility and his integrity, discount the irresponsibility of his apolitical stance. William H. Rey, for instance, argues that to call him an escapist is to overlook the clear-sighted realism which balances the ethical idealism in his outlook.[42] But his 'realism', his insight into the expediency and corruption of the politicians, is precisely what makes him escapist. The only resolve he shows is not to fight his corner. He keeps repeating, for example to his lawyer and the journalist Kulka in Act Four (DW II, 440–1), that the whole business is 'non-political', but he does so with a disregard of the wider implications that is at best naïve, at worst disingenuous. His course of action lands the institution he directs on the verge of financial ruin, and Ebenwald can fairly make that point against him at the meeting of the management committee in Act Three. It is, he says, a time when 'the director – unintentionally, of course, but very incautiously – has brought the Elisabethinum to the very brink of the abyss' (DW II, 406). That is, Bernhardi 'meant well' but did not consider practical consequences. By the end, he is not even acting on conviction but out of sheer dislike of publicity, and the escapism in this protection of his privacy becomes quite overt: he just wants peace and quiet, he says (DW II, 459), and to Flint and Winkler he uses images of flight ('Flucht', 'entfliehen': DW II, 461–2). His 'moral victory' is at the same time a moral capitulation.

But because Flint is left to put the case against Bernhardi, the force of that case – that the affair is a 'tragicomedy of obstinacy', individualism pursued to the point of destructiveness – is made to ring hollow: the rhetoric of the play supports Bernhardi as the record of his achievement does not. Because his lack of political sense is expounded by no one more convincing than Flint, his irresponsibility is never unmasked and he is allowed to seem the standard-bearer of an untainted individualism. Indeed it seems clear that Schnitzler actually intended the figure of Bernhardi to represent an ideal of disinterested integrity. His exposition of the character, set out in his letter to Charmatz, as someone who has simply done his duty as a physician without calculating the implications, has declined to be pushed into playing a political role, and has conducted himself without ever compromising his dignity (AS/Bfe. II, 1), defines attitudes that he himself repeatedly adopted. He always stood apart from public involvement in Austrian politics – a distinctive and difficult stance during the First World War (see pp. 163–6, below) – and a series of aphorisms published in 1927 in his *Buch der Sprüche und Bedenken* make the reasoning behind his attitude explicit. He saw politics as always involving the subordination of principles to calculated ends: 'It is in the nature of politics to be directed at specific goals, so that ethical motives, however often they are claimed, play no part whatsoever' (AB, 83). Protestations of political conviction, then, are hollow, a mask to cover self-seeking and self-indulgence:

> Political conviction? That is often nothing but a convenient mask behind which a rogue would like to conceal his repellent visage, to gain the freedom of that political carnival which when Ash Wednesday comes we like to call world history [auf dem politischen Faschingsrummel, den wir am Aschermittwoch Weltgeschichte zu nennen lieben], and to do his cowardly deeds unpunished or even applauded. (AB, 90)

This is the kind of view expressed in the play by the eye specialist Professor Pflugfelder. The affair would never have come to anything, he says, 'if it were not for ambition, parliamentary parties, human baseness – in a word, politics' (DW II, 417). It follows that political involvement is inherently corrupting, and anyone who involves himself with a political party inevitably degrades himself by association:

> Wer sich einer Partei anschließt, und sei sie ihren Prinzipien nach die beste von allen, der encanailliert sich in jedem Falle, – denn er hat Parteigenossen. (AB, 95)

> Anyone who joins a political party, even if in principle it is the best party of all, is bound to be contaminated, for he has fellow party members.

Bernhardi, then, represents attitudes to which Schnitzler himself assented. In 1922, in a short study of his dramatic work, Theodor Kappstein associated the objectivity and irony of Bernhardi closely with the dramatist's own way of thinking,[43] and since when Schnitzler wrote to Kappstein on 24 July he picked out the chapter on *Professor Bernhardi* as one of those that he thought particularly good (AS/Bfe. II, 282) it is reasonable to infer that he did not reject the identification. Certainly he considered Bernhardi wholly in the right in respect of his medical responsibilities; when Emil Reich argued that he has an 'ethical' obligation to tell his patient the truth, Schnitzler dismissed these doubts in his diary as 'nonsense' (Tgb., 27 December 1918), and a letter of 10 April 1924 to Edith Werner spells the point out again (AS/Bfe. II, 339–40).

The ideals of humanitarianism and individual liberty that Schnitzler believed in were increasingly under threat from the anti-Semitic and nationalist movements in Austria. It is because these factors are at work in *Professor Bernhardi* that it is anything but a non-political play. Schnitzler certainly saw the physician's calling as more productive of human happiness than the politician's, and when Sol Liptzin describes the confrontation between Bernhardi and Flint in the final act as one between 'the scientist who fearlessly pursues the path of his honest convictions, and the man of public affairs who must constantly alter his views to conform with changing political constellations',[44] it is absolutely in keeping with the playwright's intentions.

Various contemporary critics close to Schnitzler wanted to see in *Professor Bernhardi* a Viennese equivalent of *An Enemy of the People*. Berta Zuckerkandl was one who compared the two plays in 1912 (WAZ, 2 December 1912), in 1918 Auernheimer referred to Ibsen's Dr Stockmann as a 'Nordic cousin of Bernhardi' (NFP, 24 December 1918), and in 1923 Alfred Kerr, reviewing a production at the Residenztheater in Berlin, even argued that in the 'honesty' of its ending Schnitzler's play surpassed Ibsen.[45] But Bernhardi's ironies are far removed from Stockmann's solitary struggle for progress.

Schnitzler's distaste for political commitment led him to fight shy of making the work a genuine confrontation with social issues. He never wholly lost the apolitical habits of the 'Jung Wien' period, and as successive developments unfolded and the ethos of liberalism lost ever more ground, he, like Bernhardi, either fell back on irony or took refuge in privacy – in his case, the privacy of his diary.

Just these weaknesses are documented in his play. They are set in a satirical context, the sharply-observed political machinations around Bernhardi. But in satire, according to Schiller's classic definition, the deficiency of reality is contrasted with an ideal that must at least be implicit;[46] that is, satire needs to be sustained by an underlying idea against which the abuses satirized may be measured. That *Professor Bernhardi* is not merely a polemic against anti-Semitism but treats wider issues of ethical principle is its virtue, the source of its undying fascination. Its weakness is that the underlying moral amounts to no more than an opting-out of political issues altogether.

Critical Reception: Diagnosis Without Therapy

Both the banning of *Professor Bernhardi* in Vienna in 1912 and its eventual production six years later sparked off long debates in the press.[47] The argument in 1912 followed predictable lines. On the Left, the *Arbeiter-Zeitung* argued on 30 October that the ban showed up the deficiencies of the censorship system and the urgent need for reform; on the Right, the *Reichspost* published on 3 December an account signed 'H.B.' supporting the censor and dismissing the work as a defamatory and inartistic polemic; and in the Liberal *Neue Freie Presse* seven weeks later, an anonymous academic lawyer declared it a model of moral drama holding up a mirror to the world.[48] The controversy was kept alive by attempts to circumvent the ban, including the abortive attempt to mount a production in Pressburg in 1913. On 11 May 1913 *Kikeriki* carried a cartoon showing a grotesquely long-nosed Schnitzler departing from Pressburg to the strains of the folk song 'Muß i denn, muß i denn zum Städtele 'naus' (figure 6), and the affair remained a source of satirical comment. On 16 April 1914, for example, the humorous weekly *Die Muskete* carried on its front page a cartoon on 'literary Vienna' (figure 7). The caption, its wording based on a famous epigram by Grillparzer, suggested that 'Viennese style' had not developed but degenerated, the final stage of degeneration determined by financial considerations. In the foreground, beside a pious Bahr, is Schnitzler, with the railway timetable between Vienna and Pressburg in his pocket.

Schniklers „Professor Bernhardi" in Preßburg
verboten.

Muß i denn, muß i denn zum Städtele 'naus,
Und du mein Schak bleibst i-n.

6 *Kikeriki*, 11 May 1913:
cartoon on the banning of
Professor *Bernhardi* in Pressburg.

Officially, the play was banned in Austria not specifically because it treated the so-called 'Jewish question' but because of its
'tendentious and distorted' depiction of public life. This reason was
not published, however, and was explicitly formulated only in a
memorandum to the police authorities in Berlin.[49] It was widely
taken for granted that the more precise reason was Schnitzler's
treatment of anti-Semitism in clerical politics – in a nutshell, the
policy of the Christian Social party. *Die Wage*, for example, carried
an article spelling out the assumption that the ban was due to
Schnitzler's presentation of a conflict (between physician and priest,
science and church) which was sharpened by the fact that the
representative of medical science was a Jew.[50] After the further ban
in Pressburg, Berta Zuckerkandl took a similar line, arguing in the
Liberal *Wiener Allgemeine Zeitung* on 30 April 1913 that it proved
how up-to-date the play was, despite its turn-of-the-century
setting.

The anti-Semitic attack to which Schnitzler was subjected did not
let up. During the war, for instance, the *Österreichische Volks-Presse*
carried a supposedly patriotic piece on 8 January 1915, in which the
play was attacked as a betrayal of Austria: it bore no relation to

Das schreibende Wien.

[Zeichnung von Rudolf Herrmann.]

7 'Literary Vienna':
cartoon by Rudolf
Herrmann, *Die Muskete*,
16 April 1914.

„Die Entwicklung des Wiener Stils ist ganz leicht zu definieren: Von der persönlichen Note
durch die Wiener Note zur Banknote."

historical reality but was a creation of the Jewish 'fantasy' of its
'Freemason' author. After the 1918 production a rather euphoric
entry in Schnitzler's diary recorded that the review in the day's
Reichspost seemed 'more decent than usual' (Tgb., 24 December
1918); but although the piece, signed 'N.', praised the lively
dialogue it also reported that the play was written for Jews and was
repulsive to anti-Semites.

From the very first, there was a lot of argument about the extent
to which the play had polemical intentions, that is, to what extent it
was written as an attack on anti-Semitism in Austrian public and professional life. Looking through the reviews of the Berlin première,
Schnitzler noted in his diary that some reviewers had complained
that he had written a polemical play ('ein Tendenzstück'), others
that he had not (Tgb., 5 December 1912). What was widely observed by the early commentators was that the work presented a
(more or less realistic) miniature of Austrian society,[51] and both
Arthur Eloesser and Paul Goldmann (the latter an old friend, though
increasingly critical of Schnitzler's work) defined its force as essentially satirical.[52] Polemically defended by anti-clericals, *Professor
Bernhardi* was all too easily assumed to be polemically anti-clerical

itself. In *Der Morgen* for 23 December 1912, Friedrich Hertz defended Schnitzler against that kind of interpretation, which he
alleged was that adopted by the censors. Indeed that would be the
censors' attitude the next year when renewed appeals were made to
lift the ban.[53]

By 1918 Schnitzler had got himself thoroughly into the bad
books of the theatre critics reviewing for the Viennese press as a
result of the production the previous year of his play about the
world of journalism, *Fink und Fliederbusch*. The central figure is a
reporter who writes as Fliederbusch for the Liberal *Die Gegenwart*
but contributes to the weekly *Die elegante Welt* a reactionary piece
under the name 'Fink', defending a speech in parliament by a
conservative politician, Count Niederhof. When as 'Fliederbusch'
he then publishes a tirade of invective in reply to 'Fink', the son of
the editor of *Die elegante Welt* insists that 'Fink' must challenge
'Fliederbusch' to a duel. The challenge is accepted, partly through
the machinations of an aristocratic reporter who writes under the
name of 'Styx' and who is a further split personality in that he can
change from writing gossip for *Die elegante Welt* to writing ex-
posures of high society for *Die Gegenwart* (it is in effect his place
that Fink has taken, while he in turn wishes to take Fliederbusch's
place). But the need for decision and responsible self-knowledge is
avoided; Fliederbusch, and probably Styx also, will find employ-
ment on a new paper being founded by Niederhof, a figure who
regards 'convictions' as 'sentimental irrelevancies' (DW II, 629).

The first reviewers at once likened *Fink und Fliederbusch* to
Professor Bernhardi in two respects. First, it was another 'play without women'; and secondly, while again not set in the present (the
action takes place 'in Vienna at the beginning of the century'), it
showed Schnitzler venturing once more into social and political
comedy. In the latter respect it immediately attracted sharp criticism from the Christian Social press: among the reviews that appeared on 15 November, the day after the première, was one in the
Reichspost (signed 'B.') that interpreted it as supporting lack of
principle ('Gesinnungslosigkeit') and another in the *Österreichische
Volkszeitung* (signed 'l.f.') describing it as preaching a political
morality as flawed as the military morality in *Leutnant Gustl*.

As Schnitzler explained to Richard Charmatz in December 1917,
his main interest was in the psychology of the central figure, forced
to decide between two alternative positions but genuinely un-
decided about them; he claimed to have played down the satirical
implications for the press as a whole (AS/Bfe. II, 151–5). The effect
of the ending was intended to be 'grotesque', and he thought the
production in the Deutsches Volkstheater failed to achieve that

(Tgb., 14 November 1917). He recognized the farcical element in the play – the idea of a character duelling with himself is reminiscent of Holofernes in Nestroy's *Judith und Holofernes*, and indeed Auernheimer drew the parallel (NEP, 15 November 1917) – but conceded to Charmatz that he had failed to combine it successfully with comedy of character as he had intended (AS/Bfe. II, 155). Certainly many of the adverse press criticisms homed in on the farcical quality. One of the reviews that Schnitzler mentioned in his diary on 15 November with special dislike was that by Paul Frank in the same day's *Fremdenblatt*, in which the play is described as based on an essentially farcical idea incapable of sustaining a comedy. The next day, it was described as a 'crude farce' in the *Wiener Mittags-Zeitung*, in a review signed 'A.S.', and in the *Wiener Abendpost* as a farce laden down with polemical *Tendenz* or a polemical drama that degenerated into farce.

But once again it was the alleged tendentiousness that drew most of the fire; once again reviewers saw a polemic where Schnitzler insisted he had not intended one. Much of the press comment, including that in the Liberal press, centred on the picture the play presented of the press. Reviewers, including prominent critics such as Marco Brociner and Richard Specht, repeatedly declared that it was an inaccurate and unfair picture, which showed Schnitzler's ignorance of journalism.[54] More sympathetic critics argued defensively either that he was not attempting to treat all journalism – this was the argument of Salten, whose review appeared in the evening edition of the *Berliner Tageblatt* on 15 November 1917 – or that he was no more mocking genuine journalism than Molière mocks genuine religion in *Tartuffe* (Auernheimer).

The attack culminated in two pieces that appeared on 19 November, the day Schnitzler made his most bitter entry in his diary about his mistreatment at the hands of his reviewers. Bernhard Neufeld, describing the play in the *Sonn- und Montagszeitung* as an examination of the nature of journalism pursued 'almost to the point of bloodshed', asked rhetorically whether the stage was a suitable place for presenting sociological theses; and in the *Wiener Montags-Journal* the accusation that Schnitzler was writing from ignorance was built up into a sweeping generalization. In a passage that he marked in crayon on his cutting, he is derided as having been writing in Vienna for a whole generation 'without knowing more of Vienna than Jewish literary salons and literary snobs', and as 'depicting Viennese aristocrats, Viennese girls [Wiener süße Mädel], and Viennese life without having any knowledge of aristocrats, girls, or life'.

A short note (signed 'G.') in the *Wiener Montagblatt* reached the obvious conclusion that the unfavourable reception accorded the play was a direct consequence of the realism with which Schnitzler had treated the press. (Neufeld, indeed, made the same point.) Certainly some of the most generous and sympathetic assessments of the play appeared not in Viennese papers but in Germany (Oskar Bendiener in the *Karlsruher Tagblatt*, 22 November) and the Austrian provinces (Max Pirker in the *Grazer Tagespost*, 1 December).

Among all the first reviews, there was only one to which Schnitzler reacted with grateful approval. This was Auernheimer's, in which the central problem of the play is defined as being that of the 'validity of journalistic convictions and indeed of any convictions'. But to treat a subject of that kind, full of satirical implications, in a form of comedy making use (to use Schnitzler's own terms) of farcical and grotesque effects, was to court misunderstanding. The material is not shaped by Schnitzler's commitment; two of the most acute of the Viennese critics, Polgar and Oskar Maurus Fontana, both commented on the impression of relativism made by the play.[55] It is this impression of dispassionate scepticism that provided the reviewer in the *Reichspost* with the opportunity to draw a parallel with *Professor Bernhardi*, suggesting that in both plays Schnitzler adopted a pose of distant superiority over all ideological commitment.

The debate about polemical 'tendentiousness' was renewed when *Professor Bernhardi* was finally performed in Vienna in 1918, and the term *Tendenzstück* was widely used. Auernheimer argued in the *Neue Freie Presse* that it was a misapprehension not based on the play itself but created by the ban that had been imposed on it in Austria. He made the point first in a brief review (signed 'A') that appeared on 22 December 1918, and expanded on it two days later. But when Salten's review appeared in the *Fremdenblatt* on 22 December, Schnitzler noted in his diary that though he had praised the play even he had called it a 'Tendenzstück', the very action inherently 'tendentious'. Five days later, in the *Wiener Mittag*, Max Mell again discussed it as essentially tendentious, classifying it under the heading of polemical social plays ('Zeit- und Thesenstücke').[56] In his diary that day (27 December 1918), Schnitzler dismissed Mell's review as 'respectfully impudent' ('hochachtungsvoll frech'), blaming the tone on the malign influence of Hofmannsthal.

How strongly Schnitzler disagreed with the assessment of the play as polemical or tendentious can be gauged from the crayon underscorings he made on his copy of a review in *Der Morgen* for 23 December 1918, in which the reviewer ('h.l.') insisted that it was not merely a Viennese comedy nor a satire, but a *Tendenzstück*. In his letters he consistently insisted that what he had written was not a *Tendenzstück* but essentially a comedy, a 'comedy of character' ('eine Charakterkomödie') – he used the term both to Charmatz in 1913 and again to Ludwig Hirschfeld six years later.[57]

The chief bone of interpretative contention was from the first, as it has remained, Bernhardi's complex character. The complexity was praised by Berta Zuckerkandl, who defined him as a 'dualistic' character, a 'demi-hero' in whom passion and scepticism were at odds (WAZ, 2 December 1912). But other reviewers objected that at bottom he is weak, lacking the courage to fight his corner. This is at least briefly suggested, for example, in the review in the *Berliner Tageblatt* on 29 November 1912 which Schnitzler picked out as the most hostile of the first notices: under the heading 'Der unpolitische Politiker', Fritz Engel argued that while the work may look like a tendentiously polemical play of ideas ('ein Tendenzdrama'), Schnitzler has neither the strength to take up a strong position nor the stomach to show intolerance to the intolerant.

Even in these generally appreciative early reviews, certain doubts can be read between the lines as to whether the play had realized the true dramatic potential of the material. Even the *Neue Freie Presse*, which was generally sympathetic to Schnitzler's work, carried on 4 January 1913 a long review by Paul Goldmann which concludes that he has only skimmed the surface of the problem inherent in his material. Three months later, in *Die Wage*, A. Halbert again in effect accused the dramatist of dodging the issue of general principle.[58] Meanwhile in an issue of *Die Fackel* dated 1 April Karl Kraus too had made the point that the play falls short of being specific in its polemical or satiric thrust (F 372–373, 13). A regular reader of *Die Fackel*, Schnitzler recorded this attack in his diary, dismissing it as 'rather lame' ('etwas lahme Angriffe': Tgb., 1 April 1913).

In view of his dislike and mistrust of Kraus,[59] it must have been particularly galling in later years when their work was compared to Schnitzler's disadvantage. In 1917, reviewing *Fink und Fliederbusch* in *Die Wage*, Oskar Maurus Fontana stressed the ineffectiveness, as he saw it, of Schnitzler's satire of journalism by contrasting it with the 'white-hot, holy hatred' that informed Kraus's creativeness; and six years later again, Siegfried Jacobsohn, whom Schnitzler respected as an 'excellent theatre critic',[60] published in his journal *Die Weltbühne* an article, prompted by a production of *Professor Bernhardi* in the Residenztheater in Berlin, arguing that the weakness of the play was manifested in the weakness of its hero – a 'hero' only in the sense of being the title role – and that the lack of bite, the substitution of witty irony for satirical fire, was typical of Austria, the one exception being Kraus.[61]

The charge of insufficient sharpness and commitment would remain the most serious criticism levelled against Schnitzler's whole *œuvre*. When he died, it was in effect repeated even in the *Neue Freie Presse* in a laudatory front-page piece: 'He was a great diagnostician of social and political evils, without being able to prescribe the therapy, without the weapon, the gleaming scalpel, of the surgeon' (NFP, 22 October 1931). A similar charge, put in even more harshly sweeping terms, appeared the same day in the obituary in *The Times*: 'It was a pity only that in the last resort he was without a philosophy to give brilliant analysis of character a permanent meaning.'

Hofmannsthal and Theatrical Comedy

Hofmannsthal was not open to charges of triviality nor, as his work developed, of lacking a 'philosophy'. But for a long time the critics tended to think of him too just as he had been in the days of 'Jung Wien', in his case pigeon-holing him as an 'Impressionist' lyric poet. It certainly took longer for him to establish himself as a dramatist. On 2 October 1918 he wrote to Andrian that he was 'first and foremost [. . .] a Viennese playwright', and that since the age of fourteen he had thought 'of himself as 'a kind of house-dramatist to an imaginary Burgtheater' (H/Andrian, 288). But that is a clear example of his retrospective self-interpretative shaping of his biography, and gives an oversimplified picture of his development as a playwright. In fact it took a long time before he came to have real confidence in himself as a dramatist for the theatre.

His approach to the theatre was a gradual progression. The appearance of Eleonora Duse in Vienna in February 1892 provided him, so he told Felix von Oppenheimer, with 'the most powerful theatrical impression' he had received up to then (H/Bfe. I, 42), and is commemorated in two essays. Five months later, on 19 July 1892, he wrote to Schnitzler that he had been trying to write something for 'the harsh reality of the actual stage' ('für die wirkliche brutale Bühne': H/AS, 23), but the tragedy referred to in that letter, *Ascanio und Gioconda*, remained unpublished, and his early lyrical dramas exploring the limitations of the aesthetic life are fundamentally undramatic.

Drama depends on the interaction of characters and their loyalties. Hofmannsthal's early work expresses, as he came to realize, his own developing *self*-awareness ('ein Gewahrwerden seiner Selbst': A, 233), and lacks the authentic action of dramatic conflict. The central character in *Gestern*, Andrea, perceives all human life as solipsistic[62] and is himself self-centred to the point of narcissism:

> Ist nicht die ganze ewige Natur
> Nur ein Symbol für unsrer Seelen Launen?
> Was suchen wir in ihr als unsre Spur?
>   (HKA III, 26)

Is not the whole of eternal nature merely a symbol for the moods of our own souls? What do we seek in it but traces of ourselves?

Even in *Der Tor und der Tod* it is only on the brink of death that the egocentric Claudio appreciates the rewards of involvement with others and determines to 'attach himself' anew to life (HKA III, 73).

In 1894 Hofmannsthal reported to Andrian that his version of Euripides' *Alkestis* had brought him 'a little closer to the dramatic drama' he wanted to achieve (H/Andrian, 23: letter of 21 February 1894), and by the end of 1897 he was telling Bahr he had a far stronger longing for the stage than previously (H/Bfe. I, 277). But he still admitted the 'lyrical' nature of his plays and their 'distance from the truly dramatic' ('den Abstand vom wirklich Dramatischen': H/Bfe. I, 278).[63] Even after he had had one-act plays accepted by Brahm, he recognized how far he still had to go: writing to Oppenheimer on 15 May 1899, he conceded that it was appropriate to refer to them as 'poems' ('Gedichte': H/Bfe. I, 285). And writing to Brahm on 21 December 1900, over a year and a half after the failure of *Die Hochzeit der Sobeide* and *Der Abenteurer und die Sängerin* in Berlin, he signed himself with ironic resignation a 'sometime playwright' ('Ihr Hofmannsthal[,] ci-devant Theaterdichter': H/Bfe. I, 324). When the Insel-Verlag published a two-volume edition of the lyrical dramas (*Kleine Dramen*) in 1907, it still seemed self-evident to Josef Hofmiller, reviewing them together with his collected poems in the *Süddeutsche Monatshefte* early the following year, that like Musset's verse plays they were 'not conceived for the stage' (HUK, 156).

The two projects that brought him to serious full-length dramatic writing were adaptations of Sophocles and Calderón. Both plans were conceived in Varese in the autumn of 1901, and the first notes were written the following spring. The version of *Electra* was intended to be the first part of a two-part *Orestie*; the second part, *Orest in Delphi*, was never written. Calderón, on the other hand, was to remain a lifelong interest. A plan in late 1918 to undertake a series of translations for the Burgtheater came to nothing when Andrian lost his position in charge of the theatre, but Hofmannsthal continued to be occupied with *La vida es sueño* throughout the 1920s in his work on *Der Turm*.

As a letter to Marie Luise Borchardt shows, it was *Elektra* that he would later look back on as the play in which he had first begun to write drama that was really suitable for the theatre (H/Borchardt, 178: letter of 12 June 1923). What was perhaps most significant about the occasion was not that he had found his characteristic dramatic style but rather that it launched his collaboration with Max Reinhardt, who was eventually to direct more works by him than by any other contemporary dramatist.[64] It was from this time that Hofmannsthal began to develop the three theatrical genres in which he excelled: comedy, morality, and opera libretto. In these genres he found suitable media for treating what he came to call 'das Soziale' – the social dimension of human life, including the relation of the fully-developed individual personality to others and the integration of the individual in the complex structure of the wider community (to which the creative writer stands in a relationship of special responsibility). His enjoyment of observing Reinhardt at work and of discussing dramatic plans with him – he told Rudolf Pannwitz in 1918 that he always found their conversations 'extremely stimulating'[65] – would also underpin their co-operation in planning the Salzburg Festival after the First World War.

The evolution of his dramatic style was still only gradual. Even before the composition of *Elektra* Kessler, stimulated by Hofmannsthal's fictional dialogue between Balzac and Hammer-Purgstall about characters in the novel and in drama, had told him that relations *between* individuals are essentially the stuff of comedy (H/Kessler, 41). It was, however, some years before Hofmannsthal came fully to associate comedy specifically with the treatment of social interaction and integration (*das Soziale*). In 1904 he planned to follow up the success of *Elektra* by writing an Oedipus trilogy for Reinhardt, but only *Ödipus und die Sphinx* was completed (it was performed in Reinhardt's Deutsches Theater in Berlin on 2 February 1906). It was only in 1908, when he was working on the material of the comedy *Cristinas Heimreise*, that he told his father people would probably come to date his *real* writing for the theatre ('die Zeit meiner *eigentlichen* Theaterschriftstellerei') from that summer or the previous year (H/Bfe. II, 324).

Even then the evolution was not complete. Long afterwards, when Andrian saw *Cristinas Heimreise* in the Theater in der Josefstadt and wrote that it seemed to him to be 'not specifically a work for the stage' ('kein specifisches Bühnenwerk': letter of 28 April 1926), Hofmannsthal, replying on 8 May, admitted that another of

Andrian's terms, 'uneigentliches Theaterstück' (meaning, roughly, not an authentic stage play), was still accurate (H/Andrian, 372–3). But more and more his interest was to centre on comedy, and a series of notes made in February 1912 finally make explicit one of the fundamental principles of the genre, that it characteristically deals with man in a social environment. 'Die Komödie bezieht sich immer auf das Soziale. Nur das *relative* Menschliche ist komisch' ('Comedy always deals with the social. Humanity is comic only when it is seen *relatively*': RA III, 512).

One key step forward was Hofmannsthal's interest in Molière. A short spell in Paris in the summer of 1908, which included visits to the Comédie-Française, prompted him to write to Kessler about the quality of Molière's work, which he recognized as the supreme achievement in the comic genre (H/Kessler, 193: letter of 4 September 1908). His own practical work on Molière texts began with his adaptation – initially working together with Rudolf Alexander Schröder – of the 'comédie-ballet' *Le Mariage forcé* under the title *Die Heirat wider Willen*, which Reinhardt produced in Munich and Berlin in 1910. It was while he was first engaged on this that Hofmannsthal wrote to Kessler on 15 August 1909 that the work captured the whole intellectual and moral spirit of its time as completely as a morality would in the form of allegory ('[. . .] so vollständig als ein Moralitätsspiel das in der Form der Allegorie thut': H/Kessler, 258).

The stress on the moral dimension is characteristic of him. As early as 5 August 1892 he had told Marie Herzfeld that a favourite form of his was a verse *proverbe* (he uses the term in Musset's sense) with a moral ('das Proverb in Versen mit einer Moral': H/Bfe. I, 62). What had changed by 1909 was that he now related the material to the society it was rooted in; both comedy and morality would serve him as vehicles for treating the concerns of his own age. Comedy was to prove the more satisfactory because of the subtlety it permitted in representing the nuances of interaction between individuals. But at this stage he was still feeling his way: *Cristinas Heimreise* was still being revised, *Jedermann* still unfinished.

Molière remained his classic model in comedy, and by January 1911 he was writing to his father not only of Molière's historic importance for the development of modern comedy but also of his own hope that he would contribute to establishing Molière fully on the German stage in new prose translations.[66] This was written shortly before the première of *Der Rosenkavalier*, which contains motifs drawn from Molière, notably from *Monsieur de Pourceaugnac* but also from *Le Médecin malgré lui* and *Le Bourgeois gentilhomme*.[67] Reinhardt had been involved in the final stages of the production of

Der Rosenkavalier in Dresden, and a letter of 17 January 1911 to Ottonie von Degenfeld records Hofmannsthal's grateful admiration of the 'magical' effect of Reinhardt's work (H/Degenfeld, 62). It was Reinhardt's stimulus that eventually encouraged him to translate or adapt more Molière.

Reinhardt's Molière productions were not without their critics. In 1912, for example, two months after Hofmannsthal had written about the 'symbolic' quality of the situations in *Georges Dandin* in which 'the relation between the figures is crystallized' (RA III, 513), Alfred Kerr wrote that Reinhardt's production of the play reduced it to *Kitsch*.[68] But a conversation with Reinhardt in 1916 inspired Hofmannsthal to write *Die Lästigen*, and his subsequent reworking of *Le Bourgeois gentilhomme* (*Der Bürger als Edelmann*) was undertaken, as his letter of 30 June 1917 to Strauss shows, with the express intention of achieving specifically theatrical effects through Reinhardt's production (H/Strauss, 312). His increased sureness may be seen in the contrast between the gratitude with which he had thanked Strauss in July 1909 for enhancing the theatricality of *Der Rosenkavalier* (H/Strauss, 63) and the sharpness with which he requested him to leave the judgment of theatrical effectiveness in *Der Bürger als Edelmann* to himself and Reinhardt: 'I have some understanding of theatrical style, and Reinhardt of practical work in the theatre' (H/Strauss, 319: letter of 16 July 1917).

Shortly after this another influence began to affect his view of his own dramatic work, blurring the importance of Molière and other French models. On 17 February 1918 he wrote to Bodenhausen that he had been reading the first two volumes of Josef Nadler's *Literaturgeschichte der deutschen Stämme und Landschaften* and asked Bodenhausen to buy copies, at his expense, for himself and Borchardt. The work seemed likely, he wrote, to be of importance for the whole German-speaking world and have a beneficial effect on creative writers both directly and indirectly (H/Bodenhausen, 246–7). He also had a copy sent to Mell.[69] When the third volume of this work, which included chapters on Austrian Baroque literature, appeared later the same year, he had that too sent to Borchardt and told him that he had found much in it 'infinitely enlivening' (H/Borchardt, 142: letter of 10 January 1919). Two years later again, Redlich noted in his diary how strongly Hofmannsthal was under Nadler's influence,[70] and in a survey of recent books Hofmannsthal forecast that in time the work would become a classic, a standard authority ('das wahre Hausbuch der Deutschen': P IV, 498). He convinced himself that Nadler had discovered the very nature of his own work; indeed in 1921 he wrote to Nadler thanking him in those very terms.[71]

Hofmannsthal derived from Nadler a conception of a South German and Austrian ('Austro-Bavarian') Baroque tradition cent-ring on a kind of drama strong in visual effects. His ideas about this tradition are rehearsed in particular from 1919 onwards in his essays about the Salzburg Festival (see pp. 201–4, below). Nadler – as Hofmannsthal only learnt later – had a 'strong prejudice' against Reinhardt (H/Burckhardt, 97: letter of 13 October 1927), but on Hofmannsthal their influence worked together. Nadler's ethnically based view of literary history fused with the stimulus of Reinhardt, whose productions were known for his use of lavish visual effects, and also with Hofmannsthal's ever-growing cultural traditionalism and his conception of the 'idea of Austria'. Under these combined influences he adopted a mystique of an unbroken indigenous tradi-tion of drama (particularly comic drama) rooted in the Baroque, and persuaded himself that in that tradition the roots of his own work were to be found.

The whole line of argument is flawed. There was in fact no genuine continuity of the kind he came to argue, no indigenous tradition of comic drama extending from the Baroque to the present day.[72] But both his mistaken (at the very least, over-simplified) sense of an Austro-Bavarian tradition of *visual* drama and the view that he constructed of himself as a late representative of that tradition were fundamental to his later dramatic work.

What Nadler's approach offered was, in fact, a myth, the equi-valent in literary history to the political and cultural 'idea of Austria'. Hofmannsthal became, as he wrote to Strauss on 4 June 1924, 'filled with the idea – and all the more so with the insight of maturity – that the individual can produce nothing lasting that is not linked to tradition' (H/Strauss, 444). He began to parade the idea of theatrical tradition in his essays, using it quite un-critically. In 1918, for example, he argued that Reinhardt's empha-sis on the actor was evidence of his debt to a genuinely 'popular' ('volkstümlich') Viennese theatrical tradition (P III, 431); four years later he described Viennese popular drama (wrongly) as being organically derived from the *commedia dell' arte*, lifting both the idea and the phrasing from an essay by Wilhelm Kosch, another literary historian (P IV, 95).[73]

In the same uncritical spirit, he imposed on his own work, in two respects, a pattern of what he romanticized as theatrical tradi-tionalism. Firstly, he overstated the centrality in his writing of work undertaken directly for the theatre, telling Pannwitz in December 1919, for example, that adaptations such as *Alkestis*, *Elektra*, and *Das gerettete Venedig* had been undertaken with the idea specifically of extending the theatre repertory.[74] Secondly, he related his own work to Viennese theatrical tradition, and by the mid-1920s was even attempting to argue that the Viennese dialect theatre had shaped his youthful dramatic ambitions (A, 236). The 'basic theme' of the account of his career as a dramatist that he drafted for Max Pirker in 1921 was that the force of his 'home soil' ('die Kräfte des Bodens') had worked on him, drawing him to traditional theatrical forms ('zu den traditionellen Formen'), to which his 'poetic subjectivity' had been subordinated (A, 369).

This distortion also informs his correspondence with Andrian in 1918. When Andrian became director-general of the court theatres in the summer of that year, Hofmannsthal glimpsed an ideal opportunity for a renewal of the true tradition of Austrian theatre. In particular he foresaw an end to the exclusion of his own works from the Burgtheater. No doubt he had *Der Schwierige* (by now well advanced towards completion) in mind. A good deal of pent-up bitterness, partly about the contrast between the Burgtheater and what Reinhardt was achieving in Berlin, is poured out to Andrian in a letter of 28 August 1918:

> Denk nur daß während das Burgtheater in allem und jedem seine eigene Tradition verhöhnte und mit Füßen trat, den österreichischen Ton mit Füßen trat, mich mit Füßen trat, nichts kannte und propagierte als Gerhart Hauptmann und Otto Ernst (Hauptmann bekam *drei Mal* den Grillparzerpreis!!) – baute Reinhardt in partibus infidelium eine Art schöneres Burgtheater auf, mit einem höher zielenden Repertoire – nur eine Lücke darin, das Gesellschaftsstück. (H/Andrian, 271)

> Just think that while the Burgtheater was in every way spurning its own tradition, trampling on it, trampling on the Austrian voice, trampling on me, heeding and cultivating nothing but Gerhart Hauptmann and Otto Ernst (Hauptmann was awarded the Grillparzer Prize *three times!*), Reinhardt in foreign parts was constructing a kind of finer Burgtheater, with a more ambitious repertory, with only one gap – social comedy.

He returned to this matter on 2 October, in a letter already quoted. Had Andrian, he asked, reflected on how he had been treated in the nineteen years since his first plays had been performed in the Burgtheater (H/Andrian, 287)? His plays had either not been produced there or, in the case of *Jedermann*, had been given only a few performances, by contrast with long runs in German cities such as Munich and Dresden:

> In fact it was dreadful for me, because first and foremost I am certainly a Viennese playwright [weil ich ja doch gewiß primär

ein Wiener Theaterdichter bin]. From the age of fourteen I have thought of myself as a kind of house-dramatist to an imaginary Burgtheater [als eine Art Hausdichter eines imaginären Burgtheaters]; that was also what underlay my adaptations – *Elektra* (which eventually was an independent work, not an adaptation), *Venice Preserv'd*, later various Molière things. All this work – carrying on from Schreyvogel, Grillparzer, Halm, and Wilbrandt – became meaningless in relation to Berlin, where there is, after all, no tradition in the theatre. [. . .] I myself find it really strange that someone could be so systematically mistreated here [daß man hier jemanden so systematisch mißhandeln konnte], and that that someone happened to be myself. (H/Andrian, 288)

In March 1899, during Schlenther's second season in charge, the Burgtheater programme had presented a glimpse of quite different possibilities. In three and a half weeks, between 1 March and 24 March, no fewer than twelve evenings were devoted to plays by Schnitzler and Hofmannsthal: seven (1, 2, 4, 7, 12, 17, and 23 March) to a programme of one-act plays by Schnitzler (*Paracelsus, Die Gefährtin,* and *Der grüne Kakadu*), one (16 March) to *Das Vermächtnis,* and four (18, 19, 21, and 24 March) to Hofmannsthal's *Der Abenteurer und die Sängerin* and *Die Hochzeit der Sobeide.* It must have seemed as if the Viennese 'Moderns' had taken over the national theatre – a promise of classic status, which however would never be realized in the Burgtheater in their lifetime. Hence Hofmannsthal's reflection nearly twenty years later on how things had been in the 1820s and early 1830s, when Schreyvogel was Grillparzer's mentor; he could not but contrast the failure of the modern Burgtheater to encourage an indigenous dramatist such as himself. Again the argument, spelling out a chain of antecedents, is based on his characteristic emphasis on tradition (which four years later would also inform his interpretation of Grillparzer in the 'Rede auf Grillparzer').

Writing in the *Neue Freie Presse* on 18 July 1929 immediately after Hofmannsthal's death, Salten compared him to Grillparzer in a different sense. Grillparzer was another dramatist who had found it difficult to shake off a public image determined by an early success he had grown out of. Like Grillparzer, so Salten argued, Hofmannsthal underestimated the fame he enjoyed and thought himself mistreated when in fact he commanded admiration (Fiechtner 1949, 41). Certainly Hofmannsthal was both ambitious and touchy, but his view of the failings of the Burgtheater was shared by at least one prominent critic. Reviewing the first Salzburg *Jedermann* in the *Neue Freie Presse* on 27 August 1920, Auernheimer wrote that

Reinhardt had fulfilled all the responsibilities towards Hofmannsthal that the Burgtheater had failed to fulfil towards him and also towards other Austrian dramatists (*Resonanz*, 9). (Only two of Auernheimer's own comedies had so far been performed there.)

The seriousness with which Hofmannsthal planned his tactics in support of Reinhardt may be gauged from the unusual circumspection with which he secured advance approval from Beer-Hofmann of the essay 'Das Reinhardtsche Theater', in which he put his admiration of Reinhardt on public record (H/Beer-Hofmann, 137–8: letter of 25 July 1917). In practical terms, it was on Reinhardt that all his hopes of achieving a theatrical base centred. He spelt out those hopes to Andrian in the summer of 1918:

> So here everything is interlinked: all my hopes for a rebirth of Austrian theatre from the work of the *only* creative force in this area [die *einzige* productive Potenz auf diesem Gebiet], a man who moreover – it could not be otherwise – is an Austrian with his whole heart and soul; my whole destiny as a dramatist [mein ganzes Schicksal als Theaterdichter]; and yours in your new profession. (H/Andrian, 268: letter of 27 August 1918)

The next day he returned to the subject, urging on Reinhardt's behalf the possibility of collaboration, with Salzburg the crucial point of contact ('Collaboration (über Salzburg)': H/Andrian, 271). These ambitious plans for the influence he might exercise through Andrian were dashed with the establishment of the republic, but when Wildgans became director of the Burgtheater, Hofmannsthal still hoped that Reinhardt's company would be able to perform there; he imagined, so he told Andrian on 25 January 1921, an arrangement whereby Reinhardt's company would be 'guests and more-than-guests, with recurring visits and the expectation of exchange visits and so on' (H/Andrian, 319).[75] Indeed, he saw this as how *Der Schwierige* might ideally be produced.

In the very broadest terms, the schematic self-interpretation that Hofmannsthal summarized in the letter to Pirker, tracing his development out of lyric drama into the 'fulfilment of traditional theatrical demands' (A, 370), is accurate, but his self-description to Andrian as 'first and foremost a Viennese playwright' overstates his closeness to the theatre. As late as 1922 he admitted to Carl J. Burckhardt that he was still learning to appreciate the playwright's total dependence on the actor (H/Burckhardt, 98: letter of 13 October 1922), and five years later still, on 1 November 1927, he would admit to Richard Strauss – in complete contradiction of his self-description to Andrian in 1918 – that he was first and foremost a poet and not a man of the theatre ('ein Dichter, aber kein Theatraliker': H/Strauss, 520).

His repeated emphasis on tradition also obscures the crucial importance of comedy for him not merely as a form of entertainment (its main historical function in the theatre) but as a vital medium of expression. He had been attracted to large-scale dramatic forms because the theatre was a social institution and so provided a means of social engagement; it was in comedy (including the comic libretti that he wrote for Strauss) that he was able to treat *das Soziale* not just allegorically, as in the moralities and, as he would say, in *Die Frau ohne Schatten* (A, 218), but in a way that allowed him to deal with human relations and interaction – the generic point formulated in 1912 that comedy deals with man in a social environment (RA III, 512). It was precisely in the interrelations of the figures that he saw the essence of Molière; the point is one he returned to in a note written after a discussion with Andrian in 1916 in Warsaw (A, 178). This is also the principal force of the cryptic late note in *Ad me ipsum* equating his own comedies with 'the attainment of the social dimension' ('das *erreichte Soziale: die Komödien*': A, 226). So too one of the aphorisms in the *Buch der Freunde*, 'What prevented Ibsen from making comedies out of his subjects was a northern Protestant stiffness and unsociableness' (A, 63), clearly implies that comedy is the natural form for treating social problems. By the mid-1920s Hofmannsthal perceived his *œuvre* as culminating in *Der Schwierige* because that work presented a multi-perspective treatment of social relations and social integration ('Das Soziale – perspektivisch behandelt': A, 237); and when he wrote about the treatment of language in the play he defined its importance as lying in its function as the very basis of social existence ('*das* soziale Element': A, 231).

Surprisingly, when Nadler wrote an article on Hofmannsthal's treatment of society, he did not draw on the comedies. But his argument, that Hofmannsthal answers the problem of social change 'through pure creation of artistic form' ('durch reine Gestaltung': HUK, 355), is actually most pertinent to the comedies. In the late summer of 1907, at the very time when his dramatic writing was beginning to mature, Hofmannsthal wrote that comedy is always in the deepest sense about the art of living ('In der Comödie handelt es sich um reine *Lebenskunst* im tiefsten Sinn': HKA XX, 175). It is in that sense that, as Richard Alewyn perceived,[76] the comedies lie at the very centre of his work.

CHAPTER 4

Eros

Double Standards and the 'Woman Question'

No theme occupies a more central place in the art of early twentieth-century Vienna than that of sexuality, especially female sexuality. The phenomenon has received a lot of attention in recent years; what I can attempt here is only a brief summary of some of the main issues, as a preliminary to discussing the treatment of the subject by Schnitzler and Hofmannsthal.

Though relations between the sexes were generally perceived as Schnitzler's principal theme they were by no means his exclusive preserve. Among other early twentieth-century Viennese dramatists, for example, the subject looms large in the work of Wildgans: the importance of the sexual drives is histrionically proclaimed by the medical student Bonifaz Strantz in Act Three of *Armut* (1914) and forms a central theme in *Liebe* (1916). (They are also treated in *Die Sonette an Eád*, first published in 1912.) Significantly the figure of Casanova fascinated the writers of this whole generation. Reviewing the first performance of Auernheimer's verse comedy *Casanova in Wien*, which appeared (dedicated to Schnitzler) in 1924, Musil noted that Casanova had become 'an almost symbolical figure', a repository of all imaginable passion.[1] Schnitzler himself treated Casanova in *Die Schwestern* and in the related story *Casanovas Heimfahrt*. Hofmannsthal drew on Casanova's memoirs not only in *Der Abenteurer und die Sängerin*, in which the aging Baron Weidenstamm looks back on a life spent 'reaching out [. . .] for all life's pleasures' ('der mit tausend Armen / nach allen Freuden griff': D I, 268) but also in the play *Cristinas Heimreise* and its earlier version 'Florindos Werk', centring on the figure of the seducer Florindo and revised in the late summer of 1908;[2] and he even thought of giving the would-be lady-killer Neuhoff in *Der Schwierige* the name 'Neuhaus'.[3]

The drama of the time is peopled by erotic 'adventurers', from Schnitzler's Anatol and Heink in Bahr's comedy *Das Konzert* (1909) to Jaromir in *Der Unbestechliche* (1923) and Max von Reisenberg in *Komödie der Verführung* (1924). The preoccupation with sexual *mores* is a consequence not least of the flagrant corruption in the moral double standards that had long obtained in Vienna, where erotic dalliance was a way of life. At the end of the nineteenth century and in the early years of the twentieth these double standards came under attack from several quarters: most notably from Freud, from Karl Kraus, and from the burgeoning Women's Movement.

The 'social morality' of the period – the formula is Stefan Zweig's, taken from the account in his memoirs[4] – was based on the same double standards as obtained in Victorian England, the 'familiar contrast between the restrictive morality of the bourgeois family and the sexual licence of the streets'.[5] Beneath a surface veneer of virtuous respectability, practical expectations of the two sexes were determined by conventional ideas of their different 'drives' and social roles. Young men of good family were permitted and even encouraged to sow their wild oats by indulging in affairs with socially inferior girls who had no expectation of marriage. The social types with whom a young man might safely have affairs, from actresses to shop-girls, are represented scene by scene in *Anatol*. Married men might take mistresses. But the young woman whom such a man might marry, educated for a life of submissive domesticity, was required to remain impeccably chaste – an expectation that is spelt out in Schnitzler's early story 'Die Braut' where the narrator refers to 'what every one of us expects in his future wife: a wondrous, holy, virtuous contrast to the mad passion of our youthful affairs' (ES I, 87). Sheltered women, like the respectable Gabriele in *Anatol*, were left naïvely ignorant of life – Anatol tells Gabriele that too much was kept from her when she was a young girl (DW I, 47) – and a conspiracy of silence on sexual matters in particular bred, as Zweig recalls, not only ignorance but also covert preoccupation with sex.

In this atmosphere it was inevitable that Freud's findings, promoting the libido to the most important factor in human behaviour, and ascribing to women no less than to men a susceptibility to sensual and erotic stimuli, would create shock waves. How widely his theories were known must not be overstated, but the *Studies in Hysteria* (*Studien über Hysterie*) – his joint publication with Breuer – were reviewed by Berger in the *Neue Freie Presse* on 2 December 1895. His work was well known at that time in medical circles through his lectures and papers on the sexual aetiology of hysteria and neuroses,[6] and as editor of the *Internationale klinische Rundschau* Schnitzler was particularly well abreast of developments in the theory and practice of psychological medicine. The reviews he himself contributed went far beyond his own specialist field: they extended to a range of works on nervous diseases and hysteria, including Freud's translation of lectures by Charcot, and from 1899 onwards works on hypnotism, including Freud's translation of Bernheim. He found his own experiments with hypnosis 'interesting' (Tgb., 28 March 1889), and in March and April 1889 the journal carried a four-part article of his on the use of hypnosis in the treatment of loss of speech.[7] In August of the same year he wrote the first of the *Anatol* playlets, *Die Frage an das Schicksal*, in which Anatol hypnotizes Cora but shirks putting to her the 'fateful' question he has intended about her fidelity (DW I, 36–40). It is a light-hearted example of Schnitzler's use in his dramatic work of his professional knowledge of work on the human mind.

Of Freud's books, two that made a particularly strong impact in arguing the importance of sexuality for understanding the development of the human mind were *The Interpretation of Dreams* and the *Three Essays on the Theory of Sexuality* (*Drei Abhandlungen zur Sexualtheorie*). In the latter, first published in 1905, the theory of infantile sexuality is developed;[8] here Freud also presents the argument that the original impulse behind the sexual drive is to serve not reproduction but what he would later call the 'pleasure principle'. In 1909 he added to the second edition of *The Interpretation of Dreams* his conclusion that 'the majority of the dreams of adults deal with sexual material and give expression to erotic wishes'.[9] In particular he returned repeatedly to the sexual aetiology of neuroses. Privately as early as 1892, and in print by 1895, he argued that anxiety neurosis derives from sexual disturbances.[10] This conviction led him into open criticism of prevailing moral codes, since he saw nearly all neuroses as resulting from the repression of unconscious ideas, especially sexual desires, in conflict with socially-determined conscious ideas.

In 1908 Freud published in a specialist journal his essay ' "Civilized" Sexual Morality and Modern Nervous Illness' ('Die "kulturelle" Sexualmoral und die moderne Nervosität'), in which he argued that modern civilization (that is, Western society, not just Vienna) is based on the suppression of instincts – an anticipation of the argument of the 1930 treatise *Civilization and its Discontents* (*Das Unbehagen in der Kultur*). Civilized society ('die Kultur') has an 'injurious influence' as a result of 'the suppression of the sexual life of civilized peoples (or classes) through the "civilized" sexual morality prevalent in them'; the requirements of conventional morality induce neuroses in the individual. How unworkable the system is shows both in 'the "double" sexual morality which is valid for men in our society' and also in women's susceptibility to neurosis.[11] Freud's strictures on the unsatisfactory character of marriage in this climate were taken further in 1912 in an essay 'On the Universal Tendency to Debasement in the Sphere of Love' ('Über die allgemeinste Erniedrigung des Liebeslebens'), again published in a specialist journal. Here he argues that conventional respect for virtue can be sexually inhibiting; it may even be 'impossible to adjust the claims of the sexual instinct to the demands of civilization'.[12]

Exploration of neuroses and hysteria was becoming inseparable from questions of sexual morality. Though Schnitzler steered discreetly past this minefield in his medical reviews, he was very quick to reflect changing perceptions in his dramatic writing. The increasingly critical treatments of sexual *mores* with which he made his name (*Anatol*, *Liebelei*, *Reigen*) all antedate Freud's major publications. His plays are a sensitive register of the conventions and habits of the *fin de siècle*, irresponsible conventions that were all about him and by which he himself lived in his early years.

When Mizi Glümer was in Wiesbaden in 1892, for example, he reflected:

> I can't bring her back and marry her. It's impossible for purely material reasons, and I also confess that I'm still too cowardly to live in Vienna with her as my wife. – There's no need for me to explain that further; it's all in *Das Märchen*. (Tgb., 20 September 1892)

His own way of life, as documented in his early diaries, exemplifies the hypocrisies of the 'double sexual morality', with its insouciant male privilege and sexist prejudice. The restless amorality of the leisured young men of the time is captured in a rather mannered diary note written in his mid-twenties: 'I'd like to have beside me now Mizi, now Adele – even a whore; just something different' (Tgb., 13 April 1889). A year later another note asks: 'Can a woman who has ever belonged to someone else make me happy?' (Tgb., 27 September 1890). It is a rhetorical question, and three years later the answer is still the same, as he reflects on the difference between male infidelity (as practised by himself) and female infidelity (which he had discovered in Mizi Glümer):

> How different female infidelity and male infidelity are. [Wie anders ist doch Weiber- und Männer-untreue.] Essentially it was the same thing, but I brushed that aside since I was the man and the stronger of us. She – and this I am still glad of – could not break free and has become a deceitful whore [eine verlogene Dirne], driven from one lie to the next! (Tgb., 3 April 1893)

That is, he concedes that his deception of Mizi Glümer was basically no different from her deception of him; he perceives indeed that there was 'a remarkable parallelism' ('ein wunderbarer Parallelismus': Tgb., 16 April 1893) between their actions. But he condemns her nevertheless as no better than 'a deceitful whore' and a 'born whore' ('eine geborene Hure': Tgb., 21 April 1893), while himself regarding his new lover a month later as an 'instrument de plaisir' (Tgb., 26 May 1893).

The only women Anatol encounters with whom a liaison would be dangerous are the married Gabriele (with whom there seems no prospect of an affair) in the episode *Weihnachtseinkäufe* and Else, his mistress in *Agonie*. To be caught in an affair with a married woman meant a duel, possibly death, as in *Liebelei* and again in *Das weite Land*. The appearance of the deceived husband towards the end of the first act of *Liebelei* and Fritz's acceptance of their duel, which casts a shadow of impending tragedy over the party atmosphere in his flat, can perhaps strike modern audiences merely as a melodramatic device for bringing the action to a close, but in fact it is entirely consistent with the realism of the play. For though in civil law duelling was illegal, it was still common in the first half of the 1890s among men of the wealthy and professional classes, who tended to be reserve officers and so were covered by what Schnitzler regarded as the 'foolish' ideas of the military code of honour (*Jug.*, 314). He himself was threatened with a duel in connection with one of his affairs in the mid-1880s (*Jug.*, 261). Beer-Hofmann is known to have duelled twice, in 1886 and 1890, and Hofmannsthal was involved as a second in 1894.[13] Of other members of their circle, Schnitzler recorded that shortly after the *Waidhofener Beschluß* disqualified Jews from duels by declaring them without honour, Bahr duelled about the question whether Jews were 'satisfaktionsfähig' (Tgb., 30 March 1896); later the same year he also recorded that Salten had been slightly wounded in a duel (Tgb., 29 May 1896).

Schnitzler confronted the issue squarely in *Freiwild*, his next play after *Liebelei*. A cavalry officer, Karinsky, refers disparagingly to an actress; Paul Rönning, a civilian, strikes him in the face. The second act opens with an extended argument about the consequences (DW I, 297–300). Paul, who, as Schnitzler spelt out to Brahm, represents general humane values against the prejudices of a minority class (AS/Brahm, 50: letter of 30 September 1896), has no intention of fighting the duel required of him by convention. His friends defend the code: a refusal would put him beyond the pale throughout civilized society ('in der ganzen gebildeten Welt'). Paul, however, stands his ground: he ridicules the 'obligation to let oneself get shot', and also declines to flee with Anna, the actress.

Karinsky confronts him again and shoots him dead: the 'fair game' of the title finally covers not just young actresses but the individual prepared to offer rational defiance to a barbaric code. As in *Liebelei*, Schnitzler had taken on a sensitive social issue; the play was so contentious that after it had been performed he was moved to note that he himself had no intention of responding to any challenge to a duel (Tgb., 16 September 1896). Three and a half years later, his failure to issue a challenge in response to the attack on him in the *Reichswehr* following the publication of *Leutnant Gustl* was one of the reasons explicitly given for his cashiering.[14]

The alternatives for women – being protected like property as a married woman, or being treated as 'fair game' for predatory sexual exploitation as a single woman – illustrate some of the background to the feminist movement which was rapidly gaining momentum in the 1890s. Most of the causes championed by the movement had barely changed since the 1840s, when the early feminists were arguing – against a phalanx of conservative opposition, both male and female – for improvements in education (to allow women the opportunity of equal development of the personality and to end the restriction of their lives to domesticity and dependence on their husbands); an end to the marriage of convenience; and the creation of wider career openings.[15] All these demands were still un-answered at the beginning of the 1890s. On 17 May 1890 in a letter to Schnitzler, Olga Waissnix defined marriage as the only career in which women were allowed to find happiness in life (AS/Waissnix, 205). Arranged marriages were still common. Moreover, for the less privileged classes the industrialization of the city had added further problems. Housing in the new outer suburbs was cramped and squalid; at work women were exploited in factories that pro-vided sweat-shop working conditions and wretchedly low wages.

The 1890s brought a series of significant developments. The main thrust of campaigning was for equal political and social rights, better education, reform of the conventions of marriage, and im-provement in working conditions. The reduction of the franchise in 1888 (the right to vote in provincial elections was actually removed from women who had hitherto qualified by professional standing and the possession of property) led to political agitation, in par-ticular for the repeal of the so-called 'Paragraph 30' of the 1867 constitution, which barred women from membership of political organizations. In 1893 the principal organization of the bourgeois women's movement, the *Allgemeiner österreichischer Frauenverein*, was founded; its monthly, the *Dokumente der Frauen*, was launched – just before *Die Fackel* – in March 1899. The causes for which

the bourgeois movement campaigned, over and above enfran-
chisement, women's education, and opportunities in trades and
professions, included legal rights and pacifism (Bertha von Suttner's
Die Waffen nieder!, which had appeared in 1889, reached its thirtieth
printing by 1910). In education, the first grammar school for girls
in Vienna (*Mädchengymnasium*) was opened in 1892; in 1897 women
were admitted to full student membership of the Philosophical
Faculty of the university. Within the same period, the principal
organ of the 'proletarian' (Social Democrat) women's movement,
the *Arbeiterinnen-Zeitung*, was launched in 1892, edited by Adelheid
Popp, who would lead the first strike of women workers in
Vienna, in support of a claim for higher wages and a reduction of
the working day, in 1893.

Sexual freedom was not a major feminist issue. But in a culture
dominated by men, the breaking of the conventional conspiracy of
silence about female sexuality stimulated both artistic production
and intense intellectual interest. Whether enticing or dangerous, it
held the fascination of mystery. Orthodox scientific opinion tended
either to be dominated by the strict conservatism represented in
Krafft-Ebing's *Psychopathia sexualis*, first published in 1886 and
much reprinted,[16] or simply to measure the psychology of women
against male norms – an attitude that attracted Kraus's sarcasm in
1907: 'The division of the human race into two sexes has not yet
been recognized by science' (F 229, 13). Even Freud would argue in
the first of the *Three Essays on Sexuality* that the erotic life of
women, 'partly owing to the stunting effect of civilized conditions
and partly owing to their conventional secretiveness and insincerity',
was veiled in a 'still more impenetrable obscurity' than that of
men.[17] And as late as 1926, in his essay 'The Question of Lay
Analysis' ('Die Frage der Laienanalyse'), he repeated the point in his
much-quoted admission that 'the sexual life of adult women is a
"dark continent" for psychology'.[18]

In the visual arts, the mystery of this irrational force provided
Gustav Klimt with his most powerful inspiration. Kraus attacked
Klimt as derivative, characterizing his portraiture of women as
transposing the art of Fernand Khnopff onto Viennese subjects:
'Whether they are called Judith or Hygieia [an allusion to the
principal figure in 'Medicine', one of Klimt's allegorical university
paintings], Frau X or Frau Y', he wrote in 1901 (F 73, 10), 'all his
figures have the pallor of women who are professionally misunderstood, and round their darkly glowing eyes Herr Klimt has painted
unmistakable shadows in rings, or let us rather say *Schottenringe*'
('unverkennbare Schattenringe oder sagen wir lieber gleich
Schottenringe') – an allusion to the stretch of the Ringstrasse con-

taining the Stock Exchange, and so suggesting the wealthy women of the *haute bourgeoisie* who provided Klimt with his customers (and the psychologists with some of their patients).[19] In Kraus's view, Klimt's work represented the hollow decorative 'ornament' that he and Loos opposed. But the 'decorative' element in his oils is deliberate and significant. Totally lacking in the spare lines of his drawings, it has a symbolic or allegorical function; knowingly double-edged, his depiction of female figures captures central tensions of the time.

Klimt's most celebrated theme was that of the embrace. Even in the apparently romantic treatment in the early (pre-Secession) oil 'Love' ('Liebe') of 1895,[20] the figures are surmounted by figures symbolizing transience and so suggesting the fragility of happiness. 'Even when we are children', wrote Olga Waissnix in 1890, 'all our natural feelings are stifled; propriety, etiquette, and reputation are the bogeys always used to frighten us. Everything about us is costume' ('[. . .] Alles ist an uns Toilette': AS/Waissnix, 205). Or again, Zweig's memoirs recall how the conventional restrictions on young women were supported by the elaborate and corseted fashions of the time.[21] It is this restrictiveness of social 'costume' that Klimt captures in the portraits he painted in the years immediately after the scandal of the university paintings: portraits of women in decorative clothes that almost merge into an ornately decorative background, from which their eyes look soulfully out. The most striking examples are the well-known portraits 'Fritza Riedler' (1906) and especially 'Adele Bloch-Bauer I' (1907), both of which hang in the Österreichische Galerie in the upper Belvedere palace; the 'decorativeness' serves to suggest emotional imprisonment in an environment of material opulence. Only shortly after Freud's most important discoveries and Schnitzler's dramatic explorations of the relations between the sexes, Klimt evoked in a series of paintings the release of instinctual drives hitherto not acknowledged in woman – making his effect so startlingly, indeed, that in 1905 Berta Zuckerkandl speculated that if ever he were ennobled he would take the title 'Klimt von Frauentrieb' (*Marb.*, 392). In a succession of paintings he presented woman as ecstatic and voluptuous – from 'Moving Water' ('Bewegtes Wasser', 1898) and 'Medicine' (1901), the latter destroyed by fire in 1945, to the highly sensual 'Danae' of 1907–8 in which he reworked a common theme of the art of the 1890s,[22] that of fulfilment brought by a Zeus transformed into a shower of gold.

The threatening power of female sexuality – again, a theme throughout European art and literature at the time – is most fully evoked by Klimt in 'Judith I' (1901), depicting Judith in ecstatic satiation after the symbolically sinister beheading of Holofernes.[23] There is even more aggressive menace in the tense and predatory 'Judith II' (1909). The sense of threat links with a strong current of anti-feminism at the turn of the century, which in Vienna found its most influential expression in Otto Weininger's treatise *Geschlecht und Charakter* (1903). This farrago, anti-Semitic as well as misogynist, was very widely read (it went through eleven printings in six years, seventeen in all by 1918). In it Weininger presents the male principle in humanity as rational and creative, the female principle as irrational and amoral, claiming that woman's strongest need is for sex, denying the possibility of a woman genius, and deriding the movement for emancipation as unfeminine.[24] Echoes, albeit in no way misogynist, are to be found in Karl Kraus's insistence in the years 1906–11 on the essential sensuality ('Sinnlichkeit') of woman,[25] but Kraus also argued that that sensuality was being subjugated to a hypocritical moral code ('Sittlichkeit'). He attacked the double standards which made it impermissible to marry a woman who had had an affair but entirely desirable to have an affair with a woman who was married (F 229, 11) and which behind a 'mask' of moral righteousness persecuted adultery and prostitution while condoning marriage for money and turning the unloved wife into 'something between a work-horse and a sex object' (F 115, 23).

There is no misogyny in Schnitzler – nor indeed in Hofmannsthal, though *Elektra* conveys the sense of female sexuality as a dangerous force. But their very different approaches to presenting relations between the sexes, especially in their comedies, reveal some of the fundamental contrasts in their work as dramatists.

It would be much too simple to say that these contrasts simply reflect the different life experiences of the promiscuous Schnitzler and the monogamous Hofmannsthal. Rather, they lie in the different artistic intentions of the two dramatists – in particular the extent to which each is willing to shape the world recreated in his dramatic fiction to a specific moral view. 'To me', Hofmannsthal wrote to Burckhardt on 10 September 1926, 'marriage is something exalted, truly *the* sacrament – I would not like to imagine life without marriage. (Everything I think about it is said in my comedies, often in a deliberately disguised, almost frivolous way)' (H/Burckhardt, 226). That is, within the constraints of comic convention, his comedies express an unshaking conception of human relations, with marriage a supreme ('sacramental') bulwark. He uses the union of lovers, the traditional ending of comedy, to impose a moral framework, a reaffirmation of moral order.

'Marriage is good' ('Gut ist die Ehe') is the 'truth' Cristina affirms (L I, 240); abandoned by Florindo, she marries the Captain, 'in the name of God' ('in Gottes Namen'), her catchphrase. The final tableau of *Der Schwierige* is a celebration of the engagement of Hans Karl and Helene. In *Der Unbestechliche* Jaromir's attempts at infidelity are thwarted, his marriage to Anna safeguarded; Arabella finds the 'right man' in Mandryka and they commit themselves to lasting devotion (HKA XXVI, 69).

Schnitzler imposes no such moral pattern. Rather, his treatment of women in his plays shows a keen understanding of the realities of life in his times – not the practical problems of the working woman (that is the subject of the novel *Therese*) but the problems with which relations between the sexes were fraught. The unusual sympathy which informed his view of women and their problems was recognized in literary circles by the mid-1890s. It is recorded in a letter written by Lou Andreas-Salomé on 15 May 1894, after she had read *Das Märchen*,[26] and two years later by the young Hofmannsthal, who referred rather airily to Schnitzler's 'often-discussed overestimation of female personalities' (H/AS, 73: letter of 21 August 1896). From 1899 onwards at the latest, Schnitzler was quite frequently invited to speak to women's organizations in Vienna,[27] and he had regular contacts with figures associated with the Women's Movement.[28]

In his plays he repeatedly treats male characters who lack any capacity for fidelity, from Anatol, who on his own wedding morning shocks even Max by having to get rid of another woman with whom he has spent the night (*Anatols Hochzeitsmorgen*: DW I, 91), to Max von Reisenberg in *Komödie der Verführung*, who, as the young singer Judith Asrael says, 'would never be capable of sacrificing anything to a woman, no kind of happiness, not even a passing pleasure that beckoned elsewhere' ('[. . .] kein Glück, ach, nicht einmal ein Vergnügen, das Ihnen von wo anders her winkte': DW II, 909). The victims of this moral shiftlessness are the women characters – the single women betrayed, from Christine in *Liebelei* onwards, and the married women discontented in their marriages, from the elegant Gabriele in *Anatol*, with her sense of unfulfilment and secret envy of the *süßes Mädl* in the suburbs, to Genia in *Das weite Land*. One of Schnitzler's great dramatic gifts lies in his ability, within the conventions of comedy or tragicomedy, to individualize his female characters, allowing for their many-sidedness.

There is a revealing passage in *Das weite Land* – a speech omitted altogether in Stoppard's adaptation – where Friedrich Hofreiter pontificates about women:

I think it's always terribly one-sided to judge women only on their erotic effect [die Frauen nur aufs Erotische hin zu beurteilen]. We keep forgetting that in the life of every woman, even if she has lovers, there are a lot of times when she has to think of quite other things than love. She will read books, she will make music, she will organize shows for charity, she will cook, she will bring up her children – she may even be a very good mother, some-times even an excellent wife. And a hundred times more valu-able than a so-called 'respectable' woman [als eine sogenannte anständige Frau]. (DW II, 302)

The passage has a comic effect, arising not only from the irony of the situation (in his show of broad-mindedness Hofreiter is actually thinking of his own deception of his wife) but also from the shallowness of what he says: the 'other things' he can think of as a woman's tasks are still restricted to the traditional domestic sphere and the leisure activities of the well-to-do. Above all, his image of women still reduces them to functions rather than to autonomous individuals. It is a devastating exposure of male complacency.

Again and again, women in Schnitzler's works are portrayed as being deprived of the understanding they need. It is one of the main subjects of his late fiction, a theme in both *Fräulein Else* and *Therese*. Examples in his plays include notably Margarete in the one-act comedy *Literatur*, whose literary pretensions seem to have grown out of her frustration with a family not one of whom has under-stood that she could want more that 'a husband and fine clothes and a social position' (DW I, 740).

Examples such as these underlie one of the most remarkable of the articles on Schnitzler that appeared after his death in 1931 – a serious and very positive assessment by Klara Blum, praising him as a 'pioneer of equal rights'. Entitled 'Artur Schnitzler, ein Pionier des Frauenrechtes', it appeared in the Social Democrat *Arbeiter-Zeitung* on 2 November, presenting his writings as a cumulative exposé of the corruption of the old, capitalist, feudal Austria, and arguing that among the injustices he exposed were the repression and devaluation of women, whose equal rights (in society, at work, and in love) he presented as beyond question:

Schnitzler's crucial achievement was that he exposed the mon-strous injustice of the old society, above all towards women. No one else understood women as he did – women as the classic objects of that silent and courteous repression and devaluation that is typical of middle-class life. No one else sympathized so deeply and subtly with their revolt against their own subordinate, dependent and secondary role in life [. . .]

Women's claim to equal rights in society, in work and in love was something that Schnitzler took completely for granted. But it is still not taken for granted generally; and for that reason we may regard Schnitzler not as the representative of times past but rather as a pioneer, the *patient pioneer of an idea*, whose struggle is still in the forefront of attention, still in the spotlight: a pioneer of the *idea of equality in the erotic sphere*.

Schnitzler's Dramatization of Dalliance: Anatol, Liebelei, *and* Reigen

Women's rights have no place in the *Anatol* cycle. Anatol is a wealthy philanderer. When he speaks to his friend Max in *Die Frage an das Schicksal* about the compulsive infidelity of women and men alike (DW I, 31–2) he is defining the guiding principle of his perceptions: relations between the sexes are inevitably limited to the 'moment' of feeling. Both this way of thinking and its consequence, a life of trivially episodic character, are reflected in the loose structure of the work, which is made up of a series of one-act playlets featuring the successive women with whom he conducts his liaisons. These are punctuated by reflective dialogues with the bonhomous Max, in which his affairs and his character are discussed.

What Anatol sees in each young woman in his life is not so much the individual herself as a figure elaborated by his own imagination, in an atmosphere sentimentally cherished. Hofmannsthal detected this imaginative element in Anatol's character, and in a draft review which he decided not to publish but sent to Schnitzler on 23 December 1892 (H/AS, 32–3) he described him as being in his sentimental dandyism a 'Viennese poet', whose life is lovingly arranged in nostalgic longing for lost pleasures.[29] In the discarded final scene *Anatols Größenwahn* a friend remarks that to hear him speak one would think he had loved quite different women from ordinary men (DW I, 112); he replies that he has indeed, since it is he who has loved them ('Gewiß . . . denn ich war es, der sie liebte!'). Others look for a *cocotte* in every woman, he has looked in every *cocotte* for a woman ('[. . .] ich hab in jeder Kokotte das Weib gesucht!'), that is, an archetypal construct of his own wishful thinking.

The nature of his affairs is encapsulated in the programmatically entitled scene *Episode* (one of the titles alluded to in Hofmannsthal's verse prologue), where Anatol hands over to Max his mementos of his past loves. Each bears an inscription but not a name, 'for after all, any of them could be called Marie or Anna' (DW I, 52) – another illustration of the way he looks beyond the individual women to an imagined type, denying them any real individuality. His affairs are seen and discussed almost entirely from a male view-point; the women, other than the wistful but virtuous Gabriele, are essentially interchangeable to him, playing bit-parts in the comic ups and downs of his erotic career.

Yet Anatol is a brooder miscast as a Casanova. The promiscuity on which his life centres is both motivated and complicated by hypochondriac introspection. The uncomplicated Max has no illusions about romance, and reminds Anatol in *Agonie* that a love affair often ends 'earlier than we realize: many a happiness has already begun to die with the very first kiss' ('[. . .] Es gibt manches Glück, das mit dem ersten Kuß zu sterben begann': DW I, 82) – an anticipation of the idea of transience hanging over Klimt's oil 'Liebe' painted five years later. Anatol, by contrast, is constantly worried about the faithfulness or faithlessness of his various loves. The whole of the Cora episode (*Die Frage an das Schicksal*) illustrates how he clings to his illusions, fighting shy of learning the truth. He depends on sentimental atmosphere: as Max tells him, in order to feel that he understands the mystery of womankind he needs semi-darkness and the green and red light in his flat, he needs to be playing the piano (DW I, 57). That he has kept the mementos of his past which he parades in *Episode* is typical of what in another scene, *Agonie*, Max calls the 'jumble' of past, present, and future in which his mind functions ('dieser Wirrwarr von Einst und Jetzt und Später': DW I, 83). Years after a love is over he can still get jealous at some slight infidelity long ago, as he does in *Anatols Größenwahn* (DW I, 119–20). Blurring the passing of time is characteristic of his sentimental inability to face squarely up to reality – part of the imaginatively 'poetic arrangement' of his perceptions appreciated by Hofmannsthal. But as he tells Max, Anatol has always been a 'hypochondriac of love' ('ein Hypochonder der Liebe': DW I, 82); to Gabriele he describes himself as a 'frivolous melancholic' ('Leichtsinniger Melancholiker': DW I, 46). The self-ironizing descriptions are apt, and that they are formulated by Anatol himself is revealing of his deep self-absorption.

Peter Skrine defines the formal effect of the cycle as 'an original fusion of revue and monodrama'.[30] Certainly its idiom is that of light comedy; it is, indeed, precisely as an example of light comedy that Athene Seyler and Stephen Haggard approach it in their correspondence on the 'craft' of comic acting.[31] The genre determines the sketchiness with which the various women are drawn, lively

though each of them is. But it also affords a critical distance, largely
achieved through the contrast in attitudes in Anatol's exchanges
with Max, which allows us to see the self-centredness of the principal character and the hollowness of his way of life.

In *Liebelei* there is a shift both in genre and in perspective: a move
from episodic comedy towards serious drama coincides with a
shifting of emphasis away from the male viewpoint of the reflective
Anatol and the ironic Max to the emotional experience of a central
female figure. The play deals with an affair that gets out of hand.
By convention, relations between well-to-do young men and girls
from the poorer classes in the outer suburbs could never be more
than passing affairs. The convention was of long standing: half a
century earlier it had formed the basis of Nestroy's comedy *Das
Mädl aus der Vorstadt* (1841). Christine is the daughter of a musician
in the Theater in der Josefstadt – not well-off, but from a cultured
home, with Schiller on the shelves and a bust of Schubert on the
stove. She brings to her affair with Fritz Lobheimer all the romantic
idealism such influences may suggest,[32] and falls seriously in love
with him. Fritz, who lives in an elegant flat in the Strohgasse (not
in the old city centre but just outside it, round the corner from the
house where Hofmannsthal was born), fends off her attempt to
speak of her feelings. She has to pretend that she knows the social
rules and that she knows the affair 'is not for ever' (DW I, 225), but
in fact she has never accepted the limitation placed by social convention on her affection.

The conventional norm is represented in the play in two other
relationships. Christine's friend Mizi, who has worked as a dress-
maker, is having an affair with Fritz's friend Theodor. Both clearly
understand the temporary nature of their affair. In the light-hearted
mood of the first act – an act which, as Ferry Bératon observed in
his review of the première,[33] still seems closely related to the *Anatol*
playlets – Theodor spells out the ground rules to Fritz:

> THEODOR. [. . .] Du mußt dein Glück suchen, wo ich es bisher
> gesucht und gefunden habe, dort, wo es keine großen Szenen,
> keine Gefahren, keine tragischen Verwicklungen gibt, wo der
> Beginn keine besonderen Schwierigkeiten und das Ende keine
> Qualen hat, wo man lächelnd den ersten Kuß empfängt und mit
> sehr sanfter Rührung scheidet.
>
> (DW I, 219)

> THEODOR. [. . .] You must look for happiness where I have
> always looked for it, and found it too: where there are no grand
> scenes, no risks, no tragic complications, where there is no par-

ticular difficulty about starting and no pain in bringing it to an end, where the first kiss comes with a smile and you can part with gentle affection.

Mizi, who has a hard-headed understanding of what she can expect to get out of any affair, defines the rules just as clearly to Christine, warning her that girls of their kind are always going to be left in the lurch sooner or later (DW I, 256).

The other female figure with whom Christine is contrasted is a married neighbour, Katharina Binder, who stands as a monitory example of what will be in store for Christine if, like herself, she settles for the orthodox married life of the poorer classes. In just that way, we learn in *Episode,* the Cora of *Die Frage an das Schicksal* has eventually married a master carpenter. 'They find love in the city centre and get married in the suburbs', Anatol says ('In der Stadt werden sie geliebt und in der Vorstadt geheiratet': DW I, 54). Frau Binder, who thinks Mizi is a bad influence on a 'decent girl' (DW I, 241), has married a worker in a hosiery factory and has a nine-year-old daughter, and encourages Christine to marry a cousin of her own husband. The issue is fought out in an argument in Act Two (DW I, 243–4) between herself and Christine's father, who sees the conformist solution offered by Frau Binder as dismally unattractive and defends the right of youth to have its fling. Frau Binder says that a girl 'can't just wait for some Count to come along, and even if one does come along, he usually says goodbye again without having married her'. To which Weiring responds, with a rare flash of malice, by denigrating the alternative re-presented by her own humdrum existence: 'Und was hat denn so ein armes Geschöpf schließlich von ihrer ganzen Bravheit, wenn schon – nach jahrelangem Warten – richtig der Strumpfwirker kommt!' ('And what does a poor girl get in the end from being good, even if – after years of waiting – she finds her hosiery-worker!').

Clearly many real-life affairs depended on the connivance of indulgent fathers like Weiring; indeed, just two days after the première of *Liebelei* in the Burgtheater, Schnitzler noted in his diary that Mizi Reinhard's father was an 'unwitting Weiring' (Tgb., 11 October 1895). But in the play, events confirm that his position is irresponsible. Bératon summed him up in his review as offering a 'sentimental' moral lesson: 'misbehave so that at least you will have something to remember for the rest of your life'.

How deeply Fritz feels for Christine is uncertain. Peter Skrine argues that in Act Two, when he already knows that he is going to risk his life in a duel, Fritz experiences a moment of supreme fulfilment in his enjoyment of her presence;[34] there are perhaps after all, Fritz says (half to himself), 'moments that radiate an aura of eternity' ('Augenblicke, die einen Duft von Ewigkeit um sich sprühen': DW I, 252). But still, it is an enjoyment of the moment – an aesthetic experience, not a moral commitment – and it is for another woman that he is going to die.

In the last act, furthermore, the focus shifts entirely to the consequences for Christine of his behaviour. Her father has nothing better to offer than advice that she should forget Fritz. But when the warnings she has heard from the voices of realism (both from the knowingly flirtatious Mizi and from the respectable Katharina Binder) prove all too accurate, the thought that she has meant to Fritz nothing more than a 'pastime' is more than she can bear and she abandons all pretence at concealing the strength of her love:

> THEODOR (*bewegt*). Er hat Sie gewiß lieb gehabt.
> CHRISTINE. Lieb! – Er? – Ich bin ihm nichts gewesen als ein Zeitvertreib – und für eine andere ist er gestorben – ! Und ich – hab' ihn angebetet! – Hat er denn das nicht gewußt? . . . Daß ich ihm alles gegeben hab', was ich ihm hab' geben können, daß ich für ihn gestorben wär' – daß er mein Herrgott gewesen ist und meine Seligkeit [. . .]
>
> (DW I, 262)
>
> THEODOR (*moved*). I'm sure he was fond of you.
> CHRISTINE. Fond! Him? – I was nothing more to him than a pastime – and he has died for another woman! But I – I worshipped him! Didn't he even know that? Didn't he know that I gave him everything I had to give, that I would have died for him – that he was my God and my salvation?

Schnitzler first conceived the play as a *Volksstück*,[35] meaning by that term a play using dialect and presenting a realistic treatment of life among the poorer classes. The term also inevitably evokes suggestions of a link with the tradition of dialect drama in Vienna. In particular, Schnitzler knew *Das Mädl aus der Vorstadt*. The first *süßes Mädl* he himself encountered[36] is referred to in his diary with an allusion to Nestroy's title ('dieses "Mädel aus der Vorstadt"': Tgb., 27–28 November 1881), and his diary records that he saw the Nestroy play both on 19 January 1890 and again on 24 July 1891, when he saw Mizi Glümer playing in it in Baden, some twenty kilometers south-west of Vienna.[37] Just three months after that he first jotted down his plan for what would eventually become *Liebelei* (he did not settle on the final title until 9 September 1894). The only early review that followed up the link with Viennese popular drama was one by Berger, distinguishing it on

— Du, du fitzt der Arthur Schnitzler, der berühmte Dichter der „Liebelei".
— Kunftftück! Der hat uns einfach abg'fchrieben.

8   Cartoon by Theodor
Zasche, *Figaro*, 23 April 1896.

the grounds of its lack of sentimentality from the popular drama of
the generation after Nestroy. This review appeared on 14 October
1895 in the *Neue Revue* (*Montags-Revue*); three days later, writing to
Hofmannsthal about the reception of the play, Schnitzler picked out
Berger's 'shrewd review' ('die gescheite Kritik') for special praise
(H/AS, 63: letter of 17 October 1895).

Wengraf's review in the *Arbeiter-Zeitung* on 11 October 1895,
true to the paper's political line, argued that the action centres too
much on the leisured classes to achieve the kind of accurate fidelity
to everyday experience that might be looked for in full-blooded
realism, and cast doubt on the authenticity both of the characterization and of the language. Several critics, including Jacob Julius
David, accused Schnitzler of creating a Viennese equivalent of
Parisian ways.[38] There was, on the other hand, also a good deal
of testimony for his success in capturing a recognizable Viennese
reality. This is implicit, for example, in a cartoon by Theodor
Zasche that appeared in one of the Viennese magazines, *Figaro,* on
23 April 1896 (figure 8). It shows two young women standing
outside the Café Griensteidl and looking in through the windows.
'Look,' says one, 'there's Arthur Schnitzler, the famous author of

Liebelei.' 'Nothing to it,' replies the other, 'he just drew copies of us'.

Zasche, a well-known illustrator, knew Schnitzler personally. But any implication that there was 'nothing to it' did scant justice to Schnitzler's technique. The deceptive quality in it is his skill in preserving, in a work moving away from a predominantly comic mode, a graceful lightness in the dialogue. This lightness of touch is wr t gained him the high esteem he would be held in by French critics, one of whom would later describe him as a 'Viennese Parisian' ('quelle grâce captivante, quel charme exquis et léger!').[39] But *Liebelei* is in fact a work of powerful momentum, moving from the predominantly carefree banter of the opening scene to an emotional climax of tragic intensity. Many of the early reviews concentrated on the significance of the première in the development of the Burgtheater, an illustration of the new modernism taking root there, but Max Kalbeck, reviewing it in the *Neues Wiener Tagblatt* on 11 October 1895, was one critic who particularly praised the final act as 'veering decisively towards tragedy'. Schnitzler would indeed never write a more powerful play.

A recent commentator has written that 'a masterpiece such as Schnitzler's *Liebelei* [. . .] is not so very far removed from the world of Ibsen'.[40] The praise is appropriate because of the emotional intensity achieved in treating, in an explicitly Viennese setting, a social problem of real substance and currency – the first Viennese drama to achieve that combination since Anzengruber's *Das vierte Gebot* (1877), which was never performed in the Burgtheater. The production of *Liebelei* was a brave venture. From Schnitzler's diary we know that, having accepted the play in January 1895, Burckhard admitted five months later that when it was produced it would be seen as 'dangerous' (Tgb., 16 June 1895); and indeed, according to a later entry, not only the Emperor but even the supposedly modern Mitterwurzer, a celebrated actor in Ibsen, pronounced it immoral (Tgb., 5 September 1896).

Still more dangerous, of course, was *Reigen*. No sooner had Schnitzler finished writing it than he wrote to Olga Waissnix that it was 'completely unprintable' (AS/Waissnix, 317: letter of 26 February 1897). To the private printing of 1900 he appended a prefatory note repeating that its content precluded publication in the current climate of opinion;[41] and when he did risk publication three years later, the reaction of Hofmannsthal and Beer-Hofmann – they sent him a joint letter on 15 February 1903 beginning 'Dear Pornographer' ('Lieber Pornograph': H/AS, 167) – was a joking portent of the scandals to follow.[42] Even after the war, when it was finally staged in Vienna, more attention was given to the scandal the production caused than to the play itself – though at least Mell, whose reviewing Schnitzler generally disliked, provided readers of the *Wiener Mittag* (3 February 1921) with a sober appraisal of the production and a positive assessment of the artistic qualities of the play itself. Mell argued that no area of human experience was closed to art, provided always that the material drawn from life was artistically mastered, and that in Schnitzler's 'erotic dialogues' precisely this mastery had been achieved.[43] But in his concern with technical details (such as the best way to deal with the dashes that appear in the text as each encounter reaches its predetermined climax – a problem still not definitively solved) and in his emphatic rehearsal of the point that the play was not indecent, Mell failed to define just what its intention was.

That that intention still needs to be defined is clear when we read the remark of a modern commentator to the effect that *Reigen* is tame beside Hofmannsthal's *Elektra*,[44] a phrasing which wholly misses the point that its intention is to function as a sexual *comedy*. Schnitzler has backed away from the exploration of emotional consequences that he had attempted in *Liebelei,* backed away from concentrating on the viewpoint of the female victim. The sexes are given equal weight and presented with equal irony as the figures, all reduced to types, manoeuvre their calculating way, partner by partner, through the round dance of sex.

The image of the 'round dance', a variation on a familiar topos in the visual arts of the period,[45] serves to suggest a ritual quality in their affairs. Schnitzler fashions a sexual morality without a moral, presenting in dialogue form – the whole art of the play lies in the language – a recurrent pattern of resistance, persuasion, and seduction. The outcome of each encounter is known in advance, to the participants as also to the audience. That the circle begins and ends with the prostitute provides a resonant framework for the central scenes (scenes 4–6) which deal with the infidelities of the young wife and her husband. And just as in *Anatols Hochzeitsmorgen* Anatol's marriage is only seemingly an ending in the eyes of Ilona (the girl he is *not* marrying), so here the transitory nature of each infidelity underlines the sense, implicit in the structure, that the whole cycle will begin again, an eternal recurrence. Its progression is generated not by the physical consummation but by the emotional failure of each encounter.

Interpretations of *Reigen* differ widely. There are those that stress its relation to the specific society of *fin-de-siècle* Vienna, reading into it a satirical or moralistic purpose. Others argue that the stylization of the action suggests its universality: in the subordination of all other motives to the libido, lust is the great leveller, like Death in the medieval dance of death.[46] What is at issue in this debate is the whole temper of the work.

That *Reigen* – just as much as *Anatol* and *Liebelei* – mirrors Schnitzler's own times is not in doubt. He himself told Olga Waissnix that if it were dug up in a few hundred years it would cast light on one part of contemporary civilization (it was 'eine Scenenreihe, die [. . .], nach ein paar hundert Jahren ausgegraben, einen Theil unsrer Cultur eigentümlich beleuchten würde': AS/ Waissnix, 317: letter of 26 February 1897). In particular scenes 4–6 rehearse the hypocrisies of the 'double morality'.

Thus as we watch the young wife gradually peeling off her veils in the fourth scene (DW I, 337–9), we see enacted a stripping-away of the veneer of conventional respectability, a graphic illustration of the discrepancy between social convention and the reality of psychological motivation. In the impotence suffered by the young gentleman because, as he says, he 'obviously loves her too much' (DW I, 343), we see a comic example of the 'psychical impotence' later explored by Freud as an effect of conventional adulation of womanly virtue.[47] What the young man feels at the end of the scene is not affection but wondering self-congratulation at his con- quest of a 'respectable' woman ('Also jetzt hab ich ein Verhältnis mit einer anständigen Frau': DW I, 347) – an irony all the greater in that it is she who has seduced him, in an operation so carefully calculated that she has even thought to bring her own button-hook for when they have to get dressed again (DW II, 346). In the next scene we hear her husband strictly spelling out to her the conven- tional expectation of ideal wifely virtue in contrast to the fallen women and *femmes fatales* who have put themselves beyond the pale of respectability (DW I, 349–52); she still has her memories of her own infidelity ('offenbar fällt es sich ganz angenehm') and shocks him by referring to the 'pleasure' the 'fallen women' enjoy. But his own definition of marriage as a series of love-affairs (DW I, 348) amounts not to the love she is looking for but in effect to an institutionalizing of inconstancy, a denial of coherent moral identity in the reduction of life to 'episodes'. His hypocrisy is compounded in the sixth scene when the *süßes Mädel* whom he is seducing says his wife will be behaving just as he is: he reacts with outrage (DW I, 362), when he has denied even having a wife.

The whole sequence presents a succession of dramatic ironies. Of course the affairs enacted, sordid and comic at once, carry wider overtones. The amorality of Schnitzler's Vienna was, after all, symptomatic of the general disintegration of values typical of the period; the emotional emptiness of his figures as they search vainly

for companionship is part of that precarious isolation of the individual which is characteristic of a whole generation. The identity crisis
of the *fin de siècle* has a correlative in the tendency of the characters
either not to know their partners' names, as in the first two scenes
(DW I, 329), or to go through their scenes without ever speaking
names, as in the two scenes with the *süßes Mädel*.

Schnitzler succeeds in conveying such overtones, and also the
satirical implications of the play, in comedy that is again built up of
dialogue of the utmost lightness. This was appreciated by the more
perceptive critics of the earliest productions. It is, perhaps, implicit
in Mell's review where he speaks of Schnitzler's artistic mastery as
lying in his having 'dematerialized' his subject matter, positioning it
'beyond good and evil'. Certainly the point was addressed a few
weeks earlier by Herbert Ihering, reviewing the première in the
Kleines Schauspielhaus (Berlin) in the *Berliner Börsen-Courier* on
24 December 1920. *Reigen,* he wrote, reflected the contradictory
character of Vienna itself, at once seductive and corrupt. It was not,
however, a problem-play but essentially 'unproblematical': in contrast to the self-consciousness of *Anatol*, it achieved a distinctive playfulness, 'sheer lightness' ('*Reigen* aber ist das Spiel, die
Leichtigkeit selbst': TR, 281).

The special flavour of *Reigen*, however, derives from the fact that
despite its stylized construction, the 'lightness' of mood and of
language, it is firmly rooted in Viennese reality. This is achieved
not just by the use of dialect, carefully graduated: the linguistic
placing of the action up and down the social scale is enforced by a
physical placing of the action in the city. This is, indeed, done
with far more circumstantial detail than in *Anatol* or *Liebelei*.
Anatol stages his 'farewell supper' with Annie in a private room at
Sacher's, behind the Opera House, and in *Weihnachtseinkäufe*
Gabriele guesses that Anatol's *süßes Mädl* may be in Hernals, a
predominantly working-class suburb (DW I, 44), but the scene
itself is set no more precisely than 'on the streets of Vienna'.

In *Reigen*, by contrast, the action moves quite specifically from
district to district. We do not see the young prostitute's shabby room
until the final (tenth) scene, when she claims – pretends, perhaps –
to the Count that she is planning to move to the Spiegelgasse, in
the city centre (DW I, 388). But her patch is quite explicit, and it is
not there. The first scene, where she meets the soldier, is set beside
the Augartenbrücke over the Danube Canal, not far from the
northern end of the Schottenring; it emerges that she has worked
from the Schiffgasse on the less salubrious eastern side of the canal.
He has to go back to barracks, that is, to the nearby Rossauerkaserne
on the other side of the canal in the ninth district, but in the next

scene he is back in the second district, dancing at a specific café in the Prater (Swoboda: DW I, 328), leaving the maidservant to find her own way back to the ninth distict, where she works in the Porzellangasse. Because of its proximity to the university and the main hospital (Allgemeines Krankenhaus), the ninth district had a high proportion of physicians and academics in its population; the Porzellangasse intersects the lower end of the Berggasse, where Freud practised.

It is in the Porzellangasse that the third scene is set, and the social rise continues in the fourth scene, where we have moved to the other side of the city, to the Schwindgasse, a typically solid middle-class or professional address not far from the Karlsplatz and the Schwarzenbergplatz. The husband seduces the *süßes Mädel* in a private room in the Riedhof, a discreet up-market restaurant between the Wickenburggasse and the Schlösselgasse, not far from the Allgemeines Krankenhaus; it was one of Schnitzler's own regular haunts. She has first noticed him in the Singerstrasse, in the city centre, but her own background is similar to Christine's in *Liebelei*: she lives with her mother in the Josefstadt, has a brother who is a hairdresser, an elder sister who works in a flower-shop, and a younger sister who goes for walks with a boyfriend in the Strozzigasse, a stone's throw from the Theater in der Josefstadt. The poet has taken her on an excursion to Weidling am Bach, in the Vienna Woods, a few kilometers north-west of the city. Back in his rooms, she tells him she has been to the Opera House to see *Cavalleria rusticana* (still a novelty in the 1890s: it had first been sung there in 1891 and was performed several times a year) but that she does not get tickets for the Burgtheater (DW I, 368) – another social marker, as is the Count's reminiscence in the final scene that his evening has begun with a friend in Sacher's (DW I, 386).

One effect of all this detail, allied to the vivid authenticity of the dialogue throughout, is that each vignette has a striking immediacy, a distinctive purchase on reality. Schnitzler's own awareness of this may lie behind what he wrote to Brahm on 1 October 1905, in reply to Brahm's doubts about the final act of *Der Ruf des Lebens*: he had a deep affinity for the cycle of one-act plays as a form ('Der Einakterzyklus sitzt tief in meinem Wesen'), and if Brahm looked closely at his plays he would discover that many of the acts were in fact complete and rounded ('vorzüglich in sich geschlossene Stücke') in a way that none of his longer plays were (AS/Brahm, 172). That is phrased self-deprecatingly, but the cumulative effect of the single scenes is a combination of comedy and realism – the 'sheer lightness' of comedy fashioned out of the manner of realism – that is a unique achievement.

Hofmannsthal's Elektra

If by its type-characterization and the anonymity of the partners *Reigen* has overtones of the *fin-de-siècle* sense of threatened identity, so too Hofmannsthal came to see his *Elektra*, which was written six years later and again involves a treatment of sexuality, as being about the 'dissolution of the concept of individuality' (A, 201). Where Schnitzler had fashioned his material into comedy permeated with realistic detail, Hofmannsthal opted for the emotional involvement of tragic drama reworking an ancient myth. There could hardly be a greater contrast in genre and in tone. Nevertheless *Elektra* betrays an engagement with Freudian psychology at least as intense as Schnitzler's; it has been described, not unjustly, as being 'as clearly stamped with the seal of twentieth-century pathology, as Goethe's *Iphigenie* with eighteenth century humanism, and Racine's *Phèdre* with Jansenism'.[48]

The drama that brought Hofmannsthal his first big theatrical success was also the first play he had written for a specific theatre company – indeed for a specific performer. This was Gertrud Eysoldt, Reinhardt's Lulu and Salome. In a note written on 17 July 1904, three months before the première, Hofmannsthal recalled that he had first thought of Adele Sandrock for the part, but after seeing Gertrud Eysoldt in May 1903 had promised Reinhardt to write an *Elektra* 'for his theatre and for Gertrud Eysoldt' (A, 131–2). Gertrud Eysoldt radiated an effect that Bahr, writing in the *Neues Wiener Tagblatt* at the beginning of May, had summarized as a 'strange, sultry, almost eerie charm, like a creature in a Beardsley drawing'.[49] What Hofmannsthal seems to have counted on was that with her rather spare figure she would succeed in evoking the un-'feminine' strength shown by Elektra in her pursuit of revenge.[50]

The writing of the play in the late summer of 1903 belongs to a period when Bahr and Hofmannsthal were in frequent contact. Bahr had recently written his 'Dialog vom Tragischen', in which the terminology of Breuer and Freud's *Studies in Hysteria* is applied to the workings of ancient Greek tragedy, including the theory of catharsis. The discussion is in dialogue form. In it the figure of the host claims that the aim of tragedy is 'no different from what those two physicians do'. In tragedy a 'people made sick by civilization' are reminded of 'earlier, savage man' still lurking beneath the mask of civilization; it unchains this 'animal' element and lets it rage so that, purified and calmed, man can be reintegrated in docile conformity with the customs of his time.[51] When Hofmannsthal read his completed tragedy to Bahr in Rodaun in mid-September, Bahr recognized in it 'his' Greeks, 'hysterical, breathless, restless'.[52]

'Freely adapted' from Sophocles, *Elektra* is far from being just a translation. The outline of the plot is maintained but the characterization transformed. The very beginning is indicative: Hofmannsthal deletes the role of Orestes' tutor, and withholds the appearance of Orest and the revelation of his pretended death until over halfway through the play, so concentrating interest on Elektra. The opening dialogue of the servants centres on her; once she enters, she remains on stage throughout. Doing away with her chorus of sympathetic women strengthens this concentration of the focus, as well as heightening a sense of her isolation.

It is a very distinctive effect, on which Hofmannsthal himself had mixed feelings. One immediate reservation he expressed about the play in a letter of 10 November 1903 to Hans Schlesinger concerned its 'almost desperate enclosedness, its dreadful lack of light' (H/Bfe. II, 132); on the other hand, he wanted an effect of tight 'enclosure' in the staging (P II, 68), and when Maximilian Harden's critique of Reinhardt's production appeared in August 1904 in *Die Zukunft* (Berlin), observing that when Orest appeared the dramatic spell of the play was broken (HUK, 84), he wrote to Bodenhausen agreeing that the play would have been a 'purer work of art' if Orest had not appeared at all (H/Bodenhausen, 51: letter of 6 October 1904).[53]

From the notes he wrote in the year of the first performance (RA III, 443–4), it is clear that Hofmannsthal felt he had to 'defend' his modernization of Sophocles against press comments ('was in den Gazetten vorgebracht wird'). At that stage his main concern seems to have been with his formal and structural modifications, tailored to the taste of a modern audience. The most profound changes, however, are in the characterization.

Inherent in the legend is an element of savagery, which informs the intensity of Sophocles' tragedy. But in Sophocles, Electra and Orestes retain a humanity which is apparent in their joy at their reunion; Electra plots to kill Aegisthus out of pious respect for her father and brother, prays reverently for Apollo's support in the punishment of wickedness, and commands admiration by comparison with her sister; Orestes kills Clytemnestra, with her encouragement, as an act of justice. Hofmannsthal's version, drawing on the new irrationalism, especially on the power of sexuality,[54] intensifies the savagery. Sexual motivation is clearly suggested in Sophocles' characterization too, but is elaborated more explicitly by Hofmannsthal. He later admitted that he had consulted two books about the 'dark side' ('Nachtseite') of human psychology. In one, Erwin Rohde's study of early Greek religion, *Psyche: Seelencult und Unsterblichkeitsglaube der Griechen*, which had first appeared in 1894 and was reprinted in 1898 and again in 1903, he probably drew both on the account of Dionysian dancing and on that of the state of possession in which the sibyls made their prophecies.[55] The other was the *Studies in Hysteria* by Breuer and Freud, which had been published in 1895. Though he did not possess a copy – he probably borrowed one from Bahr in 1903 (H/Bfe. II, 142) – he may well have learnt something of its matter as early as 1895–96, when he attended Berger's lectures on 'Psychology and Art'.[56] The connections with contemporary psychological debate did not escape reviewers: when Reinhardt's company performed the play in Vienna in 1905, an anonymous reviewer in the *Wiener Mittags-Zeitung* (15 May 1905), praising the integrity of the 'decorative' effect in the language and production alike, defined what Hofmannsthal had achieved as 'an *Elektra* mirrored by our modern ideal of psychological art' ('eine "Elektra" im Spiegelbild unseres psycho-künstlerischen Zeitideals').

In Hofmannsthal's *œuvre*, *Elektra* can seem like an aberration. It is a far remove from the rich lyricism of his early poetry and playlets, from the gracefulness of his short stories and essays, from the moral directness of his festival plays, and from the refined delicacy of his mature comedies. When he came to define the 'impressive unity' of his writing (A, 237), the play posed obvious problems for him. He often returned to its interpretation, explaining and expounding its meaning, and Hofmannsthal scholars have leaned gratefully on his pronouncements.

He was very concerned to distance himself from the impact made by the violence of the language and in particular the repeated insistence on 'blood'. This, he told Strauss in 1911, had led the vast majority of critics to mistake the fundamental theme of *Elektra* (H/Strauss, 120: letter of 23 July 1911). One of the critiques he may have had in mind was that by Harden, which had explored the nature of Elektra as a 'hysteric' in the Freudian sense; another may have been that by Alfred Kerr, who wrote in the *Neue deutsche Rundschau* that by contrast with Sophocles' tragedy, in which the murder of the guilty satisfied the whole moral ethos of the ancient Greeks, what was satisfied in Hofmannsthal's version was rather the private thirst of an 'epileptic' for revenge (HUK, 78).[57] The critics were, no doubt, glib in applying the term 'hysteria' to Elektra. Hofmannsthal's later formulation, that she is 'obsessed' ('eine Art Besessenheit': A, 237 [1926]), is more accurate.[58] But the distinction belongs to the specialist language of psychological diagnosis, and Elektra is a fictional character, not a patient or a case-study. Hofmannsthal was essentially concerned to reject interpretations that reduced the work to nothing but a treatment of orgiastic or even – as in Paul Goldmann's review of the Berlin première (WM, 476–8) – perverted sexuality. He was already dissociating himself from this kind of approach by the time the operatic version was being planned; hence his emphatic insistence to Strauss that it was not similar to *Salome* (H/Strauss, 18: letter of 27 April 1906). In 1911 he defined the 'basic theme' in another letter which was mainly about the basic idea of their next opera on an ancient subject, *Ariadne auf Naxos*:

> What is at issue is a simple and enormous problem in life: that of constancy [Treue]. To hold fast to what has been lost, to remain constant even unto death – or to live on, to get over it, to be transformed [sich verwandeln], to sacrifice the unity of the soul and nevertheless to preserve one's self in the transformation, to remain a human being and not to degenerate into an animal without memory [und dennoch in der Verwandlung sich bewahren, ein Mensch bleiben, nicht zum gedächtnislosen Tier herabsinken]. It is the basic theme of *Elektra*, the voice of Elektra against the voice of Chrysothemis, the heroic voice against the human one. (H/Strauss, 115: letter of July 1911)

In 1916, even more simply, it was again constancy (A, 217) or the relation between constancy and action ('die Tat': P III, 354–5) that he perceived as the central issue.

All these later pronouncements were devised in hindsight, motivated by his determination to impose a consistency on his own career. The principal methodological objection to the arguments of a critic such as William H. Rey, who tries to refute the view of the play as an orgiastic celebration of mysterious irrationality, is that his interpretation is based mainly on essays and notes – 'Der Dichter und diese Zeit', *Ad me ipsum*, 'Aufzeichnungen zu Reden in Skandinavien' – all of which were written considerably later than the play itself. In insisting that the tragedy of Elektra must be interpreted not in terms of individual psychology but in the context of the problems of Hofmannsthal's poetic work as a whole,[59] Rey discounts the effect made by the text itself, to which the reactions of the early reviewers are in fact a much surer guide.

If we concentrate on the differences Hofmannsthal has made by comparison with the Sophoclean model, one striking contrast is that the heroine's unforgiving hatred for her mother (which in Sophocles has arisen at least partly from her sense of the humiliation to her birth and breeding resulting from her mother's falsehood and conduct towards her) now derives solely from her father's death – in E. M. Butler's reading, from 'her pathological fixation on her murdered father'.[60] The opening lines of the play speak of

her howling for her father (D II, 9): the first line she speaks –
indeed, the whole of her first speech – is a lament for her father (D
II, 14–16); and later, to Orest, she identifies her very being with the
spilt blood of her father ('ich bin das hündisch / vergoßne Blut des
Königs Agamemnon!': D II, 58). Her opening speech invoking her
vision of revenge is spoken as if by a 'sleepwalker' (D II, 16). To
read this as suggesting that the vision corresponds to the function
of 'wish-fulfilment' identified by Freud in *The Interpretation of
Dreams* is not to make Hofmannsthal a mere 'disciple of Freud' – a
simplification against which Rey properly warns.[61] Rather, the play
shows him coming to terms with the strength of irrational forces,
in a way coloured by the contemporary intellectual climate.

Elektra's motivation has its origins in her father's death but is
rich in sexual overtones. She not only thinks, as Sophocles' Electra
also does, of her mother lying with her father's murderer (D II, 14),
and compares the act of revenge to a bed of rest (D II, 66): she
contrasts the light of the world and the darkness of the womb from
which – to her shame – she has been born (D II, 27); she speaks of
the child preferring to think of its mother as dead rather than in bed
('lieber tot als in dem Bette': D II, 35). Obsessed with the murder
of her father and the treachery of her mother, she has come to
associate the very idea of sexual experience with Ägisthus. When
Chrysothemis affirms her wish for 'a woman's fate', Elektra rounds
on her in scorn:

> Pfui,
> die's denkt, pfui, die's mit Namen nennt! Die Höhle
> zu sein, drin nach dem Mord dem Mörder wohl ist;
> das Tier zu spielen, das dem schlimmern Tier
> Ergetzung bietet. Ah, mit einem schläft sie,
> preßt ihre Brüste ihm auf beide Augen
> und winkt dem zweiten, der mit Netz und Beil
> hervorkriecht hinterm Bett.
>
> (D II, 20)

Do not even think it, or say it! To be the cave within which the
murderer rejoices after his murder; to play the animal offering
pleasure to a still baser animal! With one she sleeps, pressing her
breasts down on his eyes, and to the other she signals as he
crawls out from behind the bed with his net and axe.

She has herself been beautiful; indeed, she has had a narcissistic
awareness of her beauty:

> [. . .] wenn ich die Lampe
> ausblies vor meinem Spiegel, fühlte ich

mit keuschem Schauder, wie mein nackter Leib
vor Unberührtheit durch die schwüle Nacht
wie etwas Göttliches hinleuchtete.

(D II, 62)

[. . .] when at my mirror I blew out the lamp, I felt a chaste
shiver as my naked body shone in its virginity through the sultry
night like something divine.

She has had expectations of fulfilment akin to her sister's, and as she
is grimly aware, it is sexual ecstasy that she has sacrificed to her
father's memory ('diese süßen Schauder / hab ich dem Vater opfern
müssen': D II, 63). Her libidinous energies have been channelled
into the hatred that is now her 'bridegroom' ('er schickte mir den
Haß, / den hohläugigen Haß als Bräutigam': D II, 63); she has
given birth only to 'curses and despair' (D II, 65).

It is indeed from revenge that her two moments of ecstasy in the
play are attained: the first through her threat to Klytämnestra,
which leaves her 'in savage intoxication' ('in wildester Trunkenheit':
D II, 41), the second – sweeping away her failure to give Orest the
axe – in her final wild, Maenad-like dance of vengeful triumph[62]
and her last speech, with its proclamation of happiness attained
('Glück': D II, 75).

She repeatedly mocks the ordinary sexuality of other women
such as that of the servants, who recall her as dismissing them to
'crawl into bed with their menfolk' (D II, 10) and as telling them
that to have borne children here is a curse (D II, 13). Indeed, she
seems to despise femininity: discounting Ägisthus as a true man
because he is a hero only in bed ('der tapfre Meuchelmörder,
er, / der Heldentaten nur im Bett vollführt'), she describes him as
effeminate ('die Memme': D II, 17), and laughs when Klytämnestra
speaks of him as a man (D II, 34).

That hers is a disturbed, even perverted sexuality is clear, and its
perversion has cost her her very identity; she is, she says, 'nothing',
she has sacrificed all that she was:

Sieh, ich bin
gar nichts. Ich habe alles, was ich war,
hingeben müssen.

(D II, 64)

When Hofmannsthal wrote in the mid-1920s that the play is about
the 'dissolution of the concept of individuality', he defined that
dissolution in Elektra's case as a consequence of her inward-looking
concentration on remaining true to herself (A, 201). This is another
phrasing designed to refine the rawness of the work. For in this
turn-of-the-century drama, the self is a fragile thing. Klytämnestra,

too, has been warned by Elektra that she is no longer herself ('Du bist nicht mehr du selber': D II, 26). She has repressed her memory of her crime, the characteristic pattern expounded in the *Studies in Hysteria*;[63] she has hysterical symptoms, and finds in her confusion that her identity is threatened:

> dann schwindelts mich, ich weiß
> auf einmal nicht mehr, wer ich bin, und das ist
> das Grauen, das heißt mit lebendigem Leib
> ins Chaos sinken [. . .]
>
> (D II, 30)

Then I feel dizzy, suddenly I no longer know who I am, and that is horror, that is like sinking alive down into chaos [. . .]

Like Sophocles' Clytaemnestra, she is haunted by dreams: she sees them as 'unhealthy', making her in effect sick ('so gut wie krank': D II, 38); she turns to Elektra as to one who 'talks like a physician' ('Sie redet wie ein Arzt': D II, 26),[64] and indeed asks her for her 'remedy against dreams' (D II, 29). The dream from which Klytämnestra seeks release by the spilling of the 'right blood' is 'demonic' ('Ein jeder Dämon läßt von uns, sobald / das rechte Blut geflossen ist': D II, 32).

In association with the idea of release by sacrificial blood-letting, this sounds an ironic echo of the opening scene, where one of the servants has spoken of Elektra as a 'demon' (D II, 11). Indeed Elektra, who knows that Klytämnestra's dreams are about the murdered Agamemnon (D II, 38), spells out that the release for which she longs will come when the axe falls:

KLYTÄMNESTRA.   [. . .] ich will nicht länger träumen.
ELEKTRA.   Wenn das rechte
                Blutopfer unterm Beile fällt, dann träumst du
                nicht länger.

> (D II, 32)

KLYTÄMNESTRA.   [. . .] I want to dream no longer,
ELEKTRA.   When the right victim falls bloodily under the axe, then you will dream no longer.

At the heart of the interplay of character in Hofmannsthal's version is the contrast between Elektra and Chrysothemis: the fundamental contrast between what in July 1911, in the letter to Strauss already quoted, he called the 'heroic' and the 'human'. It is a formulation that may betray a reminiscence of Kerr's review, in which Chrysothemis's lament for her youth ('[. . .] und kanns

nicht fassen, daß ich nicht mehr jung bin': D II, 20) is described
as the 'most human' moment of the play (HUK, 81). In 1922
Hofmannsthal would redefine the contrast as 'the heroic Elektra and
the purely feminine Chrysothemis' ('die heroische Elektra und die
nur weibliche Chrysothemis': A, 234). Against Chrysothemis's
practicality – the role given, perhaps with more sympathy, to
Zerbinetta in *Ariadne auf Naxos*[65] – is set the un-'feminine' strength
of Elektra, the quality that Gertrud Eysoldt was chosen to evoke.
The threatening contrast she presents to conventional ideals of
womanhood may well have been one of the qualities that attracted
Reinhardt to the play, as to the other plays he produced during the
1902–3 season.[66]

In Sophocles, Chrysothemis is merely weak, and indeed reminds
her sister that she too is a woman, with a woman's weakness;
Electra tries to argue her into helping to kill Aegisthus by pointing
to the emptiness of her life, including 'a dismal prospect of aging
spinsterhood', and promising as her reward a reinstatement of her
pride and 'a marriage to be proud of'.[67] Hofmannsthal expands
the motif and gives it a new centrality. While Elektra rejects her
womanhood, Chrysothemis, by contrast, repeatedly states that she
wants children (D II, 18–21); she is envious of women who have
become mothers and is herself longing for the contentment of a
'woman's destiny' ('ein Weiberschicksal': D II, 19). It is by playing
on these feelings that Elektra tries to rouse her sister to support her,
suggesting she has a strength measured in sexuality:

> Du könntest
> mich, oder einen Mann mit deinen Armen
> an deine kühlen festen Brüste pressen,
> daß man ersticken müßte! Überall
> ist so viel Kraft in dir! Sie strömt wie kühles
> verhaltnes Wasser aus dem Fels. Sie flutet
> mit deinen Haaren auf die starken Schultern
> herunter!
>
> (D II, 49–50)

With your arms you could squeeze me, or a man, to your cool
firm breasts, to the edge of suffocation! You have so much
strength, all through you! It is like cool water that has been held
back and streams out of rock – it flows down in your hair onto
your strong shoulders!

The fundamental contrast between them is articulated when she
expresses her wish to 'inject' her 'will' into Chrysothemis's 'blood'
('. . . mit meinem Willen / das Blut dir impfen': D II, 50). Though

the image is of joining forces, in the debate between two separate characters on stage, the effect is one of dramatic contrast: Elektra's 'will' (a characteristic drawn from the original), Chrysothemis's 'blood'.

Animalistic in her savagery, Elektra – who has even spoken of herself as carrying a bird of prey (D II, 11) instead of a child – distinguishes herself from brute animality by her refusal, indeed her inability, to forget, and cannot accept it when Chrysothemis tells her the past is past (D II, 20–2). In this commitment she resolves, when she believes Orest is dead, to take upon herself the deed ('das Werk') that is rightly his (D II, 47), so that when Chrysothemis refuses her help she will resolve to act alone (D II, 54).

Critics who follow the lead provided by Hofmannsthal in his retrospective interpretations and who try to demonstrate the elevated intentions behind his version tend to stress the motif of remembrance in Elektra's commitment, giving it a moral or ethical stature. But again the support lies in Hofmannsthal's notes rather than in the text: it is to be found in *Ad me ipsum*, where 'not the deed but constancy' is defined as 'decisive' ('Das Entscheidende liegt nicht in der Tat sondern in der Treue': A, 217), or in the 'Aufzeichnungen zu Reden in Skandinavien'. It is true that lack of memory, in the sense of living for the moment, is typical of the amoral figures in Hofmannsthal's plays from *Gestern* to the mature comedies,[68] including the flirtatious Antoinette in *Der Schwierige*, who admits she has 'a bad memory' (L II, 249). But the implications of Elektra's 'Ich kann nicht vergessen' are quite different from the moral commitment to which characters developing to maturity, from Claudio to Hans Karl, advance. Her 'will', her determination and commitment, is deployed in the scene with Chrysothemis in a way irreconcilable with high morality but entirely consistent with the emphasis on sexual psychology in the piece: she bears in on her sister, playing on her sexual readiness ('das warme Blut': D II, 51), until finally the idea of 'warm-blooded' emotion merges into that of the bloodiness of murder, murder presented as a passkey to sexual gratification:

ELEKTRA.   [. . .] schnell schlüpfst du aus dem blutigen Gewand
mit reinem Leib ins hochzeitliche Hemd.
CHRYSOTHEMIS. Laß mich!
ELEKTRA.   Sei nicht zu feige! Was du jetzt
an Schaudern überwindest, wird vergolten
mit Wonneschaudern Nacht für Nacht [. . .]
(D II, 53–4)

ELEKTRA.	Quickly with a pure body you slip out of your bloody garment and into your wedding shift.
CHRYSOTHEMIS.	Leave me alone!
ELEKTRA.	Do not be too cowardly! If you can overcome your shivering horror now it will be compensated by shivers of bliss night after night.

In his review of the Berlin première, Kerr made much of the weight placed by the imagery on the currents of sexuality and violence (HUK, 79–80).[69] The writing is, in fact, highly accomplished; the rhythms of the verse, often rather fragmented, are frequently reminiscent of Grillparzer. Grillparzer, a precursor also in exploring abnormal psychology, may indeed have been much in Hofmannsthal's mind around the time he wrote *Elektra* in July and August 1903: the following January he was to deliver a lecture to the Grillparzer-Gesellschaft in Vienna on Grillparzer's dramatic characters – a lecture that Schnitzler attended and indeed enjoyed (Tgb., 15 January 1904) – and the surviving notes for that lecture (P II, 72–9) show a wide-ranging familiarity with Grillparzer's work.[70] As in Grillparzer, the effect in *Elektra* is built up in part by powerful image-complexes. These include recurrent images of flames and torches. But the key symbol is that of the fatal axe, which Elektra wants to 'dig up' ('Ich grab nichts ein, / ich grab was aus': D II, 55) – a symbol of the deed at the root of her obsession. In Sophocles the chorus speaks of the axe as itself 'remembering' the deed awaiting vengeance.[71]

At the end of Hofmannsthal's version Elektra fails to give the axe to Orest (D II, 68). Heinz Politzer and Ritchie Robertson speak explicitly of a *Fehlleistung*, that is, a parapraxis or psychological failure arising, as Robertson argues, from her unconscious identification with Klytämnestra.[72] To associate the motivation directly with Freudian theory may be over-simple, since though *The Psychopathology of Everday Life* (*Zur Psychopathologie des Alltagslebens*), in which parapraxes are expounded, had appeared in a specialist journal in 1901 it was not published in book form until 1904. But certainly Hofmannsthal's own later view was consistently that Elektra's failure is psychological: in *Ad me ipsum* there is a reference, in a paragraph dealing precisely with the relation of the conscious, unconscious, and subconscious mind, to the 'difficulty of action for Elektra' (A, 226), and the 'Aufzeichnungen zu Reden in Skandinavien' (1916) refer explicitly to Elektra's *forgetting* the axe ('das Vergessen des Beiles': P III, 354). These passages must be read with caution about Hofmannsthal's habit of reconstruction in hindsight, but in the text too there is no suggestion that she fails merely because she is weak or exhausted physically[73] – physical debility would be an anti-climax in such a psychologically charged atmosphere.

This charged atmosphere is another factor that drew Hofmannsthal to writing the play for Reinhardt and his theatre. He had in mind not only the acting of Gertrud Eysoldt but also the use Reinhardt would be able to make of the (very small) Kleines Theater to produce the sense of enclosure and oppressiveness ('Enge, Unentfliehbarkeit, Abgeschlossenheit': P II, 68) that he required. The set itself, as he conceived it, had to 'concentrate and build up the symbolic atmosphere: in the claustrophobic, womb-like setting, the giant fig-tree, the bloody shadows, the single gateway to the outside'.[74]

Most of the credit for the success of the première, including the distinctive effect of Elektra's collapse after her dance of triumph, is usually given to Reinhardt.[75] The dance, however, is not Reinhardt's invention but is built into Hofmannsthal's text. In a piece written by Max Osborn in 1924, stress is also laid on the effects achieved in Reinhardt's production by 'contrasting light effects' and use of colour; again, the light symbolism is built into the stage directions, as for example on Elektra's entry (D II, 14). The effect achieved was clearly the joint product of Hofmannsthal's imagination and Reinhardt's realization.

Osborn also gives Reinhardt credit for 'apply[ing] to the stage the results of modern artistic culture', and mentions in particular his emphasis on 'the flowing lines of the Pre-Raphaelites'.[76] That Reinhardt's production suggested links with the visual arts of the period is confirmed by the review in the *Wiener Mittags-Zeitung* in 1905 which compared Hofmannsthal's conception of the ancient world with that of Beardsley and Klimt. And again the basis is there in the text. In particular a recurrent subject in the illustrations in *Ver sacrum*, of which Klimt's 'Fischblut' (1898) is the first and best-known,[77] is recalled in the image, already quoted, of flowing hair and flowing water with which Elektra – perhaps echoing Chrysothemis's earlier image of plunging into water (D II, 21) – tries to suggest to her sister the 'strength' of her sexuality ('Sie flutet / mit deinen Haaren auf die starken Schultern / herunter!': D II, 50).

Hofmannsthal's intensification of the savagery in his source fulfilled his wish, as he defined it in 1904, to achieve something opposite in style to Goethe's *Iphigenie* ('etwas Gegensätzliches zur "Iphigenie" '), something to which Goethe's phrase 'devilish humane' ('ganz verteufelt human'), used in a letter to Schiller of 19 January 1802 after rereading *Iphigenie*, would not apply (A, 131).[78] To recognize the extent to which he drew both on the art and on the psychological writings of his time need not imply reading the play as a celebration of instinctual drives or reducing it to a dramatized case history. Essentially, Hofmannsthal is doing as Goethe had done in reworking Euripides' *Iphigenia in Tauris*, shifting the emphasis from the events that are the workings of Fate and concentrating on the characters and their motives. In the narcissistic awareness of her own beauty from which Elektra has developed she has similarities to Fräulein Else in the story for which, twenty years later, Schnitzler would draw most directly on Freudian psychology:[79] Hofmannsthal's modernization of the myth transforms Sophocles' heroine into a character whose mind is fashioned out of the insights of Freudian psychology and the imagery of the Secessionists.

The Parting of the Ways (1910–11):
Der Rosenkavalier *and* Das weite Land

Reigen and *Elektra*, in their contrasting dramatic modes, show Schnitzler and Hofmannsthal exploring a common interest in instinctual drives; but the gulf between their artistic intentions is manifest in their respective choice of genre and setting. Personally, too, they had drifted away from the close contact of the Griensteidl years. By the end of 1910 their friendship had noticeably cooled. In early October, at Hofmannsthal's request, Schnitzler sent him an advance copy of *Das weite Land*; Hofmannsthal replied on 20 October, praising it warmly (H/AS, 254–5). Nine days later he wrote again: he was away from home but about to return, and would await an invitation to Schnitzler's house to enrich the evening with a reading of *Der Rosenkavalier*. Though jokingly worded, the implicit self-importance is compounded by a postscript in which he admits having left his signed copy of *Der Weg ins Freie* in a train two years earlier 'half by accident, half on purpose' and asks Schnitzler to give him another copy (H/AS, 255–6). Schnitzler, angered and hurt by the insensitive phrasing, spent a whole day phrasing his response (Tgb., 30 October 1910). He found Hofmannsthal's tactlessness 'irreconcilable with our artistic and personal relations as they have been hitherto' and declined his request (H/AS, 256–7: letter of 2 November 1910). Hofmannsthal's abject apology was accepted (H/AS, 257–9), but when Schnitzler did hear him reading *Der Rosenkavalier* at the end of the month, his reaction was cold: it was banal in content, the verse poor, and that the work was 'not without virtues as a libretto' was 'a proof of talent in someone so unmusical' (Tgb., 29 November 1910). A year later a letter, dated 22 October 1911, which ends with the vague inquiry 'What news of *Jedermann* and so forth?' (H/AS, 264) confirms that in his attitude to Hofmannsthal's writing Schnitzler had begun to assume something of the indifference he suspected Hofmannsthal felt towards his (see p. 223, below).

The two dramatic works that they had completed in 1910, *Der Rosenkavalier* and *Das weite Land*, were both first performed in 1911 and proved two of their greatest successes. The differences in genre and style confirm how far apart they now were. The contrast is all the more striking because in subject matter the two works are again akin; *Der Rosenkavalier* is indeed where Hofmannsthal comes closest to Schnitzler in reflecting some of the views and concerns of contemporary feminism. Both treat relations between the sexes and turn on a complex female character: in each case not a mere girl but a mature woman. Genia Hofreiter is thirty-one, the Marschallin in her mid-thirties.

Der Rosenkavalier, the most popular of all Hofmannsthal's works, is an opera about love and lust, youth and aging. The silver rose alluded to in the title, presented to Sophie by Octavian as a token of the love of her husband-to-be ('die Rose seiner Liebe': HKA XXIII, 45), is a symbol of perfect love, on which the whole opera provides an ironic comment. The basis of the plot is a situation in which all the relations between the sexes are unsatisfactory. The Marschallin's marriage to the Feldmarschall, whom we never see, is clearly loveless; her affair with Octavian cannot last; the engagement arranged between Baron Ochs and Sophie is artificial and cannot possibly work; and Ochs's true colours are shown in his crude advances towards Octavian when Octavian is disguised as 'Mariandel', a comic sub-plot providing a burlesque parallel to the immorality and unsuitedness of the relations between the Marschallin and Octavian.

What has driven the Marschallin into seeking consolation in her affair with Octavian is her marriage of convenience: as a young woman she was 'ordered into holy matrimony' ('in den heiligen Ehestand kommandiert': HKA XXIII, 36). As she spells out in the same passage, Sophie is now in exactly the same position. (Ironically, the parallel that the Marschallin draws between herself and Sophie will also extend to their involvement with Octavian.) Sophie is in effect being sold into marriage by her socially ambitious *nouveau riche* father – hence Ochs's shameless demands for a 'dowry' to compensate him for condescending to the misalliance (HKA XXIII, 31–3). Appalled by the discovery that he can treat her like a 'horse-trader', Sophie asks indignantly whether he thinks he has bought her ('[. . .] Ist das leicht ein Roßtäuscher / und kommt ihm vor, er hätt' mich eingekauft?': HKA XXIII, 50). In choosing Sophie, Ochs has taken into consideration both the wealth of her father, Faninal, and his uncertain health (HKA XXIII, 18); Sophie is indeed the object of a commercial calculation on both sides.

This is a world in which woman is a dependent creature. Sophie herself has explained to Octavian that while as a man he has his own identity, she by contrast 'needs a husband in order to be somebody':

> Freilich, Er ist ein Mann, da ist Er, was Er bleibt.
> Ich aber brauch' erst einen Mann, daß ich was bin.
>
> (HKA XXIII, 48)

Man is the lord of creation ('Herr der Schöpfung': HKA XXIII, 24): the phrase is used by Ochs, preening himself on his conquests. Ochs is indeed a caricature of male sexual conquest. His engagement to Sophie is no bar to promiscuity: he is at once preoccupied with 'Mariandel' and is content to liken himself to a dog on the scent (HKA XXIII, 23); the Marschallin recognizes that his intention towards 'Mariandel' is to 'debauch' her (HKA XXIII, 93). He appreciates Sophie as 'delicious' ('deliziös'), and congratulates her father on that (HKA XXIII, 49). That she is to him merely something to be enjoyed – consumed – is borne out in his later compliment to Faninal on 'serving an old Tokay to go with a young girl' (HKA XXIII, 51).

The basic structure of the opera is clearly indebted to *The Marriage of Figaro* (the role of the Marschallin corresponding to that of Mozart's Countess, the central role of Octavian to that of Cherubino, and the discomfiture of Ochs corresponding to that of Almaviva). Its lesson, however, is like a counter to *Così fan tutte*: the Marschallin has spelled out warningly in Act One how 'all men' are (HKA XXIII, 37–8). Even Octavian is following in Ochs's footsteps. Ochs encourages him to make eyes at Sophie (HKA XXIII, 55), and he does so. If he finally acts as a 'true man' ('ein rechtes Mannsbild', HKA XXIII, 96) it is in deserting the Marschallin for Sophie; she is resigned that this is the lot of woman (HKA XXIII, 97). Again the comic sub-plot mimics the thrust of the principal action: the stage business involving the behaviour of Ochs's retinue in the Faninal household in Act Two exemplifies the effects of male intrusion into the feminine world: the serving-girls are crudely pursued, their peace shattered (HKA XXIII, 56). From the Marschallin's plea to Octavian to be 'gentle and kind, unlike all men', we know that her experience brands men in general as rough:

> Oh, sei Er jetzt sanft, sei Er gescheit und sanft und gut.
> Nein, bitt' schön, sei Er nicht wie alle Männer sind.
>
> (HKA XXIII, 37)

As examples she goes on to name both Baron Ochs and her own husband, the Feldmarschall. 'The marital bedroom', runs one of Kraus's aphorisms, first published in 1913, 'is where brutality and martyrdom cohabit' (F 389–390, 35).

It has been widely recognized that although *Der Rosenkavalier* is set in the bewigged Vienna of Maria Theresia, in various respects it reflects the *mœurs* of early twentieth-century Vienna.[80] The whole 'double morality' of the period was founded on a dual view of woman, 'the two directions personified in art as sacred and profane (or animal) love' (Freud):[81] that is, she was idolized as the virtuous embodiment of moral perfection, cocooned in the 'sanctity of marriage', and at the other end of the scale was debased as a sexual object. These two opposite roles are juxtaposed in *Der Rosenkavalier*. The conventional treatment of women as objects of adoration is suggested not only by the ritual presentation of the rose but also verbally, in the way Octavian repeatedly calls the Marschallin an 'angel' (HKA XXIII, 9–10). Yet even in the Marschallin's presence – indeed, while telling her about his coming marriage – Ochs makes lecherous advances to 'Mariandel' (HKA XXIII, 19–20); it is Sophie's physical attractiveness that makes him rejoice at having 'the luck of the Lerchenaus' ('ein Lerchenauisch Glück'), and he parades his lustful anticipation of their love-making (HKA XXIII, 53–5). The Marschallin sees him as 'bad' ('schlecht': HKA XXIII, 36), even satanic, but Ochs rejoices in his immorality ('wie Jupiter selig [. . .]': HKA XXIII, 24–5).

The Marschallin's fanciful – perhaps even rather neurotic – stopping of the clocks (HKA XXIII, 40) is a suspension of reality out of keeping with her otherwise clear-sighted outlook. She has no illusions about the transience of her affair with Octavian, no illusions about her own aging. When she counters Octavian's naïvely possessive love with a warning against 'holding on too tight' and spells out to him that sooner or later ('Heut oder morgen [. . .]') he will transfer his affections to someone younger than herself (HKA XXIII, 37–9), the work unmistakably approaches a Schnitzlerian mood.

Yet all the modern elements in the characterization are embedded in a celebration of the aristocratic society of the Austria of Maria Theresia. This atmospheric recreation of an imagined eighteenth century begins with the opening *levée* scene, which is derived from Hogarth,[82] and is embellished by invented ceremony, the formal presentation of the silver rose. Other details, down to family names, are almost certainly drawn from the diaries of an eighteenth-century nobleman, Prince Johann Josef Khevenhüller-Metsch, a prominent figure at the court of Maria Theresia.[83] The effect is of a chronological dual focus, an imprecision that is increased by the eclecticism of the composition. Over and above the reminiscences of *The Marriage of Figaro*, borrowings include the 'Papa, Papa!' with which Ochs is confronted in Act Three, and which is drawn directly from Molière's *Monsieur de Pourceaugnac*. This eclecticism is also reflected in the musical idiom adopted by Strauss, which combines a Wagnerian use of *leitmotiv* with set pieces (the aria of the Italian tenor in Act One, the trio and duet at the end of Act Three), with a further blurring of focus in the anachronistic Viennese waltz. The nature and intention of the opera is to conjure up an Austria that is of the past yet also of the present, a timeless – mythical – Austria.

In the development of Hofmannsthal's career and his collaboration with Strauss, one significance of the success enjoyed by *Der Rosenkavalier* is that it shaped his further work as a librettist. *Hosenrollen* recur both in *Ariadne auf Naxos* and in *Arabella*, which indeed Hofmannsthal thought of from the first as an attempt to recapture the spirit of *Der Rosenkavalier*.[84] The eclectic traditionalism also remained a feature of the later operas: *Die Frau ohne Schatten* was conceived as a parallel to *The Magic Flute* (H/Strauss, 96: letter of 20 March 1911), the 'Vorspiel' to *Ariadne auf Naxos* centres on figures drawn from Italian comedy, and the picture-motif in *Arabella* is derived directly from *The Magic Flute*.

Das weite Land, the play immediately preceding *Professor Bernhardi* in Schnitzler's œuvre, has a contemporary setting. After the completion of *Liebelei*, *Freiwild*, and *Reigen* Schnitzler tended to concentrate less on the problems of relations across social class divisions and more on relations between the sexes within the professional and business classes; most of the action in *Das weite Land* accordingly takes place in Baden, where the Hofreiters have a villa. The distinctive rhythm of the work has been analysed by Martin Swales:[85] the alternation of group scenes and intimate dialogues between two characters suggests the causal connection between the personal relationships that develop and the conventions and way of life of the society to which the individuals belong, a society of transitional and hence uncertain moral values.

The play presents a complex network of infidelities. At the centre of the network is Friedrich Hofreiter, a tycoon. One of his friends, a pianist by the name of Korsakow, has just committed suicide out of frustrated love for Genia Hofreiter, Friedrich's faithful wife. Genia is told by another close friend, Dr Mauer, that her husband's recent affair with Adele Natter, a banker's wife, is now over; but in the second act we learn that he is now flirting with the enigmatic Erna Wahl, a modern and independent young woman, tall and self-possessed, with whom Mauer himself is in love. Mauer is about to go walking in the Dolomites, and Hofreiter arranges to go with him. There they will call on Erna, who will be staying in a hotel near Völs. Friedrich admits to Genia that his sudden decision to go on the trip to South Tyrol is to get away from her and her 'virtue' which, he says, has driven his friend Korsakow to his death (DW II, 261). This disparagement of her fidelity is a turning-point, 'an assault which is so hurtful that Genia will deliberately try to deny what she is, to become what she could not be to Korsakow'.[86] Act Two ends, then, with the situation poised on the brink of further developments which are foreshadowed in the overtones in the exchange on which the curtain falls. As Mauer and Hofreiter set off, the others plan a night-time drive: 'Let's just set off boldly into the darkness', says Erna, and Genia agrees: 'Yes, Erna, that may be the best fun of all' (DW II, 263).

The third act is set in South Tyrol, where Friedrich, Mauer, and Erna all climb the 'Aignerturm', a notoriously dangerous peak. Intoxicated, as Friedrich says, by the heady air (DW II, 286), Friedrich and Erna have fallen in love and indeed made love on the mountain; back in their hotel, which is run by Dr von Aigner, the first climber ever to have conquered the peak, Friedrich asks her to marry him. She refuses. In Act Four we learn that in Baden Genia has meanwhile drifted (she uses the image of 'sliding': DW II, 293) into an affair with Aigner's son Otto, a young naval officer. Friedrich picks a quarrel with Otto, telling him, in the presence of Erna and Genia, that he is a coward, so precipitating a duel, in which, in the short fifth act, Otto is killed.

Hofreiter is one of Schnitzler's congenital philanderers, incapable of fidelity, incorrigibly immature. How fine it would be, he tells Adele Natter, to be young again: he was young too early, it is only at forty that one could make the most of it (DW II, 250). His characteristics are mirrored in Aigner, an older man but still philandering. Aigner tells him that he first climbed the peak just after his actress wife had left him; he still cannot understand why he betrayed her. It is at this point that he makes the speech from which the title of the play is drawn, about the 'vast terrain' of the human pysche, the baffling instability and impenetrability of motivation, in which love can coexist with infidelity: controlling these forces within ourselves is artificial, 'nature' is chaotic ('Wir versuchen wohl Ordnung in uns zu schaffen, so gut es geht, aber diese Ordnung ist doch nur etwas Künstliches . . . Das Natürliche . . . ist das Chaos': DW II, 281). Where in Hofmannsthal's comedies events are governed by moral imperatives – the 'necessity' that Hans Karl describes to Antoinette in *Der Schwierige* as governing marriage

(L II, 245) – in Schnitzler the imperatives are psychological, rooted in the 'chaotic' irrationality of instinctual drives, and destructive of happiness. Thus Aigner uncomprehendingly defines the break-up of his marriage as an ineluctable necessity:

> AIGNER. Es war nur zu Ende, mein guter Hofreiter, un-widerruflich zu Ende. Sofort . . . Das fühlten wir beide. Es mußte zu Ende sein . . .
> FRIEDRICH. Es mußte –?
> AIGNER. Mußte. [. . .]
>
> (DW II, 282)

> AIGNER. It was simply all over, my dear Hofreiter, irrevocably over, at once – we both felt that. It had to be over.
> FRIEDRICH. Had to be?
> AIGNER. Had to be. [. . .]

Set against this moral shiftlessness is the earnest voice of Mauer, who commits himself whole-heartedly to Erna. When she admits that she is not attracted to security, he tells her there is more to life than 'a certain kind of adventure' (DW II, 253). He does not moralize; what he tells Erna he dislikes is the indecisive unclarity of affairs ('Herzensschlampereien'). So too to Genia in Act Four he condemns not open 'adventures', but the ambiguities of social and moral relations built on deceitfulness, 'this mixture of reticence and forwardness, of cowardly jealousy and fake nonchalance, of raging passion and vapid pleasure' ('dies Ineinander von Zurückhaltung und Frechheit, von feiger Eifersucht und erlogenem Gleichmut – von rasender Leidenschaft und leerer Lust, wie ich es hier sehe': DW II, 307–8). It is a lucid diagnosis of a moral condition recurrently captured in Schnitzler's plays from *Anatol* onwards, a ubiquitous evasiveness which Mauer is powerless to defeat and to which Genia succumbs.

Genia's stature is that of a woman who, seeing through the deceptions with which she is surrounded, preserves a moral independence based not on the copybook 'virtue' of which Hofreiter accuses her but on her own integrity. Mauer senses this when she tells him in the first act that she has toyed in the past with 'avenging' herself on her husband and he replies by saying he is sure that in her case it would have to be a serious love, compelled by 'fate' (DW II, 227). Genia prefers a lighter touch and disclaims this, but as she tells her husband, it would in fact have been impossible for her to have an affair with Korsakow – not because of moral scruples but because she could not sacrifice her integrity ('um meinetwillen':

DW I, 240). Later, when Mauer talks of the irresistible quality of Friedrich's charm, she dissents: she needs long and patient wooing ('Um mich muß man werben, lange werben': DW II, 248).

It is this integrity that Genia endangers, even sacrifices, in her affair with Otto. She knows the superficiality of social 'respectability', but when she tells Otto in Act Four that she is a mere play-actor, acting out the role of a respectable wife ('Ich spiele die anständige Frau': DW II, 294), she is deceiving herself, and Otto realizes that she still – or again – loves Friedrich. No less than Aigner and Friedrich, she too has 'slid' into moral shiftlessness, allowing affection and deception to coexist. Towards the end of the same act she tries to console Mauer with the argument that love affairs are just 'games', which he is wrong to take seriously; and it is this, coming from her, that prompts his forthright attack, already quoted, on the dishonesty of their society.

In *Das weite Land* Schnitzler follows a pattern similar to that of *Liebelei*, in that the play moves from the banter of social comedy to a tragic climax. It is one of Schnitzler's funniest plays, full of pithily epigrammatic sayings; this quality is well captured by Stoppard's version, albeit at the expense of the subtle reflectiveness of Schnitzler's more leisurely dialogue. And as in *Liebelei*, the shift in mood and genre is inherent in the drama as it unfolds: the tragedy grows directly out of the social irresponsibility reflected in the banter. Schnitzler is dealing not just with the evocation of a social atmosphere but with the consequences of individual conduct.

To Hofreiter the discovery of his wife's affair comes at first, so he tells Mauer, like a release ('eine innere Befreiung'); he is no longer the only guilty one in his own house (DW II, 303). He fights the duel, as Genia realizes, not out of genuine hate or anger, jealousy or love (DW II, 311) – still less to 'defend his honour', even if he knows that is what the courts will make of it (DW II, 319). The character whom he really wants to fight is Natter (DW II, 306–7),[87] and when that wish is frustrated he is driven to a ritual gesture of aggression, psychologically an attempt to break out of his helpless confusion. As a punishment for the infidelity of a wife whom he has himself repeatedly betrayed, it solves nothing but only confirms the moral vacuum of his way of life.

Genia derides the duel, before its outcome is known, as 'nothing but a ridiculous charade of vanity and honour' ('nichts [. . .] als eine lächerliche Eitelkeits- und Ehrenkomödie': DW II, 312). Similarly the Marschallin dismisses Octavian's discomfiture of Ochs as nothing but a 'Viennese masquerade' ('War eine wienerische Maskerad' und weiter nichts': HKA XXIII, 93). But where the Marschallin, idealized as loving 'in the right way' ('in der richtigen

Weis'), then shows her 'goodness' ('wie gut Sie ist!': HKA XXIII, 98–9) by fading gracefully out of the picture, leaving the stage to a lyrically happy ending between the two young lovers, Schnitzler has no happy ending to offer. Friedrich Hofreiter is left alone, an 'adventurer' brought face to face with the realization that he has destroyed his own happiness. Happy endings are the stuff of myth-making, not of sceptical realism.

CHAPTER 5

The End of the Monarchy

World War

Nothing is more revealing of the contrast between the sceptical realist Schnitzler and the myth-making Hofmannsthal than their response to the outbreak of the First World War. It was in Vienna that war was declared. Just one week after the death of Bertha von Suttner, who had long been lampooned as 'die Friedensbertha', the heir presumptive to the throne, Archduke Franz Ferdinand, was assassinated together with Archduchess Sophie on 28 June by a separatist at Sarajevo. The declaration of war, in the first place against Serbia, was proclaimed in an imperial manifesto headed 'An Meine Völker!' ('To our Peoples'), which was issued on 28 July and was widely reproduced in the press the next day. In this proclamation the Emperor, now in the sixty-sixth year of his reign, justified the declaration of what he presented as a defensive war, necessary for the maintenance of peace. Towards the end comes the statement which Karl Kraus would reuse in the epilogue to *Die letzten Tage der Menschheit*, in the part of the 'Voice from Above':

Ich habe alles geprüft und erwogen.
Mit ruhigem Gewissen betrete Ich den Weg, den die Pflicht
    Mir weist.

I have weighed everything up carefully.
With a clear conscience I follow the course dictated by duty.

Nearly all the leading figures in Austrian literary and intellectual life were caught up in the excitement that the declaration of war generated. The non-political atmosphere in which the 'Jung Wien' generation had been brought up left them inexperienced in political judgment, and the nostalgia for the Austrian past characteristic of the turn of the century provided a ready-made base for sentimental patriotism. In a world whose underlying values all seemed threatened by change, the war provided something to believe in.

157

Jingoistic patriotism filled an ideological gap; enthusiasm for war took over from enthusiasm for art as a surrogate religion.

Among the poets of Austria-Hungary, it was Rilke who expressed this most unambiguously. In Munich when war was declared, he celebrated the 'God of War' in the first of his 'Fünf Gesänge', proclaiming this new deity a replacement for ideas no longer really alive:

> Endlich ein Gott. Da wir den friedlichen oft
> Nicht mehr ergriffen, ergreift uns plötzlich der Schlacht-Gott
> [. . .].

> At last a god. Often we have failed to grasp the God of peace;
> so now we are grasped by the god of war . . . .

The five poems, all written in August 1914, were published in the *Kriegsalmanach 1915*, a war anthology issued by the Insel-Verlag in Leipzig in place of the customary annual *Insel-Almanach*. They were immediately preceded by three patriotic poems by Rudolf Alexander Schröder; the same volume also included an essay by Hofmannsthal, 'Die Bejahung Österreichs'.

The attitude of the majority of Austrian men of letters may be illustrated from a representative poem by Richard Schaukal, who was just four months younger than Hofmannsthal. It is taken from a slim volume of war sonnets, of which the publishers risked a print run of 3,100 copies. (This is a fair gauge of the market. Schaukal's best-known previous work, the novel *Leben und Meinungen des Herrn Andreas von Balthesser, eines Dandy und Dilettanten* [1907], had originally been published in a printing of 830 copies; in 1914, patriotic sonnets were a safe speculation.) Dated 28 July 1914, the poem is entitled 'An meine Völker!', and, like many others at the time,[1] takes the Imperial proclamation as a starting-point. It sums up the mood of the moment: the call to arms in the first quatrain, the sense of purpose in the second. This is then extended in the sestet to gratitude to the Emperor for having fulfilled a long-felt wish, and it ends – still echoing the Imperial proclamation – in celebration of the hour of greatness awaiting Austria:

> Der Kaiser ruft. Der Kaiser sei bedankt
> dafür, daß er uns alle brauchen mag.
> Wir habens lang ersehnt und sind bereit.

> Die Welt, von Haß zerwühlt, ist morsch und wankt;
> in Flammen glühend, naht ein neuer Tag,
> und Oesterreich grüßt eine große Zeit.[2]

The Emperor calls. May he be thanked for calling on us all. This is what we have longed for, and we are ready. The world, stirred up by hatred, is rotten and tottering; in glowing flames, a new day is approaching, and Austria greets a time of greatness.

The seductive exhilaration of the beginning of the war is described by Stefan Zweig in his memoirs. As never before, he recalls, people in all ranks of society felt that they belonged together; not only in Vienna but throughout Austria-Hungary there was an intoxicating realization that they were experiencing a unique moment of history.[3] The unlikeliest figures proved susceptible to the fever. Zweig himself, later a prominent pacifist, published in the *Neue Freie Presse* on 6 August an article celebrating the entry into the war of Wilhelminian Germany; even Freud declared that 'all his libido' was given to Austria-Hungary.[4] It is less surprising that the ever-enthusiastic Bahr was equally effusive: the beginning of the war, he would recall in an essay entitled 'Kriegssegen', was the greatest event any German alive had experienced.[5] On 26 August he published in the *Neues Wiener Journal* an open letter written ten days earlier, 'Gruß an Hofmannsthal', in which he imagines Hofmannsthal as a lieutenant on the eastern front, even entering Warsaw; and he foolishly reprinted this piece the next year (by which time he was perfectly well aware that Hofmannsthal was working safely in Vienna) in a volume entitled *Kriegssegen*.

The 'spiritual uplift' of whose value the 'Optimist' tries to convince the 'Nörgler', the 'grumbling' satirical commentator, in *Die letzten Tage der Menschheit*,[6] was such that enthusiasm about the war overshadowed all else and upset every criterion of judgment. Hence, for example, Schnitzler's angry diary entry for 30 October 1914, asking whether people really thought that just because men were murdering one another Wildenbruch – a late nineteenth-century Prussian author of nationalistic historical dramas – was suddenly a better poet than he himself was ('Glauben die Leute wirklich, dass, weil die Leute sich jetzt gegenseitig morden, – Wildenbruch eher ein Dichter ist, als ich?').

Among the many whose enthusiasm was instantly kindled was Hofmannsthal. On his way to his regiment when first called up in late July, he wrote to Countess Ottonie Degenfeld:

Believe me, and tell all our friends, that every one here down to the lowliest woodcutter is going into this business, and into *all that it may develop into*, with a determination, a joy even, such as I have never experienced and indeed would never have thought possible. (H/Degenfeld, 304–5: letter of 28 July 1914)

This exaltation was echoed by German as well as Austrian friends. On 17 August, for example, Kessler wrote to him from the field that the transformation of the whole people would probably be the greatest experience of their lives (H/Kessler, 384). In September, another German friend, Schröder, addressed to him a poem – subsequently published in Schröder's book of war poems, *Heilig Vaterland* – encouraging Austrian resolution after setbacks on the eastern front.[7] Hofmannsthal responded with a poem entitled 'Österreichs Antwort', containing an allusion to the national anthem (HKA I, 112); this was printed in the *Neue Freie Presse* on 24 September and the two poems were issued together as a separate leaflet by the Viennese publisher Hugo Heller. The image of the clenched fist in the first stanza and the emphasis on heroism in the rest of this poem are typical of the rampant belligerence of the first weeks of the war. In Hofmannsthal himself, at least briefly, it produced a sense of awakening comparable to that which he had portrayed twenty years earlier in *Der Tor und der Tod*. He had noted then that Claudio's attitude is 'transfigured' because his confrontation with death is the first thing that he experiences as profoundly true, putting an end to all deceptions and all 'relativity' (A, 106). Similarly he himself now discovered in the commitment and tension of the first weeks of the war an authenticity of experience such as he had not known before. He had lived for forty years, he wrote to his old friend Eberhard von Bodenhausen on 7 October, but only now was he truly alive (H/Bodenhausen, 169). He too would remember August 1914 as an event of 'beauty' (P III, 234).

Most of the best-known figures from the world of the arts and letters in Austria were caught up in war duties, though not all on war service. Andrian, for example, remained in the diplomatic service. Austrian consul-general in Warsaw until 1914, he returned there after it had fallen to the Germans. Schaukal had a senior post in the Ministry of Labour. Among the younger poets, Josef Weinheber was one of the few who were exempted altogether, since as a post office employee he was in a reserved occupation. Alfons Petzold was prevented from serving by ill health; Broch did Red Cross work in Teesdorf near Baden in Lower Austria. Wildgans was called up into the artillery but immediately suffered an attack of phlebitis; Schönberg, who enrolled as an infantryman, was also discharged on account of ill health. Schiele, whose posting as a clerk in a prison camp for Russian officers provided him with material for memorable studies of the captives, fell victim to the influenza epidemic only a few days after the final cease-fire. Rilke, following advice that Hofmannsthal gave him (H/Rilke, 82: letter of 19 December 1915), managed to get himself transferred in 1916 to the Military Records Office (*Kriegsarchiv*), where a lot of men of letters had been found a niche, but was quickly discharged. The *Kriegsarchiv* was in effect a central office of wartime propaganda; a literary group had been formed there in November 1914, with the purpose of producing patriotic publications. Others who worked in this group included Polgar, Salten, the theatre historian Richard Smekal, the poets Franz Karl Ginzkey and Albert Ehrenstein (the latter only briefly, in 1915), and (from December 1914 until November 1917) Stefan Zweig.[8]

Active combatants included Musil, who served with distinction on the Italian front and rose to the rank of captain, and Wittgenstein, who served in the artillery in Galicia, in the far north-eastern reaches of the monarchy, where some of the most bitter fighting took place. So too did Mell, who went into the field full of enthusiasm, as a letter written to Hofmannsthal on 10 July 1917 shows: he had just been in the front line, he reported, though only for twenty-four hours, and the German troops there were making a splendid impression: 'Determination, hard work, precision can be seen everywhere, and it inspires one with strength to imitate them!' (H/Mell, 122). Kokoschka volunteered for the cavalry, hated army life from the first, and was wounded on the Russian front. Theodor Kramer, one of the principal lyric poets to write about the experience of fighting, was called up in 1915, was severely wounded in Volhynia (across the Russian border from Galicia), and subsequently served till the end of the war as an officer on the Italian front. Both Wittgenstein (another to be commissioned from the ranks) and the Prague poet Karl von Eisenstein, who held a regular commission, were eventually taken prisoner on the Italian front. Hugo Zuckermann, a Zionist and one of the most popular poets of the first weeks of war, was killed on the eastern front in December 1914. Trakl, who served in the medical corps, died of an overdose of cocaine in November 1914 not long after the battle in Galicia that provides the subject of his haunting poem of suffering and waste, 'Grodek'. Others who served on the eastern front included the novelist Alexander Lernet-Holenia (as a cavalry officer) and Franz Werfel, who worked as a telephone operator until he was summoned back to Vienna, at Kessler's instigation, to work in the *Kriegspressequartier*, another of the government propaganda offices.

Every shade of opinion is represented in this roll-call, from the shrill anti-war verse of Werfel and Ehrenstein, whose affinities were with the individualism of the Expressionist movement, to the patriotic commitment of the majority – a commitment that was sustained both by opposition to the declared enemies of the country and by a very general belief that the war was being fought in a just cause.

Prime among the foreign bogey-men were the British. Anti-British sentiments were strong and well-established. Suspicion of British colonialism had reached a peak during the Boer War, and *Kikeriki* had carried many rancorous cartoons on the subject.[9] While the artists and designers of the Secession and the Wiener Werkstätte were drawing inspiration from the example of Ashbee and the Mackintoshes (the eighth Secession exhibition at the end of 1900, which was devoted mainly to the applied arts, included a Mackintosh room), in nationalist circles the British ranked as no less an enemy than the Jews. At a meeting of the *Deutscher Verein* in October 1899 one speaker drew applause by dismissing the idea that England could be counted as belonging politically to Europe and by proclaiming the ideal of a 'United States of Europe' which might emerge in the twentieth century, created in reaction against English hostility from without and Jewish hostility within.[10] In 1914–15, together with Serbia, it was above all England that was reviled by Schaukal and other lesser jingoist poets such as Ernst von Dombrowski and Richard von Kralik, who berated the 'treachery' of perfidious Albion and called for divine vengeance ('Gott strafe England').[11]

The vituperative castigation that was meted out both to Britain and other enemies and also to doubters inside Austria was founded on the conviction of being in the right. This conviction is exemplified in a series of eight poems that Wildgans wrote between August 1914 and June 1915. These were first published as pamphlets by Hugo Heller and then reprinted in book form in Hofmannsthal's *Österreichische Bibliothek*. The first and second, 'Vae victis!' and 'Das große Händefalten', both written in August 1914, presented the war as being fought in defence of human rights and justice; the fourth, 'Ihr Kleingläubigen!' was directed at the doubters, claiming the biblical God of love as a 'god of hatred'.[12]

By the fifth and sixth poems, 'Allerseelen' and 'Legende', written in November, the realities of the killing are more to the fore, though without altering the poet's support for the Austrian cause. By the end of 1914 widespread disillusion had set in as losses in the trenches mounted and almost everyone lost friends and relatives. The advance of technology meant that the war, which had been entered into in a spirit of heroic idealism, rapidly became a destructive nightmare. Its four long years cost the Austrian armed forces alone nearly one and a quarter million lives (not counting those missing).

Relatively few were sceptical from the very first. Among these were both Werfel and Schnitzler. Werfel, who at the outbreak of war was working in Leipzig as a reader for the Kurt Wolff Verlag, wrote three anti-war poems in August 1914; one of them, 'Die Wortemacher des Krieges', invoked the heady cliché of the sublime 'hour of greatness' (the 'erhabene Zeit') and presented it as ushering in destruction and despair. He continued to express his mistrust of 'hohe Heimatworte', the deceptive rhetoric and patriotic shibboleths pictured in one of his poems of early 1915 as weapons of destruction.[13]

Schnitzler had been sceptical of militarism since his student years.[14] His perception of events in August 1914 is summed up in his diary entry for 5 August, following news of the British declaration of war against Germany: 'World war. World ruin. Momentous and monstrous news' ('[. . .] Ungeheuere und ungeheuerliche Nachrichten'). He took no sides. In December 1914, when he learned that he had been falsely accused of xenophobic comments disparaging foreign authors, he had a firm denial published in Swiss newspapers (AS/Bfe. II, 60–2). Equally when Italy entered the war against Austria-Hungary in May 1915 he was disgusted with the Italians, including d'Annunzio, and he did not disguise his relief when the danger of a Russian invasion was averted.[15] He was untouched by jingoism, but after the war was over, one of the things he held against Kraus was his criticism of Austria-Hungary and her allies 'without the least sense of the injustice and villainies on the other side' (Tgb., 4 February 1919). To him the war was itself an evil. In the autumn of 1914, after watching a surgeon friend operate on two badly-wounded soldiers, he observed that suffering is the very essence of war, adding that he, moreover, saw only an infinitesimal part of it (Tgb., 13 October 1914). Regrettably his surviving letters do not include the replies he wrote to the correspondence he received from Fritz von Unruh in northern France in the early months of the war, when Unruh was full of militaristic pride and determination, was awarded the Iron Cross for bravery, and even sent Schnitzler a poem from the front.[16] But it is striking that the receipt of these letters is often not even mentioned in Schnitzler's diaries, as though he could not bring himself to register either the danger Unruh was in or the mistakenness of his enthusiasm.

Writing to his sister-in-law Elisabeth Steinrück on 22 December 1914 he noted the incongruity in a performance of *Die Meistersinger* at the Volksoper: a full house, with delight on all sides, while outside a world war was being fought (AS/Bfe. II, 69). So too Karl Kraus would register in *Die letzten Tage der Menschheit* the inexhaustibly trivial fascination of the Viennese for the theatre through every catastrophe, from the educated man in the very first scene who remarks that the assassination of Franz Ferdinand will have serious consequences for box-office takings to the figure in

Act Two who is trying to procure tickets for an operetta and grumbles that it is sold out for so many weeks ahead that the war may be over before he gets to see it.[17] As the catastrophe unfolded, the theatrical rivalries that were the stuff of Schnitzler's everyday life in Vienna appeared insignificant in perspective – 'And out there there is a world war', he adds again in parentheses on 20 June 1915 – and his diary records his sense of despairing outrage: 'Horror upon horror, injustice upon injustice, madness upon madness!' (Tgb., 6 October 1915). There are obvious similarities between the view of the war advanced by Kraus in his public polemics and Schnitzler's private critique as evidenced by diary entries in which, recording conversations with friends on the 'pointless continuing slaughter' ('die sinnlose Weiterschlächterei': Tgb., 1 July 1916), he mentions the 'lack of imagination' ('Phantasielosigkeit') that permitted the war (Tgb., 6 March 1915) and the role of journalism in sustaining it (Tgb., 26 November 1914).

Though, like Hofmannsthal, Schnitzler disliked and mistrusted Kraus, he was a regular reader of *Die Fackel*. Kraus had long seen the dangers of technological advance which was open to abuse because out of control. As early as October 1908, in his 'open letter' entitled 'Apokalypse', charting the 'feverish progress of human stupidity', he had described mankind as having become 'complicated enough to construct machinery and too primitive to make it serve us' (F 261–262, 1), and he restated this view strongly during the war, notably in aphorisms published in *Die Fackel* in January 1917 (F 448–453, 4). By 1908 his opinion of the dangerous influence of the press was also established. The true function of journalism, as formulated in an aphorism of November 1908, lay only seemingly in serving the present: in fact it consisted in destroying the intellectual and spiritual receptiveness of posterity (F 264–265, 29). During the war he recurrently presented the press, as exemplified in particular by the *Neue Freie Presse*, as perverting the imagination and so dulling the moral sense. The theme is central in his first major wartime address, 'In dieser großen Zeit', another demolition of the cliché of the 'hour of greatness', which he delivered in November 1914 and which appeared in *Die Fackel* in early December: it is the newspaper reporter who has reduced mankind to such imaginative impoverishment that it can fight a war of destruction against itself (F 404, 9).

By that time the Austro-Hungarian army had already suffered heavy losses, in Galicia especially. Among those who read Kraus's essay was Rilke, and by mid-1915 he was echoing the view that the war was fomented by the press and that its continuance was motivated by commercial profiteering.[18] Kraus continued to present it as the product of technology in the hands of commercial interests, fanned and exploited by a corrupt press, and making nonsense of unimaginative clichés about 'dying a hero's death' – the 'Heldentod' repeatedly celebrated in patriotic verse as the war went on.[19] His dissent is summed up with polemical intensity by the 'Nörgler' in the first act of the last (postwar) version of *Die letzten Tage der Menschheit*, in one of his extended arguments with the moderate 'Optimist': 'If instead of the newspaper we had imagination, technology would not be a means of making life difficult and science would not be aiming at its destruction.'[20]

Kraus shared the inhibitions of his generation towards political activity. Like Schnitzler, he distanced himself from all political and ideological affiliation; in January 1906 he had indeed described himself as 'fanatically non-political' (F 194, 7). But he openly expressed his moral outrage concerning the war; Schnitzler, by contrast, kept his thoughts unpublished. According to Hofmannsthal, Schnitzler had once claimed to have no aptitude for journalism (H/Strauss, 215: letter of 19 December 1913); in the war at least, his feeling was rather one of distaste. His diary shows that this Bernhardi-like evasion of public commitment brought from his wife as early as 30 September 1914 an accusation of selfishness, of indulging in 'self-preservation out of keeping with the times' ('eine unzeitgemäße Selbstbewahrung') and a reproof 'for not publishing essays or finding some other appropriate activity' ('dass ich nicht essayistisch auftrete oder sonst irgend eine dem Augenblick gemäße Thätigkeit suche'). To his sister-in-law he defended himself at length:

> Even if I'm not lying in a trench – if indeed I avoid even making public 'statements' about the war – I stand just as four-square in our times as anyone else; and if I don't have thoughts about fatherland, heroism, and politics suitable for leaders or newspaper articles, I have still probably thought more sensible thoughts than many of those who have been publishing essays and lyric poems. (AS/Bfe. II, 66: letter of 22 December 1914)

In fact that October he had begun to draft a number of notes, in which he tried to come to terms with the issues raised by the war (AB, 187–230). These show that he recognized the strength of feeling on both sides but that his initial resigned acceptance of the inevitability of the war rapidly gave way to a rejection of the whole enterprise as a brutal evil, sustained by sentimental dishonesty, profiteering, and politicking. The pretence of the journalists that it was somehow ennobling was unfounded (AB, 199); it was senseless butchery ('sinnlose Menschenschlächterei': AB, 211). From early 1915 onwards these notes contain some barbed aphorisms (some of them probably written late in the war or even after it). For example:

> The history of the world is a conspiracy of diplomats against common sense. (AB, 200)

> As long as there is just one man to whom war brings advantage, and he has power and influence enough to unleash war, any attempt to prevent war will be in vain. (AB, 223)

> We say he died a hero's death [den schönen Heldentod]; why do we never say he suffered a hero's maiming [eine herrliche Heldenverstümmelung]? (AB, 220)

> A time of greatness: that is the time in which the discoveries and inventions of a time of ungreatness are exploited for the killing and maiming of human beings and for the destruction of values and works dating from the time of ungreatness. (AB, 225)

The last two of these betray the influence of Kraus. But all these reflections remained in Schnitzler's private papers; he maintained his public silence. On 28 November 1915, on one of his morning walks on the edge of the Vienna Woods to the north-west of the city, he bumped into Moriz Benedikt, the editor of the *Neue Freie Presse*, whose invitation to write something for the *Neue Freie Presse* about the war he met with the succinct rejoinder 'Wouldn't be printable' ('Laßt sich nicht drucken').

Kraus respected what he saw as Schnitzler's dignified silence, and in 1918 published an epigrammatic tribute:

Arthur Schnitzler

> Sein Wort vom Sterben wog nicht schwer.
> Doch wo viel Feinde, ist viel Ehr:
> er hat in Schlachten und Siegen
> geschwiegen.[21]

What he wrote of dying [an allusion to the early novella *Sterben*] carried little weight; but where enemies are all about, there's honour to be won: throughout the battles and the victories he held his peace.

Schnitzler's refusal to enter public debate was in marked contrast to the position adopted by Hofmannsthal, of which Kraus was consistently critical.[22] If Schnitzler had no illusions about the war from the first, Hofmannsthal steadily lost the illusions he had begun with. But while Schnitzler remained silent in public, Hofmannsthal maintained a stance of public patriotism.

Having been called up for active service at the beginning of the war, he drew on the influence of well-positioned friends, including Redlich, to get himself transferred within days to the *Kriegsfürsorgeamt*, the welfare department of the War Office in Vienna, where he was appointed head of the press department.[23] At first he protested his frustration at not being at the front. On 25 September, for example, he told Helene von Nostitz that it was 'torture' to him (H/Nostitz, 132), and on 28 October he told Ottonie von Degenfeld that it sometimes made him feel consumed by impatience and shame (H/Degenfeld, 312). These claims would carry more conviction if he had not also repeatedly and disingenuously feigned resignation to having to serve where he had been 'ordered' to serve.[24] Nevertheless, he threw himself energetically into his task, and a letter of 18 October to Bodenhausen shows his concern for the urgency of welfare work, in this case the need for winter equipment (H/Bodenhausen, 177–8). His commitment to welfare can also be seen from private letters that he wrote on 11 September to Beer-Hofmann and Schnitzler asking them for charitable contributions to the Viennese *Rettungsgesellschaft*.[25]

In October he was declared medically unfit for active service, and once he was discharged from the *Kriegsfürsorgeamt* in May 1915 (again after Redlich's intercession)[26] he was free to devote himself to patriotic essayistic work. His correspondence shows, however, that by then he had already begun to be disillusioned with the war. In November 1914 he wrote to Gustav Stolper, an economist, about the muddle and irresponsible lack of planning he observed on all sides.[27] In December he published in the *Neue Freie Presse* a letter Schröder had written him describing the terrible experience of war as a loss of an Arcadian past.[28] By Easter 1915 he was expressing despair at the apparently endless killing: 'If only this horrible massacre ('dieses gräuliche Morden') would cease, thousands constantly dying', he wrote to Bodenhausen on Easter Monday 1915; 'sometimes I feel we shall never know happiness again' (H/Bodenhausen, 192–3). This met with a patriotic reproach from Bodenhausen, who replied on 8 April that it was not murder but dying for the sake of life, and therefore unavoidable ('Aber lieber Hugo, es ist doch kein Morden, es ist ein Sterben um des Lebens willen, also unvermeidlich': H/Bodenhausen, 193). But Hofmannsthal's despair grew. By the autumn of 1915 he was telling Bodenhausen that he sometimes felt he could not bear the present state of the world much longer (H/Bodenhausen, 203: letter of 27 September 1915). He had realized, as he put it to Ottonie von Degenfeld, that this war was worse even than the Napoleonic wars; he wrote of the 'inexpressible release' ('eine unsagbare Erlösung') that peace would bring (H/Degenfeld, 323: letter of 14 October 1915). On 11 November he wrote to Bodenhausen's wife expressing the hope that Fate would 'just release us alive from this most monstrous of all trials' (H/Bodenhausen, 205).

He too recognized the unhealthy state of the Austrian and Viennese press, and indeed referred on 17 November 1915, in a letter to Andrian, to its 'abject' condition and 'proverbial' vacuousness (H/Andrian, 221). The next summer, writing on 31 July 1916, he lamented how everyone seemed to have been 'infected' by a 'journalistic' outlook, short-sightedly opportunistic ('Der journalistische, momentane Geist hat alle Menschen erstaunlich inficiert': H/Andrian, 234). In the same month he wrote to Rudolf Borchardt about the 'heavy fate' that had been visited on their whole generation (H/Borchardt, 122: letter of 14 July 1916). A letter of 7 September 1916 to Andrian shows him depressed by mistakes made in the conduct of the war rather than by the principle underlying it (H/Andrian, 239), but by the end of the year Redlich noted his depression about its 'senseless continuation'.[29] By 25 January 1917 it had become 'this horror [dieses Gräuliche] that makes the entire world [. . .] seem shallow and absurd and villainous' (H/Bodenhausen, 227), and by 10 July 1917 it was simply 'this hell around us' ('diese Hölle um uns': H/Bodenhausen, 236).

Even before the outbreak of war, Hofmannsthal had already been depressed by social and political developments. His concern about the growth of materialism is reflected in the monitory depiction in *Jedermann* of the demonic power of Mammon. When the play was first produced in the Burgtheater, he took stock of its success throughout German-speaking Europe and complained that reviewers never took the trouble to compare it with the English *Everyman* to see the originality of his reworking (H/Strauss, 217: letter of 19 December 1913). The comparison, both with *Everyman* and with Hans Sachs's *Hecastus*, shows a distinctive shift of emphasis. In Hofmannsthal's version Mammon is presented from the start as the scourge of Man: Jedermann is a heartless materialist, who relies on money to make him 'godlike' (HKA IX, 44). After the appearance of Death, Mammon leaps from Jedermann's chest of money and mockingly brings home his powerlessness, his subservience to his own wealth (HKA IX, 78–80).[30]

Over and above his critical view of the materialist *Zeitgeist*, Hofmannsthal was deeply worried by political developments in Austria-Hungary, in particular the centrifugal forces that threatened the harmony and even the integrity of the monarchy. This worry is reflected, for example, in a letter of 30 April 1912 to Bodenhausen: 'Things are looking bleak here, Eberhard, bleak for our old

Austria [. . .]. We are facing dark times, everyone senses this'
(H/Bodenhausen, 144–5). Part of the problem as he saw it lay in
the declining influence of the nobility and of leading cultural and
intellectual figures. He told Andrian on 24 August 1913 that Vienna
was in the hands of a petit-bourgeois rabble, and that he foresaw
the dissolution of the empire, left without a binding principle to
sustain it (H/Andrian, 198–200). Andrian replied reproachfully,
urging him to exert his own influence in defence of the 'idea of
Austria', and defining the importance of the multinational concept
of the monarchy (H/Andrian, 201–5: letter of 18 September 1913).

Concern in Hofmannsthal's circle with the future and role of
Austria went back to the 1890s. Bahr's diary records a discussion
about it between himself and Andrian on 8 July 1896 and his plan
for monographs to help establish a 'conception of what is Austrian',
and on 29 November 1903 he was arguing with Hofmannsthal in
Rodaun 'that it was all over for Austria'.[31] Now the theme had a
new urgency, and became the principal concern of the political and
patriotic essays and addresses to which Hofmannsthal turned his
literary energies, beginning in 1914 while he was still technically a
serving officer. As in the conscious change of direction in his work
in 1902, so again now he resorted to daily newspapers as a medium
offering wide circulation for his ideas.

His first published utterance about the war, the 'Appell an die
oberen Stände' ('Appeal to the Aristocracy'), published in the *Neue
Freie Presse* on 8 September 1914, urges caution about the dangers
of continuing in the fine enthusiasm ('die schöne Berauschung') of
the first days of the war (P III, 176). His next journalistic essay,
however, 'Die Bejahung Österreichs', is entirely patriotic in tone,
'affirming' Austria-Hungary and its army at a difficult time. Later
reprinted in the *Kriegsalmanach 1915*, the piece first appeared in the
Österreichische Rundschau at the beginning of November 1914, and
prompted a conversation between Schnitzler and Auernheimer
about Hofmannsthal's conservatism. As Schnitzler summarized it in
his diary on 13 November, his 'feudalism' seemed to be growing.

At the end of the year, published in the Christmas issue of the
Neue Freie Presse, there followed 'Worte zum Gedächtnis des
Prinzen Eugen', a celebration of Eugene of Savoy, the hero of
Austria's struggle against the Turks in the late seventeenth and
early eighteenth century. This essay, which presents Eugene as 'the
greatest Austrian of all' (P III, 205), the creator of modern Austria,
motivated by a consuming love of Austria, is an example of
deliberate mythopoeia, an attempt to supply a heroic image from
Austrian history to meet the inspirational needs of the hour. An
illustrated portrait of Eugene, *Prinz Eugen, der edle Ritter*, fol-

lowed the following year, with a concluding poem presenting his spirit as ever-present in the Austrian army (P III, 317). The essay 'Grillparzers politisches Vermächtnis', which appeared on 16 May 1915, again in the *Neue Freie Presse*, uses one of the great figures in Austrian cultural history to elaborate a similarly patriotic ideal.

Hofmannsthal's reflections on the war centred more and more on its likely cultural consequences both internationally and within the monarchy. Bodenhausen, who was a leading figure in the firm of Krupp, was one of his closest confidants at this time; when he died in 1918, Hofmannsthal wrote to his widow that he had lost his 'irreplaceable best friend' (H/Bodenhausen, 252: telegram dated 8 May 1918). Another German friend also stimulated his interest in cultural politics:[32] in the summer of 1915 he read Rudolf Borchardt's address 'Der Krieg und die deutsche Selbsteinkehr' ('The War and German Self-Examination'), which had first been delivered at the end of the previous year, and told Ottonie von Degenfeld that it was 'the most impressive piece written in German' that he had read since the outbreak of the war (H/Degenfeld, 321: letter of 1 August 1915). Not long after this Redlich began to note how changed Hofmannsthal had become, earnestly committed to translating his sense of his 'profound Austrianness' ('sein tiefinnerliches Österreichertum') into practical results.[33] But the principal influence on his developing political thinking, especially in relation to a distinctive 'Austrianness', was clearly Andrian, whose Catholic conservatism was one of the main bases for Hofmannsthal's idealized image of Austria as a repository of cultural tradition.

He openly admitted his fascinated interest in Andrian's diplomatic work (H/Andrian, 233: letter of 31 July 1916). There was indeed something rather naïve in how impressed he was, but it made him eager to accept an invitation to Warsaw when Andrian returned there as Austrian envoy to the German military government. It was there in the summer of 1916 that he first gave the lecture that was subsequently published under the title 'Österreich im Spiegel seiner Dichtung', in which he expounded the 'dualism' of Austria's relationship to Germany, its separate identity and at the same time its allegiance to German culture in the wider sense ('unsere kulturelle Zugehörigkeit zum deutschen Gesamtwesen': P III, 345). It was in Austria, he argued, that the most worthwhile elements in German history were preserved; hence the 'mission' of Austria, its essentially conservative obligation to the surrounding peoples (P III, 346–7).

Andrian had long been a defender of the multinational Austria that existed under the Habsburgs. It has been suggested that he may originally have inclined to this view because his own partly Jewish descent was incompatible with the anti-Semitic line adopted by the Austrian pan-Germanists.[34] As early as 28 July 1898 he had told Hofmannsthal of his insistence on the individuality of Austrian culture, firmly defining his 'principle not to allow Vienna to be seen or treated as a German provincial centre, nor Austria as an annex of Germany' (H/Andrian, 110), and he sternly reminded Hofmannsthal that he was 'not a German but an Austrian' (H/Andrian, 144: letter of 10 March 1900). Entering the Austrian diplomatic service provided a natural outlet for his patriotism. He was schooled as a diplomat under Aehrenthal, who was Austrian Foreign Minister from 1906 to 1912. Andrian served under him in the St Petersburg embassy in 1905–6 and was appointed by him to Warsaw in 1911. Aehrenthal pursued an imperialist policy that culminated in the annexation of Bosnia and Herzegovina in 1908, and gathered round him in the Foreign Ministry a group of like-minded loyalist Austrian nationalists who after his death in 1912 exercised considerable influence under his successor, Berchtold.[35]

In his letters to Hofmannsthal Andrian continued to defend his ideal of a separate Austria as something 'far transcending the ideal of a simple nation-state', since it was based, so he argued on 18 September 1913, on 'co-operation and up to a point the mingling of the geniuses of all the peoples' of the monarchy; their very existence was 'possible only within a great empire, and therefore directly dependent on the existence of Austria itself' (H/Andrian, 204–5). Posted back to Warsaw in 1915, Andrian defended Austrian interests against Germany. Recalled to Vienna in 1916 under German pressure, he grew increasingly disillusioned by Austrian subservience to Germany and by 5 May 1918 recorded in his diary his sense of political 'hopelessness'.[36]

Schnitzler was particularly sceptical about the effect of Andrian's influence on Hofmannsthal and recorded with evident amusement the news, brought to him by Jakob Wassermann in 1915, that for all his political pretensions the diplomatic circles with which Hofmannsthal was constantly in contact did not take him seriously (Tgb., 26 November 1915). But Hofmannsthal's lecture tours were not unique. Bahr, for example, gave public addresses on the subject of Austria and toured Germany in the winter of 1915–16 with a lecture that Hofmannsthal admired as 'clever and tactful' (H/Andrian, 226: letter of 28 January 1916). Moreover, Hofmannsthal's patriotism was always tempered by the cosmopolitan breadth of his reading. In the middle of the war, in 1916, he reread a series of Molière comedies (A, 175–81), and discussed Molière with Andrian in Warsaw (A, 178). The lectures he gave were increasingly conciliatory in tone; this emerges from his notes both for lectures in

Scandinavia and for a lecture on the 'idea of Europe' ('Die Idee Europa': P III, 350–83), and as early as 31 July 1916 he wrote to Andrian that everyone in the German and Austrian press found him 'not enough of a chauvinist' ('zu wenig Chauvinist': H/Andrian, 234). What was distinctive in his approach was the cultural dimension he imparted to the 'idea of Austria'.

One of the most important of his projects to defend the integrity of Austrian culture was the *Österreichische Bibliothek*, a series of slim books which was launched in 1915 with the intention of establishing in Germany the idea of a distinctively individual Austrian culture.[37] It was published by the Insel-Verlag in Leipzig, with Hofmannsthal as general editor. As a letter of autumn 1914 to Andrian makes clear, the members of his editorial board were picked to gain support beyond Liberal circles (H/Andrian, 208). Andrian agreed to lend his name to the project in a letter which shows that they even planned an approach for support to Friedrich Funder, the editor-in-chief of the *Reichspost* (H/Andrian, 210: letter of 7 December 1914). The final committee included a number of writers of strongly patriotic persuasion: Wildgans, Kralik, Mell, and others. The first volume, *Grillparzers politisches Vermächtnis*, with Hofmannsthal's essay of that title as foreword, appeared in July 1915. Over the next fourteen months twenty-five more appeared; among these Wildgans's *Österreichische Gedichte* was issued towards the end of 1915 as Volume 12. To the end Hofmannsthal saw the enterprise as an exercise in cultural propaganda: it was, he told Andrian, a 'patriotic publication' aimed at readers outside Austria (H/Andrian, 243: letter of 24 October 1916).

Together with his editorial activity, he continued to write further essays arguing the cultural mission of Austria. These included both 'Österreich im Spiegel seiner Dichtung' and the 1917 essay 'Die österreichische Idee', in which the essential character of Austria is defined in its historical and geographical role as both a boundary between eastern and western Europe and at the same time a meeting-place of cultures (P III, 404–5). Written in the belief that the war was about to end (Hofmannsthal uses the phrase 'zu Ende des Krieges': P III, 401), this essay reflects a number of ideas that were in general currency[38] and argues that the essential cultural task of Austria as a country was to effect a synthesis, a compromise between its German elements – no longer thought of in nationalist terms – and Slav elements ('dieses nicht mehr scharf-nationale Deutsche mit slawischem Wesen zum Ausgleich zu bringen'), and hence to promote a supranational politics of reconciliation within Europe (an 'übernationale europäische Politik': P III, 405). In this notion of an internationalism based on the preservation of specifically Austrian qualities we can already see the ideological base for Hofmannsthal's involvement in the Salzburg Festival after the war.

The empire was about to disappear, as the map of Europe was redrawn and countries like Czechoslovakia, Romania, and the Kingdom of the Serbs, Croats, and Slovenes (later Yugoslavia) came into being. By 1917, taking stock was painful. Karl Kraus summed up the consequences of 1914 in a poem that appeared in *Die Fackel* in October 1917 with the sharply ironic title 'Der allgemeine Verteidigungskrieg' ('The Defensive World War'):

> Da zehn Millionen Menschen begraben,
> so bleib' ich der Menschheit weiter gewogen.
> Nur möcht' ich das gute Gewissen nicht haben,
> mit dem sie in jenen Krieg gezogen!
>
> (F 472–473, 1)

Now that ten million human beings have been buried, I still remain well-disposed to humankind. But I wouldn't like to have the clear conscience with which they entered that war!

Franz Joseph had died at the end of 1916, but the allusion is to his proclamation announcing war against Serbia in July 1914, 'An meine Völker!' Hofmannsthal, by contrast, was not concerned to apportion blame; his thinking was dominated by profound pessimism at the threatened break-up of the monarchy. He saw the rising tide of separatism, and a letter of 10 July 1917 to Bodenhausen sums up his gloom: it represented 'the last agony of the thousand-year-old Holy Roman Empire' (H/Bodenhausen, 235), that is, of a divinely ordained institution, for which even a new German *Reich* including the German-speaking Austrians would be no substitute.

It was Andrian who perceived the potential significance of Hofmannsthal's commitment as an essayist during the war for the development of his later writing. 'From the point of view of your development', he wrote on 31 August 1916, 'I think it very possible that your present work is a necessary preparation for what will be your true poetic life's work' (H/Andrian, 238). Certainly the conception of the 'idea of Austria' and the defence of the values he saw threatened would be among the most powerful elements determining the character of his postwar work.

The Birth of the Republic

In mid-October 1918 Karl Kraus published in *Die Fackel* an excerpt from the epilogue to *Die letzten Tage der Menschheit*; the first complete version of the tragedy, in which the war is presented in apocalyptic terms as 'the last days of mankind', was published between December 1918 and August 1919.[39] After the war, the image of apocalypse became a cliché: Paul Zifferer, for example, wrote to Hofmannsthal on 24 November 1920: 'The wreck of Austria is the centre of the apocalypse [des Weltunterganges] we are living through' (H/Zifferer, 89).

Schnitzler had seen the war from its outbreak as spelling 'world ruin' (Tgb., 5 August 1914), and as it drew to a close and the consequences of defeat became clear, the idea of 'apocalypse' (he too uses the word 'Weltuntergang') crops up repeatedly in his diary: on 1 August 1918, on 20 October 1918, and on 19 May 1919. Hofmannsthal's concern meanwhile continued to centre on the cultural implications of the loss of the war and the break-up of the monarchy, which he had perceived in advance as a 'cataclysm' (H/Bodenhausen, 235: letter of 10 July 1917).

Even Schnitzler could summon up little enthusiasm when within days of the armistice the Republic was declared in November 1918. The political upheaval was overshadowed by violence on the streets of Vienna. 'A historic day is over,' he noted that evening. 'At close quarters it does not seem very splendid' (Tgb., 12 November 1918). Hofmannsthal told Ottonie von Degenfeld that the event confirmed all that he had foreseen for over a year (H/Degenfeld, 375: letter of 26 November 1918). If he acknowledged that a German victory would have been disastrous,[40] one of the reasons must have been his conviction of the importance of preserving Austrian independence from Germany. He continued to see in the breakdown of the old political structure a disruption of historical continuity; the point is made, for example, in a letter of 11 May 1919 to Carl J. Burckhardt (H/Burckhardt, 14). Two months earlier, following a reflection on Viennese society at the time, he had confessed to Burckhardt that he was engaged in reading Spengler's *Der Untergang des Abendlandes*, the first volume of which had been published the previous year (H/Burckhardt, 7–8: letter of 11 March 1919). In 1923 he could still refer tersely to a general assumption that the age was one of decline ('Wenn unsere Epoche eine des Untergangs sein soll . . .': A, 234).

Circumstances in Austria could hardly have been less propitious politically. The punitively harsh cease-fire conditions had included Austrian vacation of Tyrol south of the Brenner Pass, and it was under protest that the cease-fire was signed on 3 November, eight days before the Allies signed the final cease-fire with Germany. Even Schnitzler, the most balanced and unnationalistic of observers, was appalled at the terms imposed, which he regarded as nonsensical (Tgb., 11 November 1918).

On 11 November parliament approved a draft proclamation of a democratic republic of 'German Austria' (Deutschösterreich) as an integral part of the German republic, and the last Habsburg Emperor, Karl I, signed a formal renunciation of his share in the government of Austria. The republic of Deutschösterreich would have had over ten million inhabitants, and would have included German-speaking Bohemia ('Deutschböhmen') and the Sudetenland (western Silesia and northern Moravia), but it was radically reduced in size by the Treaty of Saint-Germain-en-Laye, the terms of which were accepted by the Austrian parliament (Nationalversammlung) on 6 September 1919 'under solemn protest to the whole world'. This treaty was signed on 10 September (ten weeks after the Treaty of Versailles between the Allies and Germany, and nine months before the Treaty of Trianon between the Allies and Hungary) and ratified in July 1920. Its terms reduced Austria to a rump republic with about six and a half million inhabitants, as against twenty-eight and a half million in the Austrian half of the Dual Monarchy (and over fifty million in the whole monarchy), and expressly proscribed the union of Austria with Germany (*Anschluss*). It laid the foundations for the unhappy history of the Austrian republic between the World Wars, a history of economic depression and persistently high unemployment; of civil unrest, with rival militias on the left and the right, culminating in the Civil War of 1934; and of government by a succession of weak coalitions until the suspension of parliament in 1933 and the establishment under Dollfuss of what has become known as 'Austro-Fascism'.

In 1919 the hardest immediate blows were two: first, the redrawing of the frontier with Italy and the loss of German-speaking South Tyrol, with over 200,000 German-speakers; and secondly, the loss to the newly-formed republic of Czechoslovakia of regions in Bohemia, Austrian Silesia, Moravia (with the German *Sprachinseln* Brünn, Iglau, and Olmütz), and the northern borders of Lower and Upper Austria, containing in all nearly three million German-speakers, all of whom had been included in the new state of 'Deutschösterreich' proclaimed by the provisional parliament on 22 November 1918. The principle of self-determination had inevitably to be sacrificed, given the practical impossibility of drawing frontiers to accommodate German-speakers who were scattered either on the northern borders of Bohemia or in the interior of Czechoslovakia. But the loss of these regions was to have severe economic consequences, and the terms of the treaty of St-Germain-en-Laye – 'the destruction treaty' ('der Vernichtungsfriede') as the *Kronen-Zeitung* called it when reporting its signature on 11 September 1919 – provoked profound and lasting resentment. When the *Reichspost* carried an article in 1920 describing the northern boundary with Czechoslovakia as a 'painful amputation' recently carried out on the body of Austria,[41] it was expressing a view that was widely shared and was by no means limited to the ultra-right-wing press. On 1 August 1922 the *Neue Freie Presse* was still referring to a 'mutilated' Austria created against the will of its people.

The 'mutilation' deprived Austria of important traditional sources of agricultural and industrial production. A substantial part of its food production had come from what was now independent Hungary, and most of its former industrial base lay in Silesia and Czechoslovakia. One effect was hyper-inflation and the collapse of the currency at the beginning of the 1920s. On 1 August 1922 (when the Austrian Krone had fallen to one thousandth the value of the Czech Krone) a front-page article in the *Neue Freie Presse* recalled that Austria depended on regularly importing coal by the train-load – eight hundred wagons a day – from Czechoslovakia, and put the blame for the currency crisis squarely on the Saint-Germain treaty.

What the crisis meant for the cultural life of Vienna can be gauged by the price of books and journals. In February 1920 one Krone bought about 25.5 pages of the issue of *Die Fackel* that appeared then (F 521–530). By July 1922 (F 595–600) each page cost 12.5 Krone; that is, the price had risen by a factor of over 300. The price spiral continued the next month: in the course of August 1922 the cover price of the *Neue Freie Presse* more than trebled. The late summer of 1922 was when the inflation peaked, and though the currency was stabilized by the Geneva Protocols later that year, the price paid included a renewed insistence on Austrian independence from Germany, and so a continuation both of economic isolation and also of vulnerability to German economic pressure.

What is less well known outside Austria is that the very boundaries of the republic were not finally settled until 1922.[42] The relation of the individual provinces (*Länder*) to the central state was already problematic, in that most of them had a long-established individual identity, which had been strengthened in the second half of the nineteenth century by the division of responsibilities between the monarchy (which retained responsibility for the military, police etc.) and the *Länder*, which had responsibility for social planning and welfare. In the immediate aftermath of the First World War there was not one province in which uncertainties did not arise either about its boundaries or even about its allegiance to the new republic.

In Vorarlberg, in the extreme west of the country, there was from the outset considerable reluctance to commit the province to

Austria. Indeed, a plebiscite in May 1919 showed a substantial majority (4:1) for negotiating incorporation in Switzerland, with which Vorarlberg is linked not only geographically but linguistically; this development foundered from lack of encouragement from the Swiss. In neighbouring Tyrol, which was briefly invaded by Bavarian troops in early November 1918, a variety of separatist policies were actively canvassed, the principal priority always being to reverse the much-resented loss of South Tyrol. Plans mooted included the declaration of an independent Tyrol, to include South Tyrol; the formation of a new neutral 'Alpine republic' (*Alpenländische Republik*) together with Vorarlberg, Salzburg, Styria, and Carinthia (the *Reichspost* reported on 4 January 1919 that this idea was being discussed); joining either Switzerland or Bavaria; linking with Italy, either as an Italian protectorate or with Italy guaranteeing the independence of a united Tyrol under the League of Nations; and *Anschluss* with Germany, which was overwhelmingly supported in a popular vote in April 1921.

In Salzburg too there was pressure for *Anschluss* with Germany. Salzburg had been incorporated in Austria only in 1816, initially as part of Upper Austria (Oberösterreich), had been a separate province only since 1849, and was the one province with a wholly German-speaking population.[43] In Carinthia (Kärnten), by contrast, there was a sizable Slovene minority, and the Kingdom of the Serbs, Croats, and Slovenes (Yugoslavia) laid claim to southern Carinthia. There was intermittent fighting from January 1919 onwards, with Yugoslav troops pushing forward to Klagenfurt and Villach on 29 April, then a new Yugoslav offensive a month later leading to the capture on 6 June of Klagenfurt, which was held until the end of July. Italy intervened to prevent further Yugoslav advances, but the issue was not settled until October 1920, when a plebiscite in the disputed districts produced a clear majority in favour of remaining in Austria. Yugoslavia also claimed southern Styria (Steiermark), and there was fighting there too in December 1918.

In Upper Austria the provisional provincial assembly (*Landesversammlung*) committed the province to membership of the new Austrian republic in November 1918. But even here, in the one province that had plentiful food in store at the end of the war, a system of transport permits prevented the free flow of supplies to the capital – an example of the tensions that existed between the provinces and the centre. In Lower Austria, of which Vienna was a part until the end of 1921, there were border clashes for nearly three years, with Czech troops in 1918–19 and with Hungarian irregulars as late as September 1921, when Bruck an der Leitha was attacked.

Disputes about the Hungarian–Austrian border centred mainly, however, on the most easterly province, the Burgenland. The so-called 'Vierburgenland', which was at first to be called 'German West Hungary' ('Deutschwestungarn'), included the predominantly German-speaking area around Pressburg (now Bratislava), but the Treaty of Trianon yielded only the Ödenburg district to Austria. Even that provoked armed resistance; after a plebiscite in December 1921 the town of Ödenburg itself (Sopron, south of Eisenstadt, the provincial capital) was finally ceded to Hungary, and there was a further small boundary adjustment in September 1922.

Not even Vienna itself was immune from speculation: in 1920 the Berlin weekly *Die Zukunft* carried an article arguing (on the basis of its international character and historic role as capital of a multi-national state) that it should be separated from 'German Austria' and made the home of the League of Nations, an internationalist republican city-state.[44]

The cumulative effect of all these uncertainties, following the disintegration of the monarchy, should not be underestimated: a generation whose sense of individual identity had long been insecure was now faced with a national identity crisis as the very integrity of Austria was under attack from north, south, east, and west.

In their responses to the rapidly-changing political situation immediately after the end of the war, Schnitzler and Hofmannsthal once again reacted very differently. Schnitzler's diaries register many conversations on political matters with friends and acquaintances in the year or so after the end of the war; these things were after all on everyone's lips. But the momentous public events were overshadowed in his life by personal worries concerning his health (particularly his hearing), his creative unproductiveness, and the deterioration of his marriage. 'The whole apocalypse [Der ganze Weltuntergang] we are facing', he noted on 20 October 1918, recording a walk he had taken in the north-western outskirts of Vienna, 'paled before my personal [. . .] bitterness'.

In the first elections in February 1919 he voted for the Social Democrats. From his diary we know that he had also voted for Social Democrat candidates both in the general election of May 1907 and in local elections in 1912;[45] but the entry for 16 February 1919 makes it clear that he did so now with little conviction, since he disliked the *Arbeiter-Zeitung* and mistrusted leanings in the party both to anti-Semitism and to 'Bolshevism'. Nevertheless, he wanted to distance himself as far as possible from the Right; he also judged it important for the Social Democrats to get a sizable minority of seats if civil unrest was to be avoided.

To the end of his life he remained wary of extremes, and in private correspondence did not conceal his disapproval both of pan-German nationalism on the Right and of 'Bolshevism' on the Left.[46] Reporting to his wife on the violence of 1927, when eighty-nine people were killed as police fired on demonstrators following the Justizpalast fire, he remained true to his contempt for the villainy of party politics ('die ganze schurkische Gemeinheit der Parteipolitik'), laying the whole blame on the party leaders, while at the same time ironizing the whole crisis as 'just one of our pleasant little Viennese revolutions' (AS/Bfe. II, 487–90: letter of 17–18 July 1927).

In his letter of 22 December 1914 to Elisabeth Steinrück, he had forecast that after the war his writing could not fail to reflect the events they were living through (AS/Bfe. II, 67), yet in fact his post-war work is mainly set in the vanished world of the pre-war years. Even in the late novel *Therese* the action ends before the beginning of the First World War.[47] By contrast with Hofmannsthal's pre-occupation with political developments and cultural politics, it is also remarkable how little Schnitzler's letters after the war – at least those that have been published – touch on the events of the moment, how much they turn instead on his own writings and their reception. True to his lifelong apolitical habits, he did not react to external crisis by publicly confronting it; rather, he re-worked old material or else turned inward, for example in devoting himself from October 1918 to January 1920 to dictating his auto-biography, which he had been preparing during the war. He re-mained in the public eye, particularly at the very start of the republic, when the Viennese productions of *Professor Bernhardi* and *Reigen* created public furore. He was the first president of the Austrian P.E.N.-Zentrum – at first hardly more than a dining club – of which Hofmannsthal was also a member; in 1927 Schnitzler, by then honorary president, wrote to Wildgans expressing his dis-satisfaction at its inactivity.[48] But despite his continuing alertness, he published only four more new plays after the end of the war. None of those achieved a major success either with the critics or at the box-office.

In the events of 1918–20 Hofmannsthal saw all his worst fears realized; a letter of June 1920 to Carl J. Burckhardt expresses the 'despair, resignation, abhorrence, disgust, revulsion' he had felt for six years 'in a world slowly collapsing and then rotting' ('[. . .] in einer langsam zusammenstürzenden, dann verwesenden Welt': H/Burckhardt, 40). Though by comparison with Schnitzler he enjoyed considerable public success, especially through the Salzburg Festival, he continued to find the postwar environment threatening. In a letter of 4 June 1922 to Willy Haas, for example, he wrote that his position as an artist was 'infinitely precarious' in the modern world (H/Haas, 47). He too took refuge in autobiographical reflections, schematizing his own development, fashioning as it were his own myth of his career: it was in April 1921 that he wrote his letter to Max Pirker, dividing his career as a dramatist into three periods (A, 369–70). In the same year he started adding again to his notes *Ad me ipsum*; significantly, some of the earliest new notes were those concerning the creation of myths (A, 233). He too remained suspicious of the effects of 'Bolshevism'. That in the mid-1920s this informed his characterization of Olivier in *Der Turm* is spelt out in a letter to Jella Oppenheimer explicitly associating the figure of Olivier with the disruptiveness of revolution, including the 1917 Bolshevik Revolution.[49] By this time he may also have made contact with the reactionary social theorist Othmar Spann,[50] the author of an influential book entitled *Der wahre Staat* (1921) which would later provide some of the theoretical basis for the non-democratic 'corporate state' (*Ständestaat*) proclaimed by Dollfuss in 1933. Based on lectures given by Spann at the University of Vienna in 1920, this book advances a romantic idea of a 'corporative' (explicitly anti-Marxist, but also anti-capitalist) state, which is conceived as a 'universalist' counter to a modern democratic 'individualism' whose roots lie in the Renaissance.[51]

Hofmannsthal's distress at postwar developments was all the more acute because of his commitment to the 'idea of Austria'. The overthrow of the monarchy in 1918 had spelt an end to the hopes of Catholic conservatives, and Andrian impressed on him the disastrous consequences likely to follow from the break-up of Austria-Hungary. Three months after the revolution Andrian wrote:

> It may be well known that the Austria of Franz Joseph has slipped badly away from the Austrian ideal, but if the work of four centuries is simply cancelled there will be even more repression, misery, and barbarism [Culturlosigkeit] than there has already been in Austria since Königgrätz. (H/Andrian, 296: letter of 13 February 1919)

The collapse of his political hopes threw Andrian into a despair which continued to spill out in his letters to Hofmannsthal. Thus on 6 April 1924 he wrote that their 'position as Austrians having to write in German, primarily for a German public', was hard enough; it was simply not true that they *were* Germans, any more than that Maeterlinck was a Frenchman (H/Andrian, 354). A *Festschrift* published that year in honour of Hofmannsthal's fiftieth birthday under the title *Eranos* included one of Andrian's very few late poems, a sonnet addressed to Hofmannsthal, 'The Poet of Austria' ('Dem Dichter Österreichs'),[52] but to the end of his life Hofmannsthal also continued to receive from Andrian letters insisting that the declaration of the republic in November 1918 had reduced Austria to a 'beggar state' ('zu einem Bettelstaat') and sealed its disintegration (H/Andrian, 426: letter of 22 September 1928). Hofmannsthal's letters to other friends, in particular Carl J. Burckhardt, testify to his own depression at the position, which he found had a quite 'deadening' effect on him (H/Burckhardt, 233: letter of 25 November 1926); and reading Andrian's letters must have contributed to his inability to overcome his fear that the break-up of the monarchy had undermined his very purpose and function as an artist. Just two months after Andrian's letter of 22 September 1928, he wrote to Josef Redlich of the despair he himself felt:

> Eben weil ich mit dem Zusammenbruch Österreichs das Erdreich verloren habe, in welches ich verwurzelt bin, [. . .] weil mein eigenes dichterisches Dasein in diesem Zusammensturz fragwürdig geworden ist (und fragwürdig werden mußte, sieht man es für mehr an, als für ein bloßes Litteratendasein) [. . .] (H/Redlich, 116: letter of 28 November 1928)

> Precisely because with the collapse of Austria I have lost the empire in which I have my roots, [. . .] because my own existence as an imaginative writer is called into question by this collapse – inevitably so, if that existence is to be seen as more than that of a mere *littérateur* [. . .]

One result of the apparent precariousness of Austria as a political entity and the critical weakness of the Austrian economy was an upsurge of nostalgia for happier bygone days. As ever, the mood was satirically reflected in *Kikeriki*, which carried on 29 August 1920 a mock small ad: 'Come back the past, all is forgiven' ('Vergangenheit kehre zurück, alles vergeben!').

Its effects were felt throughout the cultural life of Vienna. In the theatre, a high proportion of the plays (not just new plays) produced there in the period between the wars were set in the period before the First World War.[53] The shelves of the bookshops similarly reflected a vogue for the past: not only historical novels enjoyed ever-increasing popularity[54] but also scholarly productions in the field of literature and local history. In particular, there was an intensification of the interest, already in evidence at the turn of the century, in the 'Old Vienna' of the Biedermeier age and earlier.

This continuity of interest is exemplified in a series launched in 1920, 'Theater und Kultur', with which both Hofmannsthal and

Bahr were associated. Edited first by Smekal and from 1921 by Pirker, this series consisted of small monographs and collections of documents to do with the Viennese theatre; the second volume was a volume on Raimund, compiled by Smekal, to which Hofmannsthal contributed a foreword. Early in the following year, quite independently, a collection of documents edited by Paul Wertheimer concerning the history of the theatre in Vienna (*Alt-Wiener Theater*) was published. At the same time a Viennese local historian, Gustav Gugitz, was producing substantial documentary studies on aspects of the popular theatre in the late eighteenth and early nineteenth centuries: in 1920 *Der Weiland Kasperl* (*Johann La Roche*) and in 1925, co-authored with Emil Karl Blümml and published by the Viennese firm of Anton Schroll & Co., *Alt-Wiener Thespiskarren*. Schroll, a firm that had originally specialized in art and art history (at the turn of the century their list had included the important journal *Der Architekt*), also published complete editions of the major Viennese dramatists of the previous century: a seventeen-volume edition of Anzengruber (1920–22) was followed by editions of Raimund in seven volumes (1924–34) and of Nestroy in fifteen volumes (1924–30). The historical and critical edition of Grillparzer, which had been launched in 1909, appeared under Schroll's imprint from 1916 onwards and made steady progress, with twelve volumes being published in the years 1923–30.

In the same period Blümml and Gugitz also produced collections of essays on other aspects of local cultural history (*Altwienerisches*, 1920; *Von Leuten und Zeiten im alten Wien*, 1922); other works of popular scholarship in this field – publications drawing on documentary material but designed to appeal to the general educated reading public – included Karl Kobald's *Alt-Wiener Musikstätten* (1918) and Friedrich Reischl's *Wien zur Biedermeierzeit* (1921). The Biedermeier period was the subject of numerous books, including Kobald's illustrated biographies of Beethoven (1927) and Schubert (1928) and historical biographies by Joseph August Lux (*Beethovens unsterbliche Geliebte*, 1926; *Franz Schuberts Lebenslied*, 1928). The strength of interest in local history and folklore left its mark on the Nestroy and Anzengruber editions, which were mainly the work of a Viennese schoolmaster, Otto Rommel. Rommel tends to concentrate on exploring continuities within what he presents as an essentially popular theatrical tradition; this is at the expense of the commercial character of the suburban theatres, which in fact, far from being peculiar to Vienna, were strictly comparable in repertory and organization to the commercial theatres in mid-nineteenth-century London and Paris.[55]

The pervasive fascination of local history and local cultural history also showed in a vogue for illustrated volumes of poems about Vienna, dwelling especially on the Vienna of the past. Collections of this kind produced by poets of conservative temper included Lux's *Zwölf Wiener Elegien* (1921), Ginzkey's *Balladen aus dem alten Wien* (1923), and Wildgans's *Wiener Gedichte*, which appeared in 1926, illustrated with drawings by a friend of Schnitzler's, Ferdinand Schmutzer.

These examples are indicative of the climate in which Hofmannsthal's conservatism developed, finding expression in interpretations of Viennese cultural history such as the Raimund essay of 1920 and the commemorative 'Rede auf Grillparzer', a lecture he gave in Hanover in 1922. In the last years of his life he felt that the driving motivation for his writing was, as he put it to Carl J. Burckhardt, the Austria of the past, struggling for regeneration (H/Burckhardt, 246: letter of 15 July 1927). Hence the spirit of nostalgic retrospection that informs his last libretto for Richard Strauss, *Arabella*. This grew partly out of his plans – initially developed in drafts for a play *Der Fiaker als Graf* (HKA XXVI, 133–63) – to attempt a recreation of the mood of the 1870s and 1880s, in conscious parallel, as he admitted to Andrian, to the recreation of the eighteenth century in *Der Rosenkavalier* (H/Andrian, 361: letter of 28 August 1924). His stylized treatment of the past is part of that myth-making endeavour that he recognized was central to his work after 1914 (A, 233), and essentially served the 'idea of Austria': the marriage of Arabella and Mandryka, symbolical of a coming-together of Austrian and Czech culture, represents a projected re-establishment of the multinational character idealized by Hofmannsthal in the vanished monarchy and now associated with the aim of cultural conservatism, a restoration of spiritual values.

In 1927, at the end of the Munich address 'Das Schrifttum als geistiger Raum der Nation', Hofmannsthal made explicit his idea of a 'conservative revolution', presenting it as a reversal of a process going back to the Renaissance and the Reformation – that is, restoring the spiritual authority he associated with the pre-Renaissance Catholic Church and Holy Roman Empire, an alliance whose underlying significance was encapsulated in the 'idea of Austria'. The final paragraph sums up the historical process against which the 'conservative revolution' was proposed as a counter:

I am speaking of a process we are in the middle of, a synthesis, gradual and splendid if one could view it from outside, dark and testing when one is in the middle of it. We can call the process gradual and splendid if we recall that the long period of development from the convulsions of the Age of Enlightenment down to our own time is only one part of it, and that it actually begins as an inner reaction against that intellectual revolution in the sixteenth century that we usually refer to by its twin aspects, the Renaissance and the Reformation [als eine innere Gegenbewegung gegen jene Geistesumwälzung des sechzehnten Jahrhunderts, die wir in ihren zwei Aspekten Renaissance und Reformation zu nennen pflegen]. The process of which I am speaking is nothing less that a conservative revolution on a scale unknown in European history. (P IV, 412–13)

If his cultural politics have their roots in the Chandos Letter and their summation in 'Das Schrifttum als geistiger Raum der Nation', they also inform his work in the theatre immediately after the war – only hinted at, perhaps, in his celebration of the Austrian aristocracy in *Der Schwierige* but given polemical expression in his support for the Salzburg Festival.

CHAPTER 6

Cultural Conservatism in the Theatre

Hofmannsthal's Return to Drama: Der Schwierige

After the war, the direction of Hofmannsthal's work was largely governed by his views on political developments and their implications in terms of cultural history. Put unsympathetically, it means that the character of his late work was determined by a desire 'to create a controlled allegorical universe that would reinforce an increasingly fixed political ideology'.[1]

While his concern to publicize his cultural conservatism informed his practical involvement in the Salzburg Festival, in his creative writing he was able to devote himself to traditional dramatic forms. From mid-1917 he enjoyed a resurgence of productiveness, and wrote to Andrian on 27 September, during his work on *Der Schwierige*, about how important this productiveness was to him after a three-year gap; he was taking up the threads from *Cristinas Heimreise* and *Der Rosenkavalier* in the confidence that he was on the right course (H/Andrian, 252). Certainly the play marks a significant development in his career, a renewed concentration on creative writing rather than speech-making and journalism. But even in comedy his absorption in political and historical thinking meant that his work was now strongly coloured by his concern with the changing society of his time.

On 16 August 1917, while he was working on *Der Schwierige*, he talked about it to Josef Redlich, who summarized in his diary what he had said:

> Hugo told me a lot about a comedy he is working on, set among the Austrian aristocracy and obviously conceived as an ironically philosophical piece [eine [. . .] offenbar ironisch-philosophisch gedachte Komödie]. He sees this as a type of dramatic writing in which he can achieve the topmost heights [eine Art dramatischer Dichtung, in der er glaubt, das Höchste leisten zu können].[2]

185

As he learned to refine his use of comic form over the years, one of his main debts was to Molière, and a work that in a sense functioned as a preparatory study for *Der Schwierige* was the one-act comedy *Die Lästigen* (1916), which was based loosely on *Les Fâcheux* and which he wrote under the stimulus of a conversation with Reinhardt about 'social comedy' ('Gesellschaftscomödie').[3] The very title *Der Schwierige* locates the play as belonging to a tradition of comedies treating characters who are hard to please or at odds with their fellows, the most illustrious antecedent being *Le Misanthrope*. The tone of the finished work, however, is essentially that of the *Konversationsstück* (comedy of manners) long established as a staple of the Burgtheater repertory. Hofmannsthal's debt to the Burgtheater would be clearly seen by a critic such as Herbert Ihering when he reviewed Berlin productions of *Der Schwierige* in 1921 and 1930.[4]

Hofmannsthal's own awareness of this traditional pattern is reflected in his repeated use of the term 'Gesellschaftscomödie': in his very first notes about the play, made in December 1909 after a discussion with Reinhardt,[5] and again in September and October 1917, during his work on the first act, in letters to Auernheimer and Andrian.[6] To Andrian he glossed the term on 4 October as meaning 'a comedy featuring well-bred people' ('eine Comödie die unter wohlerzogenen Menschen spielt': H/Andrian, 253) – practically a definition of the comedy of manners. In the letter to Auernheimer he also used the term 'Conversationscomödie'; two years later, writing to Schnitzler, he referred to the work as a 'Gesellschaftslustspiel' (H/AS, 287: letter of 2 November 1919), reflecting (as the letter spells out) his awareness that he was depicting a specific society, the traditional form being used to reflect his traditionalist conception of the old order in Austria. *Der Schwierige* is, as he told Marie Luise Borchardt in December 1921, a play that *looks* entirely unremarkable ('ein so normales gewöhnlich *aussehendes* Stück': H/Borchardt, 163), but the 'comedy of conversation' that he fashioned within that framework is one in which conversation is not merely the medium but also one of the subjects of the play.

Though the principal setting is a Viennese salon, the plot has some unusual twists. The 'difficult man' of the title, Count Hans-Karl Bühl, has returned to Vienna from the front, his life altered by a visionary experience when a trench collapsed over him under fire and he saw the young countess Helene Altenwyl as his wife. He now has a new sense of the meaning of human life and of marriage. At the age of nearly forty he has become aware of lasting truths that are inexpressible but he also realizes that life is dependent on language ('Durchs Reden kommt ja alles auf der Welt zustande': L

II, 258). As a result he is left with a sense of inadequacy in communication, which leads him to declare, with self-ironizing hyperbole, 'that it is impossible to open one's mouth without causing the most hopeless confusion' (L II, 312). His elder sister Crescence (the name is pronounced with the second syllable nasal, to rhyme with French *naissance*) persuades him to go to a soirée at the Altenwyls' home to plead on behalf of her son Stani for Helene's hand. Once there, he tells Helene of his admiration for a circus clown, Furlani, whose act consists in creating confusion on all sides, but always with style and elegance – something of the feeling we have about Hans Karl himself. He tries to say a formal farewell to Helene, and he also tries to bring about a reconciliation between Antoinette Hechingen, a married woman with whom he has had an affair in the past, and her husband, whose integrity and bravery he has learned to value during the war. First Helene and then Antoinette are wooed by the pushful North German Baron Neuhoff, but he is summarily rebuffed by each of them in turn. When Hans Karl returns in Act Three, matters are brought to a head by Helene, who overcomes her scruples and herself proposes to him; then, since he is unwilling to face her father's insistence that he make a speech in the *Herrenhaus* (the Upper House of the Austrian parliament), they leave together, so that when the final curtain falls the traditional tableau of young lovers is conspicuously lacking – a consequence, Stani says, of their 'bizarre' character.

Though socially superior to Anatol and Schnitzler's other men-about-town, Hans Karl belongs to the familiar type of the elegant philanderer. In Hofmannsthal's preliminary notes of 1910 he was already explicitly conceived as a ladies' man ('der Freund vieler Frauen').[7] It is of course in conformity with universal comic tradition that the action of the play turns on flirtation and marriage. But the construction of *Der Schwierige* – flirtation centring on Antoinette, proposals of marriage on Helene – systematically contrasts Hans Karl with his nephew Stani and the Prussian Neuhoff. Hans Karl has had an affair with Antoinette, Stani is having an affair with her, Neuhoff tries to start an affair with her; Stani decides to marry Helene, Neuhoff proposes marriage to her, Hans Karl actually becomes engaged to her. In each case the decisiveness of the other two men contrasts with his own apparent evasiveness; indeed, even when proposing to him in Act Three, Helene herself is unsure of whether he is capable of love ('Jetzt weiß ich zwar nicht, ob du jemand wahrhaft liebhaben kannst [. . .]': L II, 299). To Antoinette, Hans Karl denies being a philanderer, a 'Frauenjäger' (L II, 244), but she makes short work of this protestation, saying that his claim to be 'not a ladies' man, just a friend, a *real* friend' is merely a trick, and asking how one and the same person can be 'so charming and at the same time so monstrously vain and selfish and heartless'. Helene, who perceives the parallel between Hans Karl and the clown Furlani, draws worrying conclusions about his relations with women and the implications for herself:

> HANS KARL. Alle andern lassen sich von einer Absicht leiten und schauen nicht rechts und nicht links, ja, sie atmen kaum, bis sie ihre Absicht erreicht haben: darin besteht eben ihr Trick. Er aber tut scheinbar nichts mit Absicht – er geht immer auf die Absicht der andern ein. Er möchte alles mittun, was die andern tun, soviel guten Willen hat er, so fasziniert ist er von jedem einzelnen Stückl, was irgendeiner vormacht: wenn er einen Blumentopf auf der Nase balanciert, so balanciert er ihn auch, sozusagen aus Höflichkeit.
> HELENE. Aber er wirft ihn hinunter?
> HANS KARL. Aber wie er ihn hinunterwirft, darin liegts! Er wirft ihn hinunter aus purer Begeisterung und Seligkeit darüber, daß er ihn so schön balancieren kann! Er glaubt, wenn mans ganz schön machen tät, müßts von selber gehen.
> HELENE (*vor sich*). Und das hält der Blumentopf gewöhnlich nicht aus und fällt hinunter.
>
> (L II, 221)

> HANS KARL. All the others are driven on by some purpose, and don't look left or right – indeed, they hardly breathe – until they've done what they set out to do. That *is* their trick. But he seemingly does nothing on purpose; he always falls in with what the others are planning. He wants to do whatever it is they are doing; he has so much good will, he is so fascinated by every little trick they perform. If someone balances a flowerpot on his nose, he balances one too, as it were from sheer politeness.
> HELENE. But he drops it?
> HANS KARL. But the point is the *way* he drops it! He drops it out of sheer enthusiasm and delight that he can balance it so beautifully. He believes that if only you did it really beautifully, it would stay up all on its own.
> HELENE (*to herself*). And usually the flowerpot can't take that, so it falls to the ground.

This dialogue has been widely recognized as a key passage in the play. There is no indication that Hans Karl is aware of the parallel between Furlani and himself; he is far from preening himself. It is we who make the connection, and Helene who brings it into the open by seeing the practical implications in her own case, as symbolized in the flowerpot. What the passage introduces is a fundamental contrast between moral concerns (intentions and consequences) and the aesthetic approach, in which intentions and consequences are subordinated to 'beauty'. At this stage Hans Karl still defends the aesthetic approach, and his admiration of Furlani's dropping of the flowerpot underlines all the doubts the two women express about his morals.

One of the ways in which *Der Schwierige* is distinguished from the *Konversationsstück* as it lived on in the plays of Schnitzler is the seriousness with which marriage is advanced as the moral counter-weight to philandering. The argument between Hans Karl and Antoinette in Act Two re-enacts a sequence in the early lyric drama *Der Tor und der Tod*. Claudio has just spoken his 'decisive' lines about constancy ('Ich will die Treue lernen, die der Halt / Von allem Leben ist [. . .]') and 'tying himself down' in moral commitment ('Gebunden werden – ja! – und kräftig binden': HKA III, 73). His past loves have been no more than an exchange of empty words ('Es war ein Tausch von Schein und Worten leer'), exemplified in piles of old love-letters that he kept in a drawer.[8] Hans Karl is congenitally reluctant to commit himself – 'ich binde mich so ungern' is one of the first things he says to his sister (L II, 151) – and his own past affair with Antoinette is recorded in letters they have exchanged during the war. This correspondence ended with a letter he wrote to Antoinette from the field hospital, in which, according to Antoinette (this is relayed to Hans Karl by her maid, Agathe, in Act One) he brought their affair to an end (L II, 169).

By contrast with the rather black-and-white simplicity of Claudio's decision, the issue is less clearly resolved in *Der Schwierige*. To Antoinette, Hans Karl himself defines marriage as the 'institution that transforms what has happened by chance and is impure into something that is necessary, lasting and valid' ('das Institut [. . .], das aus dem Zufälligen und Unreinen das Notwendige, das Bleibende und das Gültige macht: die Ehe': L II, 243) – a moment of solemnity quickly punctured by Antoinette's indignant protest that he is trying to pair her off with her own husband ('Ich spür, du willst mich verkuppeln mit meinem Mann'). In III, 10 he finally announces his betrothal but even then his hesitant formulation, 'Sie hat sich – ich hab mich – wir haben uns miteinander verlobt' ('She has – I have – we have got engaged': L II, 305) seems to underline a reluctance to accept responsibility, and the absence of the happy couple at the final curtain, in pointed reversal of the standard happy ending of comedy, reinforces the sense of uncertainty.

The extra ingredient in Hans Karl's character that most clearly differentiates the play from the stock comedies of manners it resembles is his sensitivity to nuances of language and his concern with problems of language. Thanks to the copious preliminary notes and drafts that Hofmannsthal would keep for all his works, we know that, like Chandos, Hans Karl was conceived as undergoing a crisis of identity. One of the earliest notes on the play, sketching the scene in Act One between Hans Karl and his secretary Neugebauer, explicitly compares him to Chandos as someone who has lost his grip on conventional values ('die kuranten Wertungen [. . .] sind ihm abhanden gekommen (vgl. "Ein Brief")') and who appears as a man 'who has become completely disorientated', the action of the play being intended to lead to a 'cure' for his 'difficulty'.[9] As with Chandos, the crisis is associated with language. The skill of the old retainer Lukas in reading his moods intuitively is explained in an early draft of the scene in which Lukas expounds his duties to the new servant Vinzenz: Lukas says in the draft that 'he is handicapped in expressing himself' ('weil er im Ausdruck behindert ist').[10] In the finished play, the problematic quality of language as a medium of communication is comically reflected in Hans Karl's telephone conversation with Hechingen (L II, 202–3), physical mishearing providing a comic correlative of deeper misunderstandings.

But it is again in the figure of Furlani that the theme is most suggestively presented: Hans Karl explicitly derives more pleasure from Furlani's silent mime than from the cleverest conversation ('Mich unterhält er viel mehr als die gescheiteste Konversation von Gott weiß wem': L II, 212). His mistrust of language, reflected in a characteristic reticence, even a tendency to silences, is based on the inexpressible quality of significant experience: although, as he observes to Helene in II, 14, 'everything comes about as a result of speech', what ultimately matters in life is inexpressible ('[. . .] in einem Leben, wo doch schließlich alles auf das Letzte, Unaussprechliche ankommt': L II, 258). In this insight he is clearly related to Chandos, whose plight is summarized in *Ad me ipsum* in the phrase 'Anstand des Schweigens' ('the propriety of silence': A, 215), and indeed Hofmannsthal himself linked the two works in respect of their treatment of language (A, 231). The insight is also close to Wittgenstein's insistence on the limitations of language in the *Tractatus logico-philosophicus*, the final version of which was written in the summer of 1918, while Wittgenstein was on leave from the Italian front – that is, while *Der Schwierige* was still awaiting completion.[11]

Much of one's assessment of the significance of the play depends on one's assessment of Hans Karl. We are offered alternative views: Neuhoff dismisses him as vanity and shallowness personified (L II,

230); Helene, defending him against Neuhoff (L II, 255–6), clearly admires him as the very ideal of aristocratic sensibility. His sensitivity towards language suggests that he has also something of an artistic temperament,[12] and this is underlined by the parallel with the circus *artiste* Furlani.

In 1926 Hofmannsthal listed *Der Schwierige* as an example of the explicitly autobiographical quality of his writing ('das Biographische des œuvre': A, 237). There are certainly features of his own taste reflected in Hans Karl's quirks, an obvious example being his jealous defence of his privacy,[13] but that is only one of the layers of irony in this 'ironically philosophical' piece. Hofmannsthal's own formulation, recorded in a note of 1926 as providing a key to Hans Karl's character, is 'intentional indirectness', a strategy adopted in a 'world bereft of nuance': 'Absichtliche Mittelbarkeit. (Haltung des "Schwierigen" in einer nuancenlosen Welt)' (A, 239).

It is because of the brashness of the world around them that both Hans Karl and Helene cultivate a deliberate reserve. Crescence comments on the courteous 'distance' Hans Karl preserves between himself and other people (L II, 152); Helene ironically defines her own good manners as 'just a form of nerves, to keep people at arm's length' (L II, 223). She explains her understanding of Hans Karl's admiration for Furlani by admitting that she too finds anything where the underlying intention or purpose shows through 'a bit vulgar' ('Ich find auch alles, wo man eine Absicht merkt, die dahintersteckt, ein bißl vulgär': L II, 222). Their imperturbable social case is, in short, a pose; not for nothing did Hofmannsthal at one stage envisage the title of the play as being in the plural, '*Die Schwierigen*'.[14] In Helene's case the real tension ('Anspannung') behind her 'good manners' is seen by Neuhoff (L II, 252). Similarly the 'nonchalance' that Hans Karl admires in Furlani also conceals 'tension' (L II, 222); one of the implications of the mirroring of his character in Furlani is that he too has a social front that is an 'act', essentially artificial.

One result of this front in Hans Karl's case is the constant misunderstanding he feels he is exposed to. The credibility of this claim is built up in the opening scenes, as Crescence's airy declarations are contrasted with the intuitive understanding of Lukas, but increasingly it emerges that in fact some of the other characters see his underlying intentions clearly.[15] In I, 6 Agathe defines the alleged gist of his wartime letter of farewell to Antoinette: one man is like another, and she should accept her husband again (L II, 169). Hans Karl insists that none of those words were in the letter, and Agathe replies: 'Auf die Worte kommts nicht an. Aber den Sinn haben wir gut herausbekommen' ('The words don't matter. But we got the meaning'). In the second act it emerges that she is right: Hans Karl's talk of the beginning of their affair as arbitrary ('Da ist jemand gekommen – der war – zufällig ich') and his eulogy of marriage (L II, 241–5) correspond closely to the 'meaning' Agathe has imputed to his letter. Or again when Hans Karl defends himself to Antoinette in II, 10–11, denying he is a seducer and ladies' man, the weakness he displays in finishing up by kissing her on the forehead (L II, 250) undermines his defence. Moreover, not only has she been right in accusing him of attempting to 'pair her off' with her own husband (L II, 243), there are two other passages in that same scene in which her clear-sightedness about him is evident.

First she says his seductive trick is to pretend to be a 'real friend', and that he plays on 'everything he is and everything he is not' ('Damit kokettierst du, so wie du mit allem kokettierst, was du hast, und mit allem, was dir fehlt': L II, 244). When it comes to his scene with Helene (II, 14) that is exactly the line he takes, failing to press Stani's case and urging her to take someone who is 'fine and noble, and a man – everything I am not' ('einen ganz andern, der ein braver, nobler Mensch ist – und ein Mann: das ist alles, was ich nicht bin': L II, 262). Ostensibly he is renouncing her, but by the end of the evening they will be engaged.

Secondly, after he has been talking to Antoinette about the seriousness of marriage, she deduces that he is about to marry Helene Altenwyl. He says Helene has not even been in his thoughts, that he is talking only about Antoinette herself, but she is un-impressed: it is precisely of Helene, she says, that he has been thinking (L II, 246). The point is the same one as earlier: the words don't matter; she has grasped the underlying meaning. And again she is quite right: Helene has indeed been at the centre of Hans Karl's thoughts throughout. In the first act Crescence discusses her with him in Scene 3 and talk of her possible marriage to Neuhoff and her affection for himself induces the tell-tale opening of his desk drawers that betrays his irritation (L II, 155–6). (Because his interest in her has been signalled since early in the first act Benjamin Bennett's argument that he decides to marry her 'entirely on the spur of the moment'[16] is unconvincing.) He talks of her again with Neuhoff in I, 12 and with Stani in I, 13 and I, 16 – the latter the scene in which Stani announces his decision to get engaged to her, which leads to the further scene with Crescence establishing Hans Karl's 'programme' for the evening (I, 18). In the second act his first conversation is the key dialogue with Helene about Furlani, ending with his request for a private talk. This request leads so directly into the opening words of II, 14 – 'Yes, I do want to talk to you' ('Ja, ich habe mit Ihnen zu reden': L II, 258) – that it is as though his mind has been on nothing else in the meantime, confirming Antoinette's perception in II, 10. Antoinette also makes a similar point about Helene, 'running after' Hans Karl but making it look as though she were avoiding him (L II, 232–3).

Even the brash Vinzenz, commenting on Hans Karl's strict rule that members of his family have to be announced, sees the underlying point. His formulation, 'Da will er sie sich vom Leibe halten' ('He wants to keep them off his back': L II, 148) is crude and vulgar, as is his prying into what must be behind it ('Was steckt da dahinter?'). But his conclusion is shrewd enough; the formality is part of Hans Karl's cultivation of 'distance'. There is a two-way comic effect constantly at work: on the one hand the judgments and assumptions of the other characters seem comically oversimplified by comparison with Hans Karl's circumspection and discretion; on the other hand, his sense of being misunderstood is repeatedly called into question by the accuracy with which the other characters see through him. The effect is one of sustained uncertainty, which is both a source of comedy and also part of the unusual subtlety and richness in the characterization of Hans Karl. One does well to heed Stani's words in I, 10: 'Pardon, Onkel Kari, bei dir darf man nichts wörtlich nehmen' ('Excuse me, uncle, nothing you say may be taken literally': L II, 188) – a point he repeats in similar terms to Hechingen in the final act (L II, 275).

Once one has acknowledged this, Hans Karl's actions fall into place as an enactment of 'intentional indirectness'. His reluctance to be direct and his lack of eloquence – what Stani calls his lack of 'Suada' – are not a weakness but contribute, as Stani says, to his attractive elegance ('Du gehst nie auf die Sache aus und hast so gar keine Suada, das ist gerade das Elegante an dir': L II, 180). Helene too talks of his likeable 'awkwardness' ('Die Ungeschicklichkeit, die ihn so liebenswürdig macht': L II, 255), and admits that it is not all it seems ('freilich ist alles ein Versteckenspiel'). He is like Furlani, who 'seemingly [scheinbar] does nothing on purpose' but rather 'falls in with what the others are planning'. Hans Karl may at first be reluctant to commit himself to going to the Altenwyls' soirée ('ich binde mich ungern'), but in the end his attendance follows Furlani's pattern: *seeming* to accept Crescence's 'programme', presenting Stani's suit and pleading Hechingen's cause, but in fact cutting his usual elegant figure – surrounded, as Neuhoff enviously says, by women (L II, 230) – and achieving none of his 'seeming' goals. He presses Hechingen's case, but that he does not subconsciously want to do so is shown in his 'almost unconscious' parting embrace of Antoinette (L II, 250). His wooing on Stani's behalf is hardly more than pretence; indeed he barely even goes through the motions, quickly telling Helene *not* to choose either Neuhoff or Stani (L II, 262). His ostensible 'programme', in short, is at odds with his *real* (more or less subconscious) intentions, which are concealed beneath the veneer of diffident elegance, and it is his *real* intentions that he follows.

The title that Hofmannsthal contemplated for the play in 1910, '*Der Mann ohne Absicht*', a title suggested by his reading of Kierkegaard,[17] can only have been conceived ironically. The ambiguity with which the word *Absicht* was fraught was an old joke. This emerges from a postcard sent by Hofmannsthal and Beer-Hofmann to Schnitzler from Salzburg on 18 July 1900 (H/AS, 142): 'Ganz zufällig sind wir beide hier, aber natürlich absichtlich. Hugo / Absicht ist ein gelungener Zufall oder umgekehrt. Richard' ('We are both here quite by coincidence – but of course on purpose. Hugo / "Purpose" is happy coincidence, or *vice versa*. Richard'). When Neuhoff accuses Hans Karl of constant 'calculation' ('in allem und jedem Berechnungen'), Helene rejects the charge (L II, 255); but though it is certainly too crudely phrased, it is yet another example where oversimplification contains at least a grain of truth. Like Furlani, Hans Karl only *seemingly* does nothing on purpose; the self-confident Stani, Neuhoff, and Vinzenz are ineffectual by comparison, and it is he, not Neuhoff or Stani, who wins Helene.

This is an important point because it colours Hofmannsthal's presentation of the other main theme of the play, Hans Karl's coming to terms with the modern world. A representative of the old order, friendly with the suggestively-named Altenwyls, and cosseted by the faithful Lukas who corresponds to the old retainers Hofmannsthal found portrayed in Bauernfeld's plays (P I, 162), he is confronted with new values embodied in representatives of the new order, also symbolically-named: Neuhoff, the secretary Neugebauer, and the servant Vinzenz (who at one stage was to be called 'Nowak',[18] though the suggestion of triumph in 'Vinzenz' is if anything even more sinister). Each of them in his own way is pushful and graceless. The figure of the academic 'celebrity' at the salon, Brücke, is also just as unlovable as Vinzenz in his obvious wish to use Hans Karl for his own ends. Though they are drawn from different levels of society, each of these figures represents features of a brash new world of self-interest; together they represent the changes threatening the old order. In Neuhoff, a further threat is represented, the shift in political strength within German-speaking Europe since 1866. Comparison with Hofmannsthal's much-quoted wartime essay in tabular form,

'Preuße und Österreicher' (P III, 407–9),[19] written while he was engaged in his main spell of work on *Der Schwierige* in 1917, shows how clearly Neuhoff embodies characteristics that Hofmannsthal regarded as typically Prussian (self-confidence, fluency, fondness for abstractions, lack of historical sense), in contrast to the supposedly typically Austrian qualities of Hans Karl (traditionalism, evasiveness, self-irony, wit).

Any interpretation relating the comedy to the world of postwar Europe has to take into account the problem of when the action is set – specifically, whether it is set after the war, as is suggested by the way Vinzenz speaks in the opening scene of Hans Karl's position 'nach der Kriegszeit' (L II, 149) and by the fact that throughout the play the war is spoken of in the past,[20] or whether the war is still in progress, as is suggested not only by the possibility that Hans Karl may make a speech in the *Herrenhaus* (which did not meet after October 1918) but also by the dates of his affair with Antoinette: we learn from Crescence that that began two years ago (L II, 162), and the letters Hans Karl returns to Antoinette date from June 1915 onwards (L II, 172).[21] Julius Bab put his finger on the problem as soon as the text was published: he had never read a play in which it was so unclear when the action was set.[22]

The uncertainty is almost certainly a consequence of the long genesis of the work. At least the first act was written in 1917, and by mid-November of that year, after a visit to Rodaun, Ottonie von Degenfeld knew about Hans Karl's planned farewell to Helene (H/Degenfeld, 343: letter of 14 November 1917). The following summer, indeed, Hofmannsthal told Bahr that the whole play had been written in 1917 'except for details in the last act'.[23] In fact, however, though he had prepared a detailed scenario,[24] he stopped further work because, as he later told Andrian, Reinhardt was unable to provide a suitable cast (H/Andrian, 290: letter of 2 October 1918). Though he mentioned the play to Schnitzler among his work in progress in January 1918 (Tgb., 11 January 1918) and later told Wildgans it had been finished that year (H/Wildgans, 30: letter of 14 February 1921), he actually completed it only *after* the war. In August 1919 he spent some time in the Salzkammergut 'in order to finish the third act' (H/Burckhardt, 24: letter of 2 December 1919), and on 16 September he told Andrian he was working on that act (H/Andrian, 307). Two days later he wrote to Richard Strauss that he was giving the text a final polishing (H/Strauss, 384). But not until two days after that, on 20 September 1919, did he begin his full manuscript of the last act.[25] On 31 October he ended a letter to Bodenhausen's widow by saying that he was going to work on his comedy, which he still had to finish (H/Bodenhausen, 253), and on

2 November he told Schnitzler that he was still making improvements (H/AS, 287). He completed the manuscript as late as 2 August
1920.[26] The play was serialized in the *Neue Freie Presse* between
April and September 1920, but the text was subjected to considerable
further filing and revision (substantial cuts being made in Act Two,
and the second half of Act Three being largely rewritten and in part
expanded) before the first edition in book form appeared the following year. In particular, he added the passages in III, 8 and III, 11
about Hans Karl's impending speech in the *Herrenhaus*, which are
entirely lacking in the serialized version.[27]

Between the conception of the play and its completion, the whole
structure of the society it depicts had been revolutionized. It is true,
as Bennett says, that the unruffled elegance of high society reflected in the play is reminiscent of a passage in the 'Appeal to the
Aristocracy' that Hofmannsthal published in the *Neue Freie Presse* in
September 1914, calling for a continuation of social graces, even a
demonstrative maintenance of high standards of good living (P III,
179–80);[28] and when he was working on it in 1917 there may well
have been an element almost of defiance in the evocation of threatened social graces. But despite the dates mentioned in the text there
is no very strong case for arguing that in the finished work the
action is still necessarily set during the war and that 'the audience is
meant to know this'.[29] Hofmannsthal himself told Carl Zeiss in
1917 or 1918 that the play is based on the assumption that the war is
over.[30] Though this statement predates the completion of the text,
the lack both of uniforms and of any allusions to action still in
progress suggests that whatever else he wanted his audience to be
aware of, he was precisely *not* striving to evoke a wartime mood.
On the contrary, the final effect – as Bab recognized very clearly in
1921 – is of a projection into the postwar period of a society that by
then no longer existed.

Hofmannsthal acknowledged even in 1917 that the aristocratic
society he was depicting was no longer intact in reality ('eine in der
Realität gar nicht mehr vorhandene Aristokratie'),[31] and when he
was writing the final act in 1919, he was well aware that he was
producing an affectionate portrait of a disappearing order of life.
The conscious artifice of this procedure is reflected in the sentimental tone in which he wrote about it to Schnitzler on 2 November:

> At no other time, perhaps, could I have portrayed the society it
> depicts, the aristocratic society of Austria, so lovingly in all its
> charm and with all its real quality as in the historical moment
> in which, though until just recently it existed and was even

powerful, it is dissolving quietly and wraith-like into nothing, like a cloud of mist left over in the morning. (H/AS, 287)

In short, the depiction of aristocratic society is consciously unrealistic, indeed idealized, and this did not escape contemporary reviewers. Salten, for example, reviewing the first Viennese production in the *Neue Freie Presse* on 18 April 1924, noted that there was no reflection at all of the social revolution to come (TR, 530–1). To the extent that such an idealized society is made to stand for certain qualities amid the threatening changes of the postwar world, the process is essentially – indeed, overtly – mythopoeic.

In that framework, the rivalry between Hans Karl and Neuhoff for the hand of Helene (and indeed for the affections of Antoinette) takes on a wider significance. Especially what Neuhoff describes as their 'duel' ('Zweikampf') over Helene (L II, 257) – an inflated description, but basically accurate – amounts to a playing-out, on the personal level, of a national rivalry, the political contrast being projected onto the comic action. Hans Karl's victory over Neuhoff in this 'duel' is part and parcel of the political mythopoeia underlying the play: it represents a victory of supposedly traditional Austrian characteristics over supposedly unattractive Prussian characteristics which in political terms amounts to the purest wishful thinking.

It is because of this idealizing intention that Hofmannsthal saw that his greatest difficulty in writing the comedy lay in achieving the required effect of 'discretion' (H/Andrian, 253: letter of 4 October 1917). Achieving comic effects while maintaining an atmosphere of elegance also requires subtle production and performance. Hofmannsthal was well aware of the problem, and admitted to Andrian on 2 October 1918 that the play would be 'inexpressibly difficult to cast because everything would have to be so natural and so elegant' (H/Andrian, 290). The main difficulty – one that still needs to be resolved in every new production – lies in the central character of Hans Karl, who, far from being a stock 'comic figure', has to appear genuinely charming and also sensitive. But the problem was not to prove insuperable. When writing to Andrian on 2 October 1918, Hofmannsthal seems to have imagined either Harry Walden or Arnold Korff in the part (H/Andrian, 290). Three years later, when he submitted the play to Wildgans at the Burgtheater, he again mentioned both these names, together with Anton Edthofer of the Deutsches Volkstheater. All three had, however, left Vienna, and he was by now imagining yet another actor, Albert Bassermann, playing Hans Karl in a production by Reinhardt (H/Wildgans, 31: letter of 14 February 1921). There were, then, at least four actors whom he considered capable of playing the part, as well as Gustav Waldau, who in fact played it when it was first produced in Munich in 1921 and again when Reinhardt's company performed it in Vienna in 1924.

Yet, however charmingly acted, Hans Karl is a problematic figure to bear the significance invested in his role. His function as a representative of threatened values combines uneasily with the implications of his characterization as a (more or less reformed) philanderer, whom Antoinette – the one to see through the erotic hypocrisies most clearly[32] – accuses in II, 10 of being cynical and untrustworthy. Moreover, Neuhoff's description of him in II, 2 as the arch-exemplar of a totally outmoded society cut off from the intellectual currents of present-day reality (L II, 230) also contains at least an element of truth. Prince Arduin in Schnitzler's *Komödie der Verführung*, a postwar comedy set just before the war, is unlike Hans Karl in that when war breaks out he decides to leave Europe. But his reasoning – that in the postwar world his position will be a mere irrelevancy (DW II, 954) – is entirely consistent with Neuhoff's analysis in *Der Schwierige*. As a figure of patriotic fun, Neuhoff is depicted as gratingly verbose and opportunistic, and as thoroughly deserving his comeuppance from Helene and Antoinette. But that does not mean that everything he says is wrong. That Hans Karl is indeed an outdated figure, out of touch with the changing realities, shows, for example, in his summarily impatient disregard for the philosopher Brücke at the end of Act Two. It may be, as Bennett argues, that his mind is on avoiding an uncomfortable interview with Crescence,[33] but even if Brücke is a pompous ass, the way Hans Karl brushes him aside signals an uncomprehending refusal to fashion a 'bridge' with someone who, as he has been told, is a prominent representative of the intellectual and also political life of the times (L II, 215).

This self-insulation from intellectual and political reality – the political equivalent of the selfishness of which Antoinette accuses him in his private life – is borne out in his refusal to make his speech in the *Herrenhaus*, the motif added by Hofmannsthal after the serialization of the 1920 version. He insists to the last that it would be pointless (L II, 312), and his ducking of the social responsibility the speech would entail is underlined by his absence at the final curtain. In this light it is revealing that of all Hofmannsthal's friends it was Andrian (particularly awake to the political implications) who argued that Hans Karl has 'a wretched part' to play in the last act[34] – a criticism that Hofmannsthal overruled.

Given the interweaving of personal and political significances, Hans Karl's lack of political commitment inevitably raises questions about his personal affairs too. The pointed absence of the happy couple at the final curtain, avoiding the ceremonial union of lovers, produces the effect of a distinctly open ending. To Neuhoff, Helene may present his elusiveness as a virtue (L II, 255), but his characteristic avoidance of directness – it always makes him a little uneasy, he says, if he is asked something directly (L II, 294) – is double-edged. The audience may be left remembering the embarrassed awkwardness both of his reply to her proposal (L II, 299–300) and of his admission to Crescence of their engagement (L II, 305) and may ask whether there is any evidence that he is now capable of commitment in the form of fidelity to Helene. The question is, of course, unanswerable; the final curtain falls and speculation is idle.

Der Unbestechliche

Though Hofmannsthal's last prose comedy *Der Unbestechliche* ('The Incorruptible One') is also full of ironies, it is a less subtly crafted play than *Der Schwierige*, and in keeping with its origin as an occasional work designed expressly as a vehicle for Max Pallenberg, it aims at a rather lighter tone. Hofmannsthal's letter of 26 May 1922 to Hans Kestranek, however, places it explicitly in the line of high comedies ('comedies of a higher kind'), in which he treated 'real characters' within a comic action – a line going back to *Cristinas Heimreise*, *Der Rosenkavalier*, and *Der Schwierige* (HKA XIII, 238). While planning it he again used the terms 'Gesellschaftslustspiel' (HKA XIII, 133) and 'Gesellschaftscomödie' (HKA XIII, 149), and its traditional character was not lost on contemporary critics. The review of the première in the *Wiener Zeitung*, for example, traced its ancestry back to Bauernfeld and Bahr, and described it and *Der Schwierige* together as being characterized by an 'artistic conservatism, such as the classics permitted themselves' (TR, 437).[35]

The setting is again among the Austrian aristocracy, on an estate in Lower Austria, with the faithful family servant now central to the action and comically dominant. In this case the time of the action is explicitly given as 1912, the vanished pre-war era. Writing to Marie Luise Borchardt, Hofmannsthal named among the play's antecedents *The Marriage of Figaro* (H/Borchardt, 173: letter of 21 March 1923), the reference being to Beaumarchais rather than to Mozart's opera. The 'incorruptible' servant Theodor has the same dynamic function in the plot as Figaro does, controlling the intrigue. But *Le Mariage de Figaro* is a revolutionary play, and while the title of *Der Unbestechliche* has revolutionary overtones and Theodor rails against the privilege his master enjoys (HKA XIII, 96), his activity is not disruptive: on the contrary, the outcome of the intrigue is the restoration of the domestic order which has been threatened by the philandering intentions of Jaromir.

The moral idea underlying this action is made explicit, in particular in the scene in Act One between Theodor and the Baroness, Jaromir's mother (HKA XIII, 49–55). Before his marriage Jaromir has lived a 'bachelor life of unparalleled irresponsibility and ice-cold selfishness'; now his attempted infidelity – bringing his mistresses, as Theodor says, into the house two at a time – amounts to a denial of the standards for which Theodor stands. That Theodor regards himself as functioning as an agent of a divine order is repeatedly suggested. He even reminds the Baroness that he was originally intended to be a priest. In his management of the family and their home, his honour has to be satisfied by a demonstration of the rule of moral law; the phrase he uses to express this, 'wo Gott eigentlich Wohnung hat' (literally, he will demonstrate 'where God has His dwelling-place'), underlines the divine authority he aspires to represent.[36] Jaromir has long refused to use his real name with its obvious symbolic overtones; Theodor in turn regards Jaromir's amorality as a personal slight ('eine fortgesetzte Beleidigung meiner Person') – another obvious pointer to his role as the very embodiment of moral righteousness.

The moral pattern is also brought out structurally in various ways.[37] The chaos in Theodor's absence at the beginning, when he has handed in his notice, contrasts with the orderliness of the same scene at the start of Act Five when he has resumed his 'supervision of everything' ('die Aufsicht über das Ganze': HKA XIII, 112). At the beginning of Acts Two and Three and the end of Act Four, scenes featuring Jaromir's young son, who symbolizes his father's responsibilities in his marriage, frame the episodes with the two visiting women, Melanie Galattis and Marie Am Rain. The central importance of the standards Theodor represents is also emphasized by the way he dominates the ending of each act (rather as the act-endings in *Der Schwierige* bring out in comic fashion the theme of misunderstanding).

As in *Der Schwierige*, however, the ending of the final act has an ironical character: Theodor restores the moral order by assuming a control that is actually a reversal of the social order. In this way he succeeds in preserving the standards of the aristocratic family he serves – an outcome that is rich in social and political implications since it is achieved in the teeth of Jaromir's opposition. Moreover, if Hans Karl, the 'man without purpose', outsmarts the North

German Neuhoff not only in his pursuit of Helene but also in his hold over the affections of Antoinette, so too in *Der Unbestechliche* Theodor will gain his reward not in the kind of marital respectability he imposes on Jaromir but on the contrary – as he has told the Baroness, he is no saint ('kein Heiliger': HKA XIII, 52) – in the arms of the young widow Hermine, who appears at the beginning of the final scene decked out in her new blouse in flirtatious response to Theodor's earlier request (HKA XIII, 100).

The combination of service and authority, of loyalty and scheming, of moralizing and opportunism, makes Theodor a highly original character. This was clearly seen at the time of the première by Musil, probably the most perceptive of all the theatre critics reviewing in Vienna in the early 1920s. Musil also put his finger on the weakness of the play, which he saw as Hofmannsthal's failure to develop the character of Jaromir into an adequate counterweight to Theodor.[38] *Der Unbestechliche* is a play that still acts well, but Hofmannsthal no doubt realized it needed more polishing than he was able to give it at the time of the première. Though he regarded the contraction of the middle acts that he undertook in 1923 as a gain in performance, it must have increased still further the dominance of the central role. This may, indeed, have lain behind his choice of the title *Der Unbestechliche* instead of *Theodor und das Ganze*, which he still preferred only three weeks before the première.[39] Nearly two years later he told Strauss that he was considering further work on the play (H/Strauss, 457: letter of 29 November 1924), but by then his treatment of morality and the social order was channelled into his festival plays; the theatrical centre where he commanded attention was not Vienna but Salzburg.

The Salzburg Festival: Intention and Reality

With its Baroque skyline surrounded by mountains and dominated by the fortress of Hohensalzburg, Salzburg is a town of spectacular beauty. Hofmannsthal was one of many to feel a lifetime affection for it. 'A day in Salzburg,' he wrote on 21 August 1906 to Bodenhausen, 'enchantingly beautiful, and so much the landscape of my youth and of my dreams, in many respects the background to my poetry – I can think of nothing dearer or more lovely' (H/Bodenhausen, 86).

His involvement in the Salzburg Festival was motivated partly by the frustration of his attempts to establish himself in the Burgtheater, partly by the influence of Nadler's *Literaturgeschichte der deutschen Stämme und Landschaften*. Having come to see himself as a late representative of a Baroque tradition centring on visual drama, he rehearsed Nadler's ideas in a series of essays published between 1919 and 1928 about the Salzburg Festival: opera and spoken drama were inseparable, part of a coherent Austro-Bavarian Baroque theatrical tradition which was *the* essential theatrical tradition in the German-speaking countries, enacted in an ideal Baroque framework in Salzburg before a public representing the integrity of a homogeneous culture. The first two of these essays, 'Deutsche Festspiele zu Salzburg' and 'Die Salzburger Festspiele', date from 1919. So too, probably, does 'Festspiele in Salzburg', which was published two years later; this essay is essentially a rehearsal of views derived from Nadler and is peppered with quotations from Nadler, including a description of Salzburg itself as having since the mid-seventeenth century been the leading cultural centre of the whole Alpine region between Vienna, Munich, and Innsbruck (P III, 447–8). In addition to occasional pieces about the annual repertoire, there followed ' "Das Salzburger große Welttheater" ' in 1925, 'Das Salzburger Programm' the following year, and in 1928 'Das Publikum der Salzburger Festspiele', though this last essay was published only posthumously. In these essays Hofmannsthal expounded his ideological conception of the function of the festival, advancing in particular the idea of a festival whose artistic cosmopolitanism helped preserve essentially Austrian qualities.

Michael P. Steinberg traces this 'nationalist cosmopolitanism', as he calls it, back to the eighteenth-century German Enlightenment (*Aufklärung*);[40] but the immediate source of the distinctive blend of nationalism and internationalism embraced by Hofmannsthal is to be found in the multinational character of the Austro-Hungarian monarchy in which he had his roots. It was natural for him to think of a cultural institution serving an internationalist idea while at the same time functioning as a repository of a specifically national culture. This blend of apparently contradictory ideas had, indeed, a long history in Salzburg going back to 1842, the year that the Mozart statue was unveiled and the first stirrings of the festival idea began. One of the benefits of international interest – a comparison was even made with the Olympic Games in Ancient Greece – was seen as lying precisely in the stimulation of national awareness, at that time still defined in terms of 'German' national awareness.[41] When the construction of a purpose-built Festival Theatre was being planned after the First World War, the argument was advanced again, now in relation to 'Austro-German' identity. Early in 1919 Berta Zuckerkandl published in the *Wiener Allgemeine Zeitung* an article extolling the foundation of the Festspielhaus as a commitment to the idea of cosmopolitan culture and a symbolic representation of the indestructible Austro–German spirit.[42] She continued to expound this idea, arguing the importance of the festival as a symbol and vehicle of cultural continuity, preserving spiritual values threatened by the fall of the multinational monarchy.[43]

The eventual foundation of the Salzburg Festival grew out of the collaborative work of Hermann Bahr and Max Reinhardt in the early twentieth century. Bahr talked both to Hofmannsthal and to Reinhardt and his closest colleagues about his 'Salzburg plans' in the course of December 1903, and by the end of that month was hoping that the 'Salzburger Feste' would be launched by 1905.[44] He continued in the next few years to make plans for Reinhardt's company to perform in Salzburg. Bahr moved to Salzburg in 1912 and two years later published a slim volume entitled *Salzburg* which gives a brief impressionistic history of the town, illustrated with photographs and celebrating it as a Baroque city. It was in Salzburg that he returned to the Catholic church in 1914, throwing himself into his conversion with all his customary ebullience, to the amusement of Schnitzler: 'It is said that he is now spending all his time in Salzburg shuffling around the churches on his knees' (Tgb., 13 July 1916). In the first flush of his enthusiasm, indeed, he wrote a life of Franz Joseph Rudigier, Bishop of Linz from 1853 to 1884, of such hagiographical character and effusively Catholic tone (it is even dedicated to the Archbishop of Vienna) that Hofmannsthal rejected it when he was offered it for the *Österreichische Bibliothek*. Again Schnitzler was moved to slightly malicious amusement when he was told of this by Hofmannsthal: they talked, his diary records, 'about Bahr, who gave Hugo such a militantly Catholic and pro-clerical book [ein so clerical militantes Büchl] for the *Österreichische Bibliothek* that even Poldi Andrian advised against publishing it' (Tgb., 1 August 1916).

In the summer of 1917 the Salzburger Festspielhaus-Gemeinde was founded in Vienna, and in August 1918 an artistic advisory board (*Kunstrat*) was founded. The members were Reinhardt (who had sealed his association with Salzburg in the spring of 1918 by buying Schloss Leopoldskron there), Richard Strauss, and Franz Schalk, Strauss's co-director of the Opera House in Vienna from 1919 onwards. Six months later Hofmannsthal and Alfred Roller were co-opted. In the journal of the Salzburger Festspielhaus-Gemeinde there is a good deal of idealistic internationalism,[45] but it is not seriously debated; the journal's main role was to justify the whole venture to the members of the association, who indeed increased in number from 1,769 at the beginning of 1920 to 3,129 by December 1921.

As regards repertory, the intention rehearsed by Hofmannsthal in the essay 'Die Salzburger Festspiele' was for the festival to provide 'musical and dramatic performances' – the indivisibility of the two suggested by his use of a hyphenated compound adjective in German, 'musikalisch-dramatische Aufführungen' – in a purpose-built festival theatre (P IV, 88). Though it was Hofmannsthal, not Reinhardt, who publicly argued a consistent ideological rationale for the festival, the annual repertory, including the prominence of morality plays, was largely determined by Reinhardt's taste until he was driven into exile by the *Anschluss*. Steinberg, following Broch's view, argues that to Reinhardt the Catholic morality play was essentially 'a vehicle for sensational theatrical spectacles', and that 'his participation in the stagings of *Jedermann* and *Das Salzburger große Welttheater* carried none of Hofmannsthal's ambitions of cultural reformation';[46] but in fact he was committed to the central conception of the festival repertory by the summer of 1918. On 21 July 1918 he wrote to Ferdinand Künzelmann, who was representing the Salzburger Festspielhaus-Gemeinde, that 'under the banner of Mozart, the pleasure-loving and pious genius of Salzburg, opera and drama, comedy and *Singspiel*, popular drama and also the old mysteries and Christmas plays should be blended into a noble unity'.[47] Here already are all the ingredients of Hofmannsthal's exposés of the festival programme – the combination of music, centring on Mozart, with mystery and morality plays, seen as linking with traditions of popular medieval and Baroque passion plays and Christmas plays. It was also part of Reinhardt's plan, as emphasized in the same letter, that the 'very heart of the Festival' had to be *autochthonic* art ('der Kern der Festspiele muß unbedingt eine heimische, bodenständige Kunst sein').

Hofmannsthal's essays made him the most prominent public voice of the festival idea; but he was not advancing an independent view. Though Steinberg presents him as the 'intellectual founder of the festival',[48] both Reinhardt's 1918 letter to Künzelmann and the journalism of Berta Zuckerkandl show that by the time the first of his festival essays, 'Deutsche Festspiele zu Salzburg', appeared in the issue of the *Mitteilungen der Salzburger Festspielhaus-Gemeinde* for April 1919 the ideas he was propounding were already in the air. His contribution lay rather in the systematic relation of the festival to a conservative ideology. He saw it as a first practical step in the 'conservative revolution', and indeed – so he argued in his third 'Vienna Letter' – as the first 'resurrection' of the old Europe (A, 304).

There were also other, more pragmatic, arguments for the venture, not least its potential contribution to the sickly economy of the new state.[49] Alfred Polgar, reporting on the festival for the first time in 1922, took a sceptical view of the whole enterprise: to launch a festival in a country with an economy at its last gasp, he wrote, was a piece of folly akin to holding an exhibition of paintings in a home for the blind.[50] And indeed, though the foundation stone for a grandiose festival theatre designed by Hans Poelzig was laid in August 1922, the soaring inflation of the early 1920s soon necessitated revision of the project, and the theatre was eventually completed on a different site. Even then it was critically received, in respect both of its functional efficiency and of its aesthetic appearance: Joseph August Lux wrote in the *Reichspost* on 6 June 1926 that it looked more like a garage than a festival theatre (*Resonanz*, 30).

Underlying the planning of the festival was a fixed conception of the historical significance of Salzburg itself. First and foremost, it was a town of Baroque traditions: 'the Baroque in all its forms', Max Pirker declared in 1921, was 'the very soul of Salzburg'.[51] Not only did the idea of the Baroque invoke the great age of Maria Theresia and so suggest the continuity of Austrian national culture,[52] in particular it evoked the image of a city with a long theatrical tradition. This too Pirker spelt out: 'The importance of the ancient theatrical city of Salzburg is inseparably connected with the Baroque theatre: court theatre, religious theatre, and popular theatre'.[53] Hofmannsthal even tried to portray the renewal of theatrical tradition as stretching still further back into time immemorial:

> Musikalisch theatralische Festspiele in Salzburg zu veranstalten, das heißt: [. . .] an uralter sinnfällig auserlesener Stätte aufs neue tun, was dort allezeit getan wurde; es heißt: den Urtrieb des bayrisch–österreichischen Stammes gewähren lassen [. . .]. Dem Bajuwaren wurde alles Handlung; er ist der Schöpfer des deutschen Volksspieles. ('Festspiele in Salzburg': P III, 444)

> To hold a musical and theatrical festival in Salzburg is to do once again what has always been done in the same age-old, symbolically chosen place; it is to give full rein to the basic drive of the Austro-Bavarian people [. . .]. The Austro-Bavarians turned everything into dramatic action; they are the creators of German folk-drama.

This is an argument that Reinhardt would echo over twenty years after the first festival, celebrating 'the profound pleasure in the theatre which in and around Salzburg has been firmly rooted for centuries in the medieval passion-plays, mysteries, and many folk-plays'.[54]

Secondly, standing on the border between Austria and Bavaria, the city symbolized the ethnic unity of the Austrian and German peoples. This appealed to the upsurge of pan-German sentiment in Austria after the First World War, though the guiding thought in Hofmannsthal's essays is of course not pan-Germanism (the line of thought that supported *Anschluss*) but on the contrary the independent integrity of Austria as a repository of cultural heritage. It is in this sense that what was conceived was, in the words of Hofmannsthal's essay-title, a German festival in Salzburg, 'Deutsche Festspiele zu Salzburg':

> The festival idea is the essential artistic idea of the Austro-Bavarian people [Der Festspielgedanke ist der eigentliche Kunstgedanke des bayrisch-österreichischen Stammes]. The foundation of a festival theatre on the very border between Bavaria and Austria is a symbolic expression of profound tendencies that go back half a millennium. (P III, 441)

Nevertheless, though Hofmannsthal explicitly rejected the biological 'determinism' behind Nadler's method of literary history (P IV, 495), Nadler's influence is evident in his adoption in the essay 'Festspiele in Salzburg' of the ethnic term 'Der Bajuware'.

Though Salzburg had become for him the very embodiment of the 'idea of Austria', it had in fact belonged to Austria for only just over a century. Indeed, neither his romantic view of the city's importance nor his presentation of its theatrical history stands much scrutiny. It was constantly romanticized as the 'city of Mozart', but it is well known how much Mozart in fact hated the provincialism of what in the late eighteenth century was a small town with a population of a mere 10,000 or so. This dislike can be gleaned from letter after letter that he wrote to his father in 1781. 'You yourself must admit that in Salzburg – at least for me – there isn't a pennyworth of entertainment, [. . .] nothing to stimulate my talent.'[55] He regarded Vienna, by contrast (a city twenty times larger), as 'a splendid place – for *my profession* the best place in the world', and to his father's accusations of self-indulgence he responded that he permitted himself 'no pleasures at all, except the pleasure of not being in Salzburg'.[56]

It is true that in the seventeenth and early eighteenth century theatrical treatments of classical and biblical subjects were performed both in the university and in the Archbishop's theatre,[57] but Salzburg and its environs were *not* an old-established centre of any kind of folk theatre. In his comprehensive survey of German folk drama, Leopold Schmidt stresses emphatically that the neo-Baroque festival in the town has led to quite false assumptions about the history of the Salzburg region as a theatrical centre. His findings are that in the Middle Ages Salzburg was 'surprisingly unfruitful' in drama, with few religious plays; in the Renaissance period the record of Shrovetide plays (*Fastnachtspiele*) was equally thin; there is hardly any trace of Christmas plays at the height of the Baroque age; and the one major *Volksschauspiel* performed in the second half of the eighteenth century, the *Comedie vom Jüngsten Gericht*, was imported from the Tyrol.[58] The Hanswurst of eighteenth-century Viennese popular comedy wore Salzburg peasant costume, and Hofmannsthal tries to make something of this, presenting him as a native of Salzburg ('Hanswurst [. . .] ist ein geborener Salzburger': P III, 449); but the costume is that of a figure of fun, a token not of the theatre but of rusticity. One of Mozart's complaints about the town, in the letter of 26 May 1781 already quoted, was precisely that there was no theatre worth mentioning. Even in the nineteenth century, by contrast with Pressburg, Brünn, Graz, Pest, and Prague, Salzburg was not one of the main provincial centres of theatre in Austria, where major performers toured. A report that appeared in one of the Viennese papers in 1842 admitted that the best thing about Salzburg in summer was its natural surroundings, and that in winter, while people found their way into the theatre, it was 'mostly only to be bored, for the pleasure afforded us by the few good actors is unfortunately often soured by dreadful misinterpretations of the finest plays'.[59] Other accounts from the 1840s confirm that the company was of mixed experience and that the singers were not strong.[60] As late as 1890, when Mizi Glümer was acting in Salzburg, Schnitzler was scornful of her position 'in a small provincial theatre – even if it is called "Imperial and Royal Regional Theatre"' ('an einem kleinen Provinztheater (wenn es auch k. k. Landestheater heißt)': Tgb., 19 September 1890).

The provincialism of the theatre is indicative of the provincialism of the town at that time. Bahr's fantasy of Salzburg as a cultural 'capital of Europe', written in 1900 and included in his volume *Essays* in 1912,[61] was outdone in March 1918 when Ernst Ehrens, writing of the plans for a festival theatre and focusing on the town as the birthplace of Mozart, called it 'one of the spiritual capitals of Europe – indeed of the world'.[62] Again there were precedents for such hyperbole in the 1840s: in September 1842, when the Mozart statue was unveiled, the town prided itself on having turned into an 'artistic capital', but after a week's excitement it returned to its old ways as a small provincial town.[63] The position was still very similar in 1920; even Bahr half-jokingly complained about the dreadful crowds and how the town would not be able to relax until *Jedermann* was over.[64] It is in Salzburg that Schnitzler's novel *Therese* opens; it is repeatedly referred to as a 'small town', and

Therese's father at one point considers leaving what he calls the 'boring little town' for Vienna (ES II, 628).

What visitors in the early twentieth century praised about it was always its picturesqueness and the beauty of its situation: they would describe it not as a cultural centre but as a tourist centre of antiquarian interest – a 'fascinating old-world town' which had 'sprung into being as a favourite summer and winter resort not merely for tourists, but also for those to whom the older portion of the town, [with] its many historic buildings, castle, and fine churches, proves attractive'.[65] Even those who proclaimed its uniqueness came back to the same formula: its history and beautiful position, and the association with Mozart.[66] In short, the cultural life of the town in the 1920s was not such as to make it either particularly suitable for an international festival or even particularly responsive to it. It was a provincial garrison town of about 37,000 inhabitants; Max Reinhardt himself would later look back on it as a 'philistine fishpond'.[67]

When the idea of a festival was being explored during the war by Friedrich Gehmacher, a Salzburg lawyer who was prominent in the *Mozart-Gemeinde*, and Heinrich Damisch, a Viennese music critic, the purchase of land presented difficulties because, as Gehmacher explained in 1916, they were dealing with countryfolk who were instantly mistrustful.[68] The lack of cultural commitment in the indigenous population was satirically summed up by Alfred Polgar at the end of the 1920s in an essay in his collection *Ja und Nein*, in which he gives a sketch of the typical Salzburg citizen:

> His displeasure at every disturbance of his provincial idyll is considerable and is not wholly compensated for by the pleasure of earning money. This is shown in the ambivalent attitude of the people of Salzburg to the festival now breaking over their town. On the one hand they are pleased that people and money are coming in, on the other hand they hate all the noise associated with that.[69]

Local interest in a regular festival had always centred on Mozart; there had indeed been frequent small-scale musical festivals from the late nineteenth century onwards. The Mozarteum building had been completed in 1914, and if at the end of the war there was some local resistance to the Festspielhaus project, this was in part because of loyalty to the Mozarteum and the history of past music festivals. There was also some local concern that Reinhardt might hijack the whole enterprise. The Festspielhaus was consequently planned as a centre for music and opera, 'in the spirit of the Mozart cult'.[70]

Mozart was the central figure in Berta Zuckerkandl's paean of support for the project in January 1919, and although the operatic component was always imported, mainly from Vienna,[71] the consistent intention of attracting tourism meant that the musical side of the festival inevitably remained most prominent in the long run, rather than theatrical performances. This pre-eminence of music did not date only from the 1930s, when Bruno Walter and Toscanini were among the principal luminaries; Mozart's choral and orchestral music was already central in the early years.

The major theatrical events of the 1920s were Reinhardt's productions of the two Hofmannsthal moralities. The romantic myth of the homogeneous *Volk*, which appealed to Hofmannsthal as a counter to the cultural fragmentation of German-speaking Europe, was a myth ideally suited to expression in the simple quasi-popular form of the morality play. Even when writing *Jedermann* he had been consciously attempting to adapt timeless material to recreate the effect of myth. His earliest notes for the play are headed: '*Jedermann*. An ecclesiastical play. As an epigraph, the passage from the Hebbel-Uechtritz correspondence: "I have used the Christian myth like any other"' (HKA IX, 114).[72]

There were Austrian precedents for a modern morality play, the best known being *Der Werth des Lebens* (1892) by Rudolph Lothar. This work, which treats the dawning appreciation of lasting values in a man purified through guilt, is full of echoes of Goethe's *Faust*, and its derivativeness was savagely criticized in Hans Sittenberger's study of contemporary Austrian drama.[73] But in the play's use of allegorical figures (Death and Guilt), the range of exemplary experiences the hero Wilfried goes through, and the final recognition of humane values, the pattern of a modern morality play is well-nigh complete. What Hofmannsthal achieved in *Jedermann* was essentially to exploit this pattern to serve his adoption of the 'Christian myth', so passing, as Steinberg has put it, 'from the appropriation of Greek mythology (the Elektra myth [. . .]) to Catholic mythology, rooted in the tradition of the morality play'.[74]

The material is international, the English *Everyman* on which Hofmannsthal's work is principally based being related to a well-known Dutch version. But conceiving his adaptation from the start as an exercise in recapturing the spirit and immediacy of folk theatre, he originally planned it as a work in Viennese dialect, and indeed wrote to Strauss about it in those terms on 27 April 1906 (H/Strauss, 20). When Reinhardt first produced it in Berlin in 1911, it was not a great success, and it was only after the war, in Salzburg, that it took on new significance, of two kinds. First, as Auernheimer recorded in his review in the *Neue Freie Presse* for

27 August 1920, the postwar audience was receptive to the depiction of the dangers of Mammon (*Resonanz*, 12); secondly, the production succeeded in appealing to a sense of national cultural solidarity. This is a point that Hermann Broch puts more fancifully in *Hofmannsthal und seine Zeit* where he suggests that Jedermann became, as Steinberg summarizes it, 'an allegory for Austria herself, the martyred country fallen from grace, humbly but desperately seeking salvation through a theatrical embrace of Christian piety'.[75]

Reinhardt's production in front of the cathedral was planned, as he informed the Archbishop of Salzburg in July 1920, to use 'a simple podium, without special décor',[76] in keeping with the simplicity of the material. Matching the style of the production to the dramatic idiom, he concentrated on achieving a didactic effect accessible to the widest possible public. Adopting the morality play in this spirit was an equivalent to the development of the critical *Volksstück* of Fleisser, Horváth, and Brecht. Indeed, it was possible in the 1920s to regard *Jedermann* explicitly as a kind of 'Volksstück': it was, so Ernst Decsey wrote in the *Neues Wiener Tagblatt* on 27 August 1927, 'a *Volksstück* which can be performed anywhere with the most profound effect, even on village stages or in barns' (*Resonanz*, 46).

The production of *Jedermann* was, as Reinhardt would later express it, a 'smash hit' (he used the English term),[77] and for the most part it was glowingly received by the critics. Various accounts sum up the effect of the performance as a combination of elements: the medieval play revived, combining high seriousness with a homely idiom; the great actors, including Moissi (Jedermann) and Helene Thimig (Werke); the lavish Baroque setting of the Domplatz, transformed into a theatre; the sunset, with thunder rolling in the background; and the admixture of religious feeling.[78] The success of the production gave credence to claims that the 'Baroque' spirit intended had been recreated.[79] The conscious link with folk theatre provided a justification for reworking Hofmannsthal's *Jedermann* in Salzburg dialect, as was done in 1921, with Hofmannsthal's agreement, by Franz Löser. In the 1920s there also developed a whole school of Austrian morality plays, dealing with Christian themes. The most important exponent was Hofmannsthal's friend Max Mell: *Das Wiener Kripperl von 1919*, set in Vienna, was published in 1921, and *Das Apostelspiel* (1923) was one of the main successes of the 1925 festival. Joseph August Lux, one of many Austrian writers to settle in Salzburg, had turned his hand to the genre shortly after the end of the war, and continued to write in the same vein into the early 1930s.[80] Another work that had its première at the Salzburg Festival was *Das Perchtenspiel*

(1928), a one-act play in a country setting by Richard Billinger. Hofmannsthal had admired Billinger's early poems since shortly after the war, had written to Mell about them (H/Mell, 159: letter of 1 September 1920), and through Mell continued to have occasional contact with him.

We are fortunate that among the reviewers attending the early years of the festival was Alfred Polgar. Though far from kindly disposed to Reinhardt's commercial sense, Polgar had recognized as early as 1911 that as a producer he was nothing less than a genius,[81] and he acknowledged the powerful mixture of sacred and profane achieved by the whole ambience.[82] This was exactly the effect that Hofmannsthal sought to recreate when he wrote *Das Salzburger große Welttheater*, which was performed instead of *Jedermann* in 1922.

Some tense negotiations were needed before the première of Hofmannsthal's second morality was allowed to take place in Fischer von Erlach's Kollegienkirche. The dramatist, however, was determined on the setting and told Emil Ronsperger that this church and its special character, the 'Baroque atmosphere of a solemn enclosed space', was an 'absolute precondition' of his work (HKA X, 197: letter of 9 October 1921). Yet he also conceived *Das Salzburger große Welttheater* as a 'popular' ('volksmäßig') play (P IV, 266), a revival of a genuinely popular form of drama, 'die halbvergessene volkstümliche Form' (P IV, 269). This is difficult to reconcile with his choice of Calderón's *El gran teatro del mundo* as his main source, but it links with his idealized notion, drawn from popular theatre, of a coherent theatre public. In the third of his 'Vienna Letters', published in *The Dial* in March 1923, he claimed that what Reinhardt had achieved in his production was precisely to unite the motley international audience and to create a unified and naïvely receptive public (A, 300). Two years later the picture was simplified still further, when he contrasted the integrity of the public in Salzburg with Vienna, where there was a gulf between the outlying districts and the centre with its more pretentious artistic institutions which did not appeal to the common people ('[. . .] der "Stadt" mit ihren unvolksmäßigen Kunstanstalten': P IV, 268).

The première took place in a blaze of publicity. Joseph Gregor wrote shortly beforehand that Salzburg was preparing itself for a theatrical event unparalleled for over a century, and that never in memory had a theatrical event been the subject of such lively advance discussion.[83] Schnitzler was sceptical about Hofmannsthal's motives during all the preparations. His diary records a conversation he had with Stefan Zweig on 2 June 1922 about Bahr,

Hofmannsthal, and the latter's 'unsufferable scheming' in Salzburg: the news was, he noted, that Hofmannsthal was handing over his royalties for *Das Salzburger große Welttheater* to the fund for the restoration of the Kollegienkirche simply in order to secure use of the church (*Chrstk.*, 47–8). In fact, he donated half his royalties,[84] and the production, in which, as one critic wrote, 'every opportunity was shrewdly grasped to underline the spoken word with visual effects',[85] clearly succeeded in achieving the effects he was aiming for.

The basic idea underlying the play is the enactment of human life as a series of roles, providentially dispensed, with Death as the director arranging the exits. This scheme is drawn directly from Caldcrón. It is sct up in Hofmannsthal's version in a prose scene which functions rather like the Prologue in Heaven in Goethe's *Faust*; indeed the status of the scene as a 'prologue' is humorously drawn out by *Vorwitz* (HKA X, 16) – a comic figure added by Hofmannsthal, whose name implies curiosity combined with a knowing pertness. The events are to be enacted 'symbolically' ('gleichnisweise', another reminiscence of Goethe's *Faust*), and the title of the play, 'Do good under God', introduces an action whose gist is summarized in quotations from the commandments (HKA X, 15–16).

The events of the play proper are foreshadowed in this prologue when one of the souls being given roles is allotted that of a beggar and protests against the unequal apportioning of lots, drawing on the language of Schiller's rebellious Karl Moor and supported by the Mephistophelean 'Adversary' (*Widersacher* – another figure added by Hofmannsthal), in the legalistic jargon of egalitarianism (HKA X, 19–21). The role of beggar is finally accepted after persuasion from an angel.

The language of the prologue is stylized, rich in literary and biblical allusions, often poetic in its construction but with Austrian inflections. The play proper is in rhymed verse of varying metre, mainly five-footed and six-footed lines but also, as in *Jedermann*, the four-footed couplets (*Knittelvers*) of the old German Shrovetide plays. (The apportioning of unequal lots was a familiar theme of the sixteenth century.)[86] By comparison with the rather studied archaisms of *Jedermann*, lively differentiation is added in the dialect of the countryman, and the dialogue is punctuated by the ironic commentary of *Vorwitz*. Linguistically the text displays a virtuoso command of rhythm, allusion, and register, but these literary skills are harnessed to an over-simple moral pattern.

As the action unfolds, the figures display their characteristics: the vanity of Beauty, the isolation of Wisdom (in a nun's habit), the imperiousness of the King, the materialism of the Rich Man, the complacency of the industrious but acquisitive Countryman. (The German word is 'Bauer' and is usually translated 'Peasant', but the status of the figure is higher than that implies; Eichendorff, whose translation of the Calderón original Hofmannsthal consulted,[87] uses the word 'Landmann'.) When the Beggar enters, representing a life of misery, he is rejected by Beauty as unaesthetic and is not to be pacified by the pronouncements of Wisdom. Spurred on by the Adversary, the Beggar plays Esau to the King's Jacob; he threatens like Samson to destroy the whole settled order of things, which is built on a chain of mutual dependence, the Countryman as the provider of food being no less essential than the King as the guarantor of peace.[88] The Beggar demands a new world order and rejects the Rich Man's defence of the existing order (HKA X, 36–7). The Rich Man, to whom he has nothing to offer, offers him nothing in return, in an echo of *King Lear*: nothing shall come of nothing (HKA X, 39); the Countryman offers him poorly paid work felling trees and chopping wood but then piles on further duties keeping 'order' in the woodland. This triggers the Beggar's rebellion. With axe poised he confronts all the other characters, but when Wisdom prays for him he is suddenly converted in an access of light, accepts the world as a divine comedy ('Gottes Spiel': HKA X, 50), and rejects the Adversary. He now looks for a 'new order' not in this world but on a higher plane.

The passing of time – a matter which dismays Beauty – heralds the end of the play and the moment of judgment. The figures are taken off one by one by Death, who is greeted with gladness only by the Beggar (HKA X, 62). The Beggar grasps that all the earthly things have been stage properties, the roles mere masks. In an enactment of the dictum that the last shall be first, he is the first to be allowed into the divine palace, followed by Wisdom, and the Rich Man alone is denied entrance into the kingdom of heaven.

The ideological overtones in the disrupted world of the 1920s are unmistakable.[89] Hofmannsthal explicitly saw the underlying theme of the work as the threat of chaos to the world order ('die Drohung des Chaos an die geordnete Welt': A, 296), and he recognized that his principal innovation in adapting the material lay in the figure of the rebellious Beggar (A, 296), representing the disruptive materialism against which the play as a whole was designed as a spiritual buttress. The political implications were brought out in Reinhardt's production, particularly in the way Moissi, to the dramatist's apparent approval, lent a Russian air to the figure of the Beggar, so suggesting the spectre of Bolshevism (A, 304). This is exactly how Auernheimer, reviewing the première in the *Neue Freie*

Presse on 17 August 1922, interpreted the play, which he summed up as 'another *Jedermann*, more artistically constructed and [. . .] dramatically more lively'; contrasting Hofmannsthal's Beggar with Calderón's, he concluded that Hofmannsthal's more recalcitrant figure was a product of the immediate past and represented communism (TR, 390–1).

Despite its linguistic subtlety, *Das Salzburger große Welttheater* presents mankind with black-and-white unsubtlety. The crucial moral turning-point, the visionary conversion that cuts short the Beggar's attack on privilege, is pychologically unmotivated – *dramatically* unconvincing. Hence the failure of the play to oust *Jedermann* from its central place in the Salzburg programme: the hardening of Hofmannsthal's missionary intention leads him not to elevate morality into drama but to reduce drama to simplistic morality. Even the sceptical Polgar, writing in the *Prager Tagblatt* on 19 August 1922, admitted that staging the production in the Kollegienkirche achieved the sense of 'community' aimed at: 'Somehow the seated individual feels his individuality reduced. Just by being there he becomes part of a community.' But Polgar too found that the final submission of the beggar was unconvincing, and added that this showed in Moissi's playing: 'After his transformation the role rightly has no more interest for him. He dutifully executes the heart-searching – orders are orders – but (like us) without knowing why' (*Resonanz*, 17–19).

The production of *Das Salzburger große Welttheater* was subjected to other criticisms, which in two respects amounted to attacks on the whole enterprise of the festival. One line of attack was frankly anti-Semitic. Anti-Semitic voices had already been raised after the production of *Jedermann* in 1920; *Kikeriki*, for example, carried a piece on 12 September 1920 purporting to report that the cathedral in Salzburg was being renamed the synagogue, the Domplatz renamed the 'Neuer Judenschulplatz', the statue of Mozart transformed into a monument to Max Reinhardt, and so on. After *Das Salzburger große Welttheater* the open abuse was far worse. Year by year, the anti-Semitic papers in the Salzburg area mounted increasingly vindictive attacks not only on Reinhardt and Moissi (who was widely though wrongly assumed to be Jewish) but also on Hofmannsthal. In 1922 the *Freie Salzburger Bauernstimme*, for example, expressed surprise that a Jew could have written a Catholic mystery play, and the *Deutscher Volksruf* reported that the content of *Das Salzburger große Welttheater* was 'entirely in the spirit of the fellow-members of the author's race'.[90] A few months later, the Christian Social *Salzburger Chronik* for 4 and 5 February

1923 reported favourably a protest at the first congress (*Gautagung*) of the Salzburg *Antisemitenbund* against performances of works by the 'Jew Hofmannsthal'. The organ of the *Antisemitenbund*, a weekly entitled *Der Eiserne Besen*, continued to protest against the influence of the 'Semites Reinhardt, Moissi, Hofmannsthal' (22 March 1924) – but especially against Reinhardt, 'who produces his Jewish "works of art" on cathedral squares and in houses of Christian worship' (10 September 1923). Similarly in 1926 the *Deutscher Volksruf* trumpeted the rhetorical question 'Must the director of the Festival in a German city be a Jew?' (6 February 1926).

Often the prejudice of the times revealed itself in omission rather than in overt attacks. When the foundation stone of the Festspielhaus was laid in August 1922, the journalist Rudolf Holzer made a speech on behalf of the Festspielhaus-Gemeinde, of which he was a founder-member; Berta Zuckerkandl, writing in the *Wiener Allgemeine Zeitung* on 26 August, protested that he made special mention of Richard Strauss but none at all of Reinhardt or Hofmannsthal (*Resonanz*, 20).

Anti-Semitism fed on suspicion that the festival was being run as an entrepreneurial enterprise, and indeed the high prices that the audience had to pay militated against any sense of genuine 'community' such as Hofmannsthal argued for. It was not the first time in Hofmannsthal's career that he had been criticized for an exclusiveness produced by high prices: in 1912 the point had been made by Ludwig Sternaux about the première of *Ariadne auf Naxos* in Berlin.[91] But the issue was far graver in Salzburg, where the exclusiveness was so obviously at odds with the idea of the festival as attracting the indigenous 'Volk'. This was eloquently set out in a vigorous article that appeared in *Der Merker* on 15 September 1920. The author, writing under the initials 'J.B.', argued that the production of *Jedermann* was a transparently speculative artifice acted in front of a public unfamiliar with the Salzburg context and unresponsive to the religious material, sitting in expensive seats from which the true 'Volk' were excluded; while the physical setting guaranteed splendid effects, it would have been better by moonlight without the theatricals.[92] Else Lasker-Schüler wrote no less critically to Herwath Walden that the production of *Jedermann* was unartistic: 'Life and death, sin and judgment, Heaven and Hell – all are degraded to a spectacle, [. . .] for the sensation of a rich sensation-hungry public.'[93] As inflation spiralled, the impossibility for the local man in the street to pay for admission was even clearer by the time *Das Salzburger große Welttheater* was produced, and the point was forcefully made in the *Salzburger Chronik* on 12 and 13 August 1922.[94]

As a result, far from catering for an autochthonic 'popular' public, performances were attended by an audience composed largely of tourists, the artificiality of the occasion made even clearer by the fondness of women visitors for dressing up in local costume.[95] The way the festival took root affords an example of the 'invention of tradition' analysed by Eric Hobsbawm – invented ritual establishing itself by suggesting significant continuity with the past.[96] Its commercial success depended on a strong element of nostalgic escapism, and in fact this had been built into Reinhardt's calculations even before the end of the war:

> I believe that with its wonderfully central location, the splendour of its setting and its architecture, its historic monuments and memories, and not least because of its virginal, unspoiled quality, Salzburg is destined to become a place of pilgrimage for those countless people who long to be redeemed by art from the bloody horror of our times.[97]

The escapist note continued to be sounded even by those genuinely appreciative of the cultural fare, such as Gerhart Hauptmann, to whom the town still seemed a place of 'pilgrimage' in 1928, a peaceful refuge amid the postwar disintegration of Europe.[98]

Eventually Salzburg's dependence on tourism had damaging consequences, in that the festival was particularly vulnerable both to inflation – tourism declined markedly in 1925[99] – and later to the economic pressure imposed on Austria by Nazi Germany in 1933 with the 'Tausendmarksperre' (a tax of 1,000 RM levied on German citizens visiting Austria), which had the effect of reducing the tourist industry by over three quarters.

The most sustained and outspoken rejection of the festival came from Karl Kraus. It formed part of long satirical campaigns that he waged against Hofmannsthal and Reinhardt. He attacked Hofmannsthal for derivative eclecticism, preying on tradition; the point was made most succinctly in his 1923 poem 'Goethe und Hofmannsthal' (F 622–631, 73). The campaign against Reinhardt would culminate in 1935 in the essay 'Die Handschrift des Magiers' (F 912–915, 34–62) which contrasts Reinhardt's ostentatious lifestyle and what Kraus regarded as his artistic barrenness, and draws parallels to the rise of the populist Hitler.[100] The essay 'Vom großen Welttheaterschwindel', which first appeared in print in *Die Fackel* in November 1922,[101] attacks 'the holy trinity of Messrs Reinhardt, Moissi, and Hofmannsthal'. His criticism is directed against the commercialism of the festival (in this it runs parallel to the charges of exploitation of the church setting that were made in the anti-Semitic press) coupled with what he would call Reinhardt's

'Tapeziererträume', his theatre of décor in contrast to the service of the text that informed Kraus's own readings in his 'Theater der Dichtung'. This was a time when Kraus's readings of Nestroy were at their height: in November 1921 he had read *Der Zerrissene* for the first time; in June 1922 *Der Talisman*; in November 1922 *Der böse Geist Lumpazivagabundus*. Hofmannsthal, by contrast, tried to represent Reinhardt's work as being linked to the 'popular' ('volkstümlich') theatre of Vienna by virtue of its visual effect – a view that he had spelt out in the 1918 essay 'Das Reinhardtsche Theater' (P III, 431) but that carries little conviction, particularly by comparison with Nestroy. In June 1923 there followed Kraus's poem 'Bunte Begebenheiten' (F 622–631, 65–7), which essentially reworks the jokes in the essay 'Vom großen Welttheaterschwindel' and presents Reinhardt as exploiting the ecclesiastical setting in order to cash in on the tourist trade.

Kraus's case is satirically exaggerated; nevertheless, the doubts raised by him and others about Reinhardt's entrepreneurial methods concern not just the one production but by implication the integrity of the whole festival. They have to be set against the general critical acclaim that greeted Reinhardt's productions and the impressive development and survival of the festival as an institution. Undeniably it was founded on a basis of ideological muddle and historical error. The idea of Salzburg as a traditional cultural centre was at odds with the historical facts, while the much-touted notions of Austro-German 'Volkstümlichkeit' were based on disreputable ethnic theories and hopelessly mingled both with protestations of cosmopolitan internationalism and with a 'Baroque' tradition that in truth had little to do with popular theatre. Yet the stimulus that the whole complex of ideas afforded Hofmannsthal is a striking demonstration of the inspirational power of misunderstanding. By comparison with the mainstream of modern drama both *Jedermann* and *Das Salzburger große Welttheater* may seem old-fashioned. By 1922, after all, Brecht's career was well under way; indeed in that very year he was awarded the Kleist Prize. But *Jedermann*, having been performed at the first Salzburg Festival in 1920 and again in 1921, and then annually from 1926 until the *Anschluss*, has remained the lynchpin of the festival, still performed in the setting chosen by Reinhardt; and as Martin Stern has reminded us, of all the works of Brecht, only *Die Dreigroschenoper* can compete with it in popular success.[102]

CHAPTER 7

Post mortem

Friends and Critics

Neither Hofmannsthal nor Schnitzler felt at home in the 1920s. Hofmannsthal tried to reflect the crisis of the age in his dramatic writing, and even if his romantic conservatism imposed an artistic straitjacket on his serious work (in particular *Das Salzburger große Welttheater* and *Der Turm*) this was counterbalanced by his achievements in comedy, *Der Schwierige*, *Der Unbestechliche*, and *Arabella*. Schnitzler had no such compensation. His prose fiction continued to be well received, but he was well aware of his waning creative powers as a dramatist, and his preference for writing about the Vienna of 1900 rather than the problems of the present increased his sense of isolation. Hofmannsthal once wrote that creative writers tend to rework their experience from one part of their life (P I, 160–1); to none does this apply more than to Schnitzler.

Precisely because he depended on reliving time past, the death of Hofmannsthal, the outstanding poet of 'Jung Wien', clearly affected him deeply. His distress was reported by Beer-Hofmann in a brief personal memoir that appeared in the *Neue Freie Presse* on 21 July 1929 (Fiechtner 1949, 346), and five days after the funeral in Rodaun he himself wrote very frankly of his feelings to Hedwig Fischer, the daughter of the publisher:

> I feel it very deeply that he is no longer alive. Let us at such times not shrink from grand words – I loved him deeply, not only because of the many creative writers I admire he was in my opinion perhaps the most 'real' and because, although ten years younger than I, he was a companion of my youth, but because he was the most remarkable human being and, despite all his problematic qualities, an intensely human one [auch weil er der merkwürdigste und dabei, bei mancher Problematik seines Wesens, ein höchst menschlicher Mensch war] [. . .] (*Chrstk.*, 9)

218

The 'problematic' qualities had, however, weighed heavily on their friendship, which had steadily deteriorated. Despite all their contact for nearly forty years they had never used the intimate form of address – no doubt partly a consequence of the age difference. The only members of the Griensteidl circle to whom Schnitzler used 'du' were Bahr and Lothar, who were only one year and three years younger than himself respectively, and Hofmannsthal did not use 'du' to Bahr, Beer-Hofmann, or Salten, all older than himself. (The men of letters with whom he did come to use 'du' tended to be slightly younger than he was: Borchardt, Schröder, the novelist Robert Michel.) But it is also symptomatic of the difference in their social backgrounds. Many of those with whom he was on 'du' terms belonged, like himself, to the aristocratic classes: Edgar Freiherr Karg von Bebenburg, Felix Baron Oppenheimer, Leopold Freiherr von Andrian-Werburg, Georg Freiherr zu Franckenstein, Clemens Freiherr zu Franckenstein, Harry Graf Kessler, Eberhard Freiherr von Bodenhausen-Degener. Schnitzler's envious sense of a class difference between himself and Hofmannsthal was in evidence in his diary as early as the mid-1890s, when he tried to analyse the 'very slight but undeniable irritation' he felt towards the younger man:

> [. . .] But I think that some of his airs and the fads he affects also contribute to my irritation [dass zu meiner Gereiztheit auch manche Allüren und Marotten von ihm beitragen]: his fondness for some of the externals of an aristocratic way of life and aristocratic opinions, his obvious preference for the company of 'young gentlemen'. Of course my irritation is also fed by my consciousness that *I* do not ride, that I cannot fence decently, and that I cannot shoot at all – in short that my parents neglected the physical side of my education (at which I would surely not have been bad). As a result my longing for 'elegance' (which in any case has subsided a lot recently) can never be wholly satisfied. (Tgb., 29 July 1896)

Moreover, Hofmannsthal's unpredictable moods, which he always explained as the effect of 'nerves', made him a demanding friend. Even at the age of twenty he was already ruthless about avoiding appointments. 'If the Sandrocks, Schnitzler etc. want to visit me,' he wrote to Beer-Hofmann from Strobl (to the east of Salzburg) in 1894, 'please don't strain your tact to get me out of it. Simply send a telegram, and *if I want* I can just continue and pretend I never got it' (H/Beer-Hofmann, 36–7: letter of 25 August 1894). Strauss met similarly firm treatment, as, for instance, when Hofmannsthal refused point-blank to have any dealings with Count

Seebach, the director of the Opera House in Dresden, about details in *Der Rosenkavalier*, writing that all external dealings should 'uniformly' be left to Strauss (H/Strauss, 79: letter of 12 July 1910). The *Buch der Freunde*, it may be remembered, includes the aphorism: 'A certain degree of arrogance is a useful ingredient of genius' (A, 18).

Hofmannsthal's egocentricity shows even in an expression of gratitude to Schnitzler such as the remark in a letter of 15 March 1900, written when he was planning a play (never completed), 'Paracelsus und Dr. Schnitzler': 'I am keenly aware that in my contact with you *nothing whatsoever* is unfruitful; nothing, even the smallest detail, that cannot be made something of later' (H/AS, 135). He also resented it that when he and Schnitzler met it was he who nearly always seemed to have to fit in with Schnitzler's convenience. On 28 March 1902 this resentment exploded in a letter written, he said, with tears in his eyes 'not from emotion but from anger'; he claimed to be giving vent to feelings he had been holding back for ten years (H/AS, 155). Increasingly, too, he complained that they saw each other too rarely.[1] In fact, however, he himself would often decline meetings on account either of his work or of his 'nerves', and he could do so with uncompromising frankness, as when he asked Schnitzler on 15 November 1897: 'Please excuse me and don't be cross: but why should I want to meet [Ludwig] Fulda?' (H/AS, 97). And when in another bout of exasperation just before the war he complained that he always had to make the effort to go to see Schnitzler (H/AS, 273: letter of 27 March 1914), Schnitzler could very reasonably reply the following day that it was in the natural course of things for Hofmannsthal to come to Vienna but not for him to travel out to Rodaun.

If Schnitzler suspected that behind Hofmannsthal's self-preservation there lay an element of self-importance, the suspicion can only have been enforced by the directness with which even in the 1890s the younger man, not one to indulge in uncritical effusiveness, sometimes criticized his work. In a letter of 16 July 1896, for example, Hofmannsthal subjected a draft of *Freiwild* to an ostensibly diffident but in fact damning critique, suggesting it was ineffective and the dialogue insufficiently individualized (H/AS, 69–70). Though the letter was not mentioned in Schnitzler's diary, thirteen days later there followed the long entry about his 'irritation'. Even Hofmannsthal's praise tended to be qualified by detailed criticism – for example, in his letter of 13 November 1903 on *Der einsame Weg* (H/AS, 177) – and must sometimes have seemed to verge on the condescending. A short note written on 22 December 1900 illustrates this: Hofmannsthal expresses his admiration of

Schnitzler's productiveness by calling him 'the Kotzebue of the short story' ('Man kann Sie nun ruhig den Kotzebue der Novelle nennen': H/AS, 145) – faint praise indeed, and Hofmannsthal must have known that Schnitzler would perceive the disrespect between the lines.

It was inevitable that their friendship was touched by rivalry. Traces of envy are certainly to be found often in Schnitzler's diaries. He was suspicious first of Hofmannsthal's greater intimacy with Beer-Hofmann (Tgb., 28 August 1894); just over a year later, noting a certain tension in their relations, he put the blame on the influence of Hermann Bahr:

> Hugo is too close to Bahr. That evidently prevents him from having genuine and constant warmth towards me. Despite good will – despite the best of will – on both sides, there is no deeper relationship between us [kein tieferes Verhältnis zwischen uns] as there could be and perhaps ought to be. (Tgb., 21 December 1895)

Analysing his 'irritation' in 1896, he admitted in one of his passages of self-punishing honesty that besides Hofmannsthal's 'airs' and 'fads' one cause lay in his own longing for his friend's good opinion: 'It is probably crossness that I am so strongly influenced in my opinion of myself by what I guess to be Hugo's opinion about me and that I often think I notice that he thinks less well of me than I would wish' (Tgb., 29 July 1896). Four years later he noted that his liking was decreasing ('Er ist mir jetzt weniger sympathisch') because of what he found a false note, a tendency to aim for effect, in Hofmannsthal's conversation (Tgb., 2 November 1900).

Schnitzler's trust was finally undermined by Hofmannsthal's reaction to *Der Weg ins Freie*. In his diary on 1 January 1909 he noted concisely a parting of the ways ('unsre Wege gehen getrennt'). But they continued to meet quite frequently, even during the war, when Schnitzler was out of sympathy with Hofmannsthal's pro-pagandist work. After one such meeting, when Hofmannsthal and his wife had visited the Sternwartestrasse and Hofmannsthal had been recounting his experiences in Poland, Schnitzler summed up in his diary his ambivalent verdict: 'Personally fascinating as usual – for the most part, probably, on account of his suspect quality' ('durch das bedenkliche seines Wesens': Tgb., 25 July 1916). By the end of the war, his view of Hofmannsthal had deteriorated into embittered wariness. When Mell published in *Der Wiener Mittag* adverse reviews of two productions in the Deutsches Volkstheater, Schnitzler blamed Hofmannsthal's influence. 'The closer to Hugo, the more hostile and malicious the attitude to me', he wrote in his diary on 27 December 1918 after reading Mell's review of *Professor Bernhardi*. Some four months later, after a review of *Der Ruf des Lebens*, he refers to Mell as Hofmannsthal's 'satellite' and complains sourly: 'It is impossible for anyone who is influenced by him to assert himself sympathetically or even objectively towards me' ('Keiner kann sich mir gegenüber mit Sympathie, ja nur objektiv behaupten, der von ihm influenzirt wird': Tgb., 5 May 1919). After the war Hofmannsthal was conscious of the growing coolness between them, and wrote reproaching Schnitzler for his reluctance to open his heart to him, regretting that he never saw him except from afar or that they would do no more than exchange a few words. 'I should love to spend an hour walking in the open air with you again – can't we manage that? I think of you often and with affection; after all, you are a whole part of my life' (H/AS, 294: letter of 19 March 1921).

In the final analysis the greatest barrier between them was the inequality in their assessment of each other's gifts and creative achievements. Like all the rest of their circle, Schnitzler was from the first hugely impressed by Hofmannsthal's precocious talent: 'Loris is simply stupendous!', he noted in his diary on 21 June 1891. He unreservedly accepted that the young poet was artistically the most significant figure in their circle (Tgb., 22 August 1894), and his wife would later recall his mixed feelings towards Hofmannsthal around the turn of the century, with envious admiration side by side with ironic amusement at Hofmannsthal's manner.[2] Though he would be critical of much that Hofmannsthal wrote in later years, he always remained keenly aware of the superiority of his innate gifts. In 1907 he named him, together with Liliencron and 'perhaps' Heinrich Mann, as one of only three creative writers alive who were of the first rank (Tgb., 21 April 1907). Over twenty years later, after reading the novel *Andreas*, he noted simply in his diary on 19 August 1930: 'We have lost in him the greatest creative writer of our time' ('Der grösste Dichter dieser Zeit ist mit ihm dahin': *Chrstk.*, 51).

It was rare for critical comparisons to be published that came out in Schnitzler's favour;[3] and insecure as he always felt of his own achievements, he inevitably measured himself against the younger man, so that both his admiration and his resentment were fuelled by his self-doubts. His diary chronicles in detail his constantly evolving reactions to Hofmannsthal's personality and work, and indeed his fascination with them; in the late 1920s (the material breaks off in 1927) he even had selected diary entries about

Hofmannsthal typed out in series, with a title-page bearing the autograph heading 'Hugo v. Hofmannsthal'.[4]

While Hofmannsthal published sixtieth-birthday tributes to Schnitzler both in the first of his 'Vienna Letters' in the American monthly *The Dial* and also in the *Neue Rundschau*, Schnitzler had long diagnosed Hofmannsthal's 'immense indifference' towards his work (Tgb., 28 December 1918). In fact their correspondence contains several letters in which Hofmannsthal praises his writing. Among the plays, he particularly admired *Das weite Land* (H/AS, 254–5: letter of 20 October 1910), but he was generally more appreciative of the prose fiction. This shows repeatedly in their correspondence, from his early admiration of *Frau Berta Garlan* (H/AS, 178: letter of 8 December 1903) to the summary of Schnitzler's position as a rare 'master of narrative' ('ein Meister der Erzählung'), written on 10 July 1928 (H/AS, 308). After reading one of Schnitzler's stories, 'Die Weissagung', Hofmannsthal encouraged him to write a novel (this is recorded in Schnitzler's diary entry for 27 December 1905), and it is ironic that he initially disliked *Der Weg ins Freie*, a work with which Schnitzler identified himself so closely that their correspondence on the subject twice became very sharp.[5] He was perceptive in perceiving the autobiographical element in *Casanovas Heimfahrt*, which is another work that he praised warmly (H/AS, 282: letter of 17 August 1918). The long letter of 10 July 1928 is largely devoted to praise for *Therese*, and his last extant letter to Schnitzler, written on 3 June 1929, records not only his rereading of a number of Schnitzler's prose works but also his view that *Fräulein Else* is even better than *Leutnant Gustl* and his admiration of Schnitzler's distinctive style (H/AS, 312).

But the writers who recurrently occupied Hofmannsthal's thoughts were the Olympians, from Plato and Sophocles to Calderón, Molière, and Goethe; nothing in his letters suggests that he really took Schnitzler's creative work with the same kind of seriousness. A tribute like the one he wrote for *The Dial* can only have seemed like further condescension, for rather than extolling Schnitzler he reduced his work to its 'typical' qualities, in the manner of the standard critical clichés: he had 'long been looked upon as Vienna's representative dramatic author', but his plays touched on 'only one phase' of the theatrical life of Vienna, namely the *Konversationsstück* traditional in the Burgtheater.[6]

Schnitzler's reservations about Hofmannsthal's writing centred on his dramatic work. For the early lyrical work he had genuine admiration. His diary records that he appreciated both the depth and the formal perfection of *Der Tor und der Tod* when Hofmannsthal read it aloud to himself, Beer-Hofmann, and Salten on 15 October 1893, and also the 'beauty' of the poems in *terza rima* that Hofmannsthal read on 2 August 1894. As late as 11 March 1926 he wrote to Hofmannsthal recording the deep emotion with which he had reread a number of his poems, recognizing both their originality and their lasting quality (H/AS, 306), and there is unfeigned praise too in a diary note of 17 November 1916, written after a rereading of *Der Abenteurer und die Sängerin*: 'This was genuinely a new voice!' ('Hier war wirklich ein neuer Ton angeschlagen!'). He had indeed liked *Der Abenteurer und die Sängerin* well enough to read it himself to Mizi Reinhard on 30 January 1899. But when Hofmannsthal first read it aloud in the autumn of 1898, while he conceded that it had its beauties and even 'good theatrical moments', this was tempered with the caveat that it was not 'a proper play' ('voll Schönheiten und Schönheit, mit guten theatr. Momenten, ohne ein rechtes Stück zu sein': Tgb., 30 October 1898). A year later he was still more succinctly critical of the dramatic technique of *Das Bergwerk zu Falun* ('dramatisch Schwächen': Tgb., 29 October 1899). Even *Elektra*, though much more dramatic, did not win his unstinted approval. Later, after rereading it in March 1909, he would tell Hofmannsthal he found it was 'simply admirable' (H/AS, 244), but after first seeing it in Berlin on 11 February 1904 he summarized it in his diary as a work of artifice rather than of art: while admittedly a piece of artifice of high class ('Kunststück höchsten Ranges'), it revealed nothing of the 'soul of the poet' as a work of art should. In this he was echoing the verdict of Alfred Kerr, who had summed it up two months earlier as a product of 'artistry' (HUK, 82). Writing to Hofmannsthal on 25 March 1909 he stressed that he preferred it 'un-Straussed' ('unverstrausst': H/AS, 244), but when it was finally staged in the Burgtheater in 1923 he found that the music had 'sucked the spirit' out of it, so that it was no longer bearable as a stage play (*Chrstk.*, 48).

His verdicts became ever harsher, especially after the offence Hofmannsthal gave him over *Der Weg ins Freie*. Though even in his sixties he could still write expressing 'loving admiration' after reading an essay on Schiller that Hofmannsthal had contributed to the Christmas 1925 issue of the *Neue Freie Presse* (H/AS, 304: letter of 26 December 1925), his judgment was more often ambivalent at best. An example already alluded to is his grudging acknowledgement of the effectiveness of *Der Rosenkavalier* after Hofmannsthal had read the text to a circle of family and friends:

> The whole thing thin in content; indeed, banal. In the erotic sphere, the non-sensual element exaggerated to the extent of

coarseness. The humour aridly grotesque, the verse strikingly poor. Nonetheless, not without positive qualities as a libretto, which is a real proof of talent in such an unmusical man. (Tgb., 29 November 1910)

In particular he reacted with sharpening distaste to traces he perceived in Hofmannsthal's work of what he had long regarded as his snobbery in real life. As early as 20 August 1898 he had defined in his diary Hofmannsthal's 'slightly snobbish tendency'. To his wariness on the score of Hofmannsthal's social pretentiousness the war added suspicion not only about his self-important would-be diplomatic activity but also about his closeness to the clerical camp. On 20 July 1916, for example, the 'Catholicizing snobbery' ('Katholisirender Snobism') in the Hofmannsthal household is recorded in his diary. A little later, this is sharpened into 'snobbery' *tout court*. The word 'Snobismus' crops up in the diary on 26 April 1917, on 11 January 1918 (on the latter occasion after a conversation that had touched on Hofmannsthal's work on *Der Schwierige*), and again twice in the early months of 1922. On 15 January, after reading Hofmannsthal's 'Worte zum Gedächtnis Molières' (P IV, 81–6) he wrote that he could hardly read any of his occasional work without 'inner resistance' on account of the 'pretentiousness, affectation, and snobbery', which he found increasingly intolerable, and on 18 March, after attending the première of *Josephslegende* in the Opera House in Vienna, he recorded his dislike of the text because of its 'artificiality [Gewolltheit], snobbery, and pretentiousness' (*Chrstk.*, 47).

Hofmannsthal's own background was not that of the hereditary (and in part landed) aristocracy of *Der Rosenkavalier*, *Der Schwierige*, and *Der Unbestechliche*, and the ever-sceptical Schnitzler detected pretentiousness and falsity in Hofmannsthal's idealization of that aristocracy. After a conversation with Salten about *Der Schwierige* on 30 July 1920, he noted in his diary that in it Hofmannsthal's 'lifelong disease, his snobbery, bursts out in its strongest literary expression' ('In ihm kommt die Lebenskrankheit Hugos, der Snobismus, zu heftigstem, literarischen Ausbruch': *Chrstk.*, 45). And though he went to the Viennese première in the Theater in der Josefstadt on 16 April 1924 the diary entry for that day records simply that he had still not warmed to it ('Meine Sympathie für das Stück wurde nicht größer': *Chrstk.*, 49). Among the many pieces of ephemeral journalism that appeared in the Viennese press immediately after his death, one of which Schnitzler would most certainly have been scornful is an article in which, on the basis of his jealous defence of his privacy, he is himself compared to Hans Karl.[7]

More searching than dislike of social pretension was a critical sense, which grew in the last ten years or so of Hofmannsthal's life, of artistic pretentiousness, a falsity in his writing. This is reflected in his dismissal both of the opera version of *Die Frau ohne Schatten* (Tgb., 8 October 1919) and of the prose story as artificial and without warmth – the story damningly summed up in the diary entry for 26 October 1919: 'High qualities in details, but as a work quite insupportable because of a kind of ethical *parvenu* character, mannerism, artifice, lack of inner warmth' ('[. . .] eine Art von ethischem Parvenuethum, Manierismus, Künstelei, innere Kälte'). He also drafted a longer critique, elaborating on the same reservations, which has been published from his notes (AB, 490–1.)

He repeatedly noted his sense that Hofmannsthal's work lacked genuine inner warmth. He had never understood Hofmannsthal's fondness for reworking ideas and works of other writers ('Seine fast unverständliche Neigung zu literar. Aneignungen': Tgb., 12 December 1902). In this he struck a similar note to Karl Kraus who in the very first number of *Die Fackel* included an attack on Hofmannsthal as a collector of secondhand treasures, continued to question his genuine originality and to lable him (like Klimt) as an 'eclectic', and contrasted him with the authentic originality of Nestroy by referring to him as a modern 'adapter'.[8] Schnitzler's recurrent charge, which he would discuss with Berta Zuckerkandl, was that Hofmannsthal's works were written not from 'inner necessity' but out of extrinsic motives; *Das Salzburger große Welttheater* was one example (11 February 1922: 'nicht aus inneren Notwendigkeiten'). A year later he made the same objection to *Der Unbestechliche* (16 March 1923: 'ohne jede innere Nötigung geschrieben'). Hofmannsthal's very character was now seen as calculating and opportunistic ('zwecktrüb', 22 July 1924).[9] Even when writing to Hofmannsthal he could not conceal his reservations about *Der Turm*, of which Hofmannsthal had send him a signed copy of the luxury edition:[10] in his letter of 16 November 1925 Schnitzler admitted that in places he 'would have wished for less long-windedness' (H/AS, 303). After first reading it on 30 October he had dismissed it summarily in his diary as 'a high-level superfluity' ('Eine Überflüssigkeit auf sehr hohem Niveau': Chrstk., 50).

The ups and downs of their personal relations and of their attitudes to each other's work are symptomatic of fundamental differences in their whole approach to writing and to the theatre, exemplified in the contrast between Schnitzler's close relations with the realist Brahm and Hofmannsthal's loyal admiration of Max Reinhardt's ability to 'translate' what lay between the lines of the dramatic text – its symbolical and metaphysical implications – into theatrical effects.[11] Schnitzler once formulated Hofmannsthal's besetting 'fault' as an inability to distinguish between the everyday and the ineffable: 'Hugo is one of those who present everything as equally mysterious, whether someone is thinking of death or going into the coffee-house' (Tgb., 1 October 1896). What his criticisms of *Die Frau ohne Schatten*, *Der Schwierige*, and *Der Turm* spell out is that he could not relate sympathetically to Hofmannsthal's tendency to myth-making.

Yet that tendency was at the heart of those very poetic and imaginative qualities that Schnitzler admired and envied. As early as 1893 Hofmannsthal defined the 'basic tragic myth' as founded in the search for unity of a world broken down into individuals ('Der tragische Grundmythus: die in Individuen zerstückelte Welt sehnt sich nach Einheit [. . .]': A, 106). Profoundly influenced as he was by the fragmentation of values and by the undermining of the personality in the Vienna of Freud and Mach, he came to regard the mythopoeic impulse as something crucial in the creative process (see pp. 24–5, above). And if Schnitzler thought his work pretentious, the answer lay partly in one of his own aphorisms: 'What looks like megalomania is not always a form of mental sickness; often enough it is merely the comfortable mask adopted by someone despairing at himself' ('Was uns als Größenwahn erscheint, ist nicht immer eine Geisteskrankheit; – oft genug ist es nur die bequeme Maske eines Menschen, der an sich verzweifelt': AB, 50).

Obituaries

It was widely realized that the deaths of Hofmannsthal and Schnitzler marked the end of a chapter in Austrian literary and cultural history. Numerous obituaries of Schnitzler in 1931 alluded to Hofmannsthal as well, noting the passing of a specifically Austrian note with which the two dramatists together were peculiarly associated. The point was made in newspapers from the *Solothurner Zeitung* in Switzerland (24 October 1931) to the *Danziger Neueste Nachrichten* and the *Oder-Zeitung* (Frankfurt an der Oder) in northern Germany, both of which carried on 23 October an article by Felix Panten coupling their names as 'two representatives of a whole culture'.

Hofmannsthal's death two years earlier had come as a particular shock because of its suddenness and his relative youth, and it had prompted a large number of personal reminiscences stressing his personal qualities, his gift for friendship, and the stimulus of his conversation (Salten, Borchardt, Wassermann).[12] Salten, writing in the *Neue Freie Presse* on 18 July 1929, also rejected the notion that he had been socially snobbish (Fiechtner 1949, 40). The obituaries and other commemorative articles were predictably laudatory, and several rehearsed the conservative slogans of his cultural politics. In the *Reichspost* for 17 July this was taken a stage further by Rudolf List, who presented his whole development as leading to the morality plays: that the religious element in his writing was limited was a consequence of the period in which he had grown up, but the address 'Das Schrifttum als geistiger Raum der Nation' pointed forward to a 'new German reality'. The *Neue Rundschau* published a special issue in November 1929 containing essays by Auernheimer, Mell, Nadler, and others. Auernheimer's essay on Hofmannsthal as an 'Austrian phenomenon', stressing his commitment to an Austria that no longer existed,[13] was one of several to sum up his achievement in relation to a specifically Austrian context. Willy Haas, writing in *Die Literarische Welt* on 26 July, had also stressed his deep links with the lost monarchy and had compared his final years in the republic to the experience of being orphaned (Fiechtner 1949, 257–9).

In later years his memory served as an icon of the patriotic conservatives. Mell depicted him as having been haunted to the end by the spectre of revolution;[14] Andrian even claimed that there were 'causal connections' between his death and the disintegration of the monarchy, which had removed the whole basis of his life and work. Continuing to argue for the distinctiveness of a specifically Austrian culture, Andrian advanced the view that a national culture, represented most clearly in literature, proves the cultural identity of a people, and that in Austria, greatness had been proportional to Austrianness ('die Austriacität'). His examples included Grillparzer and Stifter, but it was above all Hofmannsthal, especially Hofmannsthal the essayist, that he presented as a model on which the self-confidence of the new Austrian generation might be built.[15]

Even outside monarchist circles, Hofmannsthal was widely regarded as the supreme modern classic of Austrian culture.[16] Schnitzler was clearly just as 'representative' a writer, but his death did not meet a comparable critical consensus. The *Neue Freie Presse* referred to him on 22 October as 'the Viennese writer *par excellence*' ('der Wiener Dichter katexochen'), and the reports contained many references to his role at the very heart of Austrian literary culture: in Paris *Le Mois* informed its readers: 'Grand ami de Hugo von Hofmannsthal, il était au centre de toute l'activité littéraire en Autriche' (1 November). He was repeatedly described in rather sweeping terms as the greatest and most 'representative' writer or poet either of Austria or at least of Vienna,[17] but as he had had no ideological allegiance or school of followers argument raged about just what qualities and standards he had represented.

The controversy began with his funeral. In accordance with his own wishes, it was a simple ceremony. But the Sternewartestrasse was filled with crowds, and a long queue of cars followed the hearse to the Zentralfriedhof a full half-hour's drive away. Several papers were quick to point out that though many figures from the artistic and literary world were there, no major government figures had come, not even the Christian Social Minister of Education and Culture, Emmerich Czermak. Nor had the Social Democrat Mayor of Vienna, Karl Seitz. *Der Tag*, which raised this issue in its report on the funeral on 24 October 1931, also carried a sour commentary by its columnist 'Lucian':

> If it had been the president of an association of Christian Social veterans being buried, or the leading light of a dining club, they would have been there to a man, and there would not have been space enough for all the expensive official cars. But a mere writer – and a writer, moreover, who had not always written to please the crawlers and philistines! In those circumstances for anyone with an eye on his political career it is better to stay away. [. . .] Even the most convinced republicans are sometimes forced into shedding a tear for the old monarchy; at least public figures used to refrain from really crass bad manners.

Both Czermak and Seitz wrote effusive letters of condolence, which were carried in full by the press.[18] Czermak's included an assessment of Schnitzler as 'one of Austria's most important and representative writers, poets and dramatists'. But these conventional pieties cut no ice with those of liberal or left-wing sympathies. Oskar Maurus Fontana, for example, returned to the attack on 31 October in *Das Tagebuch*:

> The President of the Republic was absent. He had not even sent a deputy. And why? 'Just a fool and a poet', runs the line in Nietzsche – and of him too the President has probably read not a word. ['Nur Narr, nur Dichter', heißt es bei Nietzsche, den der Bundespräsident auch nur vom Nichtlesen kennen dürfte.] None of the Ministers had come; two senior civil servants 'represented' the Minister of Education. The Mayor of Vienna had stayed at home too. Taken ill? Suddenly? – But unfortunately on precisely that morning the Deputy Mayors too were engaged on important and urgent official business. One member of the City Council was there, it is true; but as a physician and art-lover he would have come even without being sent. So at the official level

Vienna was totally unrepresented at the funeral of this writer who for a generation did more for Vienna than all the governments, City Councils, and political parties put together.

Kikeriki, as ever, had an anti-Semitic answer when the next issue appeared on 1 November:

Antwort

auf die Angriffe gegen die Regierung wegen ihrer Nichtteilnahme an Schnitzlers Bestattung.

> Des Heiligen Bewitzler,
> Der Sinne schwüler Kitzler,
> Das war der 'Wiener' Schnitzler!
>
> Eh Oesterreichs Behörden
> So einen 'Dichter' ehrten,
> Beschnitten müßten s' werden!

Response

to the attacks on the government for non-attendance at Schnitzler's funeral.

A mocker of what is sacred, a sultry titillator of the senses – that was what Schnitzler the 'Viennese' was. For the Austrian authorities to honour a 'poet' like that, they would have to be circumcised!

The obituaries reflect a similar range of disparate reactions. In the first days after Schnitzler's death, the press carried pious assessments by all manner of commentators, from friends like Salten (a rather self-indulgent memoir in the *Neue Freie Presse* on 22 October 1931) to past critics like Mell (a stiff and much briefer eulogy in the *Wiener Allgemeine Zeitung* on 24 October 1931) and Polgar (an impressionistic and generously favourable account of his work as a dramatist in *Die Weltbühne*).[19] Even the *Reichspost* carried an obituary by Rudolf List (22 October 1931) in which he is described as representing, together with Schönherr, the pinnacle of Naturalism in Austria. But inevitably his career was often reduced to the long-established stereotype, the chronicler of Viennese eroticism and the *süßes Mädl*. On 23 October, for example, headlines in the more down-market Viennese press referred to him as 'Der Dichter des süßen Mädels' (*Neues Wiener Extrablatt*) or 'Der Schöpfer des "Süßen Mädels"' (*Kleine Volks-Zeitung*) – the latter over a piece by Alfred Deutsch-German which began with the statement that 'the poet of Viennese women' had died. The same phrase, 'Der Dichter der Wiener Frauen', was also used in *Wort der Frau* (Vienna) on 1 November as a headline over an undiscriminating and sentimental article by Hilda Strauss-Gutmann about the female characters Schnitzler had created. This was a much more characteristic note than that struck by Klara Blum's assessment of him in the *Arbeiter-Zeitung* as a 'pioneer of women's rights' (see pp. 125–6, above).

The main bone of contention, however, was inevitably his Jewish allegiance. Jewish and Zionist newspapers, both in Vienna and outside Austria, laid claim in their own terms to his 'representative' stature, stressing his loyalty to Jewry and laying particular weight on *Professor Bernhardi* and *Der Weg ins Freie* among his works.[20] But his standing as a Jew also prompted a range of obituaries that vividly illustrate the cultural climate of the early 1930s, when Nazism was rising in Germany. His characteristically Jewish characteristics were defined favourably at one end of the political spectrum as 'Jewish scepticism' (E.F., *Sozialdemokrat* [Prague], 23 October 1931), unfavourably at the other as a 'specifically Jewish intellectuality' (Joseph Eberle, *Schönere Zukunft*, 8 November 1931). One of the most thoughtful and balanced essays was by the novelist Robert Neumann and appeared on 30 October 1931 in the *Central-Verein-Zeitung* (Berlin). Reporting that 'the greatest Jewish writer of the present' had been buried, Neumann added the observation that neither Schnitzler nor Hofmannsthal had been descended from the 'Nibelungs who conquered the "Ostmark"'. Their kinship was also summarized concisely by Ludwig Bauer in an article entitled 'Schnitzler' that appeared the following day in *Das Tagebuch* (Berlin): 'A cultivated Jew from a highly educated family, he was, together with Hofmannsthal, *the* poet of Austria.'

But if he was suspect to the extreme right wing because he was Jewish, from a left-wing viewpoint his irony lacked the teeth of true social campaigning. To a columnist ('h.g.') in the *Rote Fahne* on 23 October he had become the 'fashionable writer of the bourgeoisie'; five days later to a columnist ('Bi.') in *Der Kämpfer* (Carlsbad) his scepticism amounted to no more than resigned escapism. The appreciation in the Prague *Sozialdemokrat*, too, assessed him as standing far above Bahr or Salten, but by comparison with Karl Kraus merely weakly ironic:

He stands in the shadow of the great negator of things Austrian, Karl Kraus, and as time passes will be ever more in his shadow.

Schnitzler's work is a document of its time and in the theatre repertory it will long provide fare for connoisseurs. What it will offer to the future, other than a reminder of the past, will probably not amount to very much.

From both ends of the political spectrum, moreover, descriptions of him as a 'representative' figure tended to be qualified with riders to the effect that the world he 'represented' belonged to the past, so that both his work and its subject matter were dated. On the right, for example, this view was voiced in the *Reichspost* on 23 October in an article signed 'B.', and again in *Das neue Reich* on 7 November. On the left, also on 23 October, the columnist of the *Rote Fahne* ('h.g.') described him as having always been the 'representative' writer of a dying world, and proclaimed his work the 'swan song of the bourgeoisie'. A similar view is implicit in the front-page eulogy in the morning issue of the *Neue Freie Presse* on 22 October 1931 in which he is described as the 'incarnation' of his age. It was also expressed outside Austria, the *Neue Zürcher Zeitung* linking it on 8 November with the social tensions in postwar Austria. This article remarked on the gulf between generations, visible especially in the contrast between Vienna and the more aggressive provinces, so that Schnitzler appeared as a 'classic phenomenon of a Viennese way of thinking that now belongs to the past'.

Even the hackneyed image of his work as an erotic chronicle related it to the manners of the pre-war years; readers of the *Neues Wiener Extrablatt* on 23 October, for example, were reminded that the Vienna Schnitzler had portrayed no longer existed: he was a 'psychologist of vanished states of mind'. In the *Kleine Volks-Zeitung* the following day, in a long and generally very positive appreciation, Alfred Deutsch-German observed that the *süßes Mädel* had died long before Schnitzler. Outside Vienna, too, a similar view had been voiced in a valedictory article by Friedrich-Carl Kobbe that had appeared on 22 October in the *Hamburger Nachrichten* under the headline 'Abschied von Anatol' ('Farewell from Anatol').

That Schnitzler's appeal was also a thing of the past was disputed by Ludwig Ullmann in two articles in the *Wiener Allgemeine Zeitung* on 23 October, but nevertheless was a widely held view. A typical verdict was that expressed in a piece signed 'W.B.' that appeared in the *Chemnitzer Tageblatt* on 22 October under the headline 'Death of Arthur Schnitzler. Ten Years after the Death of Anatol' and concluded: 'To the present generation, the *new* and *genuine* youth of today, he had nothing to say; Anatol died long before he did – falling on the eastern front, or going to the dogs during the inflation, or joining the black market.' On 28 October the assessment in *Der Kämpfer* reached the regretful conclusion, 'His work will hardly outlive him'.

In truth times had overtaken him, the immense social and political changes of half a century wiping out the whole way of life in which his formative years had been spent and to which he con-

tinued to return in his works. The point was sympathetically put on
22 October in *Das kleine Blatt* (Vienna): 'It must be counted very
much to Schnitzler's credit that he never supported the war-
mongers. His tragedy was that as the last artistic witness to the
highly educated liberal bourgeoisie of Austria he had to live
through the decline of the class of which his works furnish a lasting
record.' Alternatively it could be argued that the drop in his appeal
after the war was partly a result of National Socialist agitation
against Jewish writers. This argument was raised as a matter of
concern in the *8-Uhr-Blatt* on 22 October. Nine days later it was
reported in *Der Kampfruf*, not to be rebutted, but as a matter of
congratulation. There were also protests on the extreme right
against what *Das neue Reich* called 'the synthetically effusive obituaries' in the liberal press (7 November). These protests were
particularly emphatic outside the capital, reflecting a general pattern
of stronger nationalistic and Fascist sympathies in the provinces by
contrast with 'red Vienna'. Thus the *Linzer Volksblatt*, for example,
setting itself up as a defender of provincial opinion, complained on
1 November about a radio broadcast in Schnitzler's memory that
had presented him as a model of the true Austrian:

> It has been to the advantage of listeners that the programme
> planning of RAVAG [the radio company *Radio Verkehrs AG*,
> which had been founded in 1924] has been influenced by sys-
> tematic and consistent criticism, so that the opinions even of
> listeners in the provinces are respected more than before.
>
> RAVAG judged it necessary to broadcast a special com-
> memorative programme on the late Viennese *littérateur* and
> physician Arthur Schnitzler, a high-quality and expensive pro-
> gramme which could be heard at midday on Sunday. RAVAG
> must of course have the right to provide appropriate apprecia-
> tions of art of every kind and every school, but for all one's
> respect for Schnitzler's artistic ability it is really not on to present
> him, indeed to glorify him, as the very model of a true Austrian,
> as Ernst Lothar took the liberty to do in his commemorative
> address.

The *Vorarlberger Tagblatt* published on 27 October a crudely anti-
Semitic article by one Dr H. N. which took issue with the eulogies
in the *Neue Freie Presse* in particular, dismissing all that the 'Jewish
press' had said about the works of a 'Jewish *littérateur* of a bygone
age' and particularly claims that he was the incarnation of a great
age in the history of Vienna and of Austria. This piece is worth
quoting at length as its sneering tone, its crass prejudice, and its

crude misjudgments are all characteristic of the climate of debate that would develop in the 1930s:

> Schnitzler thought of himself as a Jew, and the Jewish Community in Vienna was right to provide him with a grave of honour. But the German people has no reason to regard Schnitzler as a great German writer [Das deutsche Volk aber hat keinen Grund, in Schnitzler einen großen deutschen Dichter zu sehen], however loudly the Jewish press and those of the same ilk proclaim him to have been one. [. . .]
>
> However much the Jewish papers write about the immortality of their 'great' Schnitzler, it cannot cancel the fact that his time as a writer has passed. We really do have other concerns than the weary eroticists in Schnitzler's dramas and stories. In his will, Schnitzler has decreed that his diaries and his autobiography may be published in thirty years, and in part only in forty years. But in a generation's time Schnitzler's name will have been as totally forgotten as his plays and novellas. No immortality awaits these works, however much the Jewish press endeavours to hammer into its readers that with his death the literature not just of Austria but of the whole world has suffered an irreplaceable loss. Neither *Reigen* nor *Liebelei* nor any other work of Schnitzler's will be revived in times to come.

Once again, *Kikeriki* was not to be outdone. On 1 November it published a denigration of Schnitzler in answer to all the acclamation of his stature as the classic writer of the age:

Arthur Schnitzler

really was in a certain sense 'the representative writer of our age'; for with his indecent *Anatol* playlets he trained a whole generation of frivolous men-about-town and young wastrels, with his *Liebelei* he taught those of his race a liking for the sweet young things of Vienna [er hat durch seine 'Liebelei' seinen Rassegenossen erst den richtigen Gusto auf das 'süße Wiener Mädel' beigebracht], in his *Leutnant Gustl* and *Freiwild* he was the first to mock and insult the officers of the Austrian army, in *Professor Bernhardi* he attacked the Catholic church, and in his notori — his famous *Reigen* [durch seinen berü — hmten 'Reigen'] he reached a peak in modern pornography.

In the judgment of the Jewish press Schnitzler has consequently been the greatest Austrian writer of the last fifty years. When he appeared before the Judgment Seat the verdict on the use he put his talent to is likely to have been quite different!

Epilogue: The View from the Belvedere

No account of the interrelation of Schnitzler and Hofmannsthal with their historical and intellectual background would be complete without at least some brief indication of their standing in the years following their deaths and the role of other figures who have featured in the supporting cast in this study. The writing and the reception of their plays form part of a wider development, from the proclamation of a 'renaissance' founded in a collapse of inherited values in the late nineteenth century to the disintegration of the Dual Monarchy and its consequences. Those consequences included not only the cultural conservatism embraced by Hofmannsthal but also, as the end of the story, the further collapse of cultural, political, and indeed humane standards in the onset of Fascism.

Conjuring up a poetic analogue to the literature of the *fin de siècle* – its combination of sheltered security and erotic intensity – Hofmannsthal evoked in his verse prologue to *Anatol* (HKA I, 24–5) the ornamental gardens stretching out below the upper Belvedere palace, the eighteenth-century scene commemorated in Bellotto's painting of the view from the palace, which hangs in the Kunsthistorisches Museum in Vienna. In April 1935, just a year after the civil war, the failed Nazi *Putsch*, and the murder of Dollfuss, Josef Weinheber composed his sonnet 'Blick vom Oberen Belvedere', celebrating the same scene and apostrophizing in it an ideal of beauty, man-made and permanent, the Viennese past now functioning as a symbol of lost order.[21] Weinheber's choice of the same view for treatment within the traditionalist form of the sonnet looks like a classic example of literary continuity. But in fact his poem exemplifies a general point made by Klaus Amann in his study of the infiltration of Austrian literary and cultural institutions by the Nazis, that the shifts in the cultural and ideological climate in the 1930s resulted in the very reverse of the traditionalist continuities that have commonly been ascribed to Austrian literature.[22]

'Blick vom Oberen Belvedere' was published in Weinheber's *Wien wörtlich*, which appeared with illustrations by Marie Grengg. The book is an example of a vogue for nostalgic illustrated publications, a development of the fashion after the First World War for books dealing with local cultural history (see pp. 181–3, above). (Indeed Marie Grengg herself had also provided the illustrations for Ginzkey's *Balladen aus dem alten Wien*.) Increasingly the nostalgia had taken on a distinctive nationalist (that is, *völkisch*, pan-German) flavour. This trend was to be observed even in the 1920s – for instance (to take one example of many), in a celebration of the

Austrian landscape and Austrian architecture entitled *Aus der Ostmark. Ein Buch von Landschaft und alpinem Leben, Kultur und Geschichte*, which was edited by Gustav Bodenstein and published in 1927 by the Alpinists' Association, the Deutscher und Österreichischer Alpenverein. The Alpenverein was by then already a wholly Aryanized organization,[23] and while the term 'Ostmark' for Austria was by no means new – indeed it occurs in the last of Ferdinand von Saar's *Wiener Elegien* of 1893, in a passage regretting the exclusion of Austria from the German Confederation in 1867[24] – its use in the Alpenverein publication points forward to the development that pan-German nationalism would subsequently take until finally Austria was absorbed into the Third Reich and renamed the 'Ostmark'. The word recurs ever more frequently in the 1930s: one example (again, one of many) is an illustrated volume *Deutsche Ostmark. Zehn Dichter und hundert Bilder lobpreisen Österreich* edited by Friedrich Perkonig and published in Graz in 1936. The contributors, as well as Perkonig himself, included both Weinheber and Karl Heinrich Waggerl.

Perkonig (in Klagenfurt) and Waggerl (in Salzburg) were best known for stories set in the rural provinces, in keeping with the nationalist interest in cultivating provincial *Heimatkunst*.[25] Both had been sympathetic to Nazism since the early 1930s. In the *cause célèbre* of Gerhart Hauptmann's support of the Nazi régime in Germany, for example, both were among the signatories (as also were Mell and Ginzkey) of an open letter published in the Viennese press in November 1933 protesting against Alfred Kerr's criticism of Hauptmann.[26] Both became members of the Nazi party; Weinheber had been a member since December 1931.[27] The apparent continuity in traditional subject matter masks nothing less than a revolution in ideology.

The cultural climate of the 1930s was poisoned by the doctrines of racialism. In the press anti-Semitism was undiminished and complaints about it attacked: the very word, it was claimed, was a Liberal invention, and the real problem was Jewish 'anti-Germanism'.[28] The outlawing of the Social Democrat party in 1934, following that of the Communist Party in 1933, was designed to ensure the integrity of Austria as a political entity; but in the event the suppression of left-wing (and eventually liberal) ideas removed the main organized opposition to the doctrines of National Socialism. At the same time many writers of pacifist persuasion and overtly anti-Fascist views (including Stefan Zweig and Robert Neumann) were driven into exile; the whole world of the theatre, of literature, and of publishing was corrupted.

The reputations of Hofmannsthal and Schnitzler were blackened.

Schnitzler fell victim to the suppression of works by Jewish authors; the Salzburg Festival which Hofmannsthal had championed was condemned for being tainted by Jewish influence. At the same time many literary figures of clerical and conservative sympathies, including one as close to Hofmannsthal as Mell, were increasingly drawn into *völkisch* nationalism, in utter contrast to the civilized cosmopolitanism of the 'conservative revolution' as Hofmannsthal had conceived it.

In Germany, the Nazi takeover of the book market began in April 1933 when it was announced that the holdings of public libraries in Berlin were being revised. Stocks of certain approved works, including multiple copies of *Mein Kampf*, were to be acquired, and libraries systematically purged of Marxist writings and other works from which official support was withheld. A proportion of the books being removed would be publicly burned – what one Berlin paper called an 'auto-da-fe' of 'symbolic significance'.[29] Austrian newspapers gave prominent coverage to news of the scheme, publishing details of the official 'blacklist' and picking out the names of Austrian authors it included: Beer-Hofmann, Ehrenstein, Neumann, Polgar, Stefan Zweig, and Schnitzler (but not yet Hofmannsthal).

The implications of the new development were clearly spelled out by the more responsible Viennese newspapers. A leading article in *Das kleine Blatt* of 28 April, for example, eloquently attacked the purge and the racialist ideology behind it:

> The series of popular entertainments in the Third Reich continues. First Marxists were tortured and workers' hostels plundered, then Jews were hounded – now books are being burnt! Not even a pause for breath, they just keep fanning the flames and rolling the drums so that the people do not awake from their intoxication [nur weiter geschürt und getrommelt, damit das Volk aus seinem Rausch nicht erwache], so that they do not awake to the appalling everyday Fascist reality of hunger and slavery, of unemployment and low wages! [. . .]
>
> The German people have been called a race of thinkers and poets [das Volk der Denker und Dichter]. Their erudition, the high level of their general education, their respect for scholarship and the written word have given them an elevated place among the civilized nations. That is all past. Now they have fallen victim to brown-shirted barbarians, to whom their cultural heritage is fit for crude fireworks to beguile the people. When they speak of a 'struggle against an un-German spirit', they are destroying the true German spirit; what they are destroying on their medieval

pyres is not, as they believe, 'Jewish' or 'Marxist' books but German civilization!

The headline in *Das kleine Blatt* was 'Civilization on the Bonfire' ('Die Kultur auf dem Scheiterhaufen'). On the same day an article in *Der Abend*, headed 'The German Mind Remaindered' ('Deutscher Geist wird verramscht'), pointed out the opportunity available to book-lovers in Austria to acquire good editions at reduced prices in Austria, including Schnitzler in half-leather.

While the *Reichspost* was assuring its readers by the end of the year that the books that were being burnt in the Third Reich were the true enemies of Austria,[30] the Liberal and Social Democrat press in Vienna, including notably the *Wiener Allgemeine Zeitung*, continued to publish resolute criticism as events unfolded. A few examples must suffice. After the notorious burning of books from the university library in Heidelberg (in which works of Schnitzler featured, as well as other Austrian authors including Stefan Zweig, Werfel, and Bertha von Suttner) the *Neues Wiener Extrablatt* reported on 16 August that the works of the banned authors were in increasing demand in Heidelberg, even if their names could be mentioned in bookshops only in whispers. Seven months later, when a schoolteacher in Krems suggested that the blacklist of the Propaganda Ministry in Berlin might be adopted in Lower Austria, naming Schnitzler again together with Werfel, Zweig, Lernet-Holenia, Joseph Roth, and others, *Der Tag* published a piece ridiculing the proposal and stating very firmly that all sensible opinion in Austria was united in the view that book-burnings, 'as carried out in grand style in Hitler's Germany, must never take place in Austria' (27 March 1934). Two years later, noting the continued proscription and confiscation in Germany of books by Schnitzler and other Austrian authors (Werfel, Stefan Zweig, Salten, Freud, and now Hofmannsthal as well), *Die Stunde* (7 May 1936) suggested a ban on imports of German books into Austria.

As early as May 1933, however, the corollary of the blacklist, a canon of approved Austrian literature of *völkisch* character, had appeared in Vienna in an issue of the *Mitteilungen des Kampfbundes für deutsche Kultur*. It featured authors such as the novelist Mirko Jelusich (an active Nazi sympathizer since the late 1920s who would briefly become director of the Burgtheater in 1938 after the *Anschluss*), and also Schönherr, Ginzkey, and Maria Grengg; in June the *Völkischer Beobachter* carried a further list, an 'Austrian Parnassus' in which Perkonig, Waggerl, Weinheber, and Mell all featured.[31] Most of the authors concerned were writers of prose fiction; the mystique of the earthy rural life was inimical to drama.

(Nonetheless Franz Löser, the translator of *Jedermann* into Salzburg dialect in 1921, became in 1933 the organizer of the Austrian section of the [Nazi] Reichsverband Deutscher Schriftsteller.)[32] By 1934 the Austrian police were issuing their own blacklists in connection with library acquisitions, with Schnitzler included, though the general sale of books by Austrian authors, other than works of strongly political character, was largely unaffected in Austria until 1937.[33]

The Salzburg Festival also attracted the disapproval of the Third Reich, which imposed a near-boycott by German artists. This was partly because it represented competition with the festivals in Bayreuth and Heidelberg, partly out of racialist hostility to the 'international Jewish influence' that allegedly underpinned it. The boycott by German artists was only slightly modified in 1937 in exchange for the publication in Austria of *Mein Kampf*.[34] The loss of support resulting from the 'Tausendmarksperre' imposed in 1933 was compensated for at first by an increase in visitors from abroad,[35] but the funding in 1935 had to be more modest.[36] The press in Nazi Germany continued to attack the festival as insufficiently *völkisch* and as subsidized cultural propaganda,[37] and finally after the *Anschluss* a new Aryanized era was declared, with both Goebbels and Hess attending in 1938. The new policy, as Willi Schuh sarcastically reported in the *Neue Zürcher Zeitung* on 8 August 1938, amounted to no more than maintaining the 'festival idea' expounded by Hofmannsthal with exclusively 'Aryan' performers (*Resonanz*, p. 150) – that is, exploiting a profitable formula with no innovation other than racialism.

According to racialist thinking in Berlin, the Germans in Austria were fighting for their national integrity not only against the Jews who allegedly dominated literary life but also against a bogus conception of 'Austrianness': 'The Germans in Austria are fighting a bitter battle for their identity as Germans [um ihr Deutschtum]', declared Wilhelm Westecker in the *Berliner Börsen-Zeitung* for 7 January 1934: 'fighting against an Austrian identity invented by Dollfuss, against the Viennese literary Jews [gegen das Wiener Literatur-Judentum], against Austro-Marxism, against manifold foreign influences which want to secure this south-eastern bulwark for their own sphere of influence'. The proof of the artificiality of this Austrianness, the proof of how bereft it was of true tradition, was that its ancestry could be traced back to Schnitzler: it was 'ein Oesterreichertum [. . .], dessen Ahnherr – Schnitzler ist'. At the end of the same year, an article headed 'Jüdischer Parnaß' and signed 'E.H.R.' appeared on 7 December in another Berlin paper, *Der Angriff*, commenting on a new lexicon which had declared that the 'Jewish Parnassus' was to be found in Austria and had included an illustration of five supposedly 'German writers' ('Deutsche Dichter') in Austria, all of whom were Jews. (They included both Schnitzler and Hofmannsthal.) The writer insisted that in fact there was growing resistance in Vienna to the Jews, and listed some other (that is, non-Jewish) writers to consider, including Schönherr, Mell, Billinger, and Jelusich.

Just over a year after that, the same paper carried a review, signed 'G.B.', of two surveys of Austrian literature, both by Austrian literary historians, Franz Koch's *Gegenwartsdichtung in Österreich* and Adalbert Schmidt's *Deutsche Dichtung in Österreich*. In the study of German literature in the Austrian universities the emphasis on contemporary writing had been reduced in favour of a *völkisch* historical approach, with racialist ideas increasingly dominating. Nadler had held a chair in Vienna since 1931; with his support Koch had also been promoted to the professoriate there (as *Außerordentlicher Professor*) in 1932. (He had then gone to an established chair in Berlin in 1935.)[38] Schmidt was the principal editor between 1934 and 1936 of a monthly journal *Lebendige Dichtung*, which concentrated mainly on writers of right-wing, nationalist, and even Nazi allegiance. The review in *Der Angriff* dismisses the supposed domination of Jewish writers in Austria as organized deception, unmasked in the two studies under review:

> For a long time Austrian literature was buried from sight under the organized success of the Jews Stefan Zweig, Arthur Schnitzler, Franz Werfel, Felix Salten etc., and in critical discussion these *littérateurs* were taken to be typical representatives of Austrian writing. The extent to which that was a distortion of the true position is shown in two valuable histories of Austrian literature which have both appeared recently, and which feature a surprisingly large number of indigenous writers [bodenständiger Dichter], especially from outside Vienna. [. . .]
>
> The two books, both of which may be thoroughly recommended, provide unambiguous evidence of a new awakening in Austrian political culture [eines kulturpolitischen Erwachens in Österreich], of a national consciousness [einer völkischen Besinnung] which is knowingly turning away from the Jewish hacks and favouring those true creative writers whose work centres on the forces of blood and soil [die Kräfte des Blutes und des Bodens] and who recognize a pan-German national identity [ein gesamtdeutsches Volkstum] across the boundaries that divide separate states.[39]

The authors cited in support of this *Blut und Boden* pan-Germanism include Billinger and Mell as well as Jelusich and Weinheber.

How complete the corruption of literary and intellectual standards eventually was, even in the world of scholarship, may also be exemplied in the treatment of the classic national dramatist of Austria, Grillparzer. The critical edition of his works had been appearing in Vienna since 1909. One of the volumes of critical apparatus that was published in 1939 has a preface in which the editor, Reinhold Backmann, refers to past misunderstandings of Grillparzer by 'degenerates and Jewish louts' (he was 'von Degenerierten und Judenlümmeln verhöhnt') and draws a comparison with the 'greatest native Austrian of modern times'.[40]

In Nazi Germany, of course, anti-Semitic press attacks on Austrian literature and literary history never abated. At the end of 1936, for instance, readers of the *National-Zeitung* in Essen could read on 30 December a reminder that the 'Judaization [Verjudung] of Viennese artistic life, especially of Viennese theatrical life' was not new and that at the turn of the century the theatre of the Moderns had been dominated by Jews. Among these had been 'the Jew Arthur Schnitzler', who had 'set himself up as the literary agent of the Viennese *süßes Mädel* type' and had given free rein to sexual fantasies in *Reigen*, and also another 'descendant of the Jewish race', 'der Judenstämmling Hugo von Hofmannsthal'.

In Austria too, not least in the provinces, pan-Germanism and anti-Semitism thrived together. When two Viennese newspapers, *Der Tag* and the *Wiener Neueste Nachrichten*, carried a discussion of the idea that there was an identifiable Austrian 'race', ethnically distinct from the North Germans, the *Alpenländische Morgenzeitung* in Linz published two pieces on 12 and 13 January 1934, listing some of the examples of Austrians that had been quoted, including not only Freud and Werfel but also Schnitzler and Hofmannsthal, and concluding: 'As was only to be expected, there is *not a single Aryan among them*. Well, now at least we know that for certain people *"Austrian" is only another word for "Jew"*.'

To many conservative writers in Austria, especially Austrian traditionalists, Nazism was of course anathema. For some of them, the annexation of Austria in 1938 led to their being uprooted from their homeland completely. Auernheimer and Lux were among the first transported to Dachau on 1 April 1938;[41] Andrian went into exile in Switzerland. After the *Anschluss*, when the National Socialist Teachers' Association in Salzburg (Nationalsozialistischer Lehrerbund) demanded a 'cleansing' of Austrian libraries, the material they listed for removal included not only the works of Schnitzler and other Jewish authors but also patriotic and monarchist literature by authors such as Lux, which was duly burned in a ceremony on 30 April 1938.[42] But the position of Mell illustrates the slippery slope from (Catholic) conservatism to (racialist) nationalism. The end of the First World War saw him already in the pan–German camp; by 1922, together with both Müller-Guttenbrunn and Jelusich, he was a member of the policy committee of the Großdeutsche Volkspartei concerned with cultural politics.[43] From 1932 he was a member of the Prussian (later German) Academy of Arts, and (like others, including Schönherr) made the requisite declaration of loyalty to the Nazi régime in March 1933.[44]

In May that year, when the International P.E.N. Congress in Dubrovnik, under the presidency of H. G. Wells, criticized the persecution of writers and the burning of books in Germany, the Austrian delegates were among those who 'shared the opinion that German national affairs were outside the province of the P.E.N.'[45] The Austrian P.E.N. Club, of which Salten was now president, was the most important forum of discussion open to men of letters, and its representatives were privately criticized by Wells for failing to mount a worthy defence of Schnitzler's memory. At a general meeting held in the Hotel Imperial in Vienna on 28 June, Salten explained that he had not wanted to put Austrian colleagues in Germany at risk. A resolution condemning repression was passed, and a split followed in the Austrian P.E.N. Club.[46]

Mell had not supported the resolution and was among those who resigned. When the 'Bund der deutschen Schriftsteller Österreichs' ('League of German Writers in Austria') was founded in December 1936 to promote autochthonic Austrian literature, its president was Mell. To observers abroad, the very notion of a league of writers following the lead of the Alpenverein in 'giving blood priority over the mind', as a writer in one Swiss newspaper put it, was absurd, especially thinking of those who would find no favour: Schnitzler, Hofmannsthal, Peter Altenberg, Karl Kraus. 'The presidency of this [. . .] association of racially pure poets is in the hands of the Catholic Max Mell, who in this way provides evidence that writing delicate apostle-plays does not prevent one from being as tough as an Alpine mountaineer in matters of the mind.'[47] The committee of the League included Weinheber and Jelusich; other members included both Ginzkey and Nadler. The League is chiefly remembered for having published in 1938 a *Bekenntnisbuch österreichischer Schriftsteller* in support of the *Anschluss* with Nazi Germany.[48]

Schnitzler and Hofmannsthal were not 'political' dramatists writing with a polemical intention. Schnitzler opted out of political engagement altogether – the attitude which he explored in *Professor Bernhardi* against the background of satirically-presented intellectual and ideological hostility and which he himself maintained throughout the tragedy of the First World War. The political ideal that informed Hofmannsthal's later work was that of a 'glorious order' (P IV, 127), an ideal which the 'idea of Austria' embodied: a vision of a cultural continuity permitting the development and moral commitment of the individual. The responsibility of the poet – the duty of 'leadership' expounded as early as 1907 in the essay 'Der Dichter und diese Zeit' – lies in the imaginative creation of such an order (P II, 239–45): it is an exemplary achievement rather than one belonging to the sphere of practical politics.

If Schnitzler was too cynical about political involvement, in particular the realities of party politics, Hofmannsthal was too naïve; hence the irritation of Schnitzler and Salten at his failure to recognize the 'evil effects' of Christian Social policies (Tgb., 18 December 1914). His conception of the 'idea of Austria' was, it is true, closely tied up with his one attempt at practical political involvement during the war, but in the postwar world the 'idea of Austria' was far removed from the pressing economic, social, and political problems that beset the embattled republic. The restoration of order in *Das Salzburger große Welttheater* may seem to have parallels with the reactionary social theories of Spann, but to argue that when the Burgtheater company took a production of the play to Paris in 1930 it was 'the ideal play to represent the Corporate State'[49] is to read too narrowly political implications into Hofmannsthal's metaphor of the theatre of the world and so to over-politicize his intentions. Like the 'idea of Austria', the visionary conversion of the rebellious Beggar was attractive precisely because it was a mythical image removed from and contrasting with reality.

'Ich bin ein Dichter, weil ich bildlich erlebe', Hofmannsthal wrote in 1894: 'I am a poet because I perceive things metaphorically' (Λ, 107). The word *bildlich* has a dual sense: it also means 'pictorially'. His strong visual imagination contributed to his theatrical gifts (the contrasts of light and colour in *Elektra*, the presentation of the rose and the discomfiting of Ochs in *Der Rosenkavalier*). But at the same time his dramatic and poetic images contribute to the effect of his works as metaphors, expressive of a mythopoeic approach to the problems of his age.

In an essay on Hofmannsthal's 'political legacy', Herman Kunisch rightly stresses the moral seriousness of his thinking about the relation between imaginative writing and politics in the widest sense.[50] The political life of the 1930s shows, however, that in a narrower and more practical sense neither Hofmannsthal nor Schnitzler, the widely acknowledged 'representative' writers of pre-war Viennese culture, left any political legacy at all. Both the romantic myth-making of the one and the apolitical individualism

of the other were deeply rooted in the intellectual climate of
Vienna. The artistic 'renaissance' in the 1890s did not produce
a renaissance of values sufficient to withstand either jingoistic
nationalism or rabid racialism. On the contrary, the indulgence of
the 'Jung Wien' writers in nostalgia and their escapist detachment
from politics laid a foundation for the cultural capitulation that
preceded Austria's demise. The ultimate political legacy of the
'renaissance' of the 1890s can be seen in the catastrophe of the
late 1930s, when the humane ideals that both Hofmannsthal and
Schnitzler had stood for were swept away in Austro-Fascism and
the *Anschluss*, and their works disappeared for seven years both
from the Volkstheater, which became a 'Kraft durch Freude' theatre
in 1938, and from the Burgtheater, which was also draped with the
swastika.

It would be wrong to end the story there; the history of performance is, indeed, a story that has no ending. As soon as the Second
World War was over the canon of classics was swiftly restored: not
just the classics of German literature but also specifically Austrian
classics, symbols of the identity of the nation newly re-established.
As one of the undisputed modern masters and as a defender of the
'idea of Austria', Hofmannsthal was a focus of interest at once. The
first Burgtheater première after the liberation of Austria – a production that took place on 13 June 1945 in the Ronacher building,
as the Burgtheater had been closed by a fire in April – was *Jedermann*,
with the new director of the Burgtheater, Raoul Aslan, in the
title role; before the end of the year the Theater in der Josefstadt
presented a new production of *Der Schwierige*, with Anton Edthofer
as Hans-Karl Bühl. Herbert Steiner's fifteen-volume edition of
Hofmannsthal's works also began to appear in 1945 under the
imprint of the Bermann-Fischer Verlag while the firm was still
based in Stockholm.

The Schnitzler renaissance did not really gain momentum until
the centenary of his birth in 1962. It was only the year before that,
for example, that the six-volume edition of his works began to
appear, but since then interest has steadily increased. Rowohlt's
series of illustrated monographs (*Bildmonographien*) included a
volume on Hofmannsthal by 1967, while Schnitzler followed only
in 1976. But not long after there was even a popular biography – a
genre to which his life lends itself more than Hofmannsthal's – on
sale in paperback: Renate Wagner's *Arthur Schnitzler. Eine Biographie*,
first published in 1981 and reissued as a Fischer paperback in 1984.

By then a flood of Hofmannsthal and Schnitzler publications was
in full spate: both academic monographs and also editions of the

works and letters of both authors, including multi-volume paper-back editions of their works. Scholarly editions have culminated in the critical edition of Hofmannsthal's works still under way and in the exemplary edition of Schnitzler's diaries by the Österreichische Akademie der Wissenschaften.

The rehabilitation of the two dramatists in the theatre has followed a similar pattern: Hofmannsthal was re-established first, but by the beginning of the 1980s Schnitzler had become the most-performed Austrian dramatist in the Burgtheater after the nineteenth-century classics Grillparzer and Nestroy.[51]

The Burgtheater and the Theater in der Josefstadt have remained the two theatres that have most cultivated the work of Hofmannsthal and Schnitzler in Vienna since the end of the war. There have, for example, been several more productions of *Der Schwierige* in both theatres: in the Theater in der Josefstadt in 1954, in 1974 (produced by Ernst Haeussermann, with Peter Weck in the title role), and again in 1983; in the Burgtheater most notably in a production by Ernst Lothar (1959, with Robert Lindner in the title role). The most recent production, launched at the 1991 Salzburg Festival, had its première in the Burgtheater in September 1991, with costumes by Karl Lagerfeld (who also designed the costumes for a Burgtheater production of *Komödie der Verführung* in 1980).

Both the Theater in der Josefstadt and the Burgtheater company have also mounted productions of the other main plays, the latter most often in the smaller and more intimate Akademietheater: *Der Unbestechliche* (of which there was a notable production in the Burgtheater in 1983, which subsequently moved to the Akademietheater), *Cristinas Heimreise, Anatol, Liebelei, Professor Bernhardi, Das weite Land. Fink und Fliederbusch* was produced in the Akademietheater in 1970 and again in the Volkstheater, the former Deutsches Volkstheater, in 1982. When copyright restrictions came to an end fifty years after Schnitzler's death and *Reigen* was available for public performance, productions opened at the very beginning of 1982 in Basle, Manchester, and Munich; in Vienna, it was in the Akademietheater that a production by Erwin Axer was finally staged in November 1983.

The Theater in der Josefstadt – where for fifteen years from 1957 onwards Heinrich Schnitzler worked as a producer (his productions included one of *Liebelei* in 1968) and eventually as deputy director – became particularly well known from the early 1960s onwards for its assured style in Schnitzler productions. It was there that *Das Wort* was first performed in 1969 (a further production followed in 1984 in the Volkstheater); other productions in the Josefstadt have included one of *Freiwild* in 1987.

In the English-speaking world too, Hofmannsthal was at first better known than Schnitzler (a three-volume translation of *Selected Writings* by Hofmannsthal, including plays, was published in the USA between 1952 and 1963), but when the discovery of Schnitzler came it brought his work much wider popularity. This was partly through Tom Stoppard's translations, *Undiscovered Country* (1979) and *Dalliance* (1986), partly through television dramatizations of his stories, and partly through productions of *Reigen*. Hofmannsthal's international fame, by contrast, still rests largely on the undiminished appeal of the Strauss operas: especially *Der Rosenkavalier* (further popularized by a film made in 1960), but also *Elektra*, *Ariadne auf Naxos*, and *Arabella* (which was produced at the Salzburg Festival in 1947 and again in 1958, revived in Vienna in 1952, and also performed at Covent Garden in 1965). The text of *Der Rosenkavalier*, performed without the music, was first heard in the Schönbrunner Schlosstheater in 1961 and was produced in the Theater in der Josefstadt in 1984 (it was also performed in English at the 1983 Edinburgh Festival).

And at Salzburg, *Jedermann* has been restored since 1946 to its old position – by now a genuinely traditional position – as the unfailing annual centrepiece of the international festival that Hofmannsthal helped to create.

Bibliographical Note

The state of play as regards editions of Schnitzler and Hofmannsthal is unsatisfactory. The historical and critical edition of Hofmannsthal's works is only half completed; so is the excellent edition of Schnitzler's diaries, though it is usefully supplemented in the edition by Bernd Urban and Werner Volke of Schnitzler's notes on Hofmannsthal, *Hugo von Hofmannsthal. 'Charakteristik aus den Tagebüchern'* (Hofmannsthal-Forschungen, 3) (Freiburg i.Br., 1975). There is no complete edition of the voluminous correspondence of either writer. For this reason we are forced to use a number of editions, referred to by more or less conventional abbreviations; and in consequence, the List of Abbreviations (pp. xiii–xvii) may serve as a Bibliography of primary texts.

There is a vast amount of secondary literature, both on Schnitzler and Hofmannsthal and also on the cultural, political, and literary background. Even a selective bibliography would be excessively long, and a comprehensive bibliography of material I have consulted would be even longer; moreover, either would duplicate resources available elsewhere. For this reason I have decided that it is most economic to restrict myself to acknowledging my indebtedness point by point in the Notes.

There are, however, a number of works of which I have made regular use, and which should be mentioned separately as they form an indispensable basis for work on Schnitzler and Hofmannsthal:

On Schnitzler, Reinhard Urbach, *Schnitzler-Kommentar. Zu den erzählenden Schriften und dramatischen Werken* (Munich, 1974) is a mine of factual information and of documentary material on the genesis of the plays. An overview of Schnitzler productions in Vienna and their reception is given by Renate Wagner and Brigitte Vacha, *Wiener Schnitzler-Aufführungen 1891–1970* (Munich, 1971). Richard H. Allen, *An Annotated Arthur Schnitzler Bibliography:*

Editions and Criticism in German, French, and English 1879–1965 (Chapel Hill, N. Carolina, n.d. [1966]) provides a useful guide to early criticism of his work, but excludes reviews in daily newspapers. Secondary literature up to the mid-1980s is judiciously surveyed by Michaela L. Perlmann, *Arthur Schnitzler*, Sammlung Metzler, 239 (Stuttgart, 1987).

There is an invaluable chronological guide to Hofmannsthal's career in Günther Erken, 'Hofmannsthal-Chronik. Beitrag zu einer Biographie', *Literaturwissenschaftliches Jahrbuch der Görres-Gesellschaft*, Neue Folge, 3 (1962), pp. 239–313. In respect of Hofmannsthal's education this can be usefully supplemented by Franz Hadamowsky's catalogue to the exhibition *Hugo von Hofmannsthal* (Salzburg, 1959), which lists the lectures for which Hofmannsthal was inscribed at university (pp. 71–4). Werner Volke, *Hugo von Hofmannsthal in Selbstzeugnissen und Bilddokumenten* (Reinbek bei Hamburg, 1967) is the best biographical study. Heinz Lunzer, *Hofmannsthals politische Tätigkeit in den Jahren 1914–1917* (Frankfurt a.M. and Berne, 1981), gives full documentation and analysis of Hofmannsthal's war work. Horst Weber, *Hugo von Hofmannsthal. Bibliographie* (Berlin, 1972) provides exhaustive coverage of the publication of Hofmannsthal's writings. The volume *Hugo von Hofmannsthal. Freundschaften und Begegnungen mit deutschen Zeitgenossen*, edited by Ursula Renner and G. Bärbel Schmid (Würzburg, 1991) contains accounts and bibliographies of the reception of his plays and of the Strauss operas in Berlin (pp. 163–249); reviews of *Das Salzburger große Welttheater* are listed in the bibliographical appendix to Cynthia Walk, *Hofmannsthals 'Großes Welttheater'. Drama und Theater* (Heidelberg, 1980). Hans-Albrecht Koch, *Hugo von Hofmannsthal*, Erträge der Forschung, 265 (Darmstadt, 1989) gives a knowledgeable introduction to the secondary literature and state of research.

Among critical and biographical studies of the two dramatists' contemporaries, two in particular are outstandingly informative on cultural and intellectual life in Vienna: Edward Timms, *Karl Kraus, Apocalyptic Satirist: Culture and Catastrophe in Habsburg Vienna* (New Haven and London, 1986), and Peter Gay, *Freud: A Life for Our Time* (London, 1988), with a substantial 'Bibliographical Essay'.

A very useful reference work on Austrian political history is Walter Kleindel, *Österreich. Daten zur Geschichte und Kultur* (Vienna, 1978); *Dokumentation zur österreichischen Zeitgeschichte 1918–1928*, edited by Christine Klusacek and Kurt Stimmer (Vienna, 1984) gives an overview of the decade after the First World War documented from contemporary press coverage. Among the standard political histories of the declining years of the Habsburg empire, Arthur J. May, *The Hapsburg Monarchy 1867–1914* (Cambridge,

Mass., 1951) is particularly successful in establishing connections with the cultural background; John W. Boyer, *Political Radicalism in Late Imperial Vienna: Origins of the Christian Social Movement 1848–1897* (Chicago, 1981) is authoritative on the political climate of the Austria in which Schnitzler and Hofmannsthal grew up. A handy reference work on the feminism of the period is Daniela Weiland's *Geschichte der Frauenemanzipation in Deutschland und Österreich. Biographien, Programme, Organisationen* (Düsseldorf, 1983).

The classic study of the intellectual history of turn-of-the-century Vienna is Carl E. Schorske, *Fin-de-siècle Vienna: Politics and Culture* (Cambridge, 1981). The cultural background to the 1914–1918 war is explored in *Österreich und der Große Krieg 1914–1918. Die andere Seite der Geschichte*, edited by Klaus Amann and Hubert Lengauer (Vienna, 1989). The period between the wars is treated in a wide-ranging collection of essays in *Aufbruch und Untergang. Österreichische Kultur zwischen 1918 und 1938*, edited by Franz Kadrnoska (Vienna, 1981). Murray G. Hall, *Österreichische Verlagsgeschichte 1918–1938*, 2 vols (Vienna, 1985) is a mine of information on the publishing scene during that period. On the cultural scene in the later interwar years, *Austria in the Thirties: Culture and Politics*, edited by Kenneth Segar and John Warren (Riverside, California, 1991) can also be recommended as a collection of informative essays.

The index to the edition of Schnitzler's diaries published by the Österreichische Akademie der Wissenschaften (Vienna 1981–) is a reliable source of biographical data. Two older reference books are still very useful for factual information on the literary life and literary history of the period: the final volume, edited by Eduard Castle, of the *Deutsch-Österreichische Literaturgeschichte*, ed. Johann Willibald Nagl, Jakob Zeidler, and Eduard Castle, 4 vols (Vienna, 1899–1937), and the *Bio-bibliographisches Literaturlexikon Österreichs* by Hans Giebisch and Gustav Gugitz (Vienna, 1963).

Details of the repertories of the Viennese theatres are drawn mainly from the following: *175 Jahre Burgtheater 1776–1951. Fortgeführt bis Sommer 1954*, compiled by Josef Karl Ratislav (Vienna, n.d. [1954]); *Burgtheater 1776–1976. Aufführungen und Besetzungen von zweihundert Jahren*, compiled by Minna von Alth, 2 vols (Vienna, n.d. [1976]); *Die Wiener Hoftheater (Staatstheater), 2: Die Wiener Hofoper (Staatsoper) 1811–1974* by Franz Hadamowsky (Vienna, 1975); Karl Glossy, *Vierzig Jahre Deutsches Volkstheater* (Vienna, n.d. [1929]); Rudolf Tyrolt, *Chronik des Wiener Stadttheaters 1872–1884. Ein Beitrag zur deutschen Theatergeschichte* (Vienna, 1889); Richard S. Geehr, *Adam Müller-Guttenbrunn and the Aryan Theater of Vienna: 1898–1903. The Approach of Cultural Fascism* (Göppingen, 1973); Anton Bauer and Gustav Kropatschek, *200 Jahre Theater in der Josefstadt 1788–1988*

(Vienna, 1988), and two further books by Anton Bauer, *150 Jahre Theater an der Wien* (Vienna, 1952) and *Opern und Operetten in Wien* (Graz, 1955). – Franz Hadamowsky, *Wien: Theatergeschichte. Von den Anfängen bis zum Ende des Ersten Weltkriegs* (Vienna, 1988) gives a concise outline of the foundation, official authorization, and administration of the court theatres (including the Opera House) and of the commercial theatres up to 1918. The foundation and early years of the Salzburg Festival are documented in the first volume of a well illustrated chronicle by Edda Fuhrich and Gisela Prossnitz, *Die Salzburger Festspiele. Ihre Geschichte in Daten, Zeitzeugnissen und Bildern* (Salzburg, 1990); details of the annual programme at the festival are given in Josef Kaut, *Festspiele in Salzburg* (Salzburg, 1969); the productions of Max Reinhardt are listed in *Max Reinhardt. 'Ein Theater, das den Menschen wieder Freude gibt . . .'. Eine Dokumentation*, edited by Edda Fuhrich and Gisela Prossnitz (Munich and Vienna, 1987).

The distinctive physical structure of the expanding city in which Schnitzler and Hofmannsthal grew up is well conveyed in Donald J. Olsen's copiously illustrated study *The City as a Work of Art: London, Paris, Vienna* (New Haven and London, 1986). *Das große Groner-Wien-Lexikon*, edited by Felix Czeike (Vienna, 1974) is an authoritative source of topographical information about the Vienna of the past; I have also used two popular guidebooks dating from the early twentieth century, the *Wiener Cicerone: Illustrierter Fremden-Führer durch Wien und Umgebung*, 20th edition prepared by Franz Höllrigl (Vienna, 1911–12), and *Wien mit Umgebung und Ausflug nach dem Semmering* (Griebens Reiseführer, 8), 23rd edition (Berlin, 1914–15).

Notes

The following standard abbreviations are used in references to academic journals (see also List of Abbreviations, p. xvii):

CG   *Colloquia Germanica*
CL   *Comparative Literature*
DVLG   *Deutsche Vierteljahrsschrift für Literaturwissenschaft und Geistesgeschichte*
EG   *Études Germaniques*
GLL   *German Life & Letters*
GQ   *German Quarterly*
GR   *Germanic Review*
HB   *Hofmannsthal-Blätter*
HF   *Hofmannsthal-Forschungen*
IASL   *Internationales Archiv für Sozialgeschichte der deutschen Literatur*
JDSG   *Jahrbuch der deutschen Schillergesellschaft*
JIG   *Jahrbuch für Internationale Germanistik*
LJ   *Literaturwissenschaftliches Jahrbuch der Görres-Gesellschaft*
LK   *Literatur und Kritik*
MAL   *Modern Austrian Literature*
MK   *Maske und Kothurn*
MLR   *Modern Language Review*
NGC   *New German Critique*
ÖGL   *Österreich in Geschichte und Literatur*
OL   *Orbis Litterarum*
PEGS   *Publications of the English Goethe Society*
PMLA   *Publications of the Modern Language Association of America*
PQ   *Philological Quarterly*
WW   *Wirkendes Wort*
ZDU   *Zeitschrift für den deutschen Unterricht*

Chapter 1 Fin-de-siècle *Vienna: Irrationalism and Renaissance*

1 Arthur J. May, *The Hapsburg Monarchy 1867–1914* (Cambridge, Mass., 1951), p. 174.
2 See A, 90 (note dated 11 April 1891); Tgb., 18 April 1891.
3 Hermann Bahr, *Selbstbildnis* (Berlin, 1923), p. 240. He claimed to have learnt his ability to switch direction ('mich umschalten') in Berlin in the mid-1880s. ('An Begabung dazu hat's mir ja nie gefehlt': *Selbstbildnis*, p. 169).
4 Andrew W. Barker, '"Der große Überwinder": Hermann Bahr and the Rejection of Naturalism',

MLR 78 (1983): 617–30 (p. 617). This article provides the most balanced sympathetic assessment of Bahr's critical work. On Kraus's opposition to him see Edward Timms, *Karl Kraus, Apocalyptic Satirist: Culture and Catastrophe in Habsburg Vienna* (New Haven and London, 1986), pp. 51–3; on the foundation of *Die Zeit* see Jens Rieckmann, *Aufbruch in die Moderne: Die Anfänge des Jungen Wien. Österreichische Literatur und Kritik im Fin de Siècle* (Königstein/Ts., 1985), pp. 69–89.

5 See H/Bfe. I, 28 (undated letter [no. 11], signed 'Loris').

6 Stefan Zweig, *Die Welt von Gestern. Erinnerungen eines Europäers* (Stockholm and London, 1941), p. 54.

7 Hermann Bahr, *Prophet der Moderne. Tagebücher 1888–1904*, ed. Reinhard Farkas (Vienna, 1987), p. 154; H/AS, 213 (Schnitzler's letter of 7 August 1905); Tgb., 12 August 1905.

8 Karl Popper, *Unended Quest: An Intellectual Autobiography*, revised edn (Glasgow, 1970), p. 9.

9 Karl Kraus, *Frühe Schriften 1890–1902*, ed. Joh. J. Braakenburg, 2 vols (Munich, 1979), 1: 12–16 (p. 16): review of Hofmannsthal's *Gestern*, *Die Gesellschaft*, 8, no. 6 (June 1892), pp. 799–801.

10 Henry Wickham Steed, *The Hapsburg Monarchy* (London, 1913), p. ix.

11 Joseph Redlich, *Emperor Francis Joseph of Austria: A Biography* (London, 1929), p. 448. Lueger's election had finally been confirmed by the Emperor in April 1897.

12 Zweig, *Die Welt von Gestern*, p. 22 (see also pp. 73–4).

13 Bahr, *Selbstbildnis*, pp. 66, 297.

14 May, *The Hapsburg Monarchy 1867–1914*, p. 174.

15 Zweig, *Die Welt von Gestern*, p. 9.

16 See David S. Luft, 'Science and Irrationalism in Freud's Vienna', MAL 23, no. 2 (1990): 89–97. Luft argues that 'Freud drew on two traditions: a way of thinking which emphasized external biological reality and one that emphasized an internal reality of feelings' (p. 96); his interest in the irrational was thus strengthened by the influence of the powerful scientific tradition of the Viennese medical school, which informed a biological view of human nature.

17 Bahr, *Prophet der Moderne. Tagebücher 1888–1904*, p. 155: diary note of 27 November 1903.

18 Martin Stern, 'Der Briefwechsel Hofmannsthal – Fritz Mauthner', HB 19/20 (1978): 21–38 (pp. 33–4: Hofmannsthal's letter of 3 November 1902); Fritz Mauthner, 'Die Poesie und die Sprache', *Die Wage* 4, no. 3, 14 January 1901, pp. 43–6.

19 Hermann Bahr, *Die Überwindung des Naturalismus. Als zweite Reihe von 'Zur Kritik der Moderne'* (Dresden, 1891), p. 150.

20 Also reprinted in *Das Hermann-Bahr-Buch* (Berlin, 1913), pp. 87–101. Excerpt: WM, 147–8.

21 Sigmund Freud, *Aus den Anfängen der Psychoanalyse. Briefe an Wilhelm Fließ, Abhandlungen und Notizen aus den Jahren 1887–1902*, ed. Marie Bonaparte, Anna Freud, and Ernst Kris (Frankfurt a.M., 1962), p. 264: letter of 8 January 1900.

22 See Tgb., 26 March 1900.

23 See Michael Worbs, *Literatur und Psychoanalyse im Wien der Jahrhundertwende* (Frankfurt a.M., 1983), pp. 225–51 on Schnitzler's early work.

24 Some recent research deals with this question in detail: see Horst Thomé, 'Sozialgeschichtliche Perspektiven der neueren Schnitzler-Forschung', IASL 13 (1988): 158–87, especially pp. 163–5.

25 See Michael Hamburger, 'Hofmannsthals Bibliothek. Ein Bericht', *Euphorion* 55 (1961): 15–76 (p. 27); Bernd Urban, *Hofmannsthal, Freud und die Psychoanalyse.*

Quellenkundliche Untersuchungen (Frankfurt a.M. and Berne, 1978), pp. 39 and 125–6.

26 '"Was ist das Leben für ein Mysterium". Unveröffentlichte Briefe von Hugo von Hofmannsthal', ed. Rudolf Hirsch, NZZ, 6–7 August 1983 (no. 181): 41–2 (p. 42): letter of 22 January 1908 to Schmitz.

27 See Urban, *Hofmannsthal, Freud und die Psychoanalyse*, pp. 20 and 129.

28 See Richard Alewyn, *Über Hugo von Hofmannsthal*, 2nd edn (Göttingen, 1960), pp. 111–42.

29 Hermann Bahr, *Glossen. Zum Wiener Theater (1903–1906)* (Berlin, 1907), p. 276.

30 Carl E. Schorske, *Fin-de-siècle Vienna: Politics and Culture* (Cambridge, 1981), pp. 84 and 217.

31 See Christian M. Nebehay, *Gustav Klimt. Sein Leben nach zeitgenössischen Berichten und Quellen* (Munich, 1976), p. 114.

32 *Sonores Saitenspiel. Österreichische Lyrik seit der Jahrhundertwende*, ed. Laurenz Wiedner and Franz Taucher (Vienna, n.d.), p. 37.

33 See Timms, *Karl Kraus, Apocalyptic Satirist*, especially pp. 165–86.

34 Steed, *The Hapsburg Monarchy*, p. 203.

35 Eduard Hanslick, *Musikkritiken*, ed. Lothar Fahlbusch (Leipzig, 1972), p. 293.

36 Willi Reich, *Schoenberg: A Critical Biography*, translated by Leo Black (London, 1971), p. 50; Oliver Neighbour, Paul Griffiths, and George Perle, *The New Grove Second Viennese School* (London, 1983), p. 144.

37 See Dagmar Barnouw, 'Loos, Kraus, Wittgenstein, and the Problem of Authenticity', in *The Turn of the Century: German Literature and Art, 1890–1915*, ed. Gerald Chapple and Hans H. Schulte (Bonn, 1981), p. 258.

38 See my essay 'Erinnerung und Elegie in der Wiener Literatur 1890–1930', LK, no. 223–224, April–May 1988, pp. 153–69.

39 Schorske, *Fin-de-siècle Vienna*, p. 307.

40 E.g., Paul Wertheimer, *Neue Gedichte* (Munich and Leipzig, 1904), p. 9 ('Der Liebespark', also invoking the Belvedere gardens?); Joseph August Lux, *Wiener Sonette und andere Lieder* (Dresden, n.d. [1900]), p. 24 ('Die Gartenmauern').

41 Rudolph Lothar, 'Conrad Ferdinand Meyer', *Die Wage*, 1, no. 50, 10 December 1898, pp. 827–8 (see JW II, 927).

42 See Jens Malte Fischer, *Fin de siècle: Kommentar zu einer Epoche* (Munich, 1978), p. 40.

43 See Gerd Uekermann, *Renaissancismus und Fin de siècle. Die italienische Renaissance in der deutschen Dramatik der letzten Jahrhundertwende* (Berlin, 1985), pp. 293–314.

44 Hans Sittenberger, *Studien zur Dramaturgie der Gegenwart*, vol. 1, *Das dramatische Schaffen in Österreich* (Munich, 1898), pp. 214–18.

45 *Die Gesellschaft*, 8, no. 6, June 1892, pp. 799–801. Reprinted in Kraus, *Frühe Schriften 1892–1900*, 1: 12–16.

46 See Rolf Tarot, *Hugo von Hofmannsthal. Daseinsformen und dichterische Struktur* (Tübingen, 1970), pp. 55–6 and 371.

47 It has frequently been pointed out that Hofmannsthal strengthens the association of Chandos with Bacon by attributing to the fictional Chandos works closely related to those of the historical Bacon who is his fictional addressee and by incorporating in the text borrowings from Bacon. On the relation of Chandos to Bacon and his age see especially Michèle Pauget, *L'Interrogation sur l'art dans l'œuvre essayistique de Hugo von Hofmannsthal. Analyse de configurations* (Frankfurt a.M. and Berne, 1984), pp. 281–9; also Gotthart Wunberg, 'Francis Bacon, der Empfänger des Lord-Chandos-Briefes von Hugo von Hofmannsthal', GLL, n.s. 15 (1961–1962): 195–201; Mary

Gilbert, 'Hofmannsthal's Essays, 1900–1908: A Poet in Transition', in *Hofmannsthal: Studies in Commemoration*, ed. F. Norman (London, 1963), pp. 29–52 (pp. 35–7); Stefan Schultz, 'Hofmannsthal and Chandos: The Sources of the Chandos Letter', CL 13 (1961): 1–15; Rolf Tarot, *Hugo von Hofmannsthal. Daseinsformen und dichterische Struktur*, pp. 364–71; and Pierre-Yves Pétillon, 'Hofmannsthal ou le règne du silence. Fragments à propos de Lord Chandos', *Critique*, 31, no. 339–340 (1975): 884–908.

48 The argument about this historical perspective is developed in greater detail in my paper 'Hofmannsthal and the Renaissance; or: Once More unto "Ein Brief"', PEGS, n.s. 61 (1992). A similar case has been made by Karl Pestalozzi, *Sprachskepsis und Sprachmagie im Werk des jungen Hofmannsthal* (Zürich, 1958), pp. 116–26, and by Rainer Nägele, 'Die Sprachkrise und ihr dichterischer Ausdruck bei Hofmannsthal', GQ 43 (1970): 720–32.

49 Egon Friedell, *Kulturgeschichte der Neuzeit. Die Krisis der europäischen Seele von der schwarzen Pest bis zum ersten Weltkrieg* (Munich, 1965), pp. 230–6.

50 '"Was ist das Leben für ein Mysterium". Unveröffentlichte Briefe von Hugo von Hofmannsthal', NZZ, 6–7 August 1983, p. 41: 'Kennst Du den Roman "Dorian Gray" von Oscar Wilde? Hie und da erinnert er überraschend an unsere Art, das Leben zu sehen [. . .]' (letter of spring 1896 to Hans Schlesinger).

51 'Schnitzlers Machart bemüht sich vordeutend zu sein, wie Hofmannsthals nachstrebend ist': Alfred Kerr, 'Ödipus und der Ruf des Lebens', NR 17 (1906): 492–8. Reprinted in HUK, 155. Revised version in Kerr, *Die Welt im Drama*, 5 vols (Berlin, 1917), 2: 328–35, 288–93.

52 Kraus, *Frühe Schriften 1892–1900*, 2: 284.

53 Ferdinand von Saar, *Sämtliche Werke*, ed. Jakob Minor, 12 vols (Leipzig, n.d. [1908]), 4: 23.

54 See Horst Claus, *The Theatre Director Otto Brahm* (Ann Arbor, n.d. [1981]), p. 12.

55 *Boersen-Zeitung* (Berlin), 12 October 1895 (the production was a daring experiment 'mit dem aus dem Vollen des wiener Liebeslebens geschöpften Sittenbilde "Liebelei" von Arthur Schnitzler, dem Begabtesten und Unerschrockensten unter den wiener "Modernen"'); Albert Leitich, *Deutsche Zeitung* (Vienna), 11 October 1895 ('es ist modern, sogar schrecklich modern und – was nicht zu unterschätzen ist – es ist dem vollen Wiener Leben entnommen').

56 Ludwig Speidel, NFP, Morgenblatt, 13 October 1895; M. B—d., 'Das Wiener Drama', *Extrapost*, 14 October 1895.

57 Julius Bab, 'Die Stiltendenzen im deutschen Drama der Gegenwart', *Mitteilungen der Literarhistorischen Gesellschaft Bonn* 8, no. 5 (1915): 117–44 (p. 130).

58 E.g., (positively) 'Artur Schnitzler', *Arbeiter-Zeitung*, 22 October 1931; (negatively) Robert List, 'Arthur Schnitzler. Zum Tod des Dichters', *Reichspost*, 22 October 1931; Joseph Eberle, 'Ein vergötterter Pseudodichter', *Die schönere Zukunft*, 8 November 1931.

59 Julius Bab, 'Der Dichter des "Anatol". Zwischen Naturalismus und Neuromantik', *Berliner Volkszeitung*, Morgenausgabe, 23 October 1931.

60 Josef Körner, *Arthur Schnitzlers Gestalten und Probleme* (Zürich, Leipzig, and Vienna, 1921), p. 222.

61 See Leonhard M. Fiedler, *Max Reinhardt* (Reinbek bei Hamburg, 1975), p. 47.

62 See Martin Stern, 'Spätzeitlichkeit und Mythos. Hofmannsthals Ariadne', HF 8 (1985): 291–312.

Chapter 2 Biography in Letters and Diaries

1 See Reinhard Urbach, *Schnitzler-Kommentar. Zu den erzählenden Schriften und dramatischen Werken* (Munich, 1974), p. 185.

2 In advance of the publication of volume XII in the new standard edition of Hofmannsthal's works, the clearest summary of the genesis is Martin Stern, 'Die Entstehung von Hofmannsthals anachronistischem Gegenwartslustspiel', in the programme to the 1991 Burgtheater production of *Der Schwierige* (Programmbuch no. 78), pp. 51–77.

3 See Clemens Köttelwesch, 'Hugo von Hofmannsthal. Sämtliche Werke – Kritische Ausgabe (Arbeitsbericht)', HF 8 (1985): 315–23.

4 The 1927 version is the basis of the posthumous edition: Schnitzler, *Das Wort. Tragikomödie in fünf Akten. Fragment*, ed. Kurt Bergel (Frankfurt a.M., 1966). See pp. 5–16 on the genesis of the text.

5 See Günther Fetzer, 'Zum Stand der Planung für eine künftige Ausgabe der Briefe Hofmannsthals', HF 6 (1981): 227–32 (p. 228).

6 Egon Friedell, *Kulturgeschichte der Neuzeit. Die Krisis der europäischen Seele von der schwarzen Pest bis zum Ersten Weltkrieg* (Munich, 1965), p. 1456.

7 See Tgb., 20 September 1893. Another young woman had promised to 'try to stay faithful'; Schnitzler's comment is: 'She won't even try.'

8 Olga Waissnix (1862–1897) is the odd one out in this list. She was a respectable married woman, the wife of a hotelier in Reichenau an der Rax, *c.* 90 km. south-west of Vienna. The friendship she offered Schnitzler was strictly platonic, 'a metaphysical friendship, so to speak' (*Jug.*, 222).

9 E.g., Tgb., 26 May 1896.

10 See Tgb., 23 February 1898: 'Setzte den phantast. Einakter auf'.

11 See Tgb., 26 November 1898; see also Otto P. Schinnerer, 'The Suppression of Schnitzler's *Der grüne Kakadu* by the Burgtheater. Unpublished Correspondence', GR 6 (1931): 183–92; Renate Wagner, *Arthur Schnitzler. Eine Biographie* (Frankfurt a.M., 1984), pp. 110–11.

12 Tgb., 2 September 1900; see R. Wagner, *Arthur Schnitzler*, pp. 116–17.

13 *Wiener Zeitung*, 13 October 1924.

14 See H/AS, 286 (letter to Hofmannsthal, 1 October 1919); AS/Bfe. II, 435 (letter of 20 March 1926 to Josef Körner).

15 See Tgb., 26 September 1896.

16 Quoted in Urbach, *Schnitzler-Kommentar*, p. 155; a critique by Victor Silberer from the *Allgemeine Sport-Zeitung*, 13 February 1898, is quoted by Urbach, pp. 157–8.

17 *Das neue Volkstheater. Festschrift, herausgegeben aus Anlaß der Renovierung 1980/81* (Vienna, 1981), p. 73.

18 See Otto P. Schinnerer, 'Schnitzler and the Military Censorship: Unpublished Correspondence', GR 5 (1930): 238–46 (p. 245).

19 Theodor von Sosnosky, 'Der Fall Schnitzler. Eine unbefangene Betrachtung', *Neue Bahnen*, 1 October 1901, p. 508.

20 Robert Hirschfeld, 'Innere Zensur', *Neues Wiener Tagblatt*, 30 April 1913.

21 See Otto P. Schinnerer, 'The History of Schnitzler's "Reigen"', PMLA 46 (1931): 839–59. The reception of *Reigen* is fully documented in Alfred Poser, Kristina Poser-Schewig, and Gerhard Renner, *Schnitzlers Reigen. Zehn Dialoge und ihre Skandalgeschichte. Analysen und Dokumente* (Frankfurt a.M., 1992); the story of the scandal in Berlin forms a chapter in Ludwig Marcuse, *Obszön. Geschichte einer Entrüstung* (Munich,

1962), pp. 207–63.

22 See Otto P. Schinnerer, 'The Early Works of Arthur Schnitzler', GR 4 (1929): 153–97 (p. 185).

23 R.A.B., 'Artur Schnitzlers neues Buch', *Die Zeit* (Vienna), 6 October 1917.

24 *Neues Wiener Abendblatt*, 22 October 1931.

25 *The Times* (London), 23 October 1931.

26 Surveyed in the editorial apparatus to H/George, 234–60; and by Werner Volke, *Hugo von Hofmannsthal in Selbstzeugnissen und Bilddokumenten* (Reinbek bei Hamburg, 1967), pp. 28–36.

27 See H/Bfe. I, 337–8: letter of 15 December [1901] to Theodor Gomperz.

28 HUK, 138. See also Felix Salten, 'Der junge Hofmannsthal', NFP, 18 July 1929, reprinted in Fiechtner 1949, 37–41 (pp. 38–9); Jakob Wassermann, *Hofmannsthal der Freund* (Berlin, 1930), p. 34 (Fiechtner 1949, 106; Fiechtner 1963, 118); Willy Haas, 'Der Mensch Hofmannsthal', *Die Literarische Welt* (Berlin), 2 July 1929, reprinted in Fiechtner 1949, 254–9 (p. 254); Willy Haas, *Die Literarische Welt. Erinnerungen* (Munich, 1957), p. 44.

29 H/Kessler, 433; *Harry Graf Kessler: Tagebuch eines Weltmannes*, ed. Gerhard Schuster and Margot Pehle, Marbacher Kataloge, 43 (Marbach a.N., 1988), p. 54.

30 See H/Bfe. I, 210: letter of 1 April 1897 to Ria Schmujlow-Claassen.

31 See Wolfram Mauser, *Bild und Gebärde in der Sprache Hofmannsthals* (Vienna, 1961), pp. 47–64: 'Der Brief des Lord Chandos'.

32 Leopold Andrian, 'Erinnerungen an meinen Freund', in Fiechtner 1949, 52–64 (p. 52); Fiechtner 1963, 70–81 (p. 70).

33 Ursula Renner, 'Leopold Andrian über Hugo von Hofmannsthal. Auszüge aus seinen Tagebüchern', HB 35/36 (1987): 3–104 (p. 5): entry for 4 December 1893.

34 Hermann Bahr, *Prophet der Moderne. Tagebücher 1888–1904*, ed. Reinhard Farkas (Vienna, 1987), p. 111 (entry for 12 March 1902).

35 H. R. Klieneberger, 'Hofmannsthal and Leopold Andrian', MLR 80 (1985): 619–36 (p. 619).

36 See Michèle Pauget, *L'Interrogation sur l'art dans l'œuvre essayistique de Hugo von Hofmannsthal. Analyse de configurations* (Frankfurt a.M. and Berne, 1984), pp. 274–5.

37 On the dating of the letter see HKA III, 501.

38 See Volke, *Hugo von Hofmannsthal in Selbstzeugnissen und Bilddokumenten*, p. 77.

39 'Burgtheater-Première. Nach dem Briefe einer kleinen Berlinerin', *Velhagen & Klasings Monatshefte* 16 (1901–1902) 2: 33–44 (p. 37).

40 See Tgb., 11 January 1918.

41 See Wolfram Mauser, 'Hofmannsthals "Triumph der Zeit". Zur Bedeutung seiner Ballett- und Pantomimen-Libretti', HF 6 (1981): 141–8.

42 See Brain Coghlan, *Essays in German Literature, Music and the Theatre* (Adelaide, 1991), p. 44.

43 Bahr, *Prophet der Moderne. Tagebücher 1888–1904*, p. 163: 'In diesem Jahr hat Hugo, mit der *Elektra*, seinen ersten wirklichen Erfolg gehabt' (entry for 31 December 1903). At the time, it was the public success that most gratified Hofmannsthal: e.g., his letter of 10 November 1903 to Hans Schlesinger, 'Der sogenannte große äußere Erfolg ist also eingetreten' (H/Bfe. II, 132).

44 E.g., letters of 12 June 1909 and 23 May 1910 (H/Strauss, 53, 76).

45 See HKA, XXIV, 202–7; also Martin Stern, 'Spätzeitlichkeit und Mythos. Hofmannsthals *Ariadne*', HF 8 (1985): 291–312 (especially pp. 299–303), and Karen Forsyth, *'Ariadne auf Naxos' by Hugo von Hofmannsthal and Richard Strauss: Its Genesis and Meaning* (Oxford, 1982),

pp. 203–19.

46 See Edward Craig, *Gordon Craig. The Story of his Life* (London, 1968), pp. 181–8.

47 See Ewald Rösch, 'Komödie und Berliner Kritik. Zu Hofmannsthals Lustspielen *Cristinas Heimreise* und *Der Schwierige*', in *Hugo von Hofmannsthal. Freundschaften und Begegnungen mit deutschen Zeitgenossen*, ed. Ursula Renner and G. Bärbel Schmid (Würzburg, 1991), pp. 168–89 (pp. 170–73).

48 *Ein comedi von dem reichen sterbenden menschen, der Hecastus genannt* (1549). Hofmannsthal possessed a copy of the play in an edition of Sachs's selected works; see HKA IX, 282.

49 Heinz Lunzer, *Hofmannsthals politische Tätigkeit in den Jahren 1914–1917* (Frankfurt a.M., 1961), p. 136. See letter to Josef Redlich, 8 April 1915; letter from Redlich, 20 May 1915 (H/Redlich, 14–15); official correspondence reprinted in H/Redlich, 129–54.

50 See Rösch, 'Komödie und Berliner Kritik', pp. 181–8.

51 See Michael P. Steinberg, *The Meaning of the Salzburg Festival: Austria as Theater and Ideology, 1890–1938* (Ithaca and London, 1990), p. 146.

52 See *Chrstk.*, 89 (note 194).

53 See Steinberg, *The Meaning of the Salzburg Festival*, pp. 156–8.

54 See reviews in TR, 438–41: Emil Faktor, *Berliner Börsen-Courier*; Ludwig Sternaux, *Berliner Lokal-Anzeiger*; Norbert Falk, *BZ am Mittag* (all 22 September 1923).

55 See reviews in TR, 855–61.

56 On the development and the importance of the diary see Werner Welzig, 'Das Tagebuch Arthur Schnitzlers 1879–1931', IASL 6 (1981): 78–111.

57 His dispositions concerning his *Nachlaß* are reproduced in Gerhard Neumann and Jutta Müller, *Der Nachlaß Arthur Schnitzlers* (Munich, 1969), pp. 23–31; on the diaries see

pp. 23–6.

58 Entry for 6 April 1929, quoted by Barbara Gutt, *Emanzipation bei Arthur Schnitzler* (Berlin, 1978), p. 139.

59 Alma Mahler-Werfel, *Mein Leben* (Frankfurt a.M., 1963), p. 161 (based on a visit paid to Schnitzler on 23 March 1928).

60 The earliest cuttings in his collection that bear the heading of the 'Observer' date from May 1898.

61 See my article 'The Tendentious Reception of *Professor Bernhardi*: Documentation in Schnitzler's Collection of Press Cuttings', in *Vienna 1900: From Altenberg to Wittgenstein*, Austrian Studies, 1, ed. Edward Timms and Ritchie Robertson (Edinburgh, 1990): 108–9.

62 Neumann and Müller, *Der Nachlaß Arthur Schnitzlers*, 31: '[. . .] besonders in ihrem negirenden Theile dürfte sie [*scil*. die Sammlung] eines gewissen literar- od[er] vielmehr culturhistorischen Interesses nicht entbehren'.

63 See letter to Marie Luise Borchardt, 12 June 1923: H/Borchardt, 178.

64 Quoted from: Günther Erken, 'Hofmannsthal-Chronik. Beitrag zu einer Biographie', LJ, n.s. 3 (1962): 239–313 (p. 272).

65 Roger C. Norton, 'Hofmannsthal's "magische Werkstätte": Unpublished Notebooks from the Harvard Collection', GR 36 (1961): 50–64 (p. 59). See Brian Coghlan, '"The whole man must move at once": Das Persönlichkeitsbild des Menschen bei Hofmannsthal', HF 8 (1985): 29–47.

66 See letter from Mell, 30 October 1916: H/Mell, 117.

67 See letter of early April 1915 to Richard Strauss: H/Strauss, 256.

68 See H/Mell, 114–18. The text of Mell's essay, which remained unpublished, is given in H/Mell, 267–84. See also RA III, 648.

69 Reproduced in facsimile in *Deutschösterreichische Literaturgeschichte*, ed.

Johann Willibald Nagl, Jakob Zeidler, and Eduard Castle, 4 vols (Vienna, 1899–1937), 4: 1818–19.

70 Ritchie Robertson, '"Ich habe ihm das Beil nicht geben können": The Heroine's Failure in Hofmannsthal's *Elektra*', OL 41 (1986): 312–31 (p. 314).

71 To Carl Seelig, 14 April 1939, quoted from Ulrich Weinzierl, *Alfred Polgar. Eine Biographie* (Vienna, 1985), pp. 203–4.

Chapter 3   The Theatre

1 *Wiener Lieder und Tänze*, ed. Eduard Kremser *et al.*, 3 vols (Vienna, 1912–25), 1: 86–7. The song (music by Carl Hampe, text by J. B. Moser) was recorded in 1964 by Julius Patzak (Preiserrecords, ST-FK 50113).

2 Adam Müller-Guttenbrunn, *Das Raimund-Theater. Passionsgeschichte einer deutschen Volksbühne* (Vienna, 1897), p. 1.

3 See my essay 'Karl Kraus and the Remembrance of Things Past', in *Karl Kraus in neuer Sicht*, ed. Sigurd Paul Scheichl and Edward Timms (Munich, 1986), pp. 76–89 (p. 85).

4 Hermann Bahr, *Selbstbildnis* (Berlin, 1923), pp. 75, 287.

5 Josef Körner, *Arthur Schnitzlers Gestalten und Probleme* (Zürich, Leipzig, and Vienna, 1921), p. 222.

6 AS/Bfe. II, 751 and II, 785: letters of 19 January and 8 April 1931 to Körner.

7 'Vienna Letter', *The Dial* 73 (1922): 206–14 (p. 207); German text: A, 269.

8 'Ein Romantiker der Nerven': Rudolph Lothar, *Das Wiener Burgtheater*, Das Theater, 5 (Berlin, n.d. [1904]), p. 46.

9 See *Max Reinhardt. "Ein Theater, das den Menschen wieder Freude gibt . . .". Eine Dokumentation*, ed. Edda Fuhrich and Gisela Prossnitz (Munich and Vienna, 1987), pp. 218–22.

10 See my article 'Harbingers of Change in Theatrical Performance: Hofmannsthal's Poems on Mitterwurzer and Kainz', in *Patterns of Change: German Drama and the European Tradition. Essays in Honour of Ronald Peacock*, ed. Dorothy James and Silvia Ranawake (New York and Berne, 1990), pp. 193–206.

11 See Hilde D. Cohn, 'Hofmannsthals Gedichte für Schauspieler', *Monatshefte* 46, no. 2 (1954), 85–94.

12 Karl Glossy, *Vierzig Jahre Deutsches Volkstheater. Ein Beitrag zur deutschen Theatergeschichte* (Vienna, n.d. [1929]), p. v ('Vorbericht').

13 See *Marb.*, 384–6; see also Harold B. Segel, *Turn-of-the-Century Cabaret* (New York, 1987), pp. 183–219.

14 *Österreichische Volks-Presse*, 1 March 1913, p. 6.

15 See Richard S. Geehr, *Adam Müller-Guttenbrunn and the Aryan Theater of Vienna: 1898–1903. The Approach of Cultural Fascism* (Göppingen, 1973), pp. 135–6. Geehr gives a comprehensive account of the history of the theatre under Müller-Guttenbrunn.

16 See Geehr, *Adam Müller-Guttenbrunn and the Aryan Theater of Vienna*, p. 308.

17 Quotations from the account of the meeting in the *Deutsches Volksblatt*, 31 October 1903, pp. 9–12. A fully-documented account of the meeting is given by Geehr, pp. 349–87.

18 *Kikeriki*, 29 October 1922 (no. 42), p. 7.

19 *Deutsche Zeitung*, Abend-Ausgabe, 30 December 1899 (no. 10057), pp. 3–4; *Deutsches Volksblatt*, 31 December 1899 (no. 3951), pp. 6–7.

20 *Kikeriki-Anzeiger*, 20 April 1902, p. 3 (J.J., 'Carl Bleibtreu und A. Baumberg'); *Kikeriki*, 27 April 1902 (no. 34), p. 4 ('Zum Fall Antonie Baumberg'); 20 April 1902 (no. 32), p. 2 (J. S—a.).

21 For a full account see Peter Pulzer, *The Rise of Political Anti-Semitism in Germany and Austria*, revised edn (London, 1988), especially pp. 121–83 and 195–213; on the phenomenon within the wider context of intellectual history see Carl E. Schorske, *Fin-de-siècle Vienna: Politics and Culture* (Cambridge, 1981), pp. 116–80 ('Politics in a New Key: An Austrian Trio').

22 The announcement of the proposed foundation was carried in the morning edition of the *Deutsches Volksblatt*, 19 October 1899, p. 11.

23 See John W. Boyer, *Political Radicalism in Late Imperial Vienna: Origins of the Christian Social Movement 1848–1897* (Chicago and London, 1981), p. 418.

24 Examples from the *Österreichische Volks-Presse*, 4 January 1903, p. 1; 15 February 1903, p. 1; 23 August 1903, p. 4.

25 Pulzer, *The Rise of Political Anti-Semitism in Germany and Austria*, p. 308.

26 Kr., 'An Österreich', *Kikeriki*, no. 32, 8 August 1920, p. 2 ([. . .] 'So wirst du, armes Österreich, / Das Juden-Eldorado!'; *Reichspost*, no. 234, 25 August 1920, p. 8, and no. 241, 1 September 1920, p. 9.

27 E.g., 'Die Wiener Universität', *Kikeriki*, no. 37, 12 September 1920, p. 2.

28 Letter of 11 July 1925, quoted II/I IaaE, 93. I find no evidence to support the suggestion made by Kenneth Segar of anti-Semitism inherent in Hofmannsthal's support of the Salzburg Festival ('Austria in the Thirties: Reality and Exemplum', in *Austria in the Thirties: Culture and Politics*, ed. Kenneth Segar and John Warren [Riverside, California, 1991], pp. 360–2). Not even Schnitzler, the most sceptical of his friends, suspected him of anti-Semitism.

29 J.J., 'Carl Bleibtreu und A. Baumberg', *Kikeriki-Anzeiger*, 20 April 1902, p. 3 ('[. . .] von den

30 eigentlichen Juden pur et simple, als: Bahr, Schnitzler, Hoffmannsthal [*sic*] und noch minderen Judenjüngeln ganz zu schweigen').

30 *Kikeriki*, no. 12, 10 February 1898, p. 2: 'Unbeschnittene Theaterberichte des Dr. Hahn', reviewing '"Freiwild." Sauspiel' von Aaron Schnitzler'.

31 See AS/Bfe. II, 953.

32 Josef Karl Ratislav, *Arthur Schnitzler. Eine Studie* (Hamburg, 1911), p. 7. The passage marked reads: 'Manche Schriftsteller, die dem Judentum angehören, wie J. J. David, haben sich dem germanischen Element so assimiliert, daß man ihre Abstammung nicht errät. Anders Schnitzler, dem das Judentum eine eigentümliche Prägung als Künstler verlieh [. . .]'.

33 See Ulrich Weinzierl, 'Die Kultur der "Reichspost"', in *Aufbruch und Untergang. Österreichische Kultur zwischen 1918 und 1938*, ed. Franz Kadrnoska (Vienna, 1981), pp. 325–44 (especially pp. 328–30).

34 *Current Opinion* 56 (1914): 193–4.

35 Georg Brandes, 'Theater und Schauspiel in Deutschland', *Der Merker* 4, no. 3 (1913): 95–9; Arthur Schnitzler, 'Zum "Professor Bernhardi"', *Der Merker* 4, no. 4 (1913): 135.

36 On the genesis of the play see Sol Liptzin, 'The Genesis of Schnitzler's *Professor Bernhardi*', PQ 10 (1931): 348–55. Schnitzler approved this article in advance of its publication: see AS/Bfe. II, 789 (letter of 13 May 1931 to Liptzin).

37 See Friedrich Torberg, *Das fünfte Rad am Thespiskarren. Theaterkritiken*, 2 vols (Munich, 1966–7), 1: 229.

38 Desmond MacCarthy, 'Greatly to Find Quarrel in a Straw?', *New Statesman and Nation*, 22 August 1936, pp. 255–6.

39 See M. W. Swales, 'Arthur Schnitzler as a Moralist', MLR 62 (1967): 462–75 (pp. 463–4).

40 Hartmut Scheible rightly sees

Berthold Stauber in *Der Weg ins Freie* as an antecedent of Flint (*Arthur Schnitzler in Selbstzeugnissen und Bilddokumenten* [Reinbek, 1976], pp. 94–5). The issue of ends and means is explored in an argument between the politically ambitious Stauber and his humane father; the former rejects human kindness as a standard since, he says, it leads to sentimentality and weakness (ES I, 906).

41 Robert A. Kann, 'The Image of the Austrian in Arthur Schnitzler's Writings', in *Studies in Arthur Schnitzler*, ed. Herbert W. Reichert and Herman Salinger (Chapel Hill, 1963), p. 63.

42 William H. Rey, *Arthur Schnitzler: Professor Bernhardi* (Munich, 1971), p. 57.

43 Theodor Kappstein, *Artur Schnitzler und seine besten Bühnenwerke* (Berlin and Leipzig, 1922), p. 93 ('das ist von Schnitzlers eigenstem Geiste Spiegelung'). It was an identification rejected by Engel in his early review in the *Berliner Tageblatt* for 29 November 1912 ('Dieser Bernhardi ist nicht Schnitzler selbst; er ist nur das Ideal, das der Dichter sein möchte'); but that was a review that Schnitzler disliked.

44 Sol Liptzin, *Arthur Schnitzler* (New York, 1932), p. 193.

45 *Berliner Tageblatt*, Abendzeitung, 21 February 1923.

46 Schiller, *Werke*, Nationalausgabe (Weimar, 1943-) 20: 442–3 (*Über naive und sentimentalische Dichtung*).

47 A fuller account of the early reception may be found in my article 'The Tendentious Reception of *Professor Bernhardi*: Documentation in Schnitzler's Collection of Press Cuttings', in *Vienna 1900: From Altenberg to Wittgenstein*, Austrian Studies, 1, ed. Edward Timms and Ritchie Robertson (Edinburgh, 1990), pp. 108–25. Excerpts from selected reviews are given in an appendix, pp. 119–23.

48 'Das Zensurverbot gegen

Schnitzlers "Professor Bernhardi". Von einem hervorragenden Rechtslehrer', NFP, 19 January 1913.

49 'Für das Verbot war nicht so sehr die in der Komödie diskutierte religiöse Frage entscheidend, als vielmehr die tendenziöse und entstellende Schilderung hierländischer öffentlicher Verhältnisse.' Quoted by Glossy, *Vierzig Jahre Deutsches Volkstheater*, p. 221.

50 —ß—, 'Arzt und Priester', *Die Wage* 16, no. 1 (January 1913), pp. 24–8 (p. 24).

51 E.g., Emil Faktor, *Berliner Börsen-Courier*, Morgenausgabe, 29 November 1912; Friedrich Hertz, 'Der Fall Bernhardi. Politische Glossen zu Schnitzlers Stück', *Der Morgen* (Vienna), 23 December 1912.

52 Arthur Eloesser, 'Schnitzler und Sohn', *Das Literarische Echo*, 15, cols 475–8 (col. 477) (1 January 1913); Paul Goldmann, NFP, 4 January 1913. Goldmann stressed especially the satirical force of the characterization of Flint, '[. . .] das typische Bild des politischen Strebers [. . .] – typisch nicht für Oesterreich allein, so spezifisch österreichisch Exzellenz Flint auch sein mag. Es ist ein Meisterwerk satirischer Charakterzeichnung [. . .]'.

53 The censor insisted that the play was 'ein pamphletistisches Werk', see Glossy, *Vierzig Jahre Deutsches Volkstheater*, p. 223.

54 Examples from the Viennese papers for 15 November 1917: m.b. [= Marco Brociner], *Neues Wiener Tagblatt*; Leopold Jacobson, *Neues Wiener Journal*; —co—, *Die Zeit*. Examples from later reviews in German papers: Ludwig Hirschfeld, *Ostsee-Zeitung* (Stettin), 19 November 1917; Richard Specht, *Berliner Börsen-Courier*, Morgenausgabe, 20 November 1917; *Theater-Courier* (Berlin), 13 December 1917.

55 a.p. [= Alfred Polgar], WAZ, 16

November 1917 (also *Vossische Zeitung* [Berlin], Morgen-Ausgabe, 18 November 1917): 'Alles ist relativ'; Oskar Maurus Fontana, 'Schnitzlers Journalistenkomödie', *Die Wage*, 24 November 1917: 'Diese Lösung ist natürlich nichts als ein Notausgang in den Relativismus, als die Wald- und Wiesenweisheit eines Skeptikers'.

56 This review is reprinted in *Max Mell als Theaterkritiker*, ed. Margret Dietrich (Vienna, 1983), pp. 61–2.

57 AS/Bfe., II, 1 (letter of 4 January 1913) and II, 175 (letter of 22 February 1919).

58 A. Halbert, 'Die Tragikomödie des Starrsinns. Zu Arthur Schnitzlers "Professor Bernhardi"', *Die Wage* 16, no. 16, 19 April 1913, pp. 385–7.

59 See Reinhard Urbach, 'Karl Kraus und Arthur Schnitzler: Eine Dokumentation', LK, no. 49 (1970): 513–30; Renate Wagner, '"Und dieser Kern ist Niedrigkeit". Dokumentarisches zur Beziehung Arthur Schnitzler/Karl Kraus, unter besonderer Berücksichtigung der *Fackel*', MK 27 (1981): 322–34.

60 AS/Bfe. II, 155: letter of 24 December 1917 to Rudolph Lothar.

61 *Die Weltbühne*, 19, no. 10, 8 March 1923, pp. 276–7.

62 E.g., HKA III, 11: 'Und, wenn sich jemals zwei ins Auge sehn, / So sieht ein jeder sich nur in dem andern'.

63 On the dating of the two letters to Bahr (H/Bfe. I, 276–9) see Günther Erken, 'Hofmannsthal-Chronik. Beitrag zu einer Biographie', LJ, n.s. 3 (1962): 239–313 (p. 256).

64 See Leonhard M. Fiedler, *Max Reinhardt* (Reinbek, 1975), p. 76. Reinhardt's Hofmannsthal productions are listed chronologically in Hugo von Hofmannsthal, *Jedermann. Das Spiel vom Sterben des reichen Mannes und Max Reinhardts Inszenierungen. Texte, Dokumente,*

Bilder, compiled by Edda Leisler and Gisela Prossnitz (Frankfurt a.M., 1973), p. 120.

65 Letter of 16 January 1918. Quoted in Leonhard M. Fiedler, *Max Reinhardt und Molière* (Salzburg, 1972), p. 48.

66 'Vielleicht kann ich mit Hilfe anderer mit der Zeit diesen überaus großen (und für die Entwicklung der modernen Comödie so wichtigen) Dichter endlich auf der deutschen Bühne einbürgern, aber nur durch *Prosa*übersetzungen.' Quoted in Fiedler, *Max Reinhardt und Molière*, p. 10. Hofmannsthal's adaptations of Molière are systematically treated in Leonhard M. Fiedler, *Hugo von Hofmannsthals Molière-Bearbeitungen. Die Erneuerung der comédie-ballet auf Max Reinhardts Bühnen* (Darmstadt, 1974).

67 See HKA XXIII, 701–3.

68 Alfred Kerr, *Die Welt im Drama*, 5 vols (Berlin, 1917), 5: 161.

69 See H/Mell, 147: Mell's letter of 1 July 1918.

70 Entry for 18 September 1921, quoted in H/Redlich, 208.

71 Werner Volke, 'Hugo von Hofmannsthal und Josef Nadler in Briefen', JDSG 18 (1974): 37–88 (p. 70: letter of 16 March 1921).

72 For a fuller elaboration of the argument here, see my article 'Hofmannsthal and Austrian Comic Tradition', CG 15 (1982): 73–83.

73 Wilhelm Kosch, 'Das Volksstück von Raimund bis Anzengruber', ZDU 26 (1912): 16–28: 'Arlecchino aus Bergamo wurde zum Hanswurst aus Salzburg' (p. 16). Hofmannsthal's wording in the essay 'Komödie' is 'Harlekin aus Bergamo wird Hanswurst aus Salzburg'.

74 '[...] das Repertorium zu erweitern'. Quoted in Werner Volke, *Hugo von Hofmannsthal in Selbstzeugnissen und Bilddokumenten* (Reinbek, 1967), p. 127. Cf. the 1911 essay 'Das Spiel vor der

Menge' on his 'restoration' of *Jedermann* to the German repertory (P III, 61–2).

75 '[. . .] ein Gast- und mehr-als-Gastverhältnis zum Burgtheater [. . .], in der Form wiederkehrender Gastspiele mit Anwartschaft auf gegenseitigen Austausch u.s.f.'. On the project for Reinhardt's company to appear in the Burgtheater as a visiting company see H/Wildgans, 60–3. Wildgans was opposed to the scheme because it would amount to a downgrading of the Burgtheater company, inappropriate to their loyalty.

76 Richard Alewyn, *Über Hugo von Hofmannsthal*, 2nd edn (Göttingen, 1960), p. 80: 'Hofmannsthals Komödienwerk ist [. . .] der Haupt- und Heimweg des Dichters.'

Chapter 4 Eros

1 Robert Musil, *Theater. Kritisches und Theoretisches*, ed. Marie-Louise Roth (Reinbek, 1965), p. 157.

2 The first act is reproduced in Hofmannsthal, *Florindo*, ed. Martin Stern (Stuttgart, 1963).

3 See Michael Hamburger, 'Hofmannsthals Bibliothek. Ein Bericht', *Euphorion* 55 (1961): 15–76 (p. 72); Leonhard M. Fiedler, 'Keime des Lustspiels'. Frühe Notizen zum "Schwierigen" und zum "Unbestechlichen"', HB, no. 25 (1982): 75–85 (p. 78).

4 Stefan Zweig, *Die Welt von Gestern. Erinnerungen eines Europäers* (London and Stockholm, 1941), pp. 84–9.

5 Juliet Mitchell, *Psychoanalysis and Feminism* (Harmondsworth, 1975), p. 421.

6 On the sequence of events see Ernest Jones, *The Life and Work of Sigmund Freud*, ed. and abridged by Lionel Trilling and Steven Marcus (Harmondsworth, 1964), pp. 223–33.

7 All these writings are reprinted in Arthur Schnitzler, *Medizinische Schriften*, ed. Horst Thomé (Vienna, 1988); see especially pp. 90–3, 176–209, 210–15. On the connections between Schnitzler's medical and imaginative writings see Thomé's foreword, 'Arthur Schnitzlers Anfänge und die Grundlagenkrise der Medizin', pp. 11–59, especially pp. 31–36.

8 First publicly broached in 1896 (see Peter Gay, *Freud: A Life for Our Time* [London, 1989], pp. 92–3), and explored in his letter of 14 November 1897 to Fliess: Sigmund Freud, *Aus den Anfängen der Psychoanalyse. Briefe an Wilhelm Fließ, Abhandlungen und Notizen aus den Jahren 1887–1902*, ed. Marie Bonaparte, Anna Freud, and Ernst Kris (Frankfurt a.M., 1962), pp. 198–202.

9 *Pelican Freud Library*, ed. Angela Richards and Albert Dickson, 15 vols (Harmondsworth, 1976–86), 4: 520. Further references to Freud's works are given to this edition (abbreviated PFL).

10 PFL 10: 45–53.

11 PFL 12: 33–55. Quotations from pp. 37–8, 47.

12 PFL 7: 259.

13 See H/Beer-Hofmann, 37 (letter of 29 August 1894) and 217.

14 See Otto P. Schinnerer, 'Schnitzler and the Military Censorship: Unpublished Correspondence', GR 5 (1930): 243.

15 See *Frauenemanzipation im deutschen Vormärz. Texte und Dokumente*, ed. Renate Möhrmann (Stuttgart, 1978). Documents of the opposition in Vienna include the satirical comedy *Frauen-Emancipation* by Wilhelm Marchland (Vienna, 1840), performed in 1839 in the Theater in der Josefstadt, and the treatise *Gedanken über die angeborenen Rechte des Frauengeschlechtes* by Marie von Thurnberg [= Marie Baronin von Augustin] (Vienna, 1846).

16 On Krafft-Ebing in the context of

the *Frauenfrage* see Nike Wagner, *Geist und Geschlecht. Karl Kraus und die Erotik der Wiener Moderne* (Frankfurt a.M., 1982), pp. 74–5.

17   The last phrase ('in ein noch undurchdringlicheres Dunkel gehüllt') is mistranslated in PFL 7: 63.

18   PFL 15: 313.

19   But Freud analysed too wide a range of people, including both the 'Rat Man' and the 'Wolf Man', for later criticisms of his work as 'culture-bound', i.e., based on a restricted evidential basis (see Juliet Mitchell, *Psychoanalysis and Feminism*, pp. 419–35: 'Psychoanalysis and Vienna at the Turn of the Century') to be convincing.

20   The painting is in the Historical Museum of the City of Vienna. All the oils referred to have been widely reproduced, e.g., in Alessandra Comini, *Gustav Klimt* (London, 1975); Angelica Bäumer, *Gustav Klimt: Women* (London, 1986); Gottfried Fliedl, *Gustav Klimt 1862–1918. Die Welt in weiblicher Gestalt* (Cologne, 1989); Frank Whitford, *Klimt* (London, 1990).

21   Zweig, *Die Welt von Gestern*, pp. 78–84. See also *Die Frau im Korsett. Wiener Frauenalltag zwischen Klischee und Wirklichkeit 1848–1920*, ed. Reingard Witzmann (Catalogue: 88. Sonderausstellung des Historischen Museums der Stadt Wien) (Vienna, 1984).

22   See Bram Dijkstra, *Idols of Perversity: Fantasies of Feminine Evil in Fin-de-siècle Culture* (New York and Oxford, 1986), pp. 369–71, where the theme is interpreted as being related to the changing ecomonic environment in expressing woman's hunger for gold.

23   This painting too hangs in the Österreichische Galerie in Vienna. 'Beheading is well known to us as a symbolic substitute for castrating', Freud would write in *The Taboo of Virginity* (*Das Tabu der Virginität*, 1918) in relation to another treatment of the Holofernes story, Hebbel's tragedy *Judith*: PFL 7: 281.

24   Weininger's denigration of woman was not in itself innovative. See, for example, Dijkstra, *Idols of Perversity*, pp. 218, 239–40.

25   Karl Kraus, *Schriften*, ed. Christian Wagenkecht, 12 vols (Frankfurt a.M., 1986–89), 8: 13–38, 181–92.

26   Quoted by Barbara Gutt, *Emanzipation bei Arthur Schnitzler* (Berlin, 1978), pp. 113–14.

27   See *Marb.*, 339; Tgb., 12 November 1910; and Gutt, *Emanzipation bei Arthur Schnitzler*, pp. 166–7.

28   See Bruce Thompson, *Schnitzler's Vienna: Image of a Society* (London, 1990), pp. 69–70.

29   Headed 'Von einem kleinen wiener Buch', the draft has been published by Rudolf Hirsch, 'Hugo von Hofmannsthal, Über Schnitzlers "Anatol"', NR 82, no. 4 (1971): 795–7.

30   Peter Skrine, *Hauptmann, Wedekind and Schnitzler* (Basingstoke and London, 1989), p. 117.

31   Athene Seyler and Stephen Haggard, *The Craft of Comedy* (London, 1943), p. 28.

32   See Skrine, *Hauptmann, Wedekind and Schnitzler*, p. 125.

33   Bcraton, 'Hofburgtheater', *Wiener Salonblatt*, no. 41, 13 October 1895, pp. 8–9.

34   Skrine, *Hauptmann, Wedekind and Schnitzler*, p. 128.

35   Reinhard Urbach, *Schnitzler-Kommentar. Zu den erzählenden Schriften und dramatischen Werken* (Munich, 1974), p. 150. On the history of the term see Hugo Aust, Peter Haida, and Jürgen Hein, *Volksstück* (Munich, 1989).

36   Schnitzler himself dubbed her 'das erste süße Mädel' in his autobiography (*Jug.*, 113).

37   For a fuller discussion of the link see my article 'Changing Perspectives: The "doppelte Sexualmoral"

in 1841 and 1895. *Das Mädl aus der Vorstadt* and *Liebelei'*, in *Erbe und Umbruch in der neueren deutschsprachigen Komödie. Londoner Symposium 1987*, ed. Hanne Castein and Alexander Stillmark (Stuttgart, 1990), pp. 17–31.

38 J. J. David, 'Wiener Kunst, XII', *Das Magazin für Litteratur* (Berlin), 16 November 1895, cols 1489–92 (col. 1489). The review in *Der junge Kikeriki* (20 October 1895) summed the play up dismissively as 'künstlerische Verwienerung des Pariser Liebeslebens' (p. 3).

39 Maurice Muret, 'Un Parisien de Vienne. M. Arthur Schnitzler', *La Nouvelle Revue*, 1 August 1908, pp. 339–54 (p. 354).

40 Andrew W. Barker, 'Der große Überwinder: Hermann Bahr and the Rejection of Naturalism', MLR 78 (1983): 617–30 (p. 623).

41 Reproduced in Hartmut Scheible, *Arthur Schnitzler in Selbstzeugnissen und Bilddokumenten* (Reinbek, 1976), p. 67.

42 Otto P. Schinnerer used the material in Schnitzler's collection of press cuttings when preparing his account of the play's reception, 'The History of Schnitzler's "Reigen"', PMLA 46 (1931): 839–59; see AS/Bfe. II, 612 (letter of 2 August 1929 to Olga Schnitzler).

43 Reprinted in *Max Mell als Theaterkritiker*, ed. Margret Dietrich (Vienna, 1983), pp. 287–8.

44 Heinz Politzer, 'Hugo von Hofmannsthals "Elektra". Geburt der Tragödie aus dem Geiste der Psychopathologie', DVLG 47 (1973): 95–119 (p. 104).

45 See Dijkstra, *Idols of Perversity*, pp. 243–8.

46 Compare the conflicting approaches taken by Rolf-Peter Janz in Rolf-Peter Janz and Klaus Laermann, *Arthur Schnitzler. Zur Diagnose des Wiener Bürgertums im Fin de Siècle* (Stuttgart, 1977), pp. 55–75, and by Heinz Politzer, *Das Schweigen der Sirenen* (Stuttgart, 1968), pp. 110–41: 'Diagnose und

Dichtung. Zum Werk Arthur Schnitzlers'. Johanna Bossinade, '"Wenn es aber . . . bei mir anders wäre": Die Frage der Geschlechterbeziehungen in Arthur Schnitzlers *Reigen'*, in *Aufsätze zu Literatur und Kunst der Jahrhundertwende*, ed. Gerhard Kluge (Amsterdam, 1984), pp. 273–328, surveys the critical literature in relation to social and intellectual history.

47 PFL 7: 254 ('On the Universal Tendency to Debasement in the Sphere of Love'). Cf. Janz and Laermann, *Arthur Schnitzler. Zur Diagnose des Wiener Bürgertums im Fin de Siècle*, pp. 60–62.

48 E. M. Butler, 'Hofmannsthal's "Elektra". A Graeco-Freudian Myth', *Journal of the Warburg Institute* 2 (1938–39): 164–75 (p. 168).

49 Hermann Bahr: 'Kleines Theater. (Zum Gastspiele im Deutschen Volkstheater vom 1. bis 10. Mai 1903), *Neues Wiener Tagblatt*, 1 May 1903, pp. 2–4 (p. 4). Reprinted in Hermann Bahr, *Glossen. Zum Wiener Theater (1903–1906)* (Berlin, 1907), p. 244.

50 See Sally McMullen, 'From the Armchair to the Stage: Hofmannsthal's *Elektra* in its Theatrical Context', MLR 80 (1985): 637–51 (p. 649).

51 Hermann Bahr, 'Dialog vom Tragischen', NDR 14 (1903): 716–36 (p. 720). See Hermann Bahr, *Prophet der Moderne. Tagebücher 1888–1904*, ed. Reinhard Farkas (Vienna, 1987), pp. 134–6; on the composition of *Elektra* see H/Bfe. II, 383–5. On Bahr's reading of the *Studies in Hysteria* see Michael Worbs, *Literatur und Psychoanalyse im Wien der Jahrhundertwende* (Frankfurt a.M., 1983), pp. 139–42; on the interaction between Bahr and Hofmannsthal see Lorna Martens, 'The Theme of Repressed Memory in Hofmannsthal's *Elektra'*, GQ 60 (1987): 38–51 (pp. 39–40).

52 Bahr, *Prophet der Moderne.*

Tagebücher 1888–1904, p. 149 (entry for 13 September 1903): 'durchaus meine Griechen, hysterisch, abgehetzt, ins Ruhelose getrieben'.

53 Harden's critique is reprinted in excerpt in HUK, 82–6. On its context and influence see Worbs, *Literatur und Psychoanalyse im Wien der Jahrhundertwende*, pp. 269–72. Hofmannsthal's reaction may be coloured by his intention, never realized, of writing a companion play, *Orest in Delphi*: see Hans-Joachim Newiger, 'Hofmannsthals *Elektra* und die griechische Tragödie', *Arcadia* 4 (1969): 138–63 (pp. 157–8).

54 Steinberg's attempt to read it as 'a parable about the shattering of rational and political order' (Michael P. Steinberg, *The Meaning of the Salzburg Festival: Austria as Theater and Ideology, 1890–1938* [Ithaca and London, 1990], p. 149) is supported neither by Hofmannsthal's own pronouncements nor by the thrust of the action, in which politics plays no part.

55 See Ritchie Robertson, '"Ich habe ihm das Beil nicht geben können": The Heroine's Failure in Hofmannsthal's *Elektra*', OL 41 (1986): 312–31 (p. 323).

56 See Bernd Urban, *Hofmannsthal, Freud und die Psychoanalyse. Quellenkundliche Untersuchungen* (Frankfurt a.M. and Berne, 1978), pp. 30, 129–30.

57 The material in HUK, 77–82, forms the main part of Kerr's review 'Rose Bernd und Elektra', NDR 14 (1903): 1311–17, and is also reprinted in Alfred Kerr, *Die Welt im Drama*, 5 vols (Berlin, 1917), 1: 155–62.

58 Cf. Urban, *Hofmannsthal, Freud und die Psychoanalyse*, p. 37.

59 William H. Rey, *Weltentzweiung und Weltversöhnung in Hofmannsthals Griechischen Dramen* (Philadelphia, 1962), p. 90.

60 E. M. Butler, 'Hofmannsthal's "Elektra". A Graeco-Freudian Myth', p. 168.

61 Rey, *Weltentzweiung und Weltversöhnung in Hofmannsthals Griechischen Dramen*, pp. 18–19.

62 Ritchie Robertson argues that the brevity of the dance arises from her realization of her failure to participate in the murder ('"Ich habe ihm das Beil nicht geben können": The Heroine's Failure in Hofmannsthal's *Elektra*', pp. 313–14); but the stage direction following it spells out that it is a moment of the 'most intense triumph' (D II, 75). Bennett associates this final dance with the ineffableness of visionary experience, one of the themes of the Chandos Letter (Benjamin Bennett, *Hugo von Hofmannsthal: The Theaters of Consciousness* [Cambridge, 1988], p. 113); but it is a fulfilment of what she has anticipated, dancing in celebration of revenge for her father's death (D II, 15).

63 'Hysterics suffer mainly from reminiscences' (PFL 3: 58). See Lorna Martens, 'The Theme of Repressed Memory in Hofmannsthal's *Elektra*', p. 43.

64 Their interview, in E. M. Butler's analysis, follows the lines of 'the analysis of a neurotic patient by a physician of the Viennese school', but charged with tragic irony through the hostility of the analyst – Elektra, prompting Klytämnestra with questions – to her would-be patient ('Hofmannsthal's "Elektra". A Graeco-Freudian Myth', pp. 169–70). See Martens, 'The Theme of Repressed Memory in Hofmannsthal's *Elektra*', pp. 44–5.

65 See Steinberg, *The Meaning of the Salzburg Festival*, p. 154.

66 Sally McMullen, 'Sense and Sensuality: Max Reinhardt's Early Productions', in *Max Reinhardt: The Oxford Symposium*, ed. Margaret Jacobs and John Warren (Oxford, 1986), pp. 16–33 (pp. 21–2).

67 Quotations are from the transla-

tion by E. F. Watling in Sophocles, *Electra and other Plays* (Harmondsworth, 1953), pp. 68–117 (pp. 97–8).

68 See Ewald Rösch, *Komödien Hofmannsthals: Die Entfaltung ihrer Sinnstruktur aus dem Thema der Daseinsstufen* (Marburg, 1963).

69 'Hofmannsthal ist ein Schwelger; oft ein zarter Schwelger; hier ein Blutschwelger' (NDR 14: 1315; Kerr, *Die Welt im Drama*, 1: 158).

70 Michael Hamburger, 'Hofmannsthals Bibliothek. Ein Bericht', records only an edition presented in 1891 (p. 53), but the rhythms of Grillparzer's verse must have been taken for granted from schooldays on.

71 Sophocles, *Electra and other Plays*, p. 83.

72 Heinz Politzer, 'Hugo von Hofmannsthals "Elektra". Geburt der Tragödie aus dem Geiste der Psychopathologie', *DVLG* 47 (1973): 95–119 (p. 112); Robertson, '"Ich habe ihm das Beil nicht geben können": The Heroine's Failure in Hofmannsthal's *Elektra*', pp. 324–5.

73 Hugh Lloyd-Jones is not convincing when he argues that while Elektra's 'weakness [. . .] heightens her pathos', it is 'of no special significance that she herself cannot do the deed': Hugh Lloyd-Jones, 'Hofmannsthal's *Elektra* as a Goethean Drama', PEGS, n.s. 59 (1990): 16–34 (p. 34).

74 Sally McMullen, 'Sense and Sensuality', p. 29.

75 E.g., J. L. Styan, *Max Reinhardt* (Cambridge, 1982), p. 26: 'Sophocles' controlled and dignified tragic heroine in Reinhardt's hands became a woman consumed by the passion of a prima donna: when Orestes kills Clytemnestra and Aegisthus, Eysoldt executed a savage dance of triumph and then collapsed – an effect unimaginable in Greek tragedy.'

76 Max Osborne [*sic*], 'Stage and Scenery', in *Max Reinhardt and his Theatre*, ed. Oliver M. Sayler (repr. New York and London, 1968), pp. 133–7 (quotations from pp. 133, 135).

77 Other examples include also Kolo Moser's 'Woglinde' in vol. 4, and Wilhelm List in vol. 6. Reproductions in Christian M. Nebehay, *Ver sacrum 1898–1903*, 2nd edn (Vienna, 1981), pp. 110, 182, and 157. Hermann Ubell had commented in 1899 on Hofmannsthal's affinity to contemporary styles of painting (HUK, 65–6). The parallel between Hofmannsthal and Klimt in the context of cultural and intellectual history is summarized by Hilde Burger in H/Kessler, 504.

78 He similarly alludes to the relation to Goethe's *Iphigenie* in a slightly earlier note, dating from 1903: see RA III, 443.

79 ES II, 336–7, 362, 365.

80 See in particular Wolfram Mauser, *Hugo von Hofmannsthal: Konfliktbewältigung und Werkstruktur. Eine psychosoziologische Interpretation* (Munich, 1977), pp. 127–37, and Lilian R. Furst, 'No Bed of Roses: The Women in the "Rosenkavalier"', *Jahrbuch für Internationale Germanistik* 16 (1984): 116–20.

81 PFL 7: 251 ('On the Universal Tendency to Debasement in the Sphere of Love').

82 See HKA XXIII, 705–8. Hogarth's sequence of oils 'Marriage à la mode', including 'The Countess's Morning Levée', is in the National Gallery in London. Another Hogarth work, 'Before and After', may have served Schnitzler as a source for the fourth scene of *Reigen*: see Janz and Laermann, *Arthur Schnitzler. Zur Diagnose des Wiener Bürgertums im Fin de Siècle*, p. 61.

83 See HKA XXIII, 708–9.

84 See H/Strauss, 508 (letter of 1 October 1927), 522 (letter of 13 November 1927), 523 (letter of 5 December 1927).

85 Martin Swales, 'Schnitzler's Tragicomedy: A Reading of "Das weite Land"', MAL 10, nos 3–4 (1977): 233–45.
86 Swales, 'Schnitzler's Tragicomedy', p. 239.
87 On this element in the motivation see the discussion of the play by Klaus Laermann in Janz and Laermann, *Arthur Schnitzler. Zur Diagnose des Wiener Bürgertums im Fin de Siècle*, pp. 148–9.

Chapter 5 The End of the Monarchy

1 For an account of the poetry of the period (both patriotic and antiwar) see the articles by Albert Berger, Johann Sonnleitner, and Herbert Exenberger in *Österreich und der Große Krieg 1914–1918. Die andere Seite der Geschichte*, ed. Klaus Amann and Hubert Lengauer (Vienna, 1989), pp. 144–52, 152–8, 170–6; also my article 'Franz Werfel and Austrian Poetry of the First World War' in *Franz Werfel: An Austrian Writer Reassessed*, ed. Lothar Huber (Oxford, 1989), pp. 15–36.
2 Richard Schaukal, *1914. Eherne Sonette* (Munich, 1914), p. 16.
3 Stefan Zweig, *Die Welt von Gestern. Erinnerungen eines Europäers* (London and Stockholm, 1941), pp. 233–4. On Zweig's own attitude to the war see D. A. Prater, *European of Yesterday: A Biography of Stefan Zweig* (Oxford, 1972), pp. 71–107. Subsequent research showing Zweig's continued collaboration with the authorities is summarized by Edward Timms, *Karl Kraus, Apocalyptic Satirist: Culture and Catastrophe in Habsburg Vienna* (New Haven and London, 1986), pp. 422–3.
4 Ernest Jones, *The Life and Work of Sigmund Freud*, ed. and abridged by Lionel Trilling and Steven Marcus

(Harmondsworth, 1964), p. 426.
5 Hermann Bahr, *Kriegssegen* (Munich, 1915), p. 19.
6 Karl Kraus, *Die letzten Tage der Menschheit. Tragödie in fünf Akten mit Vorspiel und Epilog*, 'Akt-Ausgabe' (Vienna, 1919), p. 84 (Act I, sc. 12); revised version, see Karl Kraus, *Schriften*, ed. Christian Wagenknecht, 12 vols (Frankfurt a.M., 1986–89), 10: 191 (Act I, sc. 29).
7 See HKA I, 428–9.
8 On the publications and membership of this group see Kurt Peball, 'Literarische Publikationen des Kriegsarchivs im Weltkrieg 1914 bis 1918', *Mitteilungen des österreichischen Staatsarchivs* 14 (1961): 240–60; Klaus Heydemann, 'Der Titularfeldwebel. Stefan Zweig im Kriegsarchiv', in *Stefan Zweig 1881/ 1981. Aufsätze und Dokumente*, ed. Heinz Lunzer and Gerhard Renner, *Zirkular*, Sondernummer 2, October 1981, pp. 19–55; Peter Broucek, 'Das Kriegspressequartier und die literarischen Gruppen im Kriegsarchiv', in *Österreich und der Große Krieg 1914–1918*, ed. Klaus Amann and Hubert Lengauer, pp. 132–9. The group is satirized in *Die letzten Tage der Menschheit*, III, 9: Kraus, *Schriften*, 10: 337–45.
9 E.g., 'Unglaublich, aber doch wahr!', *Kikeriki*, no. 75, 18 September 1898, p. 1; 'Bald kommt der Friede', *Kikeriki*, no. 13, 13 February 1902, p. 2; 'Die Krönung König Eduard VII.', *Kikeriki*, no. 28, 27 March 1902, p. 1; 'Die unbeugsamen Oranje-Buren', *Kikeriki*, no. 44, 1 June 1902, p. 4.
10 *Deutsches Volksblatt*, Morgen-Ausgabe, 19 October 1899, p. 5.
11 Ernst von Dombrowski, *Zu Wehr und Ehr'. Vaterländische Dichtungen*, revised edn (Graz, 1915), p. 51 ('England's Flagge'). See also Schaukal, *1914. Eherne Sonette*, p. 19 ('An England') and p. 29 ('Die englische Flotte'); Richard

von Kralik, *Schwarz-gelb und Schwarz-weiß-rot* (Innsbruck, n.d.), pp. 49–53 ('An England' and 'Albion').

12 'Der Gott der Liebe ist der Gott des Hasses': Anton Wildgans, *Österreichische Gedichte*, Österreichische Bibliothek, 12 (Leipzig, n.d. [1915]), p. 22.

13 Franz Werfel, *Das lyrische Werk*, ed. Adolf D. Klarmann (Frankfurt a.M., 1967), pp. 164–5, 170.

14 See *Jug.*, 100.

15 See AS/Bfe. II, 88 (letter of 22 May 1915 to Samuel Fischer); Fritz Wittels, quoted in Peter Gay, *Freud: A Life for Our Time* (London, 1988), pp. 348–9.

16 'Der Briefwechsel Fritz von Unruhs mit Arthur Schnitzler', ed. Ulrich K. Goldsmith, MAL 10, nos. 3–4 (1977): 69–127 (pp. 95–100).

17 Kraus, *Schriften*, 10: 48, 232 (cf. 'Akt-Ausgabe', pp. 11, 128). In the final version the operetta concerned is Hugo Felix's *Husarenblut* – a satirical touch weakened by the fact that it had not been performed in Vienna since October 1894 (Theater an der Wien).

18 Rainer Maria Rilke, *Briefe*, Rilke-Archiv edition (Wiesbaden, 1950), pp. 494–5: letter of 22 August 1915 to Frl. A. Baumgarten.

19 E.g., 'Heldentod' by Richard Seyss-Inquart, brother of the later Fascist politician, in *Weltbrand 1915. Kriegspoesie*, ed. Raimund Fürlinger (Vienna, 1915), pp. 30–2.

20 Kraus, *Schriften*, 10: 209. The passage is adapted from the equivalent dialogue in the earlier 'Akt-Ausgabe' (p. 105).

21 Kraus, *Schriften*, 9: 154.

22 See Timms, *Karl Kraus, Apocalyptic Satirist*, pp. 294–301.

23 See *Schicksalsjahre Österreichs 1908–1919. Das politische Tagebuch Josef Redlichs*, ed. Fritz Fellner, 2 vols, Veröffentlichungen der Kommission für neuere Geschichte Österreichs, 39–40 (Graz, 1953–

54), 1: 241–2 (entry dated 3 August 1914); letter of 22 August 1914 to Countess Ottonie Degenfeld (H/Degenfeld, 306); Heinz Lunzer, *Hofmannsthals politische Tätigkeit in den Jahren 1914–1917* (Frankfurt a.M. and Berne, 1981), pp. 26–7. Kraus guessed that Hofmannsthal had relied on 'Protektion': F 423–425, May 1916, p. 48.

24 E.g., letters to Ottonie von Degenfeld, early September 1914: 'Man ist, wo man hinbefohlen wurde' (H/Degenfeld, 308); to Bahr, 9 September 1914: 'Schließlich steht jeder dort, wo er befohlen ist' (quoted in Lunzer, *Hofmannsthals politische Tätigkeit in den Jahren 1914–1917*, 33); to Helene von Nostitz, 25 September 1914: 'Ich [...] wurde im August zu einer militärischen Centralstelle nach Wien befohlen' (H/Nostitz, 131–2).

25 H/AS, 276; H/Beer-Hofmann, 134–5.

26 See *Schicksalsjahre Österreichs 1908–1919. Das politische Tagebuch Josef Redlichs*, 2: 29–30: entries for 6 and 17 April 1915. As he later summed up the position in a letter to Bodenhausen, he was released indefinitely and without conditions, it being his own responsibility to determine his tasks (H/Bodenhausen, 202: letter of 27 August 1915).

27 '[. . .] inmitten eines Meeres von Schwierigkeiten, Confusionen und frevelhafter, nie zu verantwortender Kurzsichtigkeit'. Quoted in Werner Volke, *Hugo von Hofmannsthal in Selbstzeugnissen und Bilddokumenten* (Reinbek, 1967), p. 141. The growing discrepancy between Hofmannsthal's private views and public utterances is pointed out by Hermann Rudolph, *Kulturkritik und konservative Revolution. Zum kulturell-politischen Denken Hofmannsthals und seinem problemgeschichtlichen Kontext* (Tübingen, 1971), p. 101.

28 *Neue Freie Presse*, no. 18070, 13 December 1914, pp. 4–5. Reprinted in P III, 496–9.

29 *Schicksalsjahre Österreichs 1908–1919. Das politische Tagebuch Josef Redlichs*, 2: 175: entry for 31 December 1916.

30 The relation of Hofmannsthal's version to his two main sources is outlined synoptically in HKA IX, 286–7; see also the introduction by Margaret Jacobs to her edition of *Jedermann* (London and Edinburgh, 1957), pp. xxvii–xxix.

31 Hermann Bahr, *Prophet der Moderne. Tagebücher 1888–1904*, ed. Reinhard Farkas (Vienna, 1987), pp. 79, 157.

32 See Jürgen Prohl, *Hugo von Hofmannsthal und Rudolf Borchardt. Studien über eine Dichterfreundschaft* (Bremen, 1973), p. 78. Borchardt's essay is also mentioned in a short piece on Borchardt that Hofmannsthal published in the *Berliner Tageblatt*, 28 November 1916 (P III, 386).

33 *Schicksalsjahre Österreichs 1908–1919. Das politische Tagebuch Josef Redlichs*, 2: 55 (entry for 24 August 1915) and 2: 80 (23 November 1915).

34 H. R. Klieneberger, 'Hofmannsthal and Leopold Andrian', MLR 80 (1985): 619–36.

35 See John Leslie, 'Österreich-Ungarn vor dem Kriegsausbruch. Der Ballhausplatz in Wien im Juli 1914 aus der Sicht eines österreichisch-ungarischen Diplomaten', in *Deutschland und Europa in der Neuzeit* (Festschrift für Karl Otmar Freiherr von Aretin), ed. Ralph Melville *et al.* (Stuttgart, 1988), pp. 661–84.

36 Quoted by Leslie, 'Österreich-Ungarn vor dem Kriegsausbruch', p. 674.

37 Steinberg overlooks this external focus when he reduces the series to an attempted 'politicization of Austrian letters': Michael P. Steinberg, *The Meaning of the Salzburg Festival: Austria as Theater and Ideology, 1890–1938* (Ithaca and London, 1990), p. 106.

38 See Brian Coghlan, *Hofmannsthal's Festival Dramas* (Cambridge, 1964), pp. 131–6. Coghlan gives an extended account (pp. 83–149) of Hofmannsthal's wartime essays as 'evidence of his attempted creation of an Austrian "myth"' (p. x).

39 See Friedrich Jenaczek, *Zeittafeln zur Fackel. Themen – Ziele – Probleme* (Munich, 1965), pp. 42–5.

40 Letter of 23 August 1919 to Ludwig von Hofmann, quoted by Martin Stern, 'Hofmannsthal und das Ende der Donaumonarchie', in *Die österreichische Literatur. Ihr Profil von der Jahrhundertwende bis zur Gegenwart (1880–1980)*, ed. Herbert Zeman, 2 vols (Graz, 1989), 1: 709–27 (p. 720).

41 Max Vancsa, 'Zur Geschichte der niederösterreichisch-böhmischen Grenze', *Reichspost*, 26 August 1920, pp. 1–2: 'Die schmerzliche Amputation, die soeben an dem Körper unseres schönen Heimatlandes vollzogen wurde [. . .]' (p. 1).

42 The following paragraphs draw particularly on the following: on state particularism, Charles A. Gulick, *Austria from Habsburg to Hitler*, 2 vols (Berkeley and Los Angeles, 1948), vol. 1, *Labor's Workshop of Democracy*, pp. 84–94 ('State Separatism'), and Anton Staudinger, 'Landesbewußtsein und Gesamtstaatsverständnis in Österreich nach den beiden Weltkriegen', *Austriaca*, numéro spécial, November 1979, *Deux fois l'Autriche: Après 1918 et après 1945*, 3, pp. 121–135; on the boundaries, *Dokumentation zur österreichischen Zeitgeschichte 1918–1928*, ed. Christine Klusacek and Kurt Stimmer (Vienna, 1984), pp. 86–100, 185–204, and Walter Goldinger, 'Der Kampf um das Staatsgebiet', in *Geschichte der Republik Österreich*, ed. Heinrich Benedikt (Vienna, 1954), pp. 60–103.

43 See statistics summarized, together with a map reproduced from 1914,

in *Österreich-Ungarn 1914* (Vienna, 1975).

44 Richard Nikolaus Coudenhove-Kalergi, 'Wien als Welthauptstadt', *Die Zukunft* 29, no. 3, 16 October 1920, pp. 61–4 (p. 62).

45 Tgb., 14 May 1907; Tgb., 23 April 1912.

46 E.g., AS/Bfe. II, 321 (letter of 21 July 1923 to Olga Schnitzler) and AS/Bfe. II, 413 (letter of 7 July 1925 to Georg Brandes).

47 It has been argued that his presentation of corrupt human relations in the novel amounts to an exploration of the reasons for the decline of the monarchy as he saw them; see R. K. Angress, 'Schnitzler's "Frauenroman" *Therese*', MAL 10, nos. 3–4 (1977): 265–82.

48 Anton Wildgans, *Ein Leben in Briefen*, ed. Lilly Wildgans, 3 vols (Vienna, 1947), 3: 168–9 (letter of 17 June 1927). See Klaus Amann, *P.E.N. Politik, Emigration, Nationalsozialismus. Ein österreichischer Schriftstellerclub* (Vienna, 1984), pp. 17–18, 144.

49 Rudolf Hirsch, 'Unbekannte Äußerungen Hofmannsthals zum "Turm"', LK, no. 135 (June 1979): 275–9 (p. 279).

50 See Walter Weiss, 'Salzburger Mythos? Hofmannsthals und Reinhardts Welttheater', in *Staat und Gesellschaft in der modernen österreichischen Literatur*, ed. Friedbert Aspetsberger (Vienna, 1977), pp. 5–19 (p. 12).

51 Othmar Spann, *Der wahre Staat. Vorträge über Abbruch und Neubau der Gesellschaft gehalten im Sommersemester 1920 an der Universität Wien* (Leipzig, 1921). The crisis of the present is repeatedly defined by Spann as a 'Gegenrenaissance' (see pp. 4, 103).

52 The text of the poem is given in H/Andrian, 499.

53 On the successive waves of the fashion for historical drama see John Warren, 'Franz Werfel's Historical Drama: Continuity and Change', in *Franz Werfel: An Austrian Writer Reassessed*, ed. Lothar Huber (Oxford, 1989), pp. 153–73.

54 See Wendelin Schmidt-Dengler, 'Bedürfnis nach Geschichte', in *Aufbruch und Untergang. Österreichische Kultur zwischen 1918 und 1938*, ed. Franz Kadrnoska (Vienna, 1981), pp. 393–407.

55 See Johann Hüttner, 'Volkstheater als Geschäft: Theaterbetrieb und Publikum im 19. Jahrhundert', in *Volk – Volksstück – Volkstheater im deutschen Sprachraum des 18.–20. Jahrhunderts*, ed. Jean-Marie Valentin (Berne, 1986), pp. 127–49.

Chapter 6 Cultural Conservatism in the Theatre

1 Michael P. Steinberg, *The Meaning of the Salzburg Festival: Austria as Theater and Ideology, 1890–1938* (Ithaca and London, 1990), p. xv.

2 *Schicksalsjahre Österreichs 1908–1919. Das politische Tagebuch Josef Redlichs*, ed. Fritz Fellner, 2 vols (Graz, 1953–54), 2: 229 (entry for 20 August 1917). The passage continues by mentioning that Hofmannsthal seemed to be 'thinking of Granville-Barker's drama *Waste* as a kind of model', but in the event, the debt to *Waste*, a tragedy centring on a prominent and ambitious politician, is slight. The link has been explored by Roger C. Norton, 'Hugo von Hofmannsthal's *Der Schwierige* and Granville-Barker's *Waste*', CL 14 (1962): 272–9.

3 Letter to Rudolf Pannwitz, 16 January 1918; quoted by Leonhard M. Fiedler, *Max Reinhardt und Molière* (Salzburg, 1972), p. 48.

4 *Berliner Börsen-Courier*, 1 December 1921 and 19 September 1930. Reprinted TR 334–5, 534.

5 Leonhard M. Fiedler, 'Keime des Lustspiels. Frühe Notizen zum

"Schwierigen" und zum "Unbestechlichen"', HB, no. 25 (1982): 75–85 (p. 77). See Martin Stern, 'Die Entstehung von Hofmannsthals anachronistischem Gegenwartslustspiel', Burgtheaterprogramme *Der Schwierige*, Programmbuch no. 78 (1991), pp. 51–77 (p. 55).

6 Rudolf Hirsch, 'Zwei Briefe über den *Schwierigen*', HB, no. 7 (1971), pp. 70–75 (p. 72) (letter of 5 September 1917); H/ Andrian, 252–3 (letters of 27 September and 4 October 1917). See Martin Stern, 'Die Entstehung von Hofmannsthals anachronistischem Gegenwartslustspiel', p. 56. The link with the *Konversationsstück* is made in the introduction to my edition of the play (Cambridge, 1966), pp. 8–11; a similar conclusion has been reached by Herbert Gamper, 'Hofmannsthal und Bauernfeld. Ein wahrscheinliches Vorbild zum *Schwierigen*', HF 8 (1985): 105–27.

7 Roger C. Norton, Hofmannsthal's "magische Werkstätte": Unpublished Notebooks from the Harvard Collection', GR 36 (1961): 50–64 (p. 62).

8 HKA III, 73. The parallel in the significance of the letters is pointed out by Rolf Tarot, *Hugo von Hofmannsthal. Daseinsformen und dichterische Struktur* (Tübingen, 1970), p. 103.

9 Martin Stern, 'In illo tempore. Über Notizen und Varianten zu Hofmannsthals Lustspiel "Der Schwierige"', WW 8 (1957–58): 115–19 (p. 119).

10 Stern, 'In illo tempore', p. 116. In this respect a note made in 1907 during work on another projected comedy, *Silvia im 'Stern'*, is revealing: 'Ich und Individuum ist identisch[,] beide Begriffe zergehen unter sprachkünstlerischer Betrachtung – können aber mit der Intuition erfaßt werden'

(Roger C. Norton, 'Hofmannsthal's "magische Werkstätte"', p. 51).

11 The link is pursued in the introduction to my edition of *Der Schwierige* (1966), pp. 21–2.

12 See my article '*Der Schwierige*: the Comedy of Discretion', MAL 10, no. 1 (1977): 1–17 (pp. 7–9). If one of Hans Karl's antecedents in comic drama is Schnitzler's *Anatol*, it may be recalled that Hofmannsthal saw Anatol as a 'Viennese poet': Hugo von Hofmannsthal, 'Über Schnitzlers "Anatol"', ed. Rudolf Hirsch, NR 82, no. 4 (1971): 795–7 (p. 796).

13 See Jakob Wassermann, *Hofmannsthal der Freund* (Berlin, 1930), p. 13 (Fiechtner 1949, 98; Fiechtner 1963, 111).

14 See Roger C. Norton, 'The Inception of Hofmannsthal's *Der Schwierige*: Early Plans and their Significance', PMLA 79, no. 1, March 1964, pp. 97–103 (p. 99), and 'Hofmannsthal's "magische Werkstätte"', p. 62.

15 On the pervasive misunderstandings between the various characters see Ronald Gray, *The German Tradition in Literature 1871–1945* (Cambridge, 1965), pp. 318–20.

16 Benjamin Bennett, *Hugo von Hofmannsthal: The Theaters of Consciousness* (Cambridge, 1988), p. 185.

17 Norton, 'The Inception of Hofmannsthal's *Der Schwierige*', p. 99. On the connection with Kierkegaard, see Michael Hamburger, 'Hofmannsthals Bibliothek. Ein Bericht', *Euphorion* 55 (1961): 15–76 (p. 72).

18 See Stern, 'In illo tempore', p. 116.

19 Possibly drawing on Hofmannsthal's view of Rudolf Borchardt; see Jürgen Prohl, *Hugo von Hofmannsthal und Rudolf Borchardt. Studien über eine Dichterfreundschaft* (Bremen, 1973), pp. 307–9. With-

in the conventions of comedy, however, the hollow clichés in which Neuhoff speaks present a parallel to the role of the victorious Olivier in *Der Turm*, as is pointed out by Tarot, *Hugo von Hofmannsthal: Daseinsformen und dichterische Struktur*, p. 403.

20 E.g., L II, 160, 184.

21 The question has occasioned lively debate. See Alfred Doppler, *Wirklichkeit im Spiegel der Sprache. Aufsätze zur Literatur des 20. Jahrhunderts in Österreich* (Vienna, 1975), pp. 67–8, 232; Adalbert Schmidt, 'Anachronistisches in Hofmannsthals Lustspiel "Der Schwierige"', in *Dichter zwischen den Zeiten* (Festschrift for Rudolf Henz), ed. Viktor Suchy (Vienna, 1977), pp. 158–66; Wolfgang Frühwald, 'Die sprechende Zahl: Datensymbolismus in Hugo von Hofmannsthals Lustspiel "Der Schwierige"', JDSG 22 (1978): 572–88; Martin Stern, 'Wann entstand und spielt "Der Schwierige"?', JDSG 23 (1979): 350–65; Martin Stern, 'Genetischer Befund als Instrument der Werkanalyse. Aus der Editionsarbeit an Hofmannsthals Lustspiel "Der Schwierige" im Rahmen der HKA', JIG, Reihe A, 11 (1981): 280–5. The debate is reviewed by Ewald Rösch, 'Komödie und Berliner Kritik. Zu Hofmannsthals Lustspielen *Cristinas Heimreise* und *Der Schwierige*', in *Hugo von Hofmannsthal. Freundschaften und Begegnungen mit deutschen Zeitgenossen*, ed. Ursula Renner and G. Bärbel Schmid (Würzburg, 1991), pp. 163–89 (pp. 182–4).

22 Julius Bab, 'Im leeren Zeitraum', *Die Hilfe*, 15 August 1921; see Ewald Rösch, 'Komödie und Berliner Kritik', pp. 181–2.

23 Hofmannsthal, 'Briefe an Freunde', NR 41 (1930): 512–19 (p. 518): '[. . .] im vorigen Sommer vollendet bis auf Kleinig-

keiten im letzten Akt' (letter of 15 June 1918).

24 H/Andrian, 252: letter of 27 September 1917; H/Strauss, 338: letter of 30 September 1917.

25 See Stern, 'Genetischer Befund als Instrument der Werkanalyse', p. 283.

26 Stern, 'Genetischer Befund als Instrument der Werkanalyse', p. 283.

27 NFP, 16 and 17 September 1920 (nos. 20135–6). The differences between the two versions are discussed in the introduction to my edition of the play (1966), pp. 13–16.

28 Bennett, *Hugo von Hofmannsthal: The Theaters of Consciousness*, p. 106.

29 Bennett, *Hugo von Hofmannsthal: The Theaters of Consciousness*, p. 363.

30 See Rösch, 'Komödie und Berliner Kritik', p. 184.

31 To Rudolf Pannwitz. Quoted by Werner Volke, *Hugo von Hofmannsthal in Selbstzeugnissen und Bilddokumenten* (Reinbek, 1967), p. 130.

32 See Frederick Alfred Lubich, 'Hugo von Hofmannsthals *Der Schwierige*: Hans Karl Bühl und Antoinette Hechingen unterm Aspekt der Sprache und Moral', *Monatshefte* 77 (1985): 47–59 (pp. 51–4).

33 See Bennett, *Hugo von Hofmannsthal: The Theaters of Consciousness*, p. 171.

34 See H/Andrian, 320: Hofmannsthal's letter of 25 January 1921.

35 Review by R.H—r [Rudolf Holzer?], *Wiener Zeitung*, 17 March 1923.

36 On this passage see Norbert Altenhofer, *Hofmannsthals Lustspiel 'Der Unbestechliche'* (Bad Homburg, 1967), p. 86.

37 On the structure see Paul Requadt, 'Hofmannsthals Komödie "Der Unbestechliche"', WW 13 (1963): 222–9, and Hans-Ulrich Lindken,

'Die Rolle des Kindes in Hofmannsthals Lustspiel "Der Unbestechliche"', ÖGL 15 (1971):
32–44.

38 M.-L. Roth, 'Un Inédit de Musil:
Le compte rendu de la première
de l'*Unbestechliche* de Hofmannsthal', EG 17 (1962): 403–5.

39 See HKA XIII, 245: letters of 20
and 22 February 1923 to Gerty
von Hofmannsthal.

40 Michael P. Steinberg, *The Meaning of the Salzburg Festival: Austria
as Theater and Ideology, 1890–1938*
(Ithaca and London, 1990), pp.
87–97.

41 Juvaviensis, 'Noch ein Wort über
das Mozartsfest', *Der Humorist*
(Vienna), no. 187, 19 September
1842, p. 755.

42 B.Z., 'Das Erste. Ein Wort
zum Mozart-Festspielhaus in
Salzburg', WAZ, no. 12227, 24
January 1919, p. 1.

43 See Berta Szeps-Zuckerkandl,
'Gespräch über Österreich'
(1920), in Fiechtner 1949, 337–8.

44 Hermann Bahr, *Prophet der
Moderne. Tagebücher 1888–1904*,
ed. Reinhard Farkas (Vienna,
1987), pp. 158–9 (entries for 6,
12, and 14 December 1903) and
162 (entry for 31 December
1903).

45 E.g., Hugo Greinz, 'Das Festspielhaus in Salzburg', MSF 4,
no. 1–2, January–February 1921,
pp. 1–6 (especially p. 3); Rudolf
Holzer, 'Warum bauen wir ein
Festspielhaus und warum in Salzburg?', MSF 4, no. 7–8, July–
August 1921, pp. 1–3 (p. 2).

46 Michael P. Steinberg, *The Mean-
ing of the Salzburg Festival*, p.
167. See Hermann Broch,
Kommentierte Werkausgabe, ed.
Paul Michael Lützeler, IX/1
(*Schriften zur Literatur, 1 – Kritik*)
(Frankfurt a.M., 1975), p. 267.

47 'Unter dem Zeichen Mozarts, des
heiteren und frommen Genius
Salzburgs, sollten hier Oper
und Schauspiel, Lustspiel und

Singspiel, das Volksstück ebenso
wie die alten Misterien und
Weihnachtsspiele zu einer
erlesenen Einheit verwoben
werden [. . .]'. Quoted by
Oskar Holl, 'Dokumente zur
Entstehung der Salzburger
Festspiele: Unveröffentlichtes aus
der Korrespondenz der Gründer',
MK 13 (1967): 148–80 (pp. 174–
8).

48 Steinberg, *The Meaning of the
Salzburg Festival*, p. 19. Cf.
also p. xi, where Hofmannsthal
is described as 'the principal
spiritual and institutional founder
of the Salzburg Festival'.

49 Hugo Greinz, 'Das Festspielhaus
in Salzburg', p. 1.

50 'Großes Theater in Salzburg!',
Prager Tagblatt, 17 August 1922,
p. 3. Quoted by Ulrich Weinzierl,
Alfred Polgar. Eine Biographie
(Vienna, 1985), p. 124.

51 Max Pirker, *Die Salzburger
Festspiele* (Zürich, Leipzig, and
Vienna, n.d. [1921]), p. 14.

52 See Michael P. Steinberg, 'Jewish
Identity and Intellectuality in fin-
de-siècle Austria: Suggestions for
a Historical Discourse', NGC,
no. 43, Winter 1988, pp. 3–33
(p. 16).

53 Pirker, *Die Salzburger Festspiele*,
p. 14.

54 '[. . .] in den mittelalterlichen
Passionen, Mysterien und vielen
Volksspielen [. . .]': quoted in
Salzburg. Stadt und Land, ed.
Jacqueline and Werner Hofmann
(Munich, 1957; repr. 1977), p.
169.

55 Mozart, *Briefe und Aufzeichnungen.
Gesamtausgabe*, ed. Wilhelm A.
Bauer and Otto Erich Deutsch, 7
vols (Kassel, 1962–75), 3: 121
(letter no. 599, 26 May 1781).

56 Mozart, *Briefe und Aufzeichnungen*,
3: 102 (letter no. 586, 4 April
1781) and 3: 155 (letter no. 621, 5
September 1781).

57 Surveyed by Artur Kutscher, *Das
Salzburger Barocktheater* (Vienna,

1924) (revised edn, *Vom Salzburger Barocktheater zu den Salzburger Festspielen* [Düsseldorf, 1939]); Heiner Boberski, *Das Theater der Benediktiner an der alten Universität Salzburg (1617–1778)* (Vienna, 1978).

58 Leopold Schmidt, *Das deutsche Volksschauspiel. Ein Handbuch* (Berlin, 1962), pp. 310–18.

59 Joseph Wer, *Der Humorist*, no. 258, 28 December 1842, p. 1043.

60 *Allgemeine Theater-Zeitung*, no. 313, 31 December 1842, p. 1375 (G.W.); *Der Humorist*, 9 February 1844, p. 140 (Rudolf Fürrich).

61 Hermann Bahr, *Essays* (Leipzig, 1912), pp. 235–41: 'Die Hauptstadt von Europa. Eine Phantasie in Salzburg'.

62 Ernst Ehrens, 'Salzburger Festspielhaus', *Die Schaubühne* 14 (1918): 225–7 (p. 225).

63 See Juvaviensis, 'Noch ein Wort über das Mozartsfest', *Der Humorist*, 19 September 1842, p. 755; 'Brief aus Salzburg', *Allgemeine Theaterzeitung*, no. 270, 11 November 1842, p. 1191.

64 *Dichter und Gelehrter. Hermann Bahr und Josef Redlich in ihren Briefen 1896–1934*, ed. Fritz Fellner (Salzburg, 1980), pp. 421, 423–4 (letters of 14 August and 26 September 1920).

65 Clive Holland, *Tyrol and its People* (London, 1909), pp. 191, 167.

66 E.g., Greinz, 'Das Festspielhaus in Salzburg', p. 2; Holzer, 'Warum bauen wir ein Festspielhaus und warum in Salzburg?', p. 2.

67 Letter to Einar Nilson, 18 October 1934, quoted by Leonhard M. Fiedler, *Max Reinhardt* (Reinbek, 1975), pp. 121–2.

68 Letter of 4 September 1916. Quoted by Holl, 'Dokumente zur Entstehung der Salzburger Festspiele', p. 161.

69 Alfred Polgar, *Auswahlband. Aus neun Bänden erzählender und kritischer Schriften* (Berlin, 1930), pp. 187–8.

70 Friedrich Gehmacher, letter of 28 January 1918 to the Stiftung Mozarteum ('[. . .] im Sinne des Mozartkultes [. . .]'). Quoted by Holl, 'Dokumente zur Entstehung der Salzburger Festspiele', p. 172. For a brief outline of the growth of musical festivals in Salzburg, see Roland Tenschert, *Salzburg und seine Festspiele* (Vienna, 1947), pp. 112–18.

71 See Pirker, *Die Salzburger Festspiele*, p. 62; also Paul Nettl, *Neue Mannheimer Zeitung*, Mittag-Ausgabe, 2 September 1925 (*Resonanz*, 22).

72 The alleged quotation ('Habe mich der christlichen Mythe wie einer anderen bedient') seems to be half-remembered from references to Christianity as a 'mythology' in two letters from Hebbel to Friedrich von Uechtritz: see Hebbel, *Sämtliche Werke*, hist.-krit. Ausgabe, ed. R. M. Werner, 24 vols (Berlin, 1901–7), 3. Abt., *Briefe*, 6: 9 (letter of 12 March 1857) and 7: 266 (letter of 25 October 1862). Hofmannsthal read Hebbel's letters in this edition in the early summer of 1903 and mentioned them enthusiastically in letters (H/AS, 170: letter of 19 June 1903; H/Beer-Hofmann, 119: letter of 29 June 1903).

73 Hans Sittenberger, *Studien zur Dramaturgie der Gegenwart*, vol. 1, *Das dramatische Schaffen in Österreich* (Munich, 1898), pp. 248–53.

74 Steinberg, *The Meaning of the Salzburg Festival*, p. 28.

75 Steinberg, 'Jewish Identity and Intellectuality in fin-de-siècle Austria', p. 4. See Hermann Broch, *Kommentierte Werkausgabe*, IX/1 (*Schriften zur Literatur*, 1 – *Kritik*), p. 266.

76 Letter of 16 July 1920; see *Hugo von Hofmannsthal: 'Jedermann. Das Spiel vom Sterben des reichen Mannes' und Max Reinhardts*

Inszenierungen. Texte, Dokumente, Bilder, ed. Edda Leisler and Gisela Prossnitz (Frankfurt a.M., 1973), p. 191.

77 Letter of summer 1942 to Joseph Chapiro, quoted in Cynthia Walk, *Hofmannsthals 'Großes Welttheater'. Drama und Theater* (Heidelberg, 1980), p. 26.

78 See Max Mell's reviews in the *Wiener Mittag*, 26 and 28 August 1920; reprinted in *Max Mell als Theaterkritiker*, ed. Margret Dietrich (Vienna, 1983), pp. 246–9; Rudolf Holzer, *Wiener Zeitung*, 26 August 1920, p. 4; Robert Konta, 'Die Salzburger August-Festtage', MSF 3, no. 9/10, October 1920, pp. 12–14. See also TR, 223–7: reviews by Joseph August Lux, *München-Augsburger Abendzeitung*, 24 August 1920; ld, *Neues Wiener Tagblatt*, 23 August 1920; and Oscar Bie, *Münchener Zeitung*, 27 August 1929.

79 E.g., Pirker, *Die Salzburger Festspiele*, p. 35.

80 See *Deutsch-Österreichische Literaturgeschichte*, ed. Johann Willibald Nagl, Jakob Zeidler, and Eduard Castle, 4 vols (Vienna, 1899–1937), 4: 1590–1648 ('Festspiele und Volkstheater'): on Lux p. 1633. Lux's work in the genre begins with *Das Fenster. Ein Spiel des Lebens in drei Aufzügen* (Leipzig, 1918).

81 Letter to Berthold Viertel, 6 July 1911; quoted in Ulrich Weinzierl, *Alfred Polgar. Eine Biographie* (Vienna, 1985), pp. 76–7.

82 Alfred Polgar, *Auswahlband. Aus neun Bänden erzählender und kritischer Schriften* (Berlin, 1930), p. 188.

83 Joseph Gregor, 'Welttheater', NFP, Morgenblatt, no. 20805, 1 August 1922, p. 1.

84 See 'Die Salzburger Festspiele 1922', MSF 5, no. 1, January–June 1922, pp. 1–2 (p. 2).

85 —e—, *Wiener Zeitung*, no. 188,

19 August 1922, p. 6.

86 E.g., Hans Sachs's several versions of *Die ungleichen Kinder Eve* between 1547 and 1558, as *Meisterlied, Fastnachtspiel*, longer play (*Comedia*), and *Schwank*.

87 See HKA X, 221.

88 Cf. Benjamin Bennett, *Hugo von Hofmannsthal: The Theaters of Consciousness*, p. 273.

89 For a sympathetic account of Hofmannsthal's achievement and intentions in the play in the context of his cultural politics, see Brian Coghlan, *Hofmannsthal's Festival Dramas* (Cambridge, 1964), pp. 150–83.

90 *Freie Salzburger Bauernstimme*, 17 August 1922, p. 3; *Deutscher Volksruf*, 17 August 1922, p. 3. Quoted in Günter Fellner, *Antisemitismus in Salzburg 1918–1938* (Vienna and Salzburg, 1979), p. 103. The material on anti-Semitism in the Salzburg press is drawn from Fellner, pp. 102–4.

91 *Die Welt am Montag*, 21 October 1912 (signed 'a.u.x.'). Quoted by Leonhard M. Fiedler, *Max Reinhardt und Molière* (Salzburg, 1972), pp. 38–9.

92 'Jedermann in Salzburg', *Der Merker* 11, no. 17, 15 September 1920, pp. 428–9.

93 Quoted by J. L. Styan, *Max Reinhardt* (Cambridge, 1982), pp. 92–3.

94 See Cynthia Walk, *Hofmannsthals 'Großes Welttheater'*, p. 117.

95 Cf. Stefan Zweig, *Die Welt von Gestern. Erinnerungen eines Europäers* (London and Stockholm, 1944), p. 360; also Bruno Walter (1947), in *Salzburg. Stadt und Land*, p. 187.

96 Eric Hobsbawm, 'Introduction: Inventing Traditions', in *The Invention of Tradition*, ed. Eric Hobsbawm and Terence Ranger (Cambridge, 1983), pp. 1–14.

97 Letter to Ferdinand Künzelmann, 21 July 1918. Quoted by Holl, 'Dokumente zur Entstehung der

Salzburger Festspiele', p. 175.

98   *Salzburg. Stadt und Land*, p. 169.

99   See Rudolf Holzer, 'Das Festspielhaus', *Reichspost*, 13 August 1925, reprinted in *Resonanz*, 26–8 (p. 28).

100 See Paul Stefanek, 'Karl Kraus versus Max Reinhardt', in *Max Reinhardt: The Oxford Symposium* (Oxford, 1972), pp. 112–23.

101 F 601–607, 1–7. It is in this essay that Kraus announced that he was leaving the Catholic church (which he did on 7 March 1923).

102 Martin Stern, 'Niemand für "Jedermann" – alle für Brecht?', *Salzburger Festspiele 1982*, Offizielles Programm (Salzburg, 1982), pp. 171–3.

Chapter 7   Post mortem

1   E.g., letters of 13 July 1910, 21 February 1913, 19 March 1921 (H/AS, 250, 272, 294–5).

2   Olga Schnitzler, *Spiegelbild der Freundschaft* (Salzburg, 1962), p. 51.

3   One example is F. O. Schmid, 'Arthur Schnitzler und die "Jung-Wiener-Schule"', *Berner Rundschau* 4, no. 3, 15 September 1909, pp. 63–74: despite Hofmannsthal's virtuosity, Schnitzler was the more genuine and significant *Dichter* ('der echtere und bedeutendere') (pp. 64–5).

4   See *Chrstk.*, 9–10, on the genesis of the typescript.

5   See Schnitzler's letters of 6 August 1908 and 2 November 1910, Hofmannsthal's of 14 September 1908 and 7 November 1910 (H/AS, 239–40 and 256–9).

6   'Vienna Letter', July 1922, *The Dial* 73, no. 2, August 1922, pp. 206–14 (p. 207). German version: A, 269.

7   Paul A. Rares, 'Max beweint Anatol. Schnitzlers Freund über die gemeinsame Jugend', WAZ, 24

October 1931, p. 4.

8   F 1, April 1899, pp. 25–7 ('dieser Edelsteinsammler aller Literaturen', p. 25); F 157, 19 March 1904, p. 23 ('einen Eklektiker von feinstem Kunstgeschmack'); F 349–350, 13 May 1912, p. 7: 'der bekanntere zeitgenössische Umdichter Hofmannsthal, der ehrwürdigen Kadavern das Fell abzieht, um fragwürdige Leichen darin zu bestatten' ('Nestroy und die Nachwelt'). On Klimt see F 73, April 1901, p. 10 ('den geübten Stileklektiker') and the scepticism about Klimt's 'originality' in F 36, March 1900, pp. 16–19.

9   *Chrstk.*, 47, 48, 49.

10 See *Chrstk.*, 96 (note 233).

11 Sally McMullen, MLR 84 (1989): 1040.

12 The principal obituary tributes are listed in Horst Weber, *Hugo von Hofmannsthal. Bibliographie des Schrifttums 1892–1963* (Berlin, 1966), pp. 60–69. Selected texts are reprinted in Fiechtner 1949 and Fiechtner 1963; there is some overlap but the selection is not identical.

13 Raoul Auernheimer, 'Hugo von Hofmannsthal als österreichische Erscheinung', NR 40, vol. 2, no. 11, November 1929, pp. 660–6.

14 'Letztes Gespräch in Rodaun 1929', in Fiechtner 1949, 267–72 (pp. 268–9), and Fiechtner 1963, 277–81 (pp. 278–9). Reprinted in Max Mell, *Gesammelte Werke*, 4 vols (Vienna, 1962), 4: 239–45 (p. 241).

15 Leopold Andrian-Werburg, 'Hofmannsthal und die österreichische Jugend', *Vaterland* 8 (1934–35), no. 8, January 1935, pp. 130–6. Martin Stern warns against the oversimple legend that the collapse of the monarchy was responsible for his death: 'Hofmannsthal und das Ende der Donaumonarchie', in *Die österreichische Literatur. Ihr Profil von der Jahrhundertwende bis zur Gegenwart (1880–1980)*, ed. Herbert Zeman, 2 vols (Graz,

1989), 1: 709–27 (p. 721).

16 E.g., Jakob Wassermann, *Hofmannsthal der Freund* (Berlin, 1930), p. 16; Fiechtner 1949, 99–100; Fiechtner 1963, 112.

17 '[Der] repräsentative Dichter Oesterreichs (Stefan Zweig, NFP, 22 October 1931); 'der repräsentativste Dichter Oesterreichs' (Karl Glossy, *Neues Wiener Journal*, 22 October); 'der repräsentative Dichter des deutschen Österreich' (Robert Neumann, *Central-Verein-Zeitung* [Berlin], 30 October); 'Oesterreichs größter Dichter' (*Unterkärntner Nachrichten*, 31 October); 'Es [*scil.* das geistige Wien] hat durch Schnitzlers Tod seinen repräsentativen Dichter verloren' (Emil Lind, *Der neue Weg* [Berlin], 1 November).

18 E.g., *Neues Wiener Tagblatt*, 28 October 1931; *Volks-Zeitung*, 31 October 1931.

19 Alfred Polgar, 'Der Theaterdichter Schnitzler', *Die Weltbühne* 27, no. 44, 3 November 1931, pp. 679–80.

20 E.g., Heinrich Glücksmann and David Feuchtwang, *Die Wahrheit* (Vienna), 30 October 1931, pp. 1–2; Sammy Gronemann, 'Arthur Schnitzler, der Jude', *Berliner Jüdische Zeitung*, Beilage, 30 October 1931.

21 Josef Weinheber, *Wien wörtlich* (Vienna, 1935), p. 85. See my article 'Architectonic Form in Weinheber's Lyric Poetry: The Sonnet "Blick vom Oberen Belvedere"', MLR 71 (1976): 73–81.

22 Klaus Amann, *Der Anschluß österreichischer Schriftsteller an das Dritte Reich: Institutionelle und bewußtseinsgeschichtliche Aspekte* (Frankfurt a.M., 1988), p. 23.

23 See Peter Pulzer, *The Rise of Political Anti-Semitism in Germany and Austria*, revised edn (London, 1988), pp. 218–19.

24 Ferdinand von Saar, *Sämtliche Werke*, ed. Jakob Minor, 12 vols (Leipzig, n.d. [1908]), 4: 24: 'Ja, da bin ich im Herzen der alten, der herrlichen Ostmark, / Deren Banner einst stolz flatterte über dem Reich – / Über dem Reich, von dem sie getrennt nun, beinahe ein Fremdling: / Östreichs Söhne, man zählt kaum zu den Deutschen sie mehr.'

25 Karlheinz Rossbacher, 'Literatur und Ständestaat', in *Staat und Gesellschaft in der modernen österreichischen Literatur*, ed. Friedbert Aspetsberger (Vienna, 1977), pp. 93–107, links the movement with the ideology of Othmar Spann and his circle.

26 See Amann, *Der Anschluß österreichischer Schriftsteller an das Dritte Reich*, pp. 35–6.

27 See Albert Berger, '"Götter, Dämonen und Irdisches": Josef Weinhebers dichterische Metaphysik' in *Österreichische Literatur der dreißiger Jahre*, ed. Klaus Amann and Albert Berger (Vienna, 1985), pp. 277–90 (p. 282).

28 See 'Jüdische Selbstzeugnisse', *Wiener Neueste Nachrichten*, 28 September 1933.

29 Wk., 'Schriftsteller auf der Schwarzen Liste', *Nachtausgabe* (Berlin), 26 April 1933.

30 *Reichspost*, 26 November 1933, pp. 1–2: 'Der Stein des Anstoßes'. See Klaus Amann, 'Im Schatten der Bücherverbrennung. Österreichische Literatur und Nationalsozialismus', *Wespennest*, no. 52 (1983), Sonderheft *Literatur und Macht*, pp. 16–25 (p. 20).

31 See Amann, *Der Anschluß österreichischer Schriftsteller an das Dritte Reich*, pp. 30, 178.

32 Amann, *Der Anschluß österreichischer Schriftsteller an das Dritte Reich*, pp. 56–7.

33 See Murray G. Hall, *Österreichische Verlagsgeschichte 1918–1938*, 2 vols (Vienna, 1985), 1: 108–22; Horst Jarka, 'Zur Literatur- und Theaterpolitik im "Ständestaat"', in *Aufbruch und Untergang. Österreichische Kultur zwischen 1918*

und 1938, ed. Franz Kadrnoska (Vienna, 1981), pp. 499–538 (especially pp. 501–2).

34   See Amann, *Der Anschluß österreichischer Schriftsteller an das Dritte Reich*, pp. 122–3; Hall, *Österreichische Verlagsgeschichte 1918–1938*, 1: 259–62.

35   See O. E. Deutsch, *National-Zeitung* (Basle), 30 August 1934 (*Resonanz*, 104–6).

36   See Richard Beer, *Volks-Zeitung* (Vienna), 25 August 1935 (*Resonanz*, 125–7).

37   E.g., —ll—, 'Festspiel-Andacht', *Stuttgarter N.S.-Kurier*, 12 August 1935 (*Resonanz*, 121).

38   See Sebastian Meissl, 'Germanistik in Österreich', in *Aufbruch und Untergang*, pp. 475–96; Hans H. Hiebel, 'Der "Anschluß der Ostmark an das Reich". Zur pränazistischen Germanistik in Österreich', ÖGL 33 (1989): 374–93.

39   G.B., 'Zeugnisse des völkischen Erwachens', *Der Angriff* (Berlin), 14 January 1936.

40   Grillparzer, *Sämtliche Werke*, hist.-krit. Ausgabe, ed. August Sauer and Reinhold Backmann, 42 vols (Vienna, 1909–48), vol. I/18 (1939), p. viii.

41   See Fritz Bock, 'Vierzig Jahre nachher', in *Wien 1938*, Forschungen und Beiträge zur Wiener Stadtgeschichte, 2 (Vienna, 1978), pp. 11–17 (pp. 16–17).

42   See Amann, 'Im Schatten der Bücherverbrennung. Österreichische Literatur und Nationalsozialismus', pp. 23–4, with quotations from reports in the *Salzburger Volksblatt*.

43   See Johannes Sachslehner, *Führerwort und Fühererblick: Mirko Jelusich. Zur Strategie eines Bestsellerautors in den Dreißiger Jahren* (Königstein/

Ts., 1985), p. 31.

44   See Amann, *Der Anschluß österreichischer Schriftsteller an das Dritte Reich*, pp. 32–5.

45   *The Times*, 27 May 1933, p. 11.

46   See Klaus Amann, *P.E.N.: Politik – Emigration – Nationalsozialismus. Ein österreichischer Schriftstellerclub* (Vienna, 1984), p. 34. Amann gives a comprehensive account of the consequences of the Dubrovnik congress (pp. 23–59). In 1933 the events were fully reported from 25 May 1933 onwards in the WAZ, which also carried several articles of editorial comment by Ludwig Ullmann between 28 May and 9 June.

47   H.L., ' "Arische" Dichter in Oesterreich', *National-Zeitung* (Basle), 7 January 1937: 'Den Vorsitz dieser [. . .] Vereinigung der rassenreinen Dichter führt der Katholik Max Mell, der damit beweist, daß man zwar zart hingehauchte Apostelspiele schreiben, aber doch in geistigen Dingen robust wie ein Bergsteiger denken kann.'

48   See Viktor Suchy. 'Literatur "März 1938" ', in *Wien 1938*, pp. 258–72 (p. 271); also Amann, *Der Anschluß österreichischer Schriftsteller an das Dritte Reich*, pp. 156–63.

49   John Warren, 'Austrian Theatre and the Corporate State', in *Austria in the Thirties: Culture and Politics*, ed. Kenneth Segar and John Warren (Riverside, California, 1991), pp. 267–91 (p. 274).

50   Hermann Kunisch, 'Hugo von Hofmannsthals "politisches Vermächtnis" ', *Jahrbuch der Grillparzer-Gesellschaft* (3. Folge), 12 (1976), pp. 97–124.

51   See 'Schnitzler und das Burgtheater', in *Burgtheater, Saison 1980/81, Planungen*, Heft 2 (1981), pp. 4–17 (p. 5).

Index

279

General Index